Post-Capita[illegible]
A Reader

POST-CAPITAL: A READER
Edited by Michelle Cotton

Mudam Luxembourg – Musée d'Art Moderne Grand-Duc Jean
Mousse Publishing

TABLE OF CONTENTS / TABLE DES MATIÈRES

FOREWORD

Suzanne Cotter
Director, Mudam Luxembourg – Musée d'Art Moderne Grand-Duc Jean

In her epoch-defining book, *The Age of Surveillance Capitalism: The Fight for a Human Future at the New Frontier of Power,* Shoshana Zuboff advances: 'If industrial civilisation flourished at the expense of nature and threatens to cost us the Earth, an information civilisation shaped by surveillance capitalism will thrive at the expense of human nature and threatens to cost us our humanity'. This cost – and its social, psychological and emotional implications – lies at the heart of *Post-Capital: Art and the Economics of the Digital Age*, which takes as its starting point how the nature of production, consumption and wealth in the digital era is transforming our experience and views of the world.

This book is published as both a reader and a catalogue to the exhibition of the same name. *Post-Capital* is a generational survey of sculpture, installation, painting, photography, video and performance by more than twenty artists from different parts of the world. Installed across three floors of the museum and extending into the public space of the city and the virtual space of the internet, the exhibition includes newly commissioned works as well as works from the Mudam Collection.

Post-Capital has been developed with reference to its context in Luxembourg, a European capital renowned for its financial sector and in which the digital economy is of strategic importance. Despite being one of the smallest countries in Europe, Luxembourg is home to people of 170 nationalities. Having made the successful transition from an industrial economy based on coal and steel and one of the founding countries of what would become the European Union, Luxembourg was ranked in 2019 as having the highest GDP per capita in the world, albeit for a country with a resident population of less than 700,000. It is forty-five kilometres from the German city of Trier, where just over two centuries ago, the philosopher and economist Karl Marx was born. Marx's notion of capitalism as a dynamic system that tends toward self-destruction is referenced in the title of this book and of the exhibition that is its source.

Post-Capital: A Reader brings together excerpts of longer texts and books on the subject of the digital age and its consequences, with respect to human freedoms and the hidden or largely invisible dynamics that are driving an evolving and unequal world order. We are privileged to be able to reproduce here contributions from some of today's most influential thinkers on the subject of our digital age and its consequences. They include Zuboff's ground-breaking essay, 'The Age of Surveillance Capitalism: The Fight for the Future at the New Frontier of Power'. The writings of James Bridle, Heike Geissler, Richard Seymour, Hito Steyerl and McKenzie Wark offer profound insights on technology's impact on our world, in which society is redefined in terms of vectors and hackers: from the increasing role of the algorithm and the inequalities of access to the psychosocial dislocation and social poverty of what Richard Seymour describes as 'the attention economy'. We are profoundly grateful to the authors for their generosity in allowing their work to be re-published here. They are accompanied by a thought-provoking essay by Michelle Cotton that introduces the framework for *Post-Capital* and situates the work of the artists in relation to the themes and perspectives that are brought forward in this book. These works are reproduced alongside insightful texts by Sarah Beaumont, Clémentine Proby, Joel Valabrega, Lauren Wetmore and Chloe Stead. The content is skilfully and intelligently brought together in the design work of Dan Solbach and his studio, to whom we extend our appreciation.

Mudam is indebted to the artists for their work, which is the inspirational point of departure for this ambitious project, and for their close and inspiring collaboration. We are also grateful to their studio assistants, galleries and collectors who have supported us with the production and loan of works in the exhibition. *Post-Capital* will travel to Kunsthal Charlottenborg, Copenhagen in 2022 and we express our gratitude to Michael Thouber, Director and Henriette Bretton-Meyer, Curator, for their collaboration and enthusiastic commitment to this project.

Michelle Cotton, Mudam's Head of Programmes and Content, developed and curated *Post-Capital* and has provided editorial direction for this publication with probing intelligence and grace. She has been supported at different stages of the project by Assistant Curators Nelly Taravel and Clémentine Proby. Joel Valabrega, Curator of Performance and Public Programmes at Mudam, curated the presentation of works by Nora Turato and Lara Favaretto and led, with Cotton, the Post-Capital Research Group, an initiative that combined the talents of our curatorial and public engagement teams (Sarah Beaumont, Caroline Hoffmann, Ioanna Madenoglu, Bob Mersch and Nelly Taravel) to research the content of this *Reader* and develop the public programme that accompanies the exhibition. The exhibition's organisation was skilfully overseen by Registrar

Marie Buisson and Head Registrar Véronique de Alzua. Technical production was led by Thierry Gratien, Sam Wirtz and Tawfik Matine El Din.

The publication of *Post-Capital: A Reader* has been expertly managed by Deborah Lambolez, Head of Publications, with Clarisse Fahrtmann, Publications Officer. Together, they have ensured, with diligence and passion, the editorial coordination and production of this important book.

The exhibition has received support from the Institut für Auslandsbeziehungen, The Italian Embassy in Luxembourg and the Mondriaan Fund. We are grateful to JCDecaux for sponsoring the production and display of Nora Turato's new poster series, created for sites across the city of Luxembourg. We also wish to extend our gratitude to the Community Garden of Bonnevoie-Kaltreis in the city of Luxembourg for their collaboration on the production of *FreePlots* (2019–ongoing) by Hito Steyerl. We thank, too, David Korecký who accompanied the production and installation of Roger Hiorns' work, *The retrospective view of the pathway* (2017–ongoing).

Accomplishing our artistic mission to produce exhibitions and publications for a diverse public that speak to our contemporary world would not be possible without the continued support of the Ministry of Culture and our many individual and corporate patrons. Finally – and most crucially – we wish to acknowledge and express our firm belief in the work of the many artists who inspire and guide us in our thinking, and who give expression and voice to realities that, while often relegated to states of invisibility, are very much present in how we make sense of and act in the world.

PRÉFACE

Suzanne Cotter
Directrice, Mudam Luxembourg – Musée d'Art Moderne Grand-Duc Jean

Dans *L'Âge du capitalisme de surveillance. Le combat pour un avenir humain face aux nouvelles frontières du pouvoir*, un livre qui a fait date, Shoshana Zuboff introduit l'idée que « si la civilisation industrielle a prospéré aux dépens de la nature et menace à présent de nous coûter la Terre, une civilisation de l'information modelée par le capitalisme de surveillance prospérera aux dépens de la nature humaine et menacera de nous coûter notre humanité ». C'est ce coût, avec ses implications sociales, psychologiques et émotionnelles, qui est au cœur de l'exposition *Post-Capital. Art et économie à l'ère du digital*, qui s'intéresse à la manière dont la nature de la production, de la consommation et de la création de richesses à l'ère numérique bouleverse notre expérience et notre vision du monde.

Ce livre se veut à la fois anthologie et catalogue de l'exposition du même nom. *Post-Capital* réunit sculptures, installations, peintures, photographies, vidéos et performances d'une vingtaine d'artistes d'une même génération venus de différentes parties du monde. Installée sur trois étages du musée, la présentation, qui comprend des œuvres spécialement commandées et des pièces de la collection du Mudam, se prolonge dans les espaces publics de la ville et le monde virtuel d'Internet.

L'exposition a été développée dans le contexte spécifique du Luxembourg, capitale européenne réputée pour son secteur financier où l'économie numérique joue un rôle stratégique majeur. Bien qu'il soit l'un des plus petits pays d'Europe, le Luxembourg compte 170 nationalités. Ayant réussi avec succès la transition d'une économie industrielle fondée sur le charbon et l'acier et étant l'un des pays fondateurs de ce qui allait devenir l'Union européenne, le Luxembourg présentait en 2019 le PIB par habitant le plus élevé au monde, et ce malgré une population résidente d'à peine 700 000 habitants. Sa capitale est située à moins de quarante-cinq kilomètres de Trèves, la ville allemande où naquit il y a un peu plus de deux siècles le philosophe et économiste Karl Marx, dont la conception du capitalisme comme système dynamique tendant à l'autodestruction est évoquée par le titre de la publication et de l'exposition.

Post-Capital: A Reader comprend des extraits de livres et de textes portant sur la question de l'ère numérique et ses conséquences sur les libertés humaines, analysées sous l'angle des dynamiques cachées ou largement invisibles qui sous-tendent un ordre mondial marqué par les dérèglements et les inégalités. Nous avons le privilège de pouvoir reproduire ici les réflexions de penseurs parmi les plus influents de notre époque sur les sujets qui nous préoccupent. Parmi ceux-ci figurent l'essai de Shoshana Zuboff mentionné plus haut ainsi que des contributions de James Bridle, Heike Geissler, Richard Seymour, Hito Steyerl et McKenzie Wark, qui offrent un aperçu des impacts de la technologie sur une société qui est redéfinie par McKenzie Wark en termes de « vecteurs » et de « hackers », du rôle croissant des algorithmes aux inégalités face à l'accès aux nouvelles technologies, en passant par la dislocation psychosociale et l'indigence des rapports sociaux dans ce que Richard Seymour a qualifié d'« économie de l'attention ». Nous sommes profondément reconnaissants aux auteurs pour la générosité dont ils ont fait preuve en nous permettant de republier leurs travaux dans cet ouvrage. Leurs écrits sont complétés par un essai de Michelle Cotton, qui expose le contexte de *Post-Capital* et situe le travail des artistes par rapport aux problématiques et perspectives présentées dans ce livre. Les œuvres des artistes sont reproduites aux côtés de textes de Sarah Beaumont, Clémentine Proby, Joel Valabrega, Lauren Wetmore et Chloe Stead. Le contenu est habilement assemblé grâce à l'expertise de Dan Solbach et de son studio, à qui nous adressons nos remerciements.

Le Mudam souhaite remercier les artistes pour leurs œuvres, qui ont inspiré ce projet ambitieux, et pour leur étroite collaboration. À ce titre, nous remercions également leurs assistants ainsi que les galeries et les collectionneurs qui nous ont soutenus en produisant ou en prêtant des œuvres.

L'exposition *Post-Capital* sera présentée à la Kunsthal Charlottenborg à Copenhague en 2022. Nous exprimons notre gratitude à Michael Thouber, directeur, et Henriette Bretton-Meyer, commissaire, pour leur collaboration et l'intérêt qu'ils ont témoigné pour ce projet.

Michelle Cotton, responsable de la programmation artistique et des contenus au Mudam, a conçu et organisé l'exposition et assuré la direction éditoriale de la cette anthologie avec intelligence et esprit. Elle a été assistée à différentes étapes du projet par Nelly Taravel et Clémentine Proby. Joel Valabrega, curatrice en charge des performances et du programme public au Mudam, a organisé la présentation des œuvres de Nora Turato et de Lara Favaretto et dirigé avec Michelle Cotton le « Post-Capital Research

Group », une initiative qui a permis de conjuguer les talents de nos équipes de commissaires et de médiateurs (Sarah Beaumont, Caroline Hoffmann, Ioanna Madenoglu, Bob Mersch et Nelly Taravel) pour mener les recherches en amont de cette anthologie et concevoir les événements publics accompagnant l'exposition. Le suivi du montage a été assuré par la régisseuse Marie Buisson et la régisseuse en chef Véronique de Alzua, avec le soutien des équipes techniques menées par Thierry Gratien, Sam Wirtz et Tawfik Matine El Din.

La publication de *Post-Capital: A Reader* a été dirigée de main experte par Deborah Lambolez, responsable des éditions, avec Clarisse Fahrtmann, chargée des éditions. Ensemble, elles ont assuré, avec diligence et passion, la coordination éditoriale et la production de cet ouvrage important.

L'exposition a reçu le soutien de l'Institut für Auslandsbeziehungen, de l'Ambassade d'Italie au Luxembourg et du Mondriaan Fund. Nous remercions JCDecaux d'avoir sponsorisé la production et la présentation de la nouvelle série d'affiches de Nora Turato, créées pour différents sites de la ville de Luxembourg. Nous souhaitons également remercier le Jardin communautaire de Bonnevoie-Kaltreis à Luxembourg pour avoir collaboré à la production de *FreePlots* (2019-en cours) de Hito Steyerl. Nous remercions en outre David Korecký, qui a accompagné la production et l'installation de l'œuvre de Roger Hiorns, *The retrospective view of the pathway* (2017-en cours).

L'accomplissement de notre mission artistique, qui consiste à réaliser des expositions et des publications en dialogue avec le monde contemporain et adressées au plus grand nombre, ne serait pas possible sans le soutien continu du ministère de la Culture et des nombreux mécènes individuels et institutionnels qui nous accompagnent. Enfin, et surtout, nous souhaitons réitérer notre foi inébranlable dans le travail des nombreux artistes qui nous inspirent et nous guident dans notre réflexion en donnant une voix à des réalités qui, bien que souvent reléguées à l'invisibilité, sont éminemment présentes dans nos manières de donner du sens et d'agir dans le monde.

ALL THAT IS SOLID MELTS INTO AIR

Michelle Cotton

Alfred Marshall defined Economics as the study of humanity in 'the ordinary business of life'.[1] This branch of knowledge concerned with the production, consumption and transfer of wealth, was understood by Marshall in 1890 not as an abstract science but something intrinsically linked to the peculiar nature of man, the economy being a product of human endeavour, psyche and desires. In a moment of crisis, when the world's largest economies are recovering from a sharp and sudden decline (with all but one of the developing economies following a similar pattern), the importance of gaining a humane perspective on this subject – which affects individuals at the deepest emotional and psychological level – is all the more apparent.[2]

Post-Capital is an exhibition that considers the contradictions, absurdities and ethical questions posed by the 'ordinary business' of contemporary life. Conceived in a moment of slowed economic growth, its starting point was the inherent paradox within the capitalist system that is both dependent upon, and threatened by technology. The title of the exhibition is borrowed from Peter Drucker's 1993 book, *Post-Capitalist Society*, a management text book that makes no reference to the internet (which became publicly accessible two years prior). Yet it describes the emergence of a system in which 'knowledge' supersedes 'land, labour and capital' in the generation of wealth.[3] Drucker links diverse sectors such as pharmaceuticals, entertainment and telecommunications, arguing that they 'have as their business the production and distribution of knowledge and information'. Even retail corporations, he argues, are making their fortunes by 'reorganising' their 'old business around information'.[4] Thus he maintains that 'knowledge' has become '*the* resource, rather than *a* resource' and that 'this fact changes – fundamentally – the structure of society. It creates new social and economic dynamics. It creates new politics'.[5]

More recently McKenzie Wark has written of the 'pervasive organising force' of information that is gathered, sorted, managed, processed, and ultimately instrumentalised by technology 'to control other things in the world'. In the 2019 book, *Capital Is Dead: Is this Something Worse?*, Wark sets out the paradox of technologies that 'made information very, very cheap and very, very abundant' whilst giving 'rise to a strange kind of political economy, one based not only on a scarcity of things but also on an excess of information'. Wark's proposition is that:

> This is not capitalism anymore; it is something worse. The dominant ruling class of our time no longer maintains its rule through the ownership of the means of production, as capitalists do. Nor through the ownership of land, as landlords do. The dominant ruling class of our time owns and controls information.[6]

This exhibition is not intended as an argument for or against technological change. Nor does it attempt to define our contemporary economic situation as 'post-capital'. It does however seek to situate a generation of artists and artistic production (broader than those assembled here) that can be seen to engage both with the subject of technological change, and also capitalism. It is an engagement that arguably begins in the late 1960s, when cybernetic theory penetrated the cultural field and the study of communications and systems of control intersected with conceptual art's own analysis of the production and commodification of art. If we go further, it holds some roots in the multi-faceted, modernist fascination with 'the machine'. Yet there was arguably a moment in the 1960s when the present discussion began in earnest, as artists started to consolidate production into rules, data sets and documents, dematerialising their work decades before the rest of us aspired to storing data in 'clouds' and working in 'paperless' offices.

> Money talk. Time is money. As sound as a dollar. Money to burn. Money won't lie.[7]

When the Covid-19 pandemic made live performance impossible, Ei Arakawa took stock of his income in a new suite of LED 'paintings'. In these works, artist fees for performances over a period of fifteen years are converted into a per-minute rate and relayed as a sequence of images of coins that light up the surface of the circular support.[8] Incandescent and ephemeral, some 'coins' are also performing 'entities' by proxy (the first in this series sings about the recent bankruptcy of his brother's tanning business). 'What is there beyond mere accounting? What is this energy?' asks Arakawa, he continues: 'There is a belief / statement that performance is beyond the value of coins. I am not chewing gum!'[9]

Marshall McLuhan classified money as 'media', comparing it to 'language' a 'store of work and experience' that 'acts also as translator and transmitter'.[10] According to McLuhan, 'Money talks' because money is a metaphor, a transfer and a bridge. Like words and language, money is a storehouse of communally achieved work, skill and experience'.[11]

Faced with the impossibility of performing, Arakawa made an image of performance, and that image was currency. It's a conceptual gesture, but also one that perfectly fits within a world in which lived experience is translated into information, a process that fragments real life and renders it as data that can be quantified and computed.

> *Pour l'instant je suis violet comme un billet de 500.*[12]

Mohamed Bourouissa's 2012 video *All-in* depicts the process of minting a coin with an image of Élie Yaffa, better known as the rap artist Booba. Partly filmed at the historic Monnaie de Paris, the film uses Booba's 2009 autobiographical song 'Fœtus' as a soundtrack, music that Bourouissa has described as embracing 'the values of capitalism through its visual codes'.[13] The song is accompanied by images of the coin being inscribed with Booba's portrait and the lyrics become integral to Bourouissa's image of the manufacture of money. The coin is symbolic of a brand in which the artist's music, image and life story are intertwined as a commodity.

During the course of the twentieth century boundaries between reality and fiction were slowly eroded, and more recent digital technology has served to accelerate this process. Martine Syms has described her on-screen chatbot avatar in the work *Mythiccbeing* (2018) as the embodiment of 'the experienced "self" and its myriad outward inflections through digital media'.[14] The work is densely layered with images and text, much of it drawn directly from Syms' own archive of photos, videos and messages on her smartphone. We are invited to interact with the chatbot via SMS, and Syms' uncanny avatar prompts us with a barrage of statements and questions in response, each assuming equal importance:

> What am I protecting 1. DESPAIR 2. UNAVAILABILITY... There's always an opportunity for failure... Part of me wants to go to Basel, part of me wants to go to Mexico... Should I go to Miami? For Thanksgiving... Athens for New Years, I don't know... Should I go to Miami?...[15]

Inasmuch as it addresses the human psyche and alludes to various issues, including identity, race and gender, *Mythiccbeing* is a work about agency and the ability of technology to augment and fictionalise narratives.

The text messages sent to *Mythiccbeing* trigger different responses and chapters of video. The chatbot elicits participation, continuously writing and re-writing its narrative, which is, as becomes apparent over time, made up of a finite reserve of stock responses. The work is a collage of fragments drawn from what McLuhan might describe as 'a store of work and experience' or what Shoshana Zuboff has referred to as an 'electronic text'; the 'textualisation of the world', in which our lives are 'digitised' and 'translated into information'.[16]

This 'electronic text' is elsewhere cut-up, collaged and given a human voice or visual permanence in the monumentally-scaled works of Nora Turato. Like a beat poet channelling the textual hysteria of the smartphone era,[17] Turato takes words and phrases from the media and her own (text-based) conversations and stitches them together into epic 'scripts'. The physical scale of her transcriptions are in direct conflict with the seemingly casual nature by which they appear set down. Quoted out of context and accentuated by the instrument of the human voice (in the spoken word performances) or visually (within the artist's books or wall paintings), language becomes volatile, provocative and incendiary.

'In the industrial age' writes McLuhan, 'the media of money and writing and clock began to converge into an organic whole again that has brought us close to the total involvement of man in his work ... [as] of an artist in his studio'.[18] The nature of work has evolved yet further today. Wark contends, there is 'no relation between the units of labour time and the units of value produced'.[19] For those engaged in the production of content – be it music, advertising or any creative endeavour – the pressure is not to manufacture units of sameness but rather 'to produce difference out of sameness'.[20] In contradistinction to the repetitions of the industrial *worker*, whose labour is seasonal or measured as they clock on and off: 'It happens when it happens ... The workplace nightmare of the worker is having to make the same thing, over and over, against the pressure of the clock; the workplace nightmare of the hacker [as Wark names them] is to produce *different* things, over and over, against the pressure of the clock'.[21]

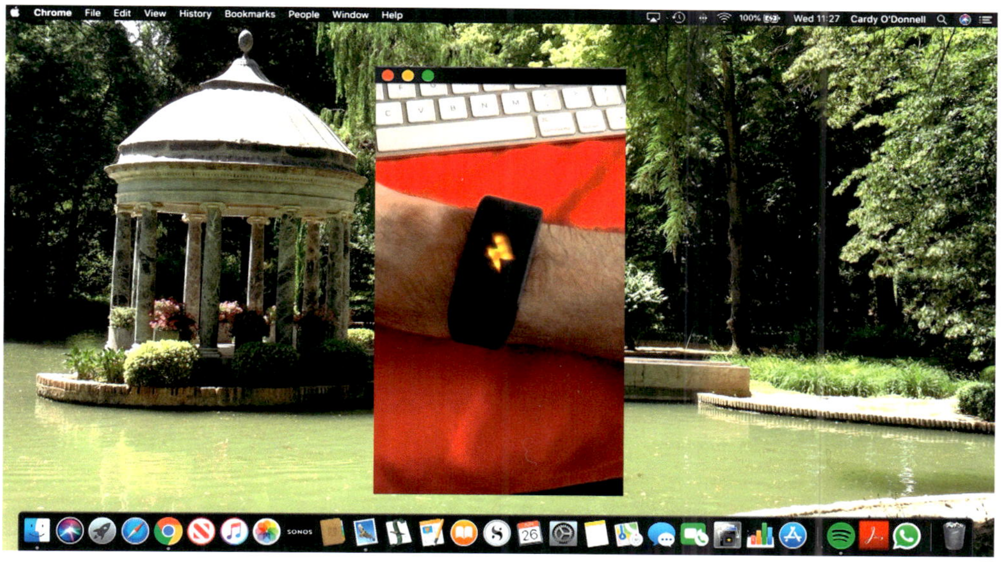

Film still from Liz Magic Laser, *In Real Life*, 2019

Cameron Rowland's series of *Handpunch* photographs (produced 2014–15) and Liz Magic Laser's 2019 five-channel video *In Real Life* can be seen to represent these two poles of contemporary labour. Whereas Rowland's photographs take the widespread use of biometric clocks to monitor employee time as their subject, Laser's work considers the round-the-clock labour of the so-called gig economy. Laser used online platforms such as Fiverr and PeoplePerHour to recruit five individuals based in Hong Kong, Nigeria, Pakistan and the United Kingdom to become both the subjects and producers of a film. Employed variously for their skills in animation, graphic design, scriptwriting, developing social media content and providing voiceover narration, the freelance workers are each alternately the focus of the five-part, 112-minute documentary, in which they undergo Laser's '30 Day Biohack Challenge'. Online consultations with a 'biohacking life coach' prescribe an array of apps and devices to address issues such as cyberslacking, weight gain or stress and to 'optimise their minds and bodies for success'. The exercise humorously demonstrates the tech industry's ingenuity for self-medication. *In Real Life* offers a study of the globalised gig economy. Yet, ultimately, this narrative serves to critique the means and conditions of its own production.[22]

The subjects of *In Real Life* might be described by Wark as 'hackers', individuals who were 'supposed to be privileged' by virtue of their creativity and technical skills. The freedom they appear to enjoy in terms of their basic working conditions – being able to choose (notionally at least) when, where, for whom and for how long they work – sets them apart from the industrial worker. The restrictive implications of a timeclock employing criminal identification technologies to log time at work (in Rowland's *Handpunch* series), or the human-scale cage fabricated by Simon Denny in the 2020 sculpture *Amazon worker cage patent drawing as virtual Aquatic Warbler cage (US 9,280,157 B2: "System and method for transporting personnel within an active workspace", 2016)* appear somewhat draconian by comparison. The latter reproduces a design patented by the online retail company Amazon to 'protect' employees in their warehouses. Yet Laser's subjects variously struggle to achieve a work-life balance and their predicament also resonates with Wark's description of the hacker who finds that their work has been 'made casual and precarious'.[23]

In Real Life chronicles the isolating experience of freelance employment in a global labour market, in which opportunities to develop relationships with clients and colleagues are limited and round-the-clock working disrupts the regular pattern of social and family life at home. The subjects appear linked through a predicament of social alienation, a condition often associated with industrial working conditions but also clearly embodied in Denny's emblematic sculpture, which can be seen as a metaphor for isolation and confinement in contemporary capitalism. Such alienating conditions are also playfully explored in Cao Fei's 2018 film *Asia One*, which is set in the eponymous warehouse of China's largest e-commerce company, Jingdong or JD.com. The film's theatrical treatment of the factory space exploits our perception of it as a somewhat hidden zone in which all movement is intensely choreographed. The warehouse or factory is 'backstage' to the (more spectacular) retail experience, out of sight and out of mind in a way that undoubtedly serves to benefit capitalism.

Asia One was made some two thousand kilometres away from the Bitcoin 'mining' facility that is the subject of Yuri Pattison's work *the ideal* (2015–ongoing). Titled partly after John Nash's theoretical concept of 'Ideal Money' – which is defined by Nash as 'money intrinsically not subject to inflation'[24] – it refers to a facility in a warehouse that

Film still from Yuri Pattison, *the ideal*, 2015–ongoing

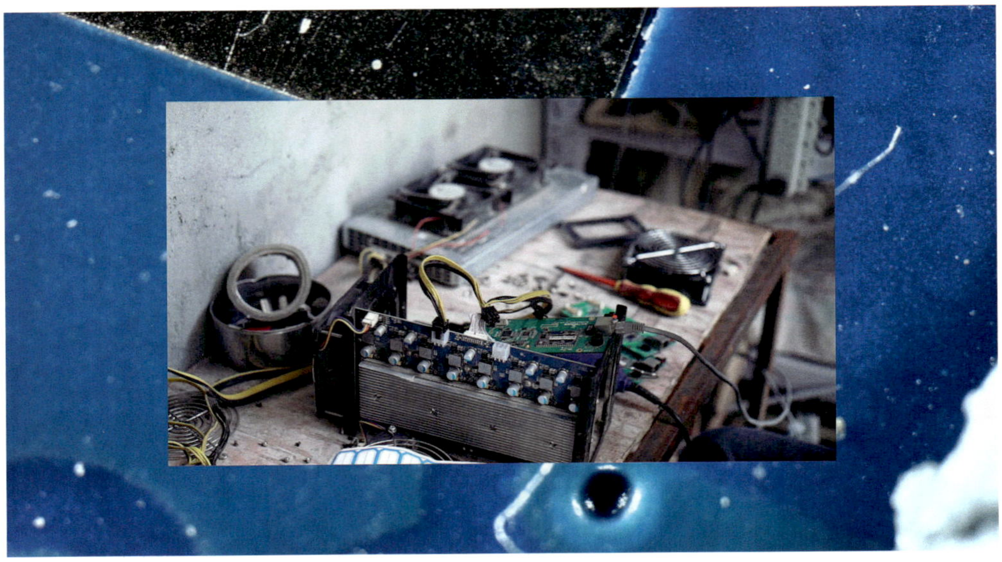

neighbours (and is powered by) a hydroelectric dam in remote mountains on the edge of the Tibetan Plateau near Kongyuxiang, Sichuan, China. The work shows the generation of cryptocurrency on an industrial scale, incorporating a video with footage filmed by an employee. Sequences showing the interior, with its deafening noise and dark corridors of shelves stacked floor to ceiling with hardware and trailing wires, are interposed with aerial views of the rural location, filmed by a drone. This back-and-forth between the mine and the surrounding natural environment calls to mind the ecological impact of the production; the daily energy consumption of Bitcoin (for 350,000 transactions) is equivalent to 0.5 percent of the world's electricity. According to one meteorologist, Bitcoin would require fourteen times the world's energy to entirely replace our daily credit card transactions.[25]

The ideal brings us closer to the material reality of cryptocurrency, drawing attention to its machinery, human labour and energy consumption. The video plays within a sculptural architecture incorporating hardware that actively mines Bitcoin, and a water-cooling system that alludes to the source of power for the facility in Kongyuxiang. This element – which recalls Hans Haacke's 1963–65 *Condensation Cube* sculpture[26] – also incorporates a number of stones from a riverbed downstream from the dam. The choice of this natural object is also significant, stones having once been used as a form of currency. *The ideal* oscillates between conditions of visibility and invisibility; moving between public and private space; light and dark; material and immaterial. As such, it mirrors the dualities inherent within Bitcoin's own 'peer-to-peer' system, which claims transparency by facilitating transactions that are publicly visible whilst providing anonymity by not identifying their real-world entities.

Elsewhere, conditions of secrecy and anonymity are part of an unofficial trade of food stamps documented in *Dropping the 10th Digit* by Shadi Habib Allah. The lightboxes illuminate photographs of scrawled notes kept behind the counters of various convenience stores in Miami. The notes serve as ledgers for the cash and non-redeemable items (such as phone credit, cigarettes, alcohol, non-prescription drugs) received in exchange for the government-issued coupons intended for buying food.[27] Their somewhat fragile, ephemeral nature seems to reflect the economic precarity behind the transactions, the customers reliant upon welfare payments and the stores having their margins squeezed by the hypermarkets built by multinational retail corporations.

These works by Rowland, Laser, Denny, Cao Fei, Pattison and Habib Allah variously give form to less-visible facets of modern production and consumption: the operations behind the counter, in the secure warehouse or the private, domestic spaces that are co-opted as workplaces by the gig economy, such as the closet in Hong Kong that served as a studio for recording the voiceover for Laser's film. Each of these works exploits the essentially visual medium of art to give focus to subjects that lack primacy, and might otherwise escape our attention. They also seem to suggest that we have arrived at the state of 'total involvement' in work that McLuhan described in 1964. Production is not only in the fields, the factories, or the offices; production happens everywhere.

Part of Lara Favaretto's ongoing, three-part work *Thinking Head* (conceived in 2017) consists of 'clandestine talks' that consider one-word topics inspired by a collection of objects (*surplus, power* and *hacker* are chosen for this exhibition). The conversations take place without an audience and in an undisclosed, private location; they are not visible or audible within the exhibition, but rather livestreamed via the internet. The visual record of this labour is discreetly limited to a single photograph that shows the location of the

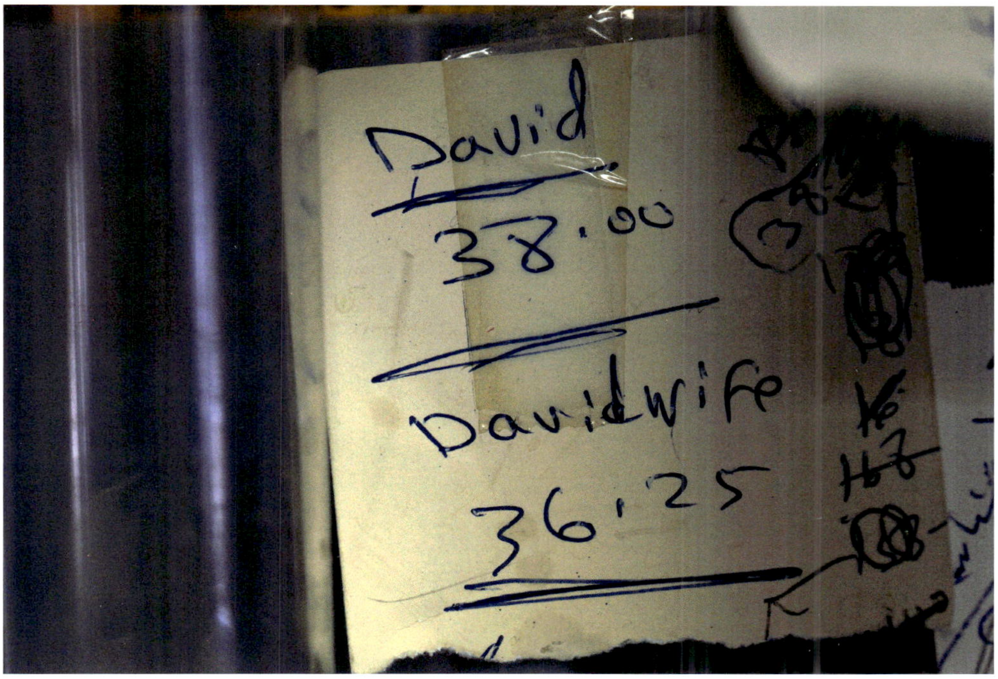

Shadi Habib Allah, *Dropping the 10th Digit*, 2018 (detail)

recording, but as an empty room. The talks can be seen to dematerialise the objects in thinking, or rather in discourse. On one level it might seem obvious that they would end up on the internet, the ultimate dumping ground for so many dematerialised things. Yet this gesture also circumnavigates the museum's participatory channels and its apparatus for engagement, inclusivity and dialogue, placing the 'content' in the public space of the internet.

Works by Guan Xiao, GCC, Nick Relph, Laura Owens, Katja Novitskova and Josephine Pryde variously refer to consumption; the more image-laden end of the supply chain, thick with visual manifestations of commodity. In the work of Guan Xiao and GCC there is a focus on material culture and hyper-consumption. Guan Xiao's somewhat totemic sculptures employ bronze casts of tree roots that are strewn with an eclectic array of high-tech, readymades and fibreglass casts of 3D-printed objects. The latter render icons or characters such as a hash mark (#) as large, physical entities. Extending over the floor with frond- or limb-like appendages or with a series of smaller elements, they appear like the flotsam and jetsam of our material excess.

Similarly, the dense succession of computer-generated images and verbose narration in GCC's video *CO-OP* satirises the politics of conspicuous consumption, with its accelerated and needless extravagance. *CO-OP* quotes from a vast number of computer-generated architectural drawings (largely showing designs for buildings in the Arabian Gulf). Such drawings are also the basis for Nick Relph's photographic series of New York buildings. Both emphasise the aspirational consumer narratives that underwrite such designs, yet in Relph's photographs, which were made by manually scanning renders wrapped around various construction sites across the city, the material is given the opposite treatment. Here it is not the speed of change and transformation that emerges, but rather the stillness of photography. Images of virtual real estate, which encapsulate so many casual consumer desires – from living with designer furniture to drinking a coffee in a landscaped precinct – are given a texture that invites close reading. The buildings appear ghost-like and overwritten with graffiti, dirt, notices and other ephemera. Collectively they describe a certain poverty in excess, perhaps indicative of a culture in which even bricks and mortar find their value in the fulfilment of digital prophecies.

Excess is also found, in digital form, in the motifs painted by Owens and the sculptures of Novitskova. Whereas Owens incorporates text and images from spam emails or internet advertising (here promoting bird feeders) within her compositions, Novitskova produces larger-than-life, two-dimensional sculptures from affective images of animals: a four-eyed, tiger-furred, jumping spider is framed by a pair of termite mounds; a bright blue cassowary stares out from under a huge, horny casque. Each is accompanied by a primary-coloured, upward-pointing arrow, a crude vector of growth that might elsewhere be used to illustrate a rising trend in stocks. The works refer to the monetisation of our attention, as McKenzie Wark writes (referencing Yves Citton), 'in a world awash in digital data, what is rare is the attention paid to it'.[28] Arresting images of the natural world – similar to those that trend online via likes and shares – are sourced from the internet and made into sculpture. They address us, somewhat insistently, head-on, and their arrow

Film still from GCC, *CO-OP*, 2014

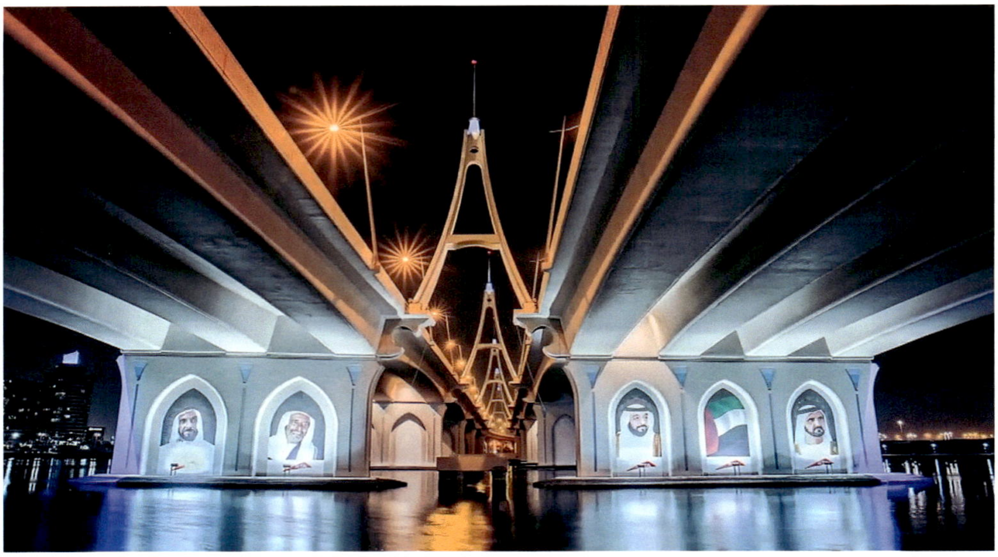

can be seen to mimic or predict their own reception. The arrow is also symbolic of a culture in which our emotions can be objectified and quantified in numerical form; experience and emotions are transcribed as 'social media', a translation that has the potential to fundamentally change 'the structure of society' and can indeed be seen to create 'new social and economic dynamics... new politics'.[29] The 'electronic text', Zuboff argues, has been 'used to survey and to control rather than to empower and to teach'.[30]

> We write to the machine, it collects and aggregates our desires and fantasies, segments them by market and demographic and sells them back to us as a commodity experience.[31]

Richard Seymour compares the economic model of social media to that of the industries profiting from gambling and addiction. 'Our social industry accounts' writes Seymour, 'are set up like enterprises competing for eyeball attention... we are all authors now', writing 'not for money, but the satisfaction of being read'. Thus 'going viral, or "trending"' can be the 'equivalent of a windfall' or 'the worst thing that can happen'.[32] Borrowing Zuboff's Foucauldian image of the 'information panopticon' Seymour describes the addictive effect of an arena in which anyone may be observed at any time and 'any person' may 'suddenly be isolated and selected for demonstrative punishment'.[33] Its mechanism of self-surveillance is also 'central' to the 'production – of endless writing – more efficient in its way than a sweatshop'. 'To inhabit the social industry', contends Seymour, 'is to be in a state of constant distractedness, a junkie fixation on keeping in touch with it, knowing where it is and how to get it'.[34]

Such dependencies and their close connection to our self-image inform Josephine Pryde's series of photographs, *Hands (Für mich),* (2014–ongoing). Colourfully manicured hands are shown touching various objects or are held against the body in a gesture that reads as something between a hand-on-heart declaration of honesty and one of self-esteem. The lighting and composition of the images invite comparisons with commercial photography. Isolated and under close scrutiny, the gestures describe an intimacy between subject and object. Several works selected for this exhibition feature smartphones or tablet computers that appear to be clutched, caressed or cradled. Accessories for a culture in which the commodity appears – in the words of Wark – 'as nothing but a vector... apotential fulfilled through the interface' of the device.[35]

In drawing attention to the smooth surfaces and soft glows of these objects, Pryde's photographs can be seen to address commodity fetishism as a mode of self-expression (be it in digital or material form). Yet they also speak to a more nebulous condition of alienation: the loneliness of a culture in which, even in genuinely social situations, people prefer solitary interactions with a machine.[36] Seymour links a decline in alcohol, nicotine and drug consumption to the rise of the smartphone, suggesting it appeared in our hands at the same moment that we abandoned cigarettes and alcohol. Yet where the latter were 'props for social interaction' the smartphone is 'an escape route, a way to connect with someone who isn't there; or is only there as a written trace, a ghost in the machine'.[37] He writes:

> The smartphone is our portal to the world, our golden ticket out of here. It holds our credit cards, music, magazines, audiobooks, maps, movies, games, tickets and keys. It is our wayfinder. It connects us to family members, workmates

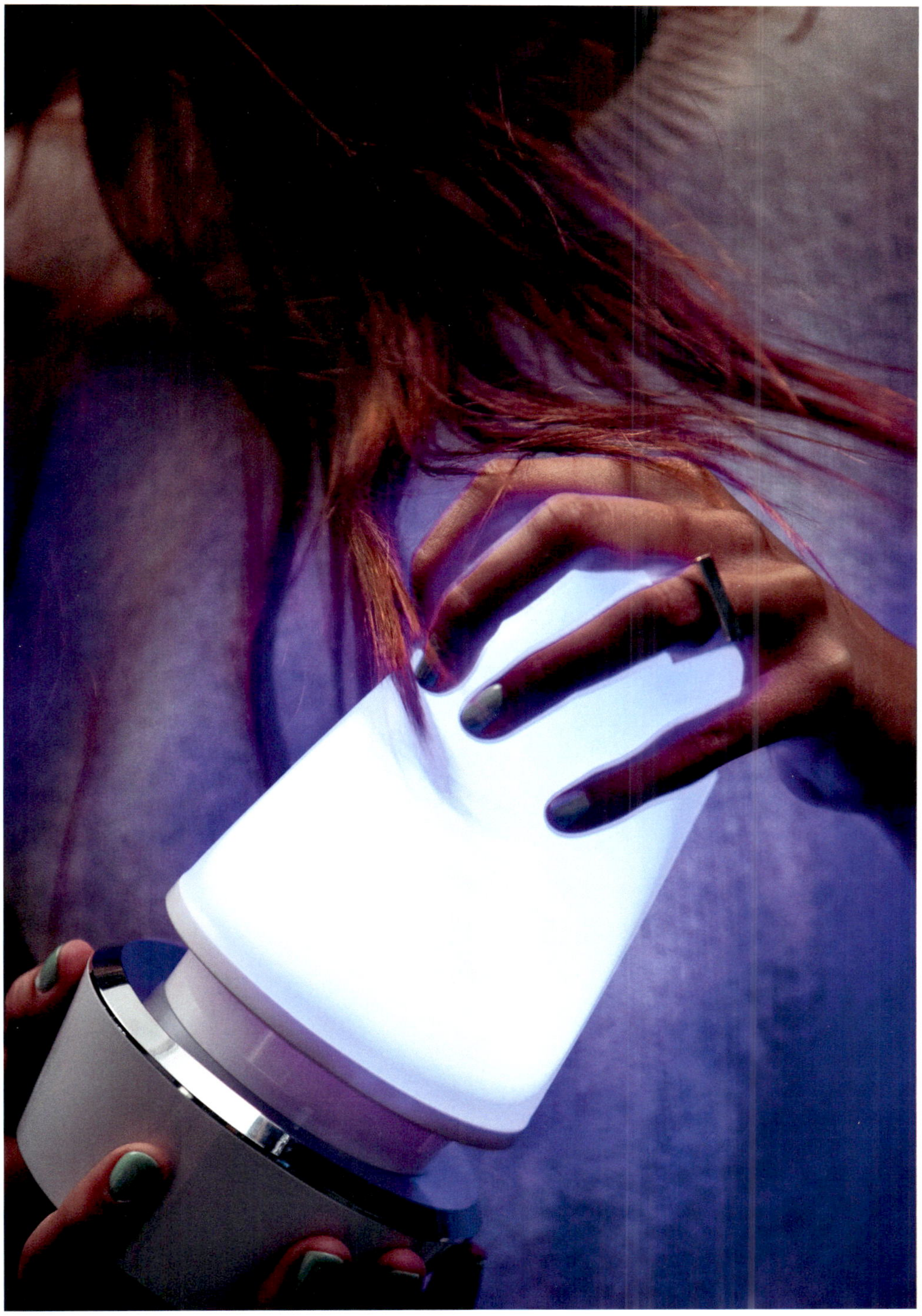

Josephine Pryde,
Küsse sind das, 2014

> and irresistible internet bullies. We use it to get dates, to get dinner. It breaks up our day... into "jittery, schizoid intervals" with constant updates. We keep it close, charged at all times. It is as though one day it's going to bring us the message we have been waiting for.[38]

The notion of property, its manifestations and relationship to power are variously explored in works by Sondra Perry, Hito Steyerl and Oliver Laric. Perry and Steyerl's works address issues of sovereignty and juridical control. *IT'S IN THE GAME* '18 *or Mirror Gag for Projection and Two Universal Shot Trainers with Nasal Cavity and Pelvis* refers to the real-life experience of Sondra Perry's twin brother, Sandy. A college basketball player, Sandy's physical likeness and statistics (and those of his teammates) became part of the intellectual property of the NCAA (National Collegiate Athletic Association), who in turn sold them to the publisher, EA Sports, for use within a videogame. Perry's mixed media installation incorporates quotes from the legal settlement established between the athletes, the NCAA and EA Sports, situating the narrative within a legacy of systemic racism.

Steyerl's installation, *FreePlots* (2019–ongoing), refers to the phenomenon of the freeport, the 'somewhat extraterritorial' storage facility that the artist has described as 'a zone of legalised extra-legality'.[39] In the essay *Duty Free Art,* Steyerl considers

Oliver Laric, 3D scan rendering of John Gibson's *Hunter and Dog*, 2013 from the website threedscans.com

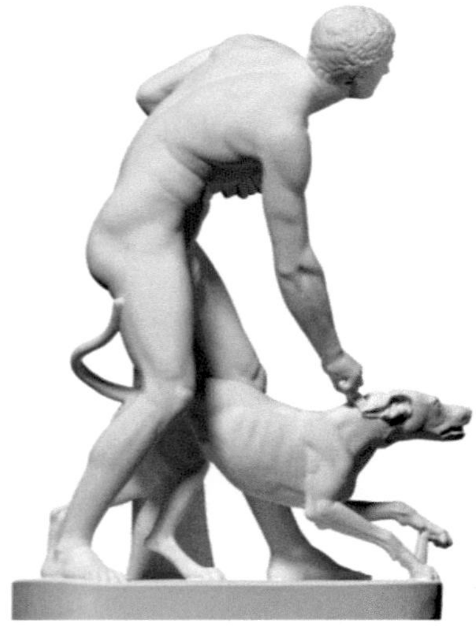

Artist: John Gibson
Period: 19th Century
Material: Stone, marble
Location: The Usher Gallery, Lincoln
Inscription: JOANNES GIBSON FACIEBAT ROMAE
Dimensions: 147.5 x 58.5 x 99.1 cm
Scanned: 2013
Scanner: Creaform Go!SCAN 3D

the priceless artworks and other goods rumoured to be stored at such facilities, proposing the freeport as 'a museum of the internet era… a museum of the dark net, where movement is obscured and data space is clouded'.[40] *FreePlots* – which takes the form of a series of planters designed to mimic the shape of freeports in Geneva and Panama – notionally exchanges the contents of this dark, dead zone for several kilos of manure-based compost and plants grown by local people via collaborations with community garden schemes. Privately-owned assets stashed in 'spaces that bypass national sovereignty'[41] are thus (symbolically) exchanged for living organisms seeded by groups of people who share a common interest in green space and in growing plants, fruits and vegetables.

Laric's website threedscans.com could be seen as an internet-era museum of an entirely opposite character. If the freeport is a 'museum of the dark net', threedscans.com might be a museum for the 'digital commons'. The objects on display, some 112 at the time of writing, are drawn from museum collections all over the world. Each is labelled with information regarding their authorship, date of creation, materials, location and dimensions, and represented via a free, downloadable 3D model. These effigies are variously based upon authorised scans or produced from hundreds of images taken by professional photographers that Laric hires and dispatches to public collections for this purpose. They are an undertaking that involves the work of lawyers, photographers, fabricators and museum professionals. Moreover, their broader, predominantly internet-based, dissemination, (be it, for example, in the work of other artists, in images posted on Instagram, the credits for a Netflix TV series or the digital scenography for an entry in the Eurovision Song Contest), are catalogued for each object.[42] The work both makes use of and extends the public museum's proposition of public access to a shared, cultural heritage. Here knowledge (in the form of objects that can be downloaded, viewed, manipulated, put within any context, and made real by anyone who knows how in any part of the world) remains in the global, public domain.

> The bourgeoisie cannot exist without constantly revolutionising the instruments of production, and thereby the relations of production, and with them the whole relations of society… Constant revolutionising of production, uninterrupted disturbance of all social conditions, everlasting uncertainty and agitation distinguish the bourgeois epoch from all earlier ones. All fixed, fast-frozen relations, with their train of ancient and venerable prejudices and opinions, are swept away, all new-formed ones become antiquated before they can ossify. All that is solid melts into air, all that is holy is profaned, and man is at last compelled to face with sober senses his real conditions of life, and his relations with his kind.[43]

Karl Marx and Friedrich Engels characterised capitalism as a dynamic system tending towards self-destruction. Wark makes the point that the sheer number of 'modifiers' (late, neo-liberal, platform, surveillance and attentional, to name a few) attached to the term 'capitalism' seem to suggest that language is failing us. What if the economic system that Marx and Engels described in 1848 was itself dematerialised and 'swept away'? Perhaps we didn't notice, suggests Wark, because the 'wonderful dream of a "post-industrial society"'[44] never materialised. Perhaps we didn't notice because the situation is not better, but worse?

> If one takes a look at the top *Fortune 500* companies, it is surprising how many of them are really in the information business. I don't just mean the technology and telecommunication companies like Apple or Google or Verizon or Cisco or the drug companies like Pfizer. One could also think of the big banks as a subset of the vectoralist class rather than as "finance capital". They too are in the information asymmetry business.[45]

Wark's name for 'the dominant ruling class of our time' is the 'vectoralist class'. Whereas the 'hacker class produces new information' i.e. 'whatever intellectual property law recognises as new'[46], the vectoralist class 'own and control the patents, the brands and celebrities that galvanise attention... the logistics and supply chains that keep information in its proprietary stacks'[47], i.e. the 'vector along which information is gathered and used'.[48] They do not, according to Wark, 'appropriate a quantity of surplus value so much as exploit an asymmetry of information'. Thus, we may obtain 'free' access to information from a search engine, assemble a social network or acquire the logistical infrastructure to run a small business, but:

> while you get that little piece of information, this ruling class gets all of that information in the aggregate. It exploits the asymmetry between the little you know and the aggregate it knows – an aggregate it collects based on information you were obliged to "volunteer".[49]

As I write, somewhere in the Czech Republic a Mikoyan Gurevich MiG-21 jet fighter aircraft acquired by Roger Hiorns in 2017 is being prepared for its next journey. Designed in the 1950s in the Soviet Union, the MiG-21 became one of the most widely produced and longest-serving combat aircraft in history. This example, which dates from the 1980s and originates in the Czech Republic, was previously buried by Hiorns on the outskirts of Prague, an act that rendered it invisible as part of an international network of subterranean aircraft that the artist conceived in 1990 and inaugurated in 2016.[50] Now exhumed, it will travel by road to Luxembourg, where it will be fitted with coils of plastic tubing and a pump that will keep a quantity of 'liquid pizza' in constant flow. Hiorns has compared the apparatus to a 'digestive' system, yet nothing is actually digested, but rather suspended in the relentless cycle of consumption around this obsolete icon of the Cold War.

The series, *The retrospective view of the pathway* (2017–ongoing) can be seen to exemplify something that James Bridle has described as the 'nexus of transparency / opacity and visibility / invisibility' in aviation. Bridle gives the example of publicly accessible websites that allow users to track thousands of planes on international flight paths in real time. The public availability of such data gives the impression of transparency whilst also serving 'to block out and erase other private and state activities, from the private jets of oligarchs and politicians to covert surveillance flights and military manoeuvres. For everything that is shown, something is hidden'.[51] According to Bridle, the opacity of this system is symptomatic of a 'new dark age' in which we are 'utterly enmeshed in technological systems', that 'shape... how we act and how we think'. 'Technological acceleration' Bridle argues, 'has transformed our planet, our societies and ourselves but it has failed to transform our understanding of these things'.[52]

The 'nexus' that Bridle describes is a subject for Hiorns' broader oeuvre; objects are often transformed by the presence of something not discernible to the eye or by a process that renders them unrecognisable. There are several examples involving aircraft. For instance, *Untitled,* 2008, presents an 'atomised passenger aircraft engine' as a pile of grey metal dust; or *Untitled (Alliance)*, 2010, which comprises two Pratt & Whitney TF33 P9 engines from a military surveillance plane secreted with anti-depressant drugs. For the sculptural intervention in the Czech Republic, Hiorns made a public artwork from an object that is deliberately hidden from view. Now unearthed and brought inside the museum, the plane becomes a piece of archaeology, a relic of this process but also a metaphor for the Cold War era and the communist system that produced the plane.

Around this object there will flow a foodstuff that can be traced back to the 6th century, when Persian soldiers of the Achaemenid Empire used their battle shields to bake flatbreads garnished with cheese and dates. The word 'pizza' is believed to derive, in part, from the Lombardic word *bizzo* or *pizzo*, meaning mouthful. This very etymology recommends its contemporary success in global capitalism as a fast food. Processed beyond recognition, in Hiorns' work it is the fleshy material in the system, flowing around the redundant machine like some abject vision of abstracted human labour. This cyborgian arrangement of machinery and pizza offers a not-so-ordinary image of the 'business of life' at this moment. This broken aircraft, hooked up to a pump like a body on life support, is animated only by that system, a technological architecture that keeps the pizza in constant flow. Hiorns' image is one that holds allusions to the past but ultimately speaks to our present. An image of terminal stasis that prompts the question: What next?

1 Economist Alfred Marshall (b. 1842, London; d. 1924 Cambridge) published *Principles of Economics* in 1890, wherein he defined economics as 'a study of mankind in the ordinary business of life; it examines that part of individual and social action which is most closely connected with the attainment, and with the use of the material requisites of wellbeing'.

2 Growth in GDP had already slowed in 2018 and 2019 to 3.6% and 2.9% in Advanced Economies and 4.5% and 3.7% for Emerging Market and Developing Economies respectively. The drop in GDP for Advanced Economies in 2020 was −4.7% with European countries (Spain, UK, Italy, France and Germany) experiencing the largest declines. It is projected to rise by 5.1% in 2021. The figures for Emerging Market and Developing Economies for 2020 and 2021 are −2.2% and 6.7%. Of these only China continued to grow in 2020 (by 2.3%). At the time of writing this essay GDP remained below end-of-2019 levels, however the US is projected to recover in the first half of 2021 and Europe / UK in 2022. The medium-term loss relative to the pre-pandemic projections is 3% for the world economy. Although smaller than that in the aftermath of the global financial crisis, low-income countries and emerging markets are projected to suffer more from the fallout than in the crisis a decade earlier when advanced economies were harder hit. Sources: *IMF World Economic Outlook* annual reports, April 2019; April 2020 and April 2021, https://www.imf.org/en/Publications/Search?series=World%20Economic%20Outlook (accessed 5 July 2021).

3 Peter F. Drucker, *Post-Capitalist Society*, New York: HarperCollins, 1993, pp. 44–45.

4 *Ibid.*, p. 182.

5 *Ibid.*, p. 45.

6 McKenzie Wark, *Capital Is Dead: Is this Something Worse?*, London / New York: Verso, 2019, p. 5.

7 *Family Dollar (Social Capital)*, 2020 lyrics by Ei Arakawa & Dan Poston; music by Arakawa, arranged by ZALA from Mish-Mosh.

8 The works refer to performances at Museum of Modern Art, New York; Tate Modern, London and the Berlin Bienniale, amongst others.

9 Ei Arakawa, *Notes on Fees & Nerf by Ei Arakawa (Sep 2, 2020)*, artist statement for the exhibition *Ei Arakawa: Fees & Nerf*, 4 September to 31 October 2020, Galerie Max Meyer, Düsseldorf.

10 Marshall McLuhan, *Understanding Media*, London / New York: Routledge, 1964, p. 152.

11 *Ibid.*, p. 147.

12 Lyric from Booba's 2009 song, 'Fœtus'.

13 Mohamed Bourouissa quoted from the interview in the documentary film *All-in*, produced by Kamel Mennour, 2013, https://www.youtube.com/watch?v=vl51Klw8USA (accessed 21 June 2021).

14 Quoted from a text written by the artist, sent to the author via email from Sadie Coles HQ, 28 May 2021.

15 Unfortunately, Syms was unable to adapt the chatbot for this presentation, and eventually took the decision to exhibit a non-interactive version of this work.

16 See Shoshana Zuboff, *In the Age of the Smart Machine: The Future of Work and Power*, New York: Basic Books, 1988 and Zuboff interviewed by Noah Kulwin: 'Shoshana Zuboff on Surveillance Capitalism's Threat to Democracy', *New York Magazine*, 24 February 2019, https://nymag.com/intelligencer/2019/02/shoshana-zuboff-q-and-a-the-age-of-surveillance-capital.html (accessed 17 June 2021).

17 I am indebted to Myriam Ben Salah for this phrase, taken from her succinct appraisal of Turato's work in Art Basel's *Curator's Picks*, September 2020, https://www.youtube.com/watch?v=DqiYbK7re8I (accessed 17 June 2021).

18 McLuhan, *op. cit.*, pp. 155–156.

19 Wark, *op. cit.*, p. 44.

20 *Ibid.*, p. 13.

21 *Ibid.*, p. 43.

22 See Catherine Taft's review of this work: 'More documentary than reality-TV show, this fascinating study of the globalised gig economy is differentiated as "art" through its ambitions of institutional critique. That is, the work points to the means and conditions of its own production and circulation'. in 'Liz Magic Laser', *Artforum*, February 2020, p. 206.

23 Wark, *op. cit.*, p. 48.

24 Mathematician John Forbes Nash Jr. (b. 1928, Bluefield, West Virginia; d. 2015, Monroe Township, New Jersey) quoted here from https://en.wikipedia.org/wiki/Ideal_money (accessed 17 June 2021). The same page claims that 'the implication bitcoin will become the single world currency, does satisfy Nash's proposal to have internationally stable money'. Pattison invokes this term somewhat ironically, viewing the situation 'as less than ideal'. Bitcoin, he explains 'has amplified and accelerated some of the worst aspects of capitalism', although he believes that cryptocurrencies have been scapegoated by the media for excesses, that 'could / should be applied more broadly in terms of a critical understanding of networked technology'. Email to the author, 31 May 2021.

25 Eric Holthaus, @EricHolthaus, Twitter, 18 February 2021. See also https://grist.org/article/bitcoin-could-cost-us-our-clean-energy-future (accessed 17 June 2021) and James Bridle, *New Dark Age: Technology and the End of the Future*, London / New York: Verso, 2018, p. 63.

26 This seminal work comprises a small amount of water within a hermetically sealed Perspex box. The state of the condensation (and thus the work's appearance) changes with the climatic conditions of its environment. It can be seen to anticipate the artist's later work on social, political and economic systems presenting a process and physical system as sculpture.

27 Namely 'Fruits and vegetables; Meat, poultry, and fish; Dairy products and Breads and cereals'. Source: US Government Services and Information, https://www.usa.gov/food-help (accessed 17 June 2021).

28 Wark refers to Yves Citton's influential book, *The Ecology of Attention*, Cambridge: Polity Press, 2017. Wark, *op. cit.*, p. 56.

29 Drucker, see note 4.

30 Zuboff interviewed by Kulwin.

31 Richard Seymour, *The Twittering Machine*, London: The Indigo Press, 2019, p. 26.

32 *Ibid.*, p. 30.

33 *Ibid.*, p. 39.

34 *Ibid.*, p. 44.

35 Wark, *op. cit.*, p. 15.

36 Pryde explains 'by mixing up the types of objects reached for and held, I wanted also to speak to objects as residues of memories and potencies and connections we make, too. So the loneliness or melancholy is also something we live and touch, maybe, and have to live and touch, too… Not including the heads of the subjects was a way to foreground another sense as part of our language… to see touching'. Email from the artist, 16 May 2021.

37 Seymour, *op. cit.*, p. 57.

38 *Ibid.*, p. 69.

39 Hito Steyerl, *Duty Free Art: Art in the Age of Planetary Civil War*, London / New York: Verso, 2017, p. 80.

40 *Ibid.*, p. 83.

41 *Ibid.*, p. 79.

42 Several of Laric's models were used in the Netflix series *Roman Empire*. The scan of John Gibson's 1847 neoclassical sculpture *Hunter and Dog* was used as part of the background animation for 'Grande Amore', an entry in the Eurovision Song Contest by the Italian group Il Volo in 2015. The same scan also appears in the video for 'MotorSport' by Migos, Nicki Minaj and Cardi B.

43 Karl Marx and Friedrich Engels, *The Communist Manifesto* originally published in German as the *Manifest der Kommunistischen Partei* in 1848. Quoted from: https://www.marxists.org/archive/marx/works/1848/communist-manifesto/ch01.htm (accessed 17 June 2021).

44 Wark, *op. cit.*, p. 116.

45 *Ibid.*, p. 45.

46 *Ibid.*, p. 43.

47 *Ibid.*, p. 13.

48 *Ibid.*, p. 3.

49 *Ibid.*, p. 55.

50 Hiorns' series *The retrospective view of the pathway* was inaugurated in 2016 with a decommissioned Hawker Siddeley Dominie T1 military plane buried at an undisclosed location close to the River Orwell on the outskirts of Ipswich, England. A second plane was buried in Haarlem, Netherlands in February 2018. The burial of the MiG-21 in Prague, in April of the same year, was the third in the series.

51 Bridle, *op. cit.*, pp. 35–36.

52 *Ibid.*, p. 2.

TOUT CE QUI EST SOLIDE SE DISSOUT DANS L'AIR
Michelle Cotton

Alfred Marshall a défini l'économie politique comme une étude de l'humanité « dans les affaires ordinaires de la vie[1] ». Cette branche de la connaissance, qui s'intéresse à la production, à la consommation et au transfert de richesse, était comprise par Marshall en 1890 non pas comme une science abstraite, mais comme quelque chose d'inhérent à la nature particulière de l'homme, l'économie étant un produit de l'effort, de la psyché et des désirs humains. En période de crise, alors que les plus grandes économies du monde se remettent à peine d'un déclin brutal et soudain (à une exception près, toutes les économies en voie de développement suivent un parcours similaire), la nécessité d'acquérir une perspective humaine sur ces problématiques – qui affectent les individus au niveau émotionnel et psychologique le plus profond – n'en est que plus apparente[2].

L'exposition *Post-Capital* se penche sur les contradictions, les aberrations et les questions éthiques liées aux « affaires ordinaires » de la vie contemporaine. Conçue à une période marquée par un fort ralentissement de la croissance économique, elle prend pour point de départ le paradoxe inhérent au système capitaliste, qui s'avère à la fois dépendant du progrès technologique et menacé par celui-ci. Le titre de l'exposition est emprunté à un livre de Peter Drucker paru en 1993, *Post-Capitalist Society*, sorte de manuel de gestion d'entreprise qui ne mentionne pas encore Internet (devenu accessible au grand public deux ans plus tôt). Pourtant, il décrit l'émergence d'un système dans lequel le « savoir » remplace « la terre, le travail et le capital » dans la création de richesse[3]. L'auteur établit un lien entre différents secteurs de l'économie tels que les laboratoires pharmaceutiques, l'industrie du divertissement et les télécommunications, affirmant que « les activités qui occupent la place centrale [sont] celles qui produisent et distribuent du savoir et de l'information ». Même les entreprises de vente au détail, affirme-t-il, font fortune en « réorganisant » leur « ancien modèle économique autour de l'information[4] ». Ainsi, il soutient que la « connaissance » est devenue « *la* ressource plutôt qu'*une* ressource » et que « ce phénomène change – fondamentalement – la structure de la société. Il crée de nouvelles dynamiques sociales et économiques. Il crée une nouvelle politique[5]. »

Plus récemment, McKenzie Wark a décrit le « prodigieux pouvoir d'organisation » que confère l'information à ses détenteurs lorsqu'elle est recueillie, triée, gérée, traitée et finalement instrumentalisée par le biais de la technologie « pour contrôler d'autres choses dans le monde ». Dans *Capital Is Dead: Is this Something Worse?* (2009), McKenzie Wark expose le paradoxe intrinsèque aux technologies qui « ont rendu l'information très, très bon marché et très, très abondante » tout en donnant « naissance à une étrange sorte d'économie politique, basée non seulement sur la raréfaction des choses mais également sur l'excès d'informations ». Sa théorie est la suivante :

> Ce n'est plus du capitalisme ; c'est quelque chose de pire. La classe dirigeante dominante de notre époque ne maintient plus son emprise par la propriété des moyens de production, comme le font les capitalistes. Ni par la propriété foncière, comme le font les propriétaires terriens. La classe dirigeante dominante de notre époque possède et contrôle l'information[6].

Cette exposition n'est pas une plaidoirie pour ou contre le changement technologique. Elle n'aspire pas non plus à définir la situation économique actuelle comme « post-capitale ». Toutefois, elle cherche à situer le travail d'une génération d'artistes (plus vaste que celles et ceux rassemblés ici) qui parlent à la fois du changement technologique et du capitalisme. Cet engagement a sans doute commencé à la fin des années 1960, lorsque la théorie cybernétique a pénétré le champ culturel et que l'étude des systèmes de communication et de contrôle a croisé la critique de la production et de la marchandisation de l'art développée par les artistes conceptuels. Pour peu que l'on remonte dans le temps, l'on notera qu'il trouve ses racines en partie dans la fascination ambivalente de la modernité pour « la machine ». Mais c'est surtout dans les années 1960 que le débat actuel a pris son essor, à mesure que les artistes ont commencé à organiser leur production artistique en fonction de règles, de séries de données et de documents, dématérialisant ainsi leur travail plusieurs dizaines d'années avant que le reste d'entre nous n'aspire à stocker ses données dans des *clouds* et à travailler dans des bureaux « sans papier ».

> *Money talk. Time is money. As sound as a dollar. Money to burn. Money won't lie.*[7]

Lorsque la pandémie de Covid-19 a rendu impossible les performances en public, Ei Arakawa a décidé de faire le point sur ses revenus dans une nouvelle série de « peintures »

Film still from Mohamed Bourouissa, *All-In,* 2012

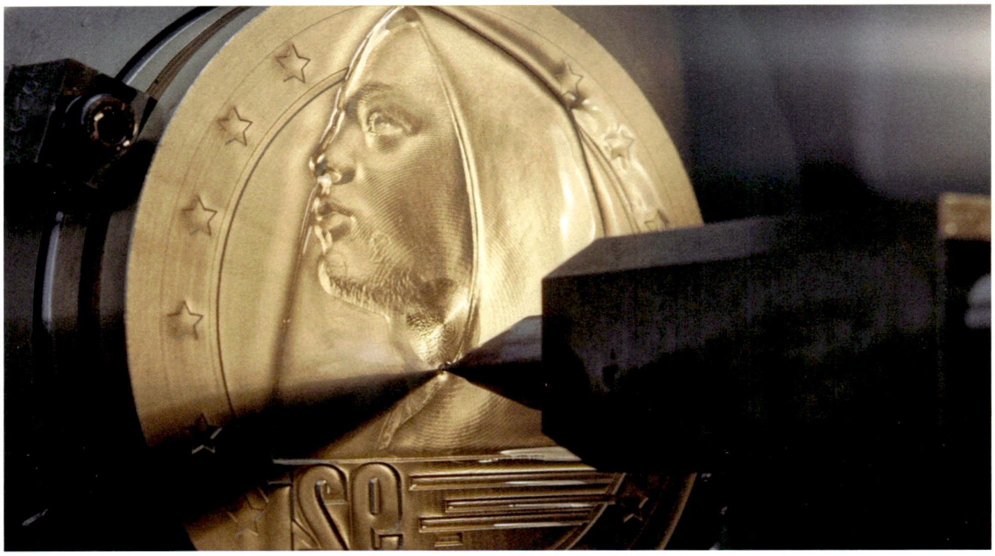

LED. Dans ces œuvres, les cachets reçus par l'artiste pour ses performances des quinze dernières années, calculés à la minute, s'affichent sous la forme d'une séquence d'images de pièces de monnaie qui éclairent la surface du support circulaire[8]. Incandescentes et éphémères, certaines de ces pièces tiennent aussi lieu d'« entités » performatives (la première de cette série entonne une chanson sur la récente faillite de l'institut de bronzage du frère de l'artiste). « Qu'y a-t-il au-delà de la simple comptabilité ? Quelle est cette énergie ?, demande l'artiste. Certains pensent / affirment que la performance se situe au-delà de la valeur des pièces de monnaie. Je ne mâche pas du chewing-gum[9] ! »

Marshall McLuhan classait l'argent dans la catégorie des « médias », à l'instar du langage, qu'il qualifiait d'« entrepôt de travail et d'expérience » qui est « aussi un traducteur et un transmetteur[10] ». Selon lui, « "l'argent parle" [...] parce que l'argent est une métaphore, un transfert, un pont. Comme les mots et le langage, l'argent est un réservoir de travail, de compétence et d'expérience communs[11] ». Face à l'impossibilité de performer, Ei Arakawa a réalisé une image de la performance, une image incarnée par l'argent. Bien que son geste soit conceptuel, il s'intègre parfaitement dans un monde où l'expérience vécue est traduite en information par le biais d'un processus qui fragmente la vie réelle et la restitue sous forme de données quantifiables et calculables.

> Pour l'instant je suis violet comme un billet de 500[12].

La vidéo *All-In* (2012) de Mohamed Bourouissa documente la frappe d'une pièce de monnaie à l'effigie d'Élie Yaffa, un rappeur mieux connu sous le nom de Booba. Tourné en partie dans le bâtiment historique de la Monnaie de Paris, le film utilise comme bande son la musique d'une chanson autobiographique du rappeur, « Fœtus », dont l'artiste dit qu'elle épouse « les valeurs du capitalisme à travers ses codes visuels[13] ». La chanson est accompagnée d'images de la pièce de monnaie sur laquelle est gravé le portrait de Booba. Les paroles de la chanson font partie intégrante de l'image de la fabrication de l'argent donnée par l'artiste, tandis que la pièce de monnaie devient le symbole d'une marque dans laquelle la musique, l'image et la vie de l'artiste s'entremêlent pour devenir une marchandise.

Au cours du XXe siècle, la frontière entre réalité et fiction s'est peu à peu érodée – un processus que les évolutions récentes de la technologie numérique n'ont fait qu'accélérer. Martine Syms décrit l'avatar qu'elle a créé à son image pour le chatbot de l'œuvre *Mythiccbeing* (2018) comme une incarnation du « "moi" vécu et de ses innombrables déclinaisons à travers les médias numériques[14] ». L'œuvre de l'artiste est une superposition complexe d'images et de textes qui proviennent majoritairement des photos, vidéos et messages qu'elle archive sur son smartphone. Alors que nous sommes invités à interagir avec le chatbot par SMS, l'étrange avatar de l'artiste nous noie sous un déluge de déclarations et de questions sans hiérarchie apparente :

> Qu'est-ce que je protège ? 1. DÉSESPOIR 2. INDISPONIBILITÉ... Il y a toujours moyen de faillir... Une partie de moi veut aller à Bâle, une autre à Mexico... Devrais-je aller à Miami ? Pour Thanksgiving... à Athènes pour le Nouvel An, je ne sais pas... Devrais-je aller à Miami ?...[15]

Dans la mesure où il sonde la psyché humaine et renvoie à des problématiques diverses telles que les questions d'identité, de race et de genre, *Mythiccbeing* est un travail sur

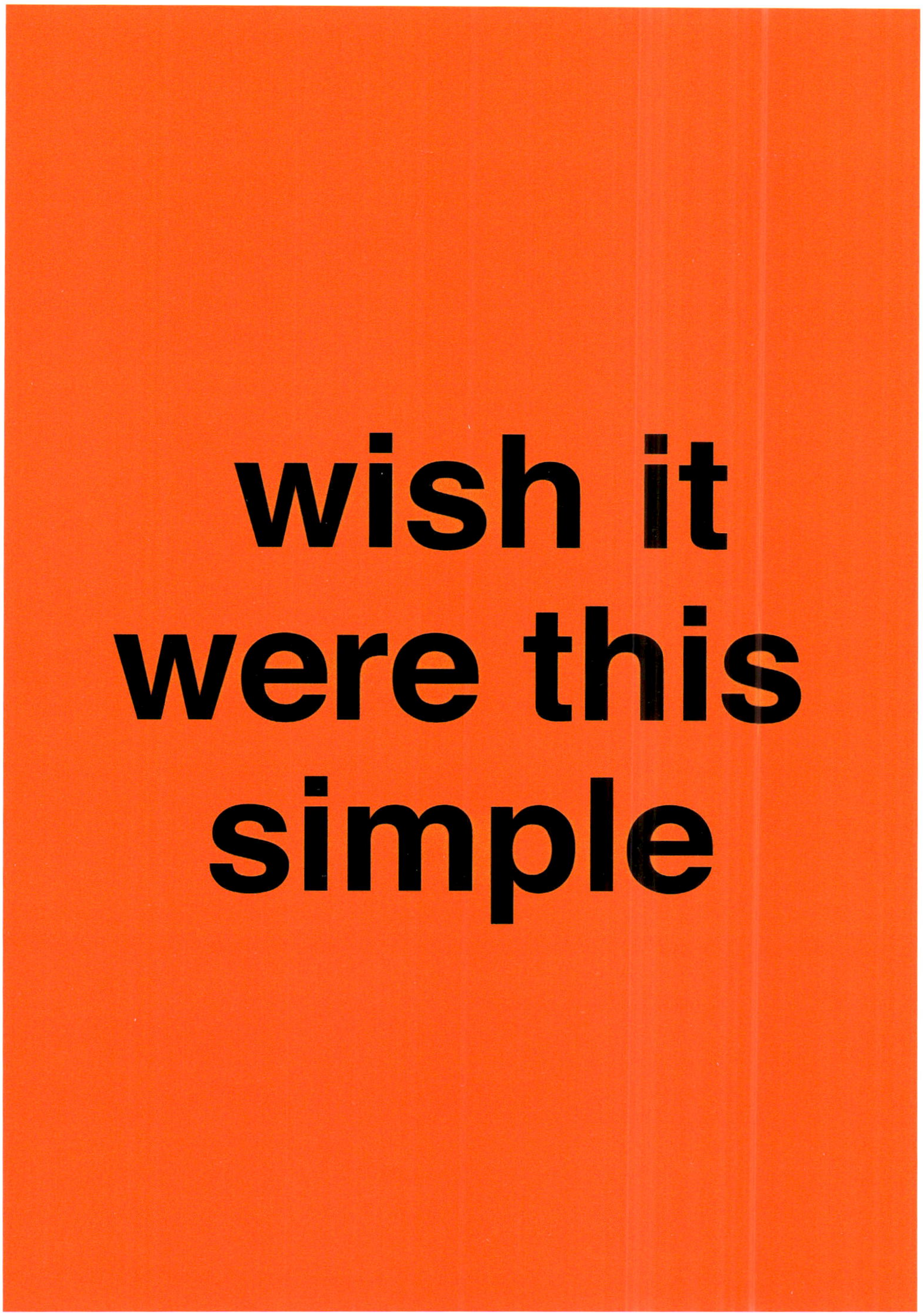

Nora Turato,
Wish it were this simple,
2021

l'autodétermination et la capacité de la technologie à augmenter et à fictionnaliser les récits.

Les SMS envoyés à *Mythiccbeing* ne suscitent pas seulement différentes réponses, mais déclenchent également différentes séquences d'une vidéo. Le chatbot sollicite la participation du spectateur, écrivant et réécrivant en permanence son propre récit, qui, comme il apparaît après un certain temps, est assemblé à partir d'un répertoire limité de réponses standardisées. L'œuvre de Martine Syms est un collage de fragments tirés de ce que McLuhan appellerait un « entrepôt de travail et d'expérience » ou de ce que Shoshana Zuboff a qualifié de « texte électronique », à savoir la « textualisation du monde » par le biais de laquelle nos vies sont « numérisées » et « traduites en informations[16] ».

Dans les œuvres monumentales de Nora Turato, ce « texte électronique » est découpé, recomposé et doté d'une voix humaine ou d'une manifestation visuelle. Telle une poète beatnik canalisant l'hystérie textuelle qui caractérise l'ère du smartphone[17], l'artiste prélève des mots et des phrases dans les médias et dans ses propres conversations (textuelles), qu'elle assemble alors en « scripts » épiques. La dimension des mots contredit la désinvolture apparente avec laquelle ils semblent avoir été choisis. Apparaissant hors contexte et accentués par la voix humaine (dans les performances « *spoken word* » de l'artiste) ou des images (dans ses livres ou ses peintures murales), ces éléments de langage deviennent volatiles, provocateurs et incendiaires.

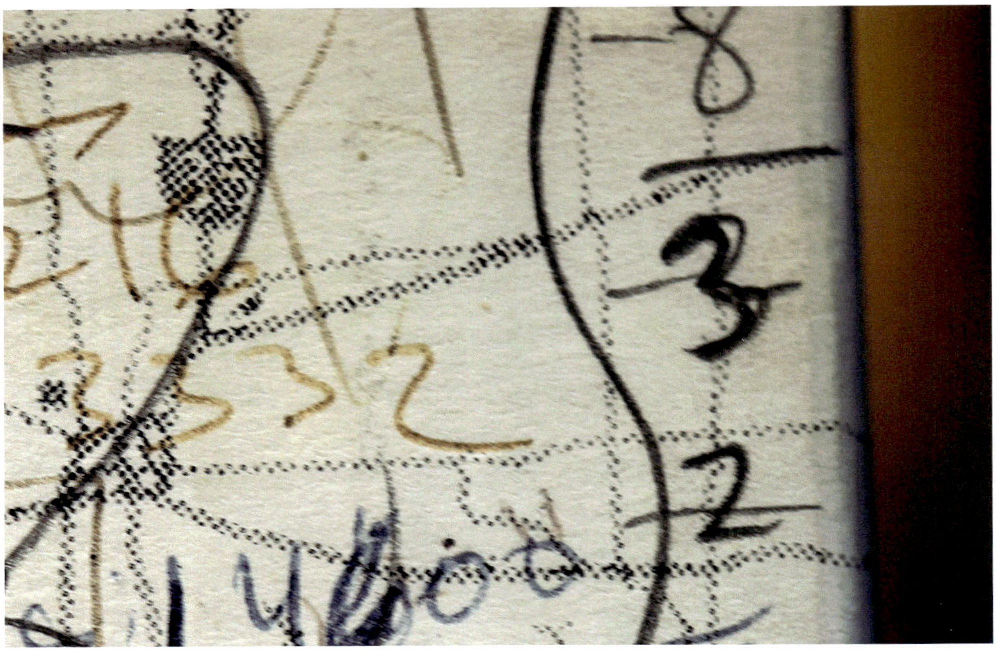

Shadi Habib Allah,
Dropping the 10th Digit,
2018

« À l'âge industriel », écrit McLuhan en 1964, « l'argent, l'écriture et l'horloge commencèrent à converger de nouveau en un tout organique qui a porté l'homme à s'engager presque aussi totalement dans son travail que [...] l'artiste dans son atelier[18]. » Depuis, la nature du travail n'a cessé d'évoluer. McKenzie Wark soutient ainsi qu'aujourd'hui il n'y a « pas [...] de relation entre unités de temps de travail et unités de valeur[19] ». Pour les producteurs de contenus – musique, publicités ou toute autre manifestation créative – le problème ne consiste pas tant à produire des unités identiques qu'à « produire de la différence à partir de l'uniformité[20] ». Contrairement aux tâches répétitives de l'ouvrier industriel, dont le travail est saisonnier ou encadré par la pointeuse, leur travail « a lieu quand il a lieu [...]. Le cauchemar professionnel de l'ouvrier est de devoir faire la même chose, encore et encore, sous la pression de la montre ; celui du hacker [c'est ainsi que McKenzie Wark nomme cette nouvelle classe de travailleurs] est de devoir produire des choses *différentes*, encore et encore, sous la pression de la montre[21] ».

La série photographique *Handpunch* de Cameron Rowland (2014/2015) et la vidéo à cinq canaux *In Real Life* (2019) de Liz Magic Laser pourraient bien représenter ces deux pôles du travail contemporain. Alors que les photographies de Cameron Rowland ont pour sujet l'usage généralisé d'horloges biométriques pour contrôler le temps de travail des employés, le travail de Liz Magic Laser s'intéresse aux conditions de travail des petites mains de l'industrie des emplois précaires. Par le biais de plateformes en ligne telles que Fiverr et PeoplePerHour, l'artiste a recruté cinq personnes basées à Hong Kong, au Nigéria, au Pakistan et au Royaume-Uni afin de produire un film dont elles seraient également les protagonistes. Choisis pour leurs compétences respectives en animation, conception graphique, scénarisation, développement de contenu pour les réseaux sociaux et narration en voix off, ces travailleurs indépendants se retrouvent ainsi à tour de rôle au centre d'un documentaire en cinq parties de 112 minutes, au cours duquel ils affrontent le « 30 Day Biohack Challenge » imaginé par l'artiste. À l'occasion de consultations en ligne, un « coach de vie spécialisé en biohacking » leur conseille une série d'applications et de dispositifs supposés les aider à résoudre les problèmes du quotidien, tels que le *cyberslacking* [qui désigne l'utilisation d'Internet au travail pour des besoins personnels], la prise de poids ou le stress afin d'« optimiser leur état d'esprit et leur corps en vue de réussir ». Ce faisant, l'artiste expose avec humour l'ingéniosité déployée par l'industrie des nouvelles technologies pour convaincre ses employés des vertus de l'automédication. Sous prétexte d'une étude de l'économie mondiale des emplois précaires, *In Real Life* critique les moyens et les conditions de sa propre production[22].

Les protagonistes de *In Real Life* appartiennent à la « classe des hackers » telle qu'elle est définie par McKenzie Wark, c'est-à-dire des individus qui sont censés être « privilégiés » en raison de leur créativité et de leurs compétences techniques. Ils se distinguent de l'ouvrier industriel par la liberté dont ils semblent jouir en termes de conditions de travail – le fait de pouvoir choisir (du moins théoriquement) quand, où, pour qui et pendant combien de temps ils travaillent. En comparaison, les restrictions imposées par l'horloge de pointage utilisant des technologies d'identification criminelle dans la série *Handpunch* de Cameron Rowland, ou par la cage à dimensions humaines de Simon Denny dans *Amazon worker cage patent drawing as virtual Aquatic Warbler cage (US 9,280,157 B2: "System and method for transporting personnel within an active workspace", 2016)* (2020),

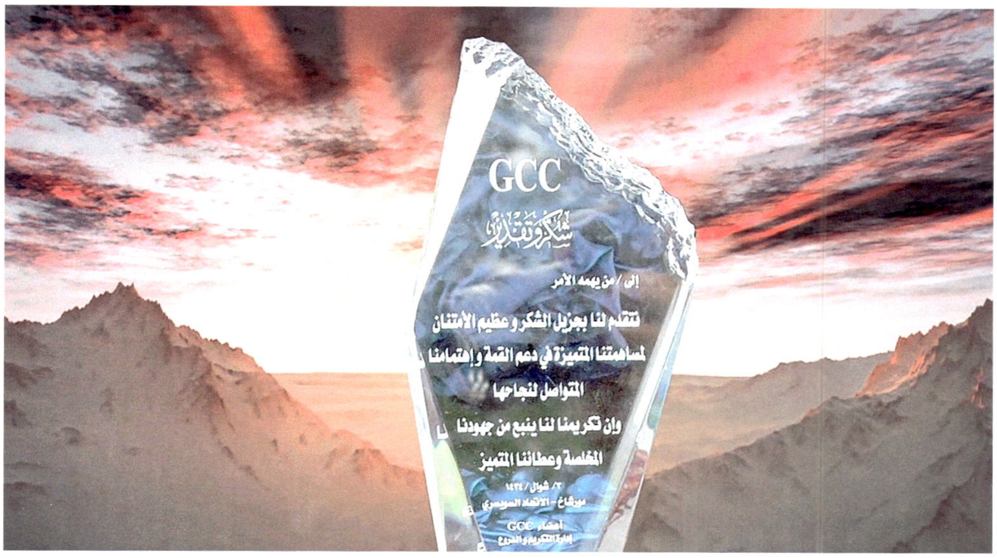

Film still from GCC, *CO-OP*, 2014

paraissent autrement plus draconiennes. Cette dernière œuvre reproduit un brevet déposé par la société de vente en ligne Amazon pour « protéger » les employés dans ses entrepôts. Pourtant, les protagonistes de Liz Magic Laser peinent à trouver un équilibre entre travail et vie personnelle, et les difficultés qu'ils rencontrent nous renvoient à la description du hacker chez McKenzie Wark, qui se désole que son travail soit « devenu informel et précaire[23] ».

In Real Life expose l'isolement du travailleur indépendant sur un marché du travail global où les possibilités de tisser des liens avec ses clients ou collègues sont limitées et où l'injonction de travailler jour et nuit perturbe le rythme régulier de la vie sociale et familiale au sein du foyer. Les protagonistes semblent liés entre eux par leur situation d'aliénation sociale, un état souvent associé aux conditions de travail industrielles, mais également incarné dans la sculpture emblématique de Simon Denny, qui peut être vue comme une métaphore de l'isolement et de l'enfermement dans le capitalisme contemporain. Ces conditions aliénantes sont également explorées avec malice dans le film *Asia One* (2018) de Cao Fei, tourné dans l'entrepôt du même nom de la plus grande société de commerce en ligne de Chine, Jingdong, ou JD.com. La théâtralisation de l'espace de l'usine joue avec notre perception de celle-ci comme une zone quelque peu obscure où tout geste est précisément chorégraphié. L'entrepôt ou l'usine constituent les « coulisses » de l'expérience client (qui est, elle, autrement plus spectaculaire). La manière dont ils sont maintenus loin des regards et des esprits sert sans nul doute les intérêts du capitalisme.

Asia One a en outre été tourné à quelque deux mille kilomètres de la « mine » de bitcoins qui fait l'objet de l'œuvre *the ideal* (2015-en cours) de Yuri Pattison. Tirant en partie son titre du concept théorique de « la monnaie idéale » développé par John Nash – que l'économiste américain définit comme « une monnaie intrinsèquement non sujette à l'inflation[24] » –, elle fait référence au dispositif d'extraction de bitcoins dans un entrepôt qui jouxte (et est alimenté en électricité par) un barrage hydroélectrique dans des montagnes reculées en marge du plateau tibétain près de Kongyuxiang, dans la province chinoise du Sichuan. L'œuvre, qui montre la génération de crypto-monnaie à échelle industrielle, comprend notamment des images filmées par un employé. Des séquences montrant l'intérieur de la mine, avec son bruit assourdissant et ses couloirs sombres bordés d'étagères remplies jusqu'au plafond d'ordinateurs et de câbles entortillés, sont entrecoupées de vues aériennes du site rural dans lequel se situe l'entrepôt, filmées par un drone. Ce va-et-vient entre la mine et le milieu naturel aux alentours évoque l'impact écologique de la production de bitcoins, dont les besoins énergétiques quotidiens (à raison de 350 000 transactions par jour) correspondent à 0,5% de l'électricité consommée à l'échelle mondiale. Selon le météorologue Eric Holthaus, si le bitcoin devait remplacer l'ensemble des transactions mondiales par carte de crédit, sa fabrication consommerait quatorze fois la production énergétique mondiale actuelle[25].

The ideal nous plonge dans la réalité matérielle de la crypto-monnaie en attirant notre attention sur les machines, le travail humain et la consommation énergétique dont elle dépend. La vidéo se déploie au sein d'une installation sculpturale comprenant des ordinateurs qui minent des bitcoins et un système de refroidissement hydraulique qui fait allusion à la source d'énergie alimentant la mine de Kongyuxiang. Cet élément – qui n'est pas sans rappeler la sculpture *Condensation Cube* de Hans Haacke de 1963-1965[26] – intègre par ailleurs des pierres provenant du lit d'une rivière en aval du barrage. Le choix de ce composant naturel est lui aussi significatif, la pierre ayant autrefois servi de

Josephine Pryde,
Sorry Not Sorry, 2016

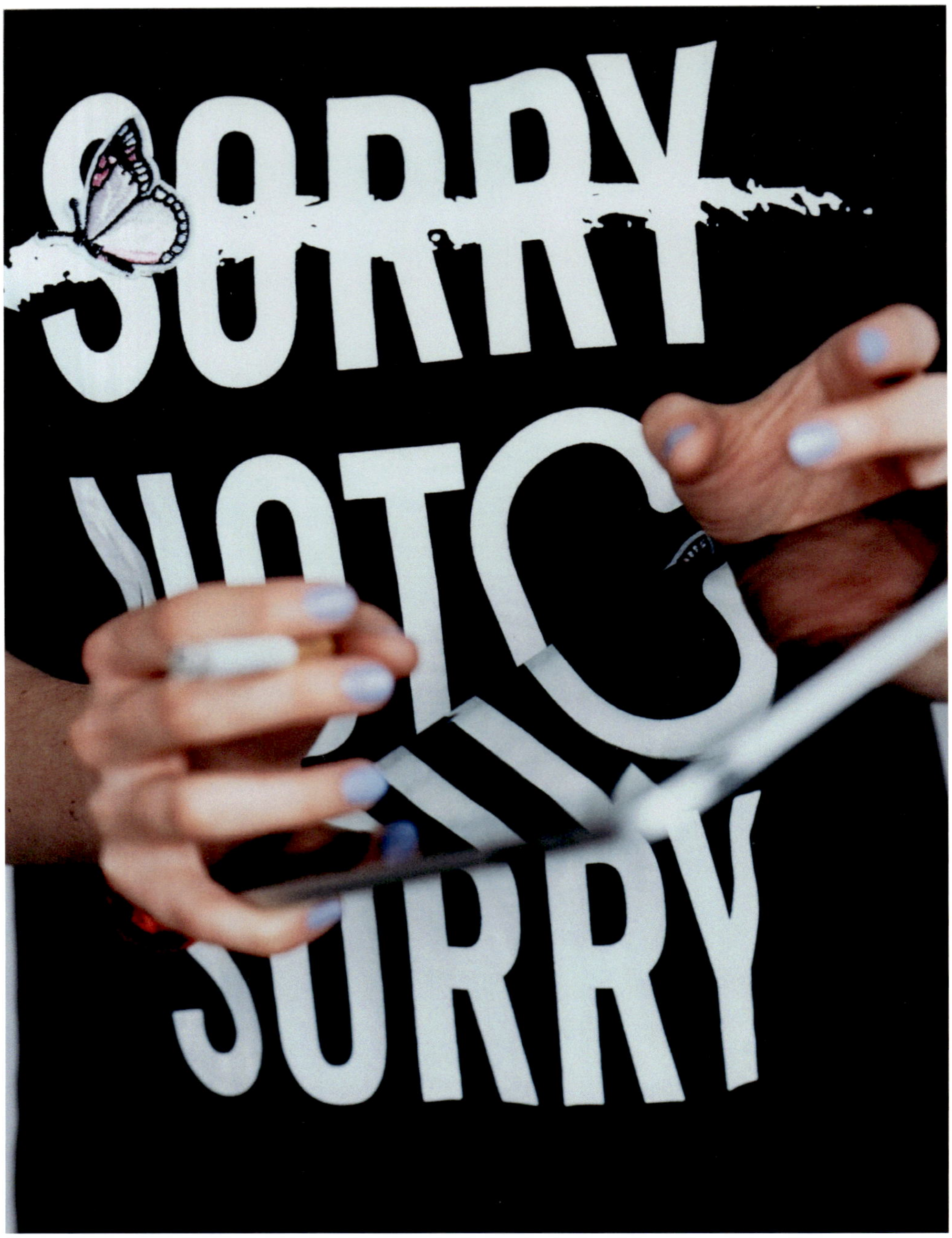

monnaie d'échange. *The ideal* oscille entre visibilité et invisibilité, espace public et espace privé, clarté et obscurcissement, matérialité et immatérialité, reflétant ainsi la nature ambivalente du protocole « *peer-to-peer* » du bitcoin, qui prétend privilégier la transparence en facilitant des transactions qui sont publiquement visibles, tout en assurant l'anonymat de ses acteurs.

Le secret et l'anonymat font partie intégrante de l'économie informelle des coupons alimentaires documentée par *Dropping the 10th Digit* (2018) de Shadi Habib Allah. Montées dans des caissons lumineux, les photographies de l'artiste montrent des bouts de papier gribouillés conservés derrière les comptoirs de certains magasins de proximité à Miami. Ces notes font office de livres de comptes où sont enregistrés les montants en espèces et les articles non éligibles (crédits téléphoniques, cigarettes, alcool, médicaments en vente libre) reçus en échange de coupons destinés à l'achat de nourriture[27]. Leur caractère fragile et éphémère reflète la précarité économique qui sous-tend ces transactions : les clients tributaires d'allocations sociales, tout comme les épiceries qui voient leurs marges se réduire avec l'arrivée d'hypermarchés implantés par les multinationales de la distribution.

Les œuvres de Cameron Rowland, Liz Magic Laser, Simon Denny, Cao Fei, Yuri Pattison et Shadi Habib Allah révèlent les faces cachées de la production et de la consommation modernes : les opérations réalisées de manière informelle dans les épiceries, ayant lieu dans des entrepôts sécurisés, ou encore dans les espaces privés et domestiques convertis en lieux de travail par les travailleurs précaires, tels que le placard à Hong Kong qui a servi de studio d'enregistrement pour la voix off du film de Liz Magic Laser. Chacune de ces œuvres exploite le medium essentiellement visuel offert par l'art pour mettre en lumière des problématiques qui, n'étant pas considérées comme prioritaires, risquent d'échapper à notre attention. Elles semblent par ailleurs suggérer que nous avons atteint l'état d'« engagement total » dans le travail décrit par McLuhan dans les années 1960. La production ne se situe plus seulement dans les champs, les usines ou les bureaux ; elle est partout.

Une partie de l'œuvre évolutive en trois chapitres *Thinking Head*, conçue par Lara Favaretto en 2017, se compose de « conversations clandestines » autour de mots clés inspirés par un ensemble d'objets (les sujets choisis pour cette exposition sont *surplus*, *pouvoir* et *hacker*). Les conversations ont lieu à l'exclusion du public, dans un lieu privé non divulgué. Ni visibles ni audibles dans l'exposition, elles sont diffusées en direct sur Internet. La trace visuelle de ce travail se résume à une seule photographie donnant à voir la pièce vide où a eu lieu l'enregistrement. Les entretiens semblent ainsi dématérialiser les objets par la pensée, ou plutôt par le discours. Si l'on peut s'attendre à ce qu'ils finissent par être accessibles sur Internet, sorte de dépotoir ultime pour tout objet dématérialisé, le choix de placer le « contenu » dans l'espace public virtuel permet également d'esquiver les dispositifs participatifs du musée et son action visant à favoriser l'engagement, l'inclusion et le dialogue.

Les œuvres de Guan Xiao, GCC, Nick Relph, Laura Owens, Katja Novitskova et Josephine Pryde renvoient de différentes manières à la consommation, aux aspects plus visibles de la chaîne d'approvisionnement, où abondent les manifestations visuelles de l'objet-marchandise. Les travaux de Guan Xiao et de GCC mettent ainsi l'accent sur la culture matérielle et l'hyperconsommation. Les sculptures aux accents totémiques de Guan Xiao prennent la forme de moulages en bronze de racines d'arbres ornés d'un assemblage éclectique d'objets high-tech, de *readymades* et de moulages en fibre de verre d'objets imprimés en 3D. Ces derniers représentent des icônes ou des caractères rendus matériels et surdimensionnés tels qu'un signe dièse (#). Recouvrant le sol de leurs extrémités en forme de frondes ou de membres, ou d'éléments plus petits, ils s'apparentent à des épaves composées des débris de nos excès matérialistes.

De même, la succession rapide d'images générées par ordinateur et de commentaires bavards dans la vidéo *CO-OP* (2014) de GCC s'amuse des codes de la consommation ostentatoire, de son extravagance vaine et outrancière. *CO-OP* utilise pour ce faire d'innombrables dessins architecturaux générés par ordinateur (dont la plupart renvoient à des projets immobiliers dans la région du golfe Arabique). Ce genre de dessin est également au cœur de la série photographique de Nick Relph sur les bâtiments new-yorkais. Alors que les œuvres du collectif et de l'artiste britannique s'attachent toutes deux à éclairer les discours consuméristes qui sous-tendent ces dessins, dans les photographies de ce dernier, réalisées en scannant manuellement des rendus architecturaux qui entourent les chantiers de construction urbains, le matériau visuel est traité de manière inverse. Ici, ce n'est pas la vitesse du changement et de la transformation qui se révèle, mais plutôt l'immobilité de la photographie. Les images de bâtiments virtuels, sur lesquels se projettent les fantasmes consuméristes les plus prosaïques (vivre entouré de meubles design, boire un café dans un quartier nouvellement aménagé...), présentent une texture qui invite à une lecture plus approfondie. Les bâtiments, recouverts de graffitis, de salissures, d'affiches et autres objets éphémères, paraissent fantomatiques. Collectivement, ils renvoient à une certaine pauvreté dans l'excès, potentiellement révélatrice d'une culture dans laquelle même les briques et le mortier tirent leur valeur de l'accomplissement de prophéties numériques.

L'excès, dans sa version numérique, caractérise également les motifs peints de Laura Owens et les sculptures de Katja Novitskova. Alors que la première intègre dans ses compositions des textes et des images provenant d'e-mails indésirables ou de publicités en ligne (en l'occurrence, pour des mangeoires pour oiseaux), la deuxième réalise des sculptures bidimensionnelles plus grandes que nature à partir d'images attendrissantes d'animaux : une araignée flanquée de quatre yeux et d'une fourrure tigrée, prête à sauter, est entourée d'une paire de termitières, tandis qu'un casoar bleu vif pointe son bec sous son énorme casque corné. Les animaux sont chacun accompagnés d'une flèche de couleur primaire pointant vers le haut, sorte de vecteur de croissance sommaire qui pourrait tout aussi bien illustrer le cours en bourse d'une action à la hausse. Ces œuvres renvoient à la monétisation de notre attention, telle qu'elle est décrite par McKenzie Wark (en référence à Yves Citton), qui constate que « dans un monde submergé de données numériques, la denrée rare, c'est l'attention que nous leur accordons[28] ». Leurs modèles – des images saisissantes de la nature semblables à celles qui font le buzz sur les réseaux sociaux grâce aux *likes* et aux partages – sont trouvés sur Internet et transformés en sculpture. Ces images s'adressent à nous avec une certaine insistance, de manière frontale, et leurs flèches semblent refléter ou prédire la manière dont elles seront perçues. La flèche symbolise par ailleurs une culture dans laquelle les émotions sont susceptibles d'être objectifiées et quantifiées sous forme numérique ; la transposition des expériences et des sentiments en « médias sociaux » a le potentiel de changer fondamentalement « la structure de la société » et pourrait bien créer « de nouvelles dynamiques sociales et économiques [...], une nouvelle politique[29] ». Le « texte électronique », écrit Shoshana Zuboff, a été « utilisé pour surveiller et contrôler plutôt que pour autonomiser et enseigner[30] » :

> Nous écrivons à la machine, elle collecte et agrège nos désirs et nos fantasmes, les segmente par marché et par démographie et nous les revend en tant qu'expérience marchande[31].

Richard Seymour compare le modèle économique des réseaux sociaux à celui des industries qui ont fait du jeu et de l'addiction leur fonds de commerce. « Nos comptes sur les réseaux sociaux, écrit-il, fonctionnent comme des entreprises rivalisant pour attirer le regard [...] nous sommes tous désormais des auteurs », qui écrivent « non pas pour l'argent, mais pour la satisfaction que procure le fait d'être lu ». Dès lors, « faire le buzz ou "*trending*" » peut être « l'équivalent d'une aubaine » ou « la pire chose qui puisse arriver[32] ». Empruntant l'image foucaldienne du « panoptique de l'information » invoquée par Shoshana Zuboff, Seymour décrit la dépendance que peut engendrer le fait d'agir dans une arène dans laquelle n'importe qui peut être observé à tout moment et où « tout un chacun » peut « soudainement être isolé et désigné à la vindicte populaire[33] ». Ce mécanisme d'auto-surveillance est également « la clé du caractère productif de l'industrie des réseaux sociaux [...] plus efficace à sa manière qu'un atelier de misère », écrit Richard Seymour. « Habiter l'industrie des réseaux sociaux, c'est se trouver dans un état de distraction constante, hanté par l'obsession, semblable à celle du toxicomane, de rester en contact avec elle, de savoir où on la trouve et comment l'obtenir[34]. »

Ces dépendances et la manière dont elles affectent l'image que l'on a de nous-mêmes alimentent la série photographique *Hands (Für mich)* (2014-en cours) de Josephine Pryde. Elle donne à voir des mains soignées aux ongles colorés touchant divers objets ou tenues près du corps dans un geste qui évoque à la fois un serment d'honnêteté et une expression d'amour-propre. L'éclairage et la composition des images invitent à des comparaisons avec la photographie commerciale. Isolés et cadrés de près, les gestes décrivent une relation d'intimité entre sujet et objet. Plusieurs œuvres choisies pour l'exposition montrent des mains qui semblent serrer, caresser ou bercer des smartphones ou des tablettes, accessoires d'une culture dans laquelle la marchandise apparaît – selon les mots de McKenzie Wark – « comme rien d'autre qu'un vecteur [...] un potentiel réalisé à travers l'interface[35] » de l'appareil.

En dirigeant l'attention sur les surfaces lisses et les lueurs rassurantes émises par ces objets, les photographies de Josephine Pryde exposent le fétichisme de l'objet-marchandise comme un mode d'expression de soi (que ce soit sous forme numérique ou matérielle). Mais elles évoquent également une sorte d'aliénation plus nébuleuse, à savoir la solitude d'une culture dans laquelle, même dans des situations d'authentique sociabilité, les individus privilégient les interactions solitaires avec la machine[36]. Richard Seymour relie ainsi la baisse de la consommation d'alcool, de nicotine et de stupéfiants à l'essor du smartphone, suggérant que celui-ci a fait son apparition au moment où nous avons arrêté la cigarette et l'alcool. Or, si ces derniers étaient des « facilitateurs d'interaction sociale », le smartphone est « une issue de secours, un moyen de se connecter à quelqu'un qui n'est pas là ou qui n'est là que sous la forme d'une trace écrite, un fantôme dans la machine[37]. » Il précise :

> Le smartphone est notre portail vers le monde, notre ticket de sortie. Il contient nos cartes de crédit, notre musique, nos magazines, nos livres audio, nos cartes, nos films, nos jeux, nos billets et nos clés. Il est notre guide. Il nous relie aux membres de notre famille, aux collègues de travail et aux irrésistibles intimidateurs qui sévissent sur Internet. Nous l'utilisons pour fixer des rendez-vous galants et commander notre dîner. Il divise notre journée [...] en « intervalles nerveux et schizoïdes » avec des mises à jour constantes. Nous le gardons à proximité, chargé à tout moment. Comme si un jour il allait nous apporter le message que nous attendions[38].

La notion de propriété, ses manifestations et son rapport au pouvoir sont explorés dans les œuvres de Sondra Perry, Hito Steyerl et Oliver Laric. Les travaux de Sondra Perry et de Hito Steyerl abordent plus particulièrement les questions de souveraineté et de contrôle juridique. *IT'S IN THE GAME '18 or Mirror Gag for Projection and Two Universal Shot Trainers with Nasal Cavity and Pelvis* (2018) de Sondra Perry fait référence à une expérience vécue par le frère jumeau de l'artiste, Sandy, qui évolue en tant que joueur de basket-ball universitaire. Il s'avère que sous ce statut, l'apparence physique et les statistiques de jeu de Sandy (et celles de ses coéquipiers) sont devenues la propriété intellectuelle de la NCAA (National Collegiate Athletic Association), qui les a revendues à la société EA Sports pour être utilisées dans un jeu vidéo. L'installation multimédia de l'artiste comprend des extraits du contrat entre les athlètes, la NCAA et EA Sports, tout en situant le récit dans le contexte historique plus large du racisme systémique.

L'installation *FreePlots* (2019-en cours) de Hito Steyerl fait quant à elle référence au phénomène du port franc, ces entrepôts de stockage « plus ou moins extraterritoriaux » que l'artiste décrit comme des « zones d'extra-légalité légalisée[39] ». Son essai « Duty Free Art » s'intéresse aux œuvres d'art et autres biens à la valeur inestimable qui sont conservés dans ces entrepôts, présentant le port franc comme modèle pour « un musée à l'ère d'Internet [...] un musée du *dark net*, dans lequel les déplacements sont dissimulés et l'espace des données brouillé[40] ». *FreePlots*, une série de jardinières reprenant la forme des ports francs de Genève et de Panama, se propose d'échanger le contenu de ces zones d'ombre ou zones mortes contre plusieurs kilos de compost à base de fumier et de plantes cultivées par la population locale en collaboration avec des associations de jardins communautaires. Les actifs privés abrités par ces « espaces qui contournent la souveraineté nationale[41] » sont ainsi (symboliquement) troqués contre des organismes vivants plantés par des collectifs ayant un intérêt commun pour l'aménagement d'espaces verts et la culture de plantes, de fruits et de légumes.

Le site web d'Oliver Laric, threedscans.com, s'apparente à un musée de l'ère Internet d'un tout autre genre. Si le port franc est un « musée du *dark net* », threedscans.com est le musée des « communs numériques ». Les objets qui y sont exposés (112 au moment de la rédaction de ce texte) proviennent de collections muséales du monde entier. Chacun est accompagné d'informations sur son auteur, la date de création, les matériaux employés, son emplacement et ses dimensions, et représenté par une maquette 3D téléchargeable gratuitement. Les images sont basées sur des scans libres de droits ou des centaines de clichés pris *in situ* par des photographes professionnels mandatés par l'artiste. Leur réalisation implique l'intervention d'avocats, de photographes, d'artisans et de professionnels des musées. Pour chaque scan, l'artiste recense par ailleurs les exemples d'utilisation suite à leur diffusion, majoritairement par le biais d'Internet (notamment dans le travail d'autres artistes, des images postées sur Instagram, le générique d'une série télévisée Netflix ou la scénographie numérique d'un participant au concours de l'Eurovision[42]). L'œuvre d'Oliver Laric exploite tout en l'élargissant la mise à disposition au public d'un patrimoine culturel partagé. Ici, la connaissance – sous la forme d'objets pouvant être téléchargés, visualisés, manipulés, placés dans toutes sortes de contextes et réalisés par quiconque sait comment s'y prendre et dans n'importe quelle partie du monde – reste dans le domaine public mondial.

> La bourgeoisie ne peut exister sans révolutionner constamment les instruments de production, ce qui veut dire les rapports de production, c'est-à-dire l'ensemble des rapports sociaux. [...] Ce bouleversement continuel de la production, ce constant ébranlement de tout le système social, cette agitation et cette insécurité perpétuelles distinguent l'époque bourgeoise de toutes les précédentes. Tous les rapports sociaux, figés et couverts de rouille, avec leur cortège de conceptions et d'idées antiques et vénérables, se dissolvent ; ceux qui les remplacent vieillissent avant d'avoir pu s'ossifier. Tout ce qui avait solidité et permanence s'en va en fumée, tout ce qui était sacré est profané, et les hommes sont forcés enfin d'envisager leurs conditions d'existence et leurs rapports réciproques avec des yeux désabusés[43].

Karl Marx et Friedrich Engels ont défini le capitalisme comme un système dynamique qui tend vers l'autodestruction. McKenzie Wark fait remarquer que le grand nombre de compléments rattachés au terme « capitalisme » (« tardif », « néolibéral », « de plateforme », « de surveillance » ou « d'attention », pour n'en citer que quelques-uns) laisse à penser que nous manquons de mots pour décrire la situation actuelle. Et si le système économique que Marx et Engels ont décrit en 1848 se dématérialisait et se « dissolvait » à son tour ? Peut-être ne l'avons-nous pas remarqué, augure Wark, parce que le « rêve merveilleux d'une "société post-industrielle[44]" » ne s'est jamais réalisé. Peut-être ne l'avons-nous pas remarqué parce que la situation actuelle n'est pas meilleure, mais pire :

> Si l'on s'intéresse aux entreprises qui figurent en tête du classement *Fortune 500*, on est surpris de voir combien d'entre elles sont actives dans le secteur de l'information. Je ne parle pas seulement des entreprises de technologie et de télécommunications, telles que Apple, Google, Verizon ou Cisco, ou des

entreprises pharmaceutiques comme Pfizer. On pourrait également considérer les grandes banques comme un sous-ensemble de la classe vectoraliste plutôt que comme "capital financier". Elles aussi opèrent dans le champ de l'asymétrie de l'information[45].

Le nom que donne McKenzie Wark à la « classe dirigeante dominante de notre époque » est celui de « classe vectoraliste ». Alors que la classe des hackers « produit de nouvelles informations », c'est-à-dire « tout ce que la loi sur la propriété intellectuelle reconnaît comme étant nouveau[46] », la classe vectoraliste « possède et contrôle les brevets, les marques et les célébrités qui galvanisent l'attention [...] la logistique et les chaînes d'approvisionnement qui lui permettent de garder l'information en sa possession[47] », c'est-à-dire le « vecteur par lequel les informations sont collectées et utilisées[48] ». Selon McKenzie Wark, elle ne « s'approprie pas tant une quantité de plus-value qu'elle n'exploite une asymétrie d'information ». Ainsi, nous pouvons accéder « gratuitement » à l'information par le biais d'un moteur de recherche, former un réseau social ou acquérir l'infrastructure logistique nécessaire à la gestion d'une petite entreprise, mais :

> [...] pendant que vous obtenez ce petit bout d'information, cette classe dirigeante obtient la somme de toutes ces informations. Elle exploite l'asymétrie entre le peu que vous apprenez et la somme de ce qu'elle apprend par ce biais – une somme d'informations qu'elle collecte sur la base des informations que vous avez été obligé de lui céder "volontairement[49]".

Au moment où j'écris ces lignes, quelque part en République tchèque, un avion de chasse à réaction Mikoyan-Gurevich MiG-21 acquis par Roger Hiorns en 2017 est en train d'être préparé pour son prochain voyage. Conçu en Union soviétique dans les années 1950, le MiG-21 est l'un des avions de combat les plus produits et les plus pérennes dans l'histoire de l'aviation. Cet exemplaire, qui a été fabriqué sous licence en République tchèque dans les années 1980, a été enterré par l'artiste dans la périphérie de Prague, un acte par lequel il devenait invisible et rejoignait un réseau international et souterrain d'avions que l'artiste a imaginé en 1990 et inauguré en 2016[50]. Désormais exhumé, il sera acheminé par voie routière jusqu'au Luxembourg, où il sera équipé d'un ensemble de tubes en plastique dans lesquels circulera un amas de « pizza liquide » propulsée par une pompe. Bien que l'artiste compare son dispositif à un système « digestif », rien n'y est vraiment digéré, la masse étant maintenue en suspens dans le cycle de consommation continue qui circule autour de cette icône obsolète de la guerre froide.

La série *The retrospective view of the pathway* (2017-en cours) illustre ce que James Bridle a décrit comme le « faisceau de liens entre transparence / opacité et visibilité / invisibilité » dans l'aviation. À titre d'exemple, James Bridle mentionne les sites web qui permettent aux utilisateurs de suivre en temps réel les trajectoires de vol de milliers d'avions de ligne. La disponibilité de ce type de données génère un sentiment de transparence tout en permettant d'« exclure et d'obscurcir d'autres activités privées et étatiques, des jets privés d'oligarques et de politiciens aux vols de surveillance secrets ou aux exercices militaires. À chaque chose qui est montrée correspond une autre chose cachée[51] ». Selon Bridle, l'opacité de ce système est symptomatique d'un « nouvel âge des ténèbres » où nous sommes « complètement empêtrés dans des systèmes technologiques » qui « façonnent [...] la manière dont nous agissons et pensons ». « L'accélération technologique », affirme James Bridle, « a transformé notre planète, nos sociétés et nous-mêmes, mais elle n'a pas réussi à transformer notre compréhension de ces choses[52] ».

Le « faisceau de liens » évoqué par James Bridle est un sujet qui parcourt toute l'œuvre de Roger Hiorns, où les objets sont souvent transformés par la présence de quelque chose qui est invisible à l'œil nu ou par un processus qui les rend méconnaissables. Plusieurs de ses interventions impliquent des aéronefs. Ainsi, *Untitled* (2008) est constitué d'un « moteur d'avion de ligne atomisé » qui prend la forme d'un tas de poussière métallique grise, tandis qu'*Untitled (Alliance)* (2010) se compose des deux moteurs Pratt & Whitney TF33 P9 d'un avion de surveillance militaire dans lesquels ont été dissimulés des antidépresseurs. Dans son intervention sculpturale en République tchèque, l'artiste a réalisé une œuvre d'art publique à partir d'un objet qu'il a délibérément soustrait à la vue du spectateur. Déterré et exposé dans un musée, l'avion devient un artefact archéologique, une relique du processus, mais aussi une métaphore de la guerre froide et du système communiste qui a généré cet avion.

La concoction alimentaire qui circule autour de l'avion trouve son origine au VIe siècle, lorsque les soldats perses de l'Empire achéménide utilisèrent leurs boucliers pour cuire des galettes garnies de fromage et de dattes. On pense que le mot « pizza » pourrait dériver du mot lombard *bizzo* ou *pizzo*, qui signifie « bouchée ». Son étymologie même pourrait expliquer son succès comme fast-food dans les sociétés capitalistes du monde entier. Transformée au point d'être méconnaissable, elle devient chez Roger Hiorns la chair qui alimente le système, une masse informe qui évoque au moyen d'une vision abjecte l'abstraction du travail à l'ère du post-capitalisme. L'association cyborgienne entre machine et pizza donne naissance à une image moins anodine qu'il n'y paraît du « commerce de la vie » à notre époque. Cet avion déglingué, relié à une pompe tel un corps maintenu artificiellement en vie, n'est animé que par ce système, ce dispositif technologique qui assure le flux constant de la pizza. Si l'image proposée par Roger Hiorns fait allusion au passé, elle n'en parle pas moins du présent. C'est l'image d'une inertie terminale qui soulève la question : et après ?

1 Il continue : « […] elle examine la partie de la vie individuelle et sociale qui a plus particulièrement trait à l'acquisition et à l'usage des choses matérielles nécessaires au bien-être. » Alfred Marshall, *Principes d'économie politique* (1890), livre I (texte de la 4e édition anglaise), trad. F. Sauvaire-Jourdan, Paris, Gordon & Breach, 1971, p. 21.

2 La croissance du PIB avait déjà ralenti en 2018 et 2019, atteignant respectivement 3,6% et 2,9% dans les économies avancées, et 4,5% et 3,7% dans les économies émergentes et en développement. En 2020, le recul du PIB des économies avancées atteignait −4,7%, parmi lesquelles les pays européens (Espagne, Royaume-Uni, Italie, France et Allemagne) enregistraient les plus fortes baisses. Il devrait augmenter de 5,1% en 2021. Les chiffres pour les marchés émergents et les économies en développement pour 2020 et 2021 sont de −2,2% et −6,7%. Parmi celles-ci, seule la Chine a continué de croître en 2020 (de 2,3%). Au moment de la rédaction de ce texte, le PIB restait inférieur aux niveaux de fin 2019, mais les États-Unis devraient se relever au premier semestre 2021, l'Europe et le Royaume-Uni en 2022. La perte à moyen terme par rapport aux projections pré-pandémiques est de 3% pour l'économie mondiale. Bien qu'elle soit moins importante qu'au lendemain de la crise financière mondiale, les pays à faible revenu et les marchés émergents devraient souffrir davantage des retombées que lors de la crise une décennie plus tôt, lorsque les économies avancées étaient plus durement touchées. Sources : Rapports annuels du FMI sur les perspectives de l'économie mondiale, avril 2019, avril 2020 et avril 2021, https://www.imf.org/en/Publications/Search?series=World%20Economic%20Outlook (consultés le 5 juillet 2021).

3 Peter Drucker, *Post-Capitalist Society*, New York, Harper Collins, 1993, p. 44-45.

4 *Ibid.*, p. 182.

5 *Ibid.*, p. 45.

6 McKenzie Wark, *Capital Is Dead: Is this Something Worse?*, Londres et New York, Verso, 2019, p. 5.

7 Extraits de l'œuvre *Family Dollar (Social Capital)* (2020). Paroles : Ei Arakawa et Dan Poston. Bande son : Ei Arakawa. Arrangement : ZALA (Mish-Mosh).

8 Les œuvres renvoient à des performances au Museum of Modern Art à New York, à la Tate Modern à Londres et à la Biennale de Berlin, entre autres.

9 Ei Arakawa, *Notes on Fees & Nerf by Ei Arakawa (Sep 2, 2020)*, déclaration d'intention de l'artiste pour l'exposition Ei Arakawa: *Fees & Nerf* du 4 septembre au 31 octobre 2020 à la galerie Max Meyer à Düsseldorf, https://maxmayer.info/artists/ei-arakawa/2 (consulté le 21 juin 2021).

10 Marshall McLuhan, *Pour comprendre les médias. Les prolongements technologiques de l'homme* (1964), trad. Jean Paré, Paris, Éditions Points, 2015, p. 166.

11 *Ibid.*, p. 161.

12 Paroles de la chanson « Fœtus » de l'album *Autopsie Vol. 3* de Booba, paru sur Because Music en 2009.

13 Mohamed Bourouissa dans un entretien dans le documentaire *All-In* (2013) produit par Kamel Mennour, https://www.youtube.com/watch?v=vl51Klw8USA (consulté le 21 juin 2021).

14 Tiré d'un texte écrit par l'artiste, envoyé par e-mail à l'auteure le 28 mai 2021.

15 L'artiste n'ayant pas été en mesure d'adapter le chatbot pour l'exposition, elle a finalement décidé d'exposer une version non interactive de ce travail.

16 Voir Shoshana Zuboff, *In the Age of the Smart Machine: The Future of Work and Power*, New York, Basic Books, 1988 ; Noah Kulwin, 'Shoshana Zuboff on Surveillance Capitalism's Threat to Democracy', entretien avec l'artiste, *New York Magazine*, 24 février 2019, https://nymag.com/intelligencer/2019/02/shoshana-zuboff-q-and-a-the-age-of-surveillance-capital.html (consulté le 17 juin 2021).

17 Je suis redevable à l'analyse pointue du travail de l'artiste que livre Myriam Ben Salah dans sa contribution aux *Art Basel Curators' Picks*, septembre 2020, https://www.youtube.com/watch?v=DqiYbK7re8I (consulté le 17 juin 2021).

18 McLuhan, *op. cit.*, p. 169.

19 Wark, *op. cit.*, p. 44.

20 *Ibid.*, p. 13.

21 *Ibid.*, p. 43.

22 « Davantage documentaire que télé-réalité, cette étude fascinante de l'économie mondialisée des petits boulots se signale comme une œuvre d'art par ses ambitions de critique institutionnelle. En d'autres termes, l'œuvre révèle les moyens et les conditions de sa propre production et diffusion. » Catherine Taft, « Liz Magic Laser », in *Artforum*, 58e année, nº 6, février 2020, p. 206.

23 Wark, *op. cit.*, p. 48.

24 John Forbes Nash Jr., « Ideal Money and the Motivation of Savings and Thrift », conférence pour la Harry Mullin M.D. Memorial Lecture, University of Scranton, 16 novembre 2011, https://www.youtube.com/watch?v=Je22xKQekCk (consulté le 21 juin 2021). La transcription de la conférence est accessible sur https://fermatslibrary.com/p/caca3495 (consulté le 21 juin 2021). La même page affirme que « l'implication selon laquelle le bitcoin deviendra la monnaie mondiale unique répond à la volonté de Nash de disposer d'une monnaie stable au niveau international ». Yuri Pattison utilise le terme de « monnaie idéale » de manière quelque peu ironique, considérant la situation comme « tout sauf idéale ». « Le bitcoin, explique-t-il, a amplifié et accéléré certains des pires aspects du capitalisme », même s'il pense que les crypto-monnaies ont été désignées comme boucs émissaires par les médias pour des excès qui « pourraient ou devraient être considérés dans un contexte plus large dans l'intérêt d'une appréciation critique de la technologie en réseau ». L'artiste dans un e-mail à l'auteure daté du 31 mai 2021.

25 Voir *Eric Holthaus*, @EricHolthaus, Twitter, 18 février 2021. Voir aussi https://grist.org/article/bitcoin-could-cost-us-our-clean-energy-future (consulté le 17 juin 2021) et James Bridle, *New Dark Age: Technology and the End of the Future*, Londres et New York, Verso, 2018, p. 63.

26 Ce travail fondateur se compose d'une boîte en Perspex étanche qui contient une petite quantité d'eau. Le degré de condensation (et donc l'aspect de l'œuvre) évolue au gré des conditions climatiques de l'environnement. On peut considérer que cette œuvre anticipe les travaux ultérieurs de l'artiste sur les systèmes sociaux, politiques et économiques qui matérialisent un processus ou un système physique sous la forme d'une sculpture.

27 À savoir « Fruits et légumes ; Viande, volaille et poisson ; Produits laitiers ; Pains et céréales ». Source : US Government Services and Information, https://www.usa.gov/food-help (consulté le 17 juin 2021).

28 Wark se réfère au livre déterminant d'Yves Citton, *The Ecology of Attention*, Cambridge, Polity Press, 2017. Wark, *op. cit.*, p. 56.

29 Drucker, cf. note 4.

30 Kulwin, *op. cit.*, https://nymag.com/intelligencer/2019/02/shoshana-zuboff-q-and-a-the-age-of-surveillance-capital.html (consulté le 17 juin 2021).

31 Richard Seymour, *The Twittering Machine*, Londres, Indigo Press, 2019, p. 26.

32 *Ibid.*, p. 30.

33 *Ibid.*, p. 39.

34 *Ibid.*, p. 44.

35 Wark, *op. cit*, p. 15.

36 Pryde explique qu'« en mélangeant les types d'objets qu'elles tentent de saisir et qu'elles tiennent, je voulais aussi parler des objets en tant que résidus de souvenirs, de potentialités et des liens que nous tissons. La solitude ou la mélancolie sont donc aussi quelque chose que nous vivons et que nous touchons, et que peut-être nous devons vivre et toucher. […] La décision de ne pas montrer la tête des modèles était un moyen de mettre en avant un autre sens qui fait partie de notre langage […] de voir le toucher. » L'artiste dans un e-mail à l'auteure daté du 16 mai 2021.

37 Seymour, *op. cit.*, p. 57.

38 *Ibid.*, p. 69.

39 Hito Steyerl, *Duty Free Art: Art in the Age of Planetary Civil War*, Verso, London / New York, 2017, p. 80. (*De l'art en duty free – L'art à l'époque de la guerre civile planétaire*, trad. française Armelle Chrétien, Dijon, Les Presses du réel, 2021.)

40 *Ibid.*, p. 83.

41 *Ibid.*, p. 79.

42 Plusieurs scans d'Oliver Laric ont été utilisés dans la série Netflix *L'Empire romain*. L'image de la sculpture néoclassique *Hunter and Dog* (1847) de John Gibson apparaît dans l'animation de fond de la présentation de la chanson « Grande Amore » par le groupe italien Il Volo lors du Concours Eurovision 2015. Le même scan figure également dans la vidéo de la chanson « MotorSport » de Migos, Nicki Minaj et Cardi B.

43 Karl Marx, Friedrich Engels, *Manifeste du Parti communiste*, 1847, Paris, Union générale d'édition 10/18, 2e édition, 1963. Cette version du texte est disponible sur https://www.marxists.org/francais/marx/works/1847/00/kmfe18470000a.htm (consulté le 15 juillet 2021).

44 Wark, *op. cit.*, p. 116.

45 *Ibid.*, p. 45.

46 *Ibid.*, p. 43.

47 *Ibid.*, p. 13.

48 *Ibid.*, p. 3.

49 *Ibid.*, p. 55.

50 La série *The retrospective view of the pathway* a été inaugurée en 2016 par l'enterrement d'un Hawker Siddeley Dominie T1 désaffecté dans un endroit tenu secret près de la rivière Orwell, dans la banlieue d'Ipswich en Angleterre. Un deuxième avion a été enterré à Haarlem, aux Pays-Bas, en février 2018. L'enterrement du MiG-21 à Prague, en avril de la même année, était le troisième de la série.

51 Bridle, *op. cit.*, p. 35-36.

52 *Ibid.*, p. 2.

Production

CAPITAL IS DEAD: IS THIS SOMETHING WORSE?

McKenzie Wark

[...] Industrial capitalism was not terribly interested in workers who think and feel. It wanted hands. It wanted muscle. It was a flesh-eating machine. Whatever disgusting and terrifying power lurks in these more recent stories does not so much eat bodies as brains. This combinatory works two ways: either your mind is erased and your body is another mind's vehicle; or your mind is subordinated to the will of another power.[1] Either way, your mind is not your own. It feels like some vile takeover. But what if this isn't just a takeover, but a whole new class relation?

Let's start thinking through this curious class relation by being very 'orthodox'. Let's start with the *forces of production*, the *relations of production* that correspond to them, the class antagonism generated out of those relations of production, and the political and culture *superstructures* that correspond to that base.[2] And let us also try to describe, just as Marx did, what may be emerging rather than what is established. If one starts with what is established, it is easy to interpret any new aspect of the situation as simply variations on the same essence. Starting with what may be emerging provides a suitable derangement of the senses, a giddy hint that all that was solid is melting into air.[3]

The thought experiment that might result is quite simple. Here's a sketch, to be elaborated upon as we go: There really is something qualitatively distinct about the forces of production that eat brains, that produce and instrumentalise and control information. This is because information really does turn out to have strange ontological properties. Making information a force of production produces something of a conundrum within the commodity form. Information wants to be free but is everywhere in chains.[4] Information is no longer scarce, it is infinitely replicable, cheap to store, cheap to transmit, and yet the whole premise of the commodity is its scarcity.

Information as a force of production calls into being particular *relations* of production and is at the same time formed by those relations. In classic Marxist style, one can look here at the evolution of legal forms.[5] In the late twentieth century 'intellectual property' emerged as almost an absolute private property right.[6] One that makes the once separate and local property forms of patent, copyright, and trademark equivalent and exchangeable forms of private property. These forms need transnational legal enforcement, precisely because information is such a slippery and abstract thing.[7]

And so, like the enclosures or the joint-stock company before it, intellectual property law becomes the form of a new kind of relation of production, more abstract than its predecessors, and one that makes not land or physical plant, but rather information itself, a form of private property. Like those preceding forms of private property, this one crystalises into a class relation. As an absolute form of private property, it creates classes of owners and non-owners of the means of realising its value. Land as private property gave rise to the two great classes of *farmer* and *landlord*. Capital as private property gave rise to the two great classes of *worker* and *capitalist*. Is there a new class relation that emerges out of the commodification of information?

For this thought experiment, let's say it does. I call those classes the *hacker class* and the *vectoralist class*. The hacker class produces new information. But what is 'new' information? It is whatever intellectual property law recognises as new. It's a strange kind of production. Where the farmer grows crops through a seasonal cycle and the worker stamps out repetitive units of commodities, the hacker has to use their time in a different way, to turn the same old information into new. Getting this done is not like the seasonal repetitions of farming or the clocking-on of the worker. It happens when it happens, including time spent napping or pulling all-nighters.[8] The workplace nightmare of the worker is having to make the same thing, over and over, against the pressure of the clock; the workplace nightmare of the hacker is to produce *different* things, over and over, against the pressure of the clock.

The characters of Peggy and Don in the TV series *Mad Men* work as mid-century prototypes.[9] It's the advertising business during the golden years of Fordism.[10] Don is a creative, struggling within the agency with its owners to become an owner too. Peggy is a secretary, a white-collar worker, and her struggle is to become a creative. Meanwhile, Joan is already at the top of the secretarial pool, managing it, but wants to become an owner. As the show progresses, the women make a little headway in this male business. By show's end, Black women are just starting to get the secretarial jobs, but the computer has arrived and will make some of them obsolete anyway. Like much of bourgeois culture, it is a small business narrative, which compresses the classes and blurs the lines between them. The prize of becoming truly ruling class is always just out of reach.

For our purposes, the interesting part is its picture of the activities of one prototype of the hacker class. The camera is fascinated by Don and Peggy actually doing their jobs. Don takes long naps on his office sofa. Sometimes he just wanders off. The material for his brilliant ad campaigns come from all sorts of incidental sources. He drinks too much, tries smoking pot. The whole office takes amphetamine shots and pulls an all-nighter, making speed-induced creative work full of tremendous energy and really bad decisions. Meanwhile Peggy manages to transition from worker to hacker because she actually knows something about how to address the desires of women, but she ends up limited and stymied in all sorts of ways by an industry that does not know the value of her difference.

The less popular series *Halt and Catch Fire* shows us the early tech industry version of the same set of activities, this same work that isn't quite regular work.[11] Hackers can't be managed like farmers or workers; they are not the same as either class. There's no relation between the units of labour time and the units of value produced. Something cooked up on the spur of the moment might have enormous value. Long hours of slog might end up being for nothing. Being exempt from routine work is not really all that glamorous in either story, as it just brings uncertainty, frustration, pressure, and (for some) madness.

Both of these shows hinge on the desire to escape from the limits of the hacker class and become owners. That's the limit to the desire the culture industry can admit for this class. And yet both these shows portray a continual treadmill of hope and failure. Like the farmer and the worker, the hacker does not usually end up owning the product of her efforts. Unless you own a drug company or a tech company or media conglomerate, you have to sell the rights to what you produce. It is not always the same as selling labour power. You might still own the intellectual property, for example. But the hacker rarely captures much of the value of what they create or invent.

Nobody else gets to be Google's Sergey Brin precisely because there is a Sergey Brin, who is not the avatar of the hacker class, but of its opposite – the *vectoralist class*. He is the real unicorn: the hacker become owner. The one that perpetuates the myth that drives a million start-ups on the path to the same desire, not realising that it is the very thing that now blocks that desire. It is highly unlikely that your start-up will be the next Google. At best, you might sell it to Google or to some other avatar of the vectoralist class.

The vectoralist class owns and controls the *vector*, a concept I use to describe in the abstract the infrastructure on which information is routed, whether through time or space.[12] A vector in geometry is simply a line of fixed length but of unfixed position. It's a way of thinking about a technology as having something about it that shapes the world in a particular way, but which can shape different aspects of the world. You can own stocks or flows of information, but far better to own the vector, the legal and technical protocols for making otherwise abundant information scarce.

If one takes a look at the top *Fortune 500* companies, it is surprising how many of them are really in the information business. I don't just mean the technology and telecommunication companies like Apple or Google or Verizon or Cisco or the drug companies like Pfizer. One could also think of the big banks as a subset of the vectoralist class rather than as 'finance capital'. They too are in the information asymmetry business. And as we learned in the 2008 crash, even the car companies are in the information business – they made more money from car loans than cars. The military-industrial sector is also in the information business. The companies that appear to sell actual things, like Nike, are really in the brand business. Walmart and Amazon compete with different models of the information logistics business.[13] Even the oil companies are in part at least in the information-about-the-geology-of-*possible*-oil-deposits business. Perhaps the vectoralist class is no longer emerging. Maybe it is the new dominant class.

One could make the case here that information was always central to capitalism and that this is just capitalism. To some extent, that may be the case. However, to even think that capitalism is about information is a fairly recent perspective. It ends up being a way of retrospectively seeing the whole course of capitalism in terms of something that only emerged as a concept and an instrumental reality as one of its late products.

The other point to clarify here is that there's a difference between information as a force of production and information as a *dominant* force of production. The vectoralist class doesn't need to own the other forces of production any more. Apple and Google don't actually make their own products. A sizable chunk of those they directly employ are not workers but hackers, people who come up with new information, whether of a technical or cultural kind, to be incorporated into products whose manufacture can be tendered out to a subordinate class of capitalists.

That might only be the case in the overdeveloped world where I happen to live.[14] Many of the world's peoples are not even workers but still peasants who are being turned into tenant farmers by the theft of their common land by a landlord class. Much of the world is also a giant sweatshop. The resistance of labour to capital is alive and well in China, India, Indonesia, and Vietnam. The older class antagonisms have not gone away. It's just that there's a new layer on top, trying to control them. Just as the capitalist class sought to dominate the landlord class as a subordinate ruling class, so too the vectoralist class tries to subordinate both landlords and capitalists by controlling the patents, the brands, the trademarks, the copyrights, but more importantly the logistics of the information vector.

The vector has also worked its way throughout the production process. This was already beginning in the so-called Fordist era. Some proposed naming it instead after the great Japanese companies that boomed in the mid-to-late-twentieth century, such as Toyota and Sony. They were the ones who figured out how to extract not just labour but also information from the labour force. It turns out that to extract not only efficiency but also quality from industrial labour, it is best to incorporate the information held by those who know the labour process best – its workers.[15] That there is a hacker class at all is in part because workers have been stripped of the information they possess about the labour process itself.

In *Capital*, Marx mostly deals with an ideal-type political economy with two classes. But in his political writings it is clear that he understands social formations as hybrids of combined and overlapping modes of production.[16] His writing on France isn't just a grand confrontation between proletariat and bourgeoisie; the scene looms large with farmers, landlords, and peasants. So here I'm simply taking my cue from the political writings and thinking a matrix of six classes, three ruling and three subordinate. The dominant classes are landlords, capitalists, vectoralists. The subordinate classes are farmers, workers, hackers.

Now imagine all the possibilities of class alliance and conflict that this generates. It turns out that politics is much less about the relation between the friend and the enemy, and much more crucially about relations among *non-friends* and *non-enemies*.[17] It's about shifting alliances of convenience between heterogeneous class interests. It's about conflicts that can take many forms, only some of them open, many of them discreet.

So how is this worse than capitalism? The vectoral infrastructure throws all of the world into the engine of commodification, meanwhile modifying the commodity form itself. There is nothing that can't be tagged and captured through information about it and considered a variable in the simulations that drive resource extraction and processing.[18] Quite simply, we have run out of world to commodify. And now commodification can only cannibalise its own means of existence, both natural and social. It's like that Marx Brothers film where the train runs out of firewood, so the carriages themselves have to be hacked to pieces and fed to the fire to keep it moving, until nothing but the bare bogies are left.[19]

It is worse also in that rather than some acephalous *multitude*, there are complex class alliances and conflicts at play.[20] The trickiest part of it is the politics of the hacker class, which after all is the class most of us here reading and writing this stuff belong to. Yes, it appears as a 'privileged' class, among those whom Bruce Robbins calls the *beneficiaries* of global relations of exploitation.[21] And it is a class that has a very hard time thinking its common interests, because the kinds of new information its various subfractions produce are all so different. We have a hard time thinking what the writer and the scientist and artist and the engineer have in common. Well, the vectoral class does not have that problem. What all of us make is intellectual property, which from its point of view is as equivalent and as tradable as pink goo.

The hacker class experiences extremes of a winner-take-all outcome of its efforts. On the one hand, fantastic careers and the spoils of some simulation of the old bourgeois lifestyle; on the other hand, precarious and part-time work, start-ups that go bust, and the making routine of our jobs by new algorithms – designed by others of our very own class. The hacker class was supposed to be a privileged one, shielded from proletarianisation by its creativity and technical skill. But it too can be made casual and precarious.

A controversial ad campaign for the website Fiverr embodied all these contradictions. It played on the desire to quit one's lousy job and become a boss, by offering the pleasure of subjecting others to the tyranny one feels as a precarious creative or technical employee these days. The ads promise a way to hire versions of your old self who are 'doers'. The most notorious ad showed a black and white picture of a hollow-cheeked, sad-eyed young woman staring directly at the viewer: 'You eat a coffee for lunch. You follow through on your follow through. Sleep deprivation is your drug of choice', it reads, concluding: 'You might be a doer'. Another slogan was 'Nothing like a safe, reliable paycheck to crush your soul'. And 'How much did you make for your boss today?' The one I most often saw defaced read 'White Collars Can Come With Leashes'. The slogans appear under pictures of a 'diverse' workforce, of course: the algorithm is in theory very tolerant about who it exploits.

The old dream of labour, that it could organise itself, is supposed to be dead. There can be no dream of the hacker class to self-organise in any way, whether like labour or in some other form. Such desires are unspeakable, even if they keep erupting in all sorts of interesting ways. Sanctioned desire is neatly summed up in the image and slogan of a cellphone company: 'Boss Revolution'. The image is of a raised fist, with a cellphone in it, in red. The only desire permissible is to become a boss, like Don Draper.

1 Boots Riley's film *Sorry to Bother You* (Significant Productions, 2018) plays out another possibility of the combinatory: workers' bodies are genetically altered with horse DNA to produce a new and more powerful species of manual labourers.
2 Karl Marx, 'Preface (to A Contribution to the Critique of Political Economy)', *Early Writings*, London: Penguin, 1992, 424ff.
3 Marshall Berman, *All that Is Solid Melts into Air: The Experience of Modernity*, New York: Penguin, 1988.
4 McKenzie Wark, *A Hacker Manifesto*, Cambridge, MA: Harvard University Press, 2004.
5 Evegeny Pashukanis, *Law and Marxism*, London: Pluto Press, 1987.
6 James Boyle, *The Public Domain*, New Haven, CT: Yale University Press, 2010.
7 Phillip Kalantzis-Cope, *The Work and Play of the Mind in the Information Age: Whose Property?*, London: Palgrave, 2017.
8 Pekka Himanen, *The Hacker Ethic*, New York: Random House, 2002.
9 Matthew Weiner et al. (executive producers), *Mad Men*, Los Angeles: Weiner Bros., 2007–15.
10 The classic Marxist study of which is Stuart Ewen, *Captains of Consciousness: Advertising and the Social Roots of Commercial Culture*, New York: Basic Books, 2001.
11 Christopher Cantwell and Christopher C. Rogers (creators), *Halt and Catch Fire*, Atlanta, GA: Gran Via Productions and Lockjaw Productions, 2014–17.
12 I borrowed the term from Paul Virilio, but the concept is closer to the work of Harold Innis, *The Bias of Communication*, Toronto: University of Toronto Press, 2008.
13 Jesse Le Cavalier, *The Rule of Logistics: Walmart and the Architecture of Fulfillment*, Minneapolis: University of Minnesota Press, 2016.
14 Leopold Kohr, *The Overdeveloped Nations*, New York: Shocken, 1978.
15 I summed up the debates around this in 'From Fordism to Sonyism: Perverse Readings of the New World Order', *New Formations* 16, 1992, pp. 4–54.
16 Karl Marx, *The Revolutions of 1848*, London: Verso, 2010; Karl Marx, *Surveys from Exile*, London: Verso, 2010; Karl Marx, *The First International and After*, London: Verso, 2010.
17 Algirdas Julien Greimas, *On Meaning: Selected Writings in Semiotic Theory*, Minnesota: University of Minneapolis Press, 1987.
18 Anna Tsing, *Friction: An Ethnography of Global Connection*, Princeton, NJ: Princeton University Press, 2005, p. 182.
19 The Marx Brothers, *Go West* (1940), directed by Edward Buzzell.
20 Michael Hardt and Antonio Negri, *Multitude*, New York: Penguin, 2005. The term has a somewhat different valence in Paolo Virno, *Multitude Between Innovation and Negation*, Los Angeles: Semiotext(e), 2008.
21 Bruce Robbins, *The Beneficiary*, Durham, NC: Duke University Press, 2017.

CAPITAL IS DEAD: IS THIS SOMETHING WORSE? [LE CAPITAL EST MORT. FAUT-IL S'EN INQUIÉTER ?]

McKenzie Wark

[...] Le capitalisme industriel ne voulait pas d'ouvriers qui réfléchissent ou ressentent des émotions. Il voulait des bras. Il voulait des muscles. C'était une machine à dévorer de la chair. Aussi répugnant et terrifiant soit-il, le pouvoir qui s'exprime dans ces épisodes plus récents ne dévore pas tant les corps que les cerveaux. C'est une logique à deux voies : soit votre cerveau est supprimé et votre corps devient alors le véhicule d'un autre cerveau, soit votre cerveau est subordonné à la volonté d'un autre pouvoir[1]. D'une manière ou d'une autre, votre cerveau ne vous appartient pas. Cela a tout d'une prise de contrôle hostile. Et s'il ne s'agissait pas simplement d'une prise de contrôle, mais d'une relation de classe entièrement nouvelle ?

Commençons par réfléchir à cette curieuse relation de classe en procédant de manière très « orthodoxe ». Commençons par les *forces de production*, les *rapports de production* qui leur sont associés, les conflits de classe engendrés par ces rapports de production, et enfin les *superstructures* politiques et culturelles qui correspondent à cette base[2]. Essayons aussi de décrire, à l'image de Marx, ce qui est susceptible d'émerger plutôt que ce qui est déjà établi. Si l'on part de ce qui est établi, il est facile d'interpréter chaque nouvel aspect de la situation comme une simple variation du même principe. Prendre comme point de départ ce qui pourrait émerger engendre un dérangement des sens salutaire, l'impression vertigineuse que tout ce qui est solide se dissout dans l'air[3].

L'exercice de réflexion qui en résulte est assez simple. En voici l'ébauche, qu'il s'agira de développer au fur et à mesure de notre réflexion : les forces de production qui dévorent les cerveaux, qui produisent, instrumentalisent et contrôlent l'information, sont dotées d'une qualité distinctive. Cela peut s'expliquer par le fait que l'information possède d'étranges propriétés ontologiques. Faire de l'information une force de production engendre une sorte de paradoxe avec le modèle connu de la marchandise. L'information veut être libre, mais elle est partout enchaînée[4]. L'information n'est plus un bien rare, elle est reproductible à l'infini, elle peut être stockée et transmise à moindres frais ; or, le principe même de la marchandise est sa rareté.

L'information en tant que force de production fait naître des *relations* de production particulières tout en étant elle-même formée par ces relations. Si l'on suivait la logique marxiste classique, on s'intéresserait dès lors à l'évolution des formes juridiques[5]. À la fin du XXe siècle, la « propriété intellectuelle » est apparue comme un droit de propriété privée quasiment absolu[6]. Un droit qui transforme des formes de propriété privée jadis séparées et locales – le brevet, le droit d'auteur, la marque de fabrique – en formes de propriété privée équivalentes et échangeables. Ces formes ont besoin d'être protégées par des lois appliquées de manière transnationale, précisément parce que l'information est une chose tellement volatile et abstraite[7].

À l'instar des formes de propriété qui l'ont précédé, telles que l'enclosure[8] ou la société par actions, le droit de propriété intellectuelle prend la forme d'un nouveau type de relation de production, plus abstrait que ses prédécesseurs, et qui ne transforme pas la terre ou l'usine en propriété privée, mais l'information en tant que telle. Comme ces formes antérieures de propriété privée, celle-ci se cristallise en une relation de classe. En tant que forme absolue de propriété privée, elle crée des classes de propriétaires et de non-propriétaires des outils nécessaires à la réalisation de sa valeur. La terre en tant que propriété privée a donné naissance aux deux grandes classes que sont les *fermiers* et les *propriétaires fonciers*. Le capital en tant que propriété privée a donné naissance aux deux grandes classes des *ouvriers* et des *capitalistes*. La marchandisation de l'information s'accompagne-t-elle de l'émergence d'une nouvelle relation de classe ?

Pour les besoins de notre exercice de réflexion, nous dirons que c'est le cas. J'appelle ces classes la *classe hacker* et la *classe vectoraliste*. La classe hacker produit de nouvelles informations. Mais qu'est-ce qu'une « nouvelle » information ? C'est tout ce que la loi sur la propriété intellectuelle reconnaît comme tel. C'est un type de production étrange. Alors que l'agriculteur fait pousser des cultures selon un cycle saisonnier et que l'ouvrier produit des unités de marchandises identiques, le hacker doit exploiter son temps différemment, afin de transformer les informations existantes en de nouvelles informations. Cette manière de faire n'a rien à voir avec les répétitions saisonnières de l'agriculture ou le pointage du travailleur. Le travail a lieu quand il a lieu, y compris pendant la sieste ou les nuits blanches[9]. Le cauchemar professionnel de l'ouvrier est de devoir faire la même chose, encore et encore, sous la pression de la montre ; celui du hacker est de devoir produire des choses *différentes*, encore et encore, sous la pression de la montre.

Les personnages de Peggy et Don dans la série télévisée *Mad Men* sont des prototypes des employés du milieu du XXe siècle[10]. Ils travaillent dans le milieu de la publicité à l'âge d'or du fordisme[11]. Don est directeur créatif et se démène avec les dirigeants de son agence publicitaire pour devenir lui-même associé. Peggy est secrétaire, col blanc, et se bat pour faire partie de l'équipe créative. Joan, quant à elle, est déjà à la tête de l'équipe des secrétaires, mais aspire à devenir associée. Au fil des épisodes, les femmes progressent à petits pas dans cet univers masculin. À la fin de la série, les femmes noires commencent tout juste à obtenir des emplois de secrétariat, mais l'avènement de l'ordinateur finira par rendre ces derniers en partie obsolètes. Comme dans nombre d'émanations de la culture bourgeoise, c'est le récit d'une petite entreprise où les classes sont comprimées et les frontières entre elles brouillées. La récompense qui consisterait à rejoindre la classe des vrais dirigeants reste toujours hors de portée.

Ce qui nous intéresse dans cette série, c'est la manière dont elle représente les activités d'un prototype de la classe hacker. La caméra suit, fascinée, Don et Peggy dans l'exercice de leur métier. Don fait de longues siestes sur le canapé dans son bureau. Parfois, il se balade. Les idées de ses brillantes campagnes publicitaires proviennent de toutes sortes de sources plus ou moins fortuites. Il boit trop, essaie la marijuana. Tout le bureau prend des amphétamines et passe des nuits blanches à produire, sous l'effet du speed, un travail créatif marqué par une énergie débordante et de très mauvaises décisions. Pendant ce temps, Peggy parvient à passer d'employée à hacker car elle est bien placée pour savoir comment répondre aux désirs des femmes, mais elle finit par être bridée et empêchée de toutes sortes de manières par une industrie qui ne reconnaît pas la valeur de sa différence.

Moins connue, la série *Halt and Catch Fire* transpose dans l'industrie technologique naissante le même type d'activités, ce même travail qui n'est pas un travail tout à fait comme les autres[12]. On ne peut pas gérer les hackers comme des agriculteurs ou des ouvriers ; ils n'appartiennent à aucune de ces deux classes. Il n'y a pas dans leur classe de relation entre unités de temps de travail et unités de valeur produite. Une idée qui germe à la faveur d'un moment peut s'avérer d'une valeur énorme ; de longues heures de travail peuvent ne rien donner du tout. Dans les deux séries, être exempté d'un travail routinier n'a rien de glamour, puisque cela n'est que source d'incertitude, de frustration, de pression et (pour certains) de folie.

Les deux séries s'articulent autour d'une volonté de dépasser les limites de la classe des hackers pour devenir propriétaires. Telle est la limite du désir que l'industrie de la culture peut accorder à cette classe. Et pourtant, ces séries dépeignent chacune un train-train quotidien fait d'espoirs et d'échecs. Comme l'agriculteur et l'ouvrier, le hacker finit rarement par être propriétaire du produit de ses efforts. À moins que vous ne possédiez un laboratoire pharmaceutique, une entreprise de technologie ou un empire médiatique, vous devez vendre les droits sur ce que vous produisez.

Cela n'équivaut pas toujours à vendre votre force de travail. Ainsi, il se peut que vous en gardiez la propriété intellectuelle, par exemple. Mais il est rare que le hacker garde en sa possession une grande partie de la valeur de ce qu'il crée ou invente.

Il n'y a qu'un Sergey Brin chez Google parce que Sergey Brin n'est pas l'avatar de la classe des hackers, mais de son opposé : la *classe vectoraliste*. C'est lui la vraie licorne : le hacker devenu propriétaire. Celui qui perpétue le mythe incitant un million de start-up à suivre le même chemin du désir, sans se rendre compte que c'est précisément celui-ci qui empêche désormais ce désir de se réaliser. Il y a très peu de chances que votre start-up soit le prochain Google. Au mieux, vous pourrez la vendre à Google ou à un autre avatar de la classe vectoraliste.

La classe vectoraliste possède et contrôle le *vecteur,* un concept que j'utilise pour décrire de manière abstraite l'infrastructure par laquelle l'information est acheminée, que ce soit dans le temps ou dans l'espace[13]. Un vecteur en géométrie est simplement une ligne d'une longueur fixe, mais dont la position peut varier. C'est une manière de penser une technologie comme possédant une propriété qui façonne le monde d'une certaine manière, mais qui peut façonner différents aspects du monde. Vous pouvez posséder des actions ou des flux d'information, mais mieux vaut posséder le vecteur, c'est-à-dire les protocoles juridiques et techniques vous permettant de raréfier des informations par ailleurs abondantes.

Si l'on s'intéresse aux entreprises qui figurent en tête du classement *Fortune 500,* il est surprenant de constater combien d'entre elles sont actives dans le secteur de l'information. Je ne parle pas seulement des entreprises de technologies et de télécommunications, telles que Apple, Google, Verizon ou Cisco, ou des entreprises pharmaceutiques comme Pfizer. On pourrait également considérer les grandes banques comme un sous-ensemble de la classe vectoraliste plutôt que comme « capital financier ». Elles aussi opèrent dans le champ de l'asymétrie de l'information. Et comme nous l'avons appris lors de la crise financière de 2008, même les constructeurs automobiles sont actifs dans le secteur de l'information : ils gagnaient plus d'argent avec les prêts automobiles qu'avec les voitures. Le complexe militaro-industriel opère lui aussi dans le secteur de l'information. Les entreprises qui semblent vendre des objets réels, telles que Nike, opèrent en réalité dans le commerce de l'image. Walmart et Amazon sont en compétition avec différents modèles du secteur de la logistique de l'information[14]. Même les compagnies pétrolières opèrent en partie au moins dans le secteur de l'information-sur-la-géologie-de-*possibles*-gisements-de-pétrole. Peut-être que la classe vectoraliste n'est plus en train d'émerger ; peut-être constitue-t-elle déjà la nouvelle classe dominante.

On pourrait faire valoir ici que l'information a toujours été au cœur du capitalisme et que c'est simplement sa véritable nature. Dans une certaine mesure, c'est peut-être vrai. Mais l'idée que le capitalisme relève de l'information est elle-même assez récente. En fin de compte, c'est une manière de considérer a posteriori toute la trajectoire du capitalisme à l'aune d'un concept et d'une réalité fonctionnelle qui sont apparus comme l'une de ses émanations tardives.

L'autre point qu'il s'agit de clarifier ici concerne la différence entre l'information en tant que force de production et l'information en tant que force de production *dominante.* La classe vectoraliste n'est plus obligée de posséder les autres forces de production. Apple et Google ne fabriquent pas leurs propres produits. La majorité des gens qu'ils emploient directement ne sont pas des ouvriers mais des hackers, des personnes qui produisent de nouvelles informations, de nature technique ou culturelle, destinées à être incorporées dans des produits dont la fabrication peut être sous-traitée à une classe subordonnée de capitalistes.

Peut-être n'est-ce vrai que pour le monde surdéveloppé dans lequel je vis[15]. De nombreux peuples à travers le monde n'ont jamais accédé au statut d'ouvriers, demeurant des paysans transformés en métayers par une classe de propriétaires de terrains qui usurpent leur terre commune. Par ailleurs, une vaste partie du monde fonctionne comme un gigantesque atelier de misère. La résistance du travail au capital se porte bien en Chine, en Inde, en Indonésie et au Vietnam. Les antagonismes de classe plus anciens n'y ont pas disparu. Tout au plus ont-ils été recouverts par l'arrivée d'une nouvelle strate qui essaie de les contrôler. Tout comme la classe capitaliste cherchait à dominer la classe des propriétaires fonciers en tant que classe dirigeante subordonnée, la classe vectoraliste essaie à son tour de subordonner à la fois les propriétaires fonciers et les capitalistes en contrôlant les brevets, les marques, les marques déposées et les droits d'auteur, mais surtout la logistique du vecteur d'information.

Le vecteur s'est aussi entièrement intégré au processus de production. Cette évolution a commencé à l'époque dite fordiste, que d'aucuns proposent de renommer d'après les grandes entreprises japonaises ayant prospéré entre le milieu et la fin du XXe siècle, telles que Toyota et Sony. Ce sont elles qui ont compris les premières comment extraire non seulement la main-d'œuvre, mais aussi les informations détenues par cette main-d'œuvre. Il s'avère que pour extraire du travail industriel non seulement du rendement mais aussi de la qualité, il est préférable d'y intégrer les informations détenues par ceux qui connaissent le mieux le processus de travail – ses ouvriers[16]. L'existence même d'une classe hacker est en partie due au fait que les ouvriers ont été dépouillés des informations qu'ils possédaient sur le processus de travail lui-même.

Dans *Le Capital,* Marx traite principalement d'une économie politique idéale à deux classes. Mais dans ses écrits politiques, il apparaît clairement qu'il comprend les formations sociales comme des formes hybrides de modes de production combinés et imbriqués[17]. Ses observations sur la France ne se limitent pas à une formidable confrontation entre prolétariat et bourgeoisie ; les agriculteurs, propriétaires fonciers et paysans y occupent une place importante. Ici, je m'inspire donc simplement des écrits politiques pour penser une matrice de six classes, dont trois dirigeantes et trois subordonnées. Les classes dominantes sont les propriétaires fonciers, les capitalistes et les vectoralistes. Les classes subordonnées sont les agriculteurs, les ouvriers et les hackers.

Maintenant, imaginez toutes les possibilités d'alliances et de conflits de classe que génère cette situation. Ce qui importe en politique, ce n'est pas tant les relations entre amis et ennemis que les relations entre *non-amis* et *non-ennemis*[18]. Il s'agit de déplacer les alliances de circonstance entre intérêts de classe hétérogènes. Il s'agit de conflits qui peuvent prendre de nombreuses formes, dont seules certaines sont publiques, quand la plupart restent discrètes.

Alors, dans quelle mesure cette situation est-elle pire que le capitalisme ? L'infrastructure vectorielle soumet le monde entier au moteur de la marchandisation, tout en modifiant le modèle même de la marchandise. Il n'existe rien qui ne saurait être étiqueté et capturé au moyen des informations qui existent à son sujet et qui ne puisse être considéré comme une variable dans les simulations qui sous-tendent l'extraction et le traitement des ressources[19]. Nous avons tout simplement épuisé les ressources planétaires pouvant être transformées en marchandises. Désormais, la marchandisation en est réduite à cannibaliser ses propres moyens d'existence, tant naturels que sociaux. Un peu comme dans ce film des Marx Brothers où le train vient à manquer de bois de chauffage : les voitures sont dépecées et jetées au feu pour le maintenir en mouvement, jusqu'à ce qu'il ne reste plus que leurs carcasses[20].

Elle est pire aussi en ce que, plutôt qu'une *multitude* acéphale, elle met en jeu des alliances et des conflits de classe complexes[21]. Son aspect le plus problématique concerne la politique de la classe des hackers, qui, après tout, est celle à laquelle appartiennent la plupart d'entre nous qui lisons ces lignes et participons à ce discours. En effet, celle-ci apparaît comme une classe « privilégiée » parmi celles que Bruce Robbins appelle les *bénéficiaires* des relations d'exploitation globales[22]. Et c'est une classe qui peine à penser ses intérêts communs parce que les types d'informations que produisent ses différentes sous-fractions divergent. Nous avons du mal à saisir ce que l'écrivain et le scientifique, l'artiste et l'ingénieur ont en commun. La classe vectoraliste, en revanche, ne connaît pas ce problème. Pour elle, ce que nous fabriquons tous, c'est de la propriété intellectuelle, qui, de son point de vue, est un article aussi interchangeable et commercialisable qu'un pot de pâte à modeler rose.

Pour ce qui est de la récompense pour ses efforts, la classe des hackers est soumise au régime du gagnant qui rafle la mise : d'une part, des carrières formidables et la perspective d'un semblant de l'ancien mode de vie bourgeois ; d'autre part, le travail précaire et à temps partiel, les start-up qui font faillite et la routinisation de nos emplois par de nouveaux algorithmes – conçus par d'autres issus de notre propre classe. La classe des hackers était censée être une classe privilégiée, protégée de la prolétarisation par sa créativité et ses compétences techniques. Or, elle aussi peut être rendue informelle et précaire.

Une récente campagne publicitaire pour le site web Fiverr incarnait toutes ces contradictions. Elle faisait appel à l'envie des utilisateurs de quitter leur emploi minable pour devenir eux-mêmes patrons et jouir à leur tour du plaisir de soumettre d'autres à la tyrannie que subit aujourd'hui l'employé créatif ou technique précaire. Les annonces faisaient miroiter la possibilité d'embaucher des « faiseurs », à savoir des versions entreprenantes de votre ancien vous. Sur la plus notoire d'entre elles figurait une photo en noir et blanc d'une jeune femme aux joues creuses, qui fixait le spectateur d'un œil triste : « Vous mangez un café pour le déjeuner. Vous allez au bout des choses. Le manque de sommeil est votre drogue de prédilection », disait le texte, avant de conclure : « Vous pourriez être une faiseuse. » Une autre affiche déclarait : « Rien de tel qu'un revenu fixe et garanti pour tuer votre âme. » Ou encore : « Combien avez-vous gagné pour votre patron aujourd'hui ? » La phrase que j'ai vue défigurée le plus souvent disait : « Les cols blancs sont admis avec leurs laisses. » Bien entendu, les slogans apparaissaient sur des images d'une main-d'œuvre « représentant la diversité » – l'algorithme étant en théorie très tolérant quant à qui il exploite.

Le vieux rêve selon lequel le travail pourrait s'organiser lui-même est censé être mort. La classe des hackers ne peut pas espérer s'auto-organiser, que ce soit comme jadis le travail d'usine ou sous une autre forme. Ces désirs sont indicibles, même s'ils continuent de se manifester de toutes sortes de manières intéressantes. Le désir sanctionné se résume parfaitement à l'image et au slogan d'une entreprise de téléphonie mobile : « *Boss Revolution* ». L'image est celle d'un poing levé qui tient un téléphone portable, le tout sur fond rouge. Le seul désir permis est celui de devenir patron, à l'instar de Don Draper.

1 Le film *Sorry to Bother You* de Boots Riley (Significant Productions, 2018) s'amuse à imaginer une autre conséquence possible de cette logique : les corps des ouvriers sont génétiquement modifiés avec de l'ADN de cheval afin de produire une nouvelle espèce plus puissante de travailleurs manuels.

2 Voir Karl Marx, « Préface », dans *Contribution à la critique de l'économie publique* (1859), trad. par Maurice Husson et Gilbert Badia, Paris, Éditions sociales, 1972, p. 17-20.

3 Marshall Berman, *Tout ce qui est solide se volatilise*, Genève, Entremonde, 2018.

4 McKenzie Wark, *A Hacker Manifesto*, Cambridge (MA), Harvard University Press, 2004.

5 Evgeny Pashukanis, *Law and Marxism*, Londres, Pluto Press, 1987.

6 James Boyle, *The Public Domain*, New Haven (CT), Yale University Press, 2010.

7 Phillip Kalantzis-Cope, *The Work and Play of the Mind in the Information Age: Whose Property?*, Londres, Palgrave, 2017.

8 Selon le *Larousse*, l'enclosure est un anglicisme qui désigne la « clôture des champs, qui s'est accompagnée du passage d'une forme communautaire à une forme individualiste d'économie agraire » ; www.larousse.fr/dictionnaires/francais/enclosure/29204 (consulté le 14 juin 2021).

9 Pekka Himanen, *The Hacker Ethic*, New York, Random House, 2002.

10 Matthew Weiner *et al.* (producteurs exécutifs), *Mad Men*, Los Angeles, Weiner Bros., 2007-2015.

11 L'étude marxiste classique sur ce sujet est de Stuart Ewen, *Captains of Consciousness: Advertising and the Social Roots of Consumer Culture*, New York, Basic Books, 2001.

12 Christopher Cantwell et Christopher C. Rogers (créateurs), *Halt and Catch Fire*, Atlanta (GA), Gran Via Productions et Lockjaw Productions, 2014-2017.

13 J'emprunte le terme à Paul Virilio, mais le concept est plus proche du travail de Harold Innis, *The Bias of Communication* [1951], Toronto, University of Toronto Press, 2008.

14 Jesse LeCavalier, *The Rule of Logistics: Walmart and the Architecture of Fulfillment*, Minneapolis, University of Minnesota Press, 2016.

15 Leopold Kohr, *The Overdeveloped Nations*, New York, Schocken, 1978.

16 J'ai résumé les débats autour de cette question dans « From Fordism to Sonyism: Perverse Readings of the New World Order », dans *New Formations*, vol. 16, 1992, p. 4-54.

17 Voir Karl Marx, *The Political Writings*, dir. David Fernbach, Londres, Verso, 2010, particulièrement *The Revolutions of 1848*, *Surveys from Exile* et *The First International and After*.

18 Algirdas Julien Greimas, *On Meaning: Selected Writings in Semiotic Theory*, Minnesota, University of Minneapolis Press, 1987.

19 Anna Tsing, *Friction: An Ethnography of Global Connection*, Princeton (NJ), Princeton University Press, 2005, p. 182.

20 Marx Brothers, *Go West*, réal. par Edward Buzzell, 1940.

21 Michael Hardt et Antonio Negri, *Multitude*, New York, Penguin, 2005. Le terme a une valence légèrement différente chez Paolo Virno, *Multitude Between Innovation and Negation*, Los Angeles, Semiotext(e), 2008.

22 Bruce Robbins, *The Beneficiary*, Durham (NC), Duke University Press, 2017.

SEASONAL ASSOCIATE

Heike Geissler

> Tote
> ASIN
> Scan tote
> Scan ASIN
> Scan ASINs until enough in tote
> Tote full
> Next tote

Tote – what does that sound like? says Hans-Peter. Let me tell you something you might not know: In German, *tote* sounds like the word for dead or death. It's like working in a crematorium, says Hans-Peter. You don't want to use these new terms quite yet, but Norman makes it clear: You can call the tote a crate, but it won't help you much because the tote's called a tote and it's called a tote everywhere. It's better to remember it right away.

Florian comes dashing in. Norman doesn't say anything, just stands silently in front of him, a punishing father who can't find the right words but conveys his low opinion of Florian entirely with his silence.

You go on trying out the new words.

> Tote.
> ASIN.
> Mark defective.
> Cubi.
> Problem solver.
> MHD goods.
> Prep.

Nothing feels real, not even the consignment of goods a forklift operator drops off beside you. Two pallets piled with shrink-wrapped brown cardboard boxes. Right now, you're in the middle of real employee life and at the same time you're in the continuation of the game that began at the test session. Norman tells Florian and Hans-Peter to release the shrink-wrap with their fish knives. They've hardly begun before he intervenes; they're working too slowly and carefully for his taste. He releases the plastic from the boxes with fast, rough movements, rips it off, balls it up, and tosses it overarm straight into the plastics container. He opens a box and pulls out a package printed with a shiny wheel rim, more throws than places it on the workstation, and elucidates the situation. Right, he says, we've got a box full of the same product. Then we leave the product in there, we don't take them all out, only one of them to scan the barcode, if you can't find it on the outside of the box. Takes too long otherwise. He moves the box around until he finds the barcode and then scans it. Watch me, he says, I'm not doing this for my own sake, I can do all this already. He enters the number of wheel rim boxes contained in the brown cardboard box. Then it looks as though the desk were throwing the brown box at Norman so that he can put the wheel rim back into its container with verve, taking no care to protect the edges. There's nothing obviously special about his motions; all you notice is the absolute unspecialness of them. Norman's movements follow a strict sense of timing; he seems to use the exact same amount of time for each activity, everything is subordinated to his sense of time, and each product to be processed is merely something that impairs the adherence to time requirements more or less than others.

[...]

You feel like you're just about part of a group. A group that's been thrown out of the saddle by a galloping donkey. Or by the cynical solemnity of a misunderstood working life.

You're playing with the products – or what is it you're doing? You're learning something about the products and how to deal with them.

You have to use strips of tape to cover up the so-called touch cutouts in the packaging of protective car-seat covers. You have to bag up unpackaged suitcases and make sure the bags have air holes. You come across a glass bathtub duck with a barcode not recognised by the computer. A new product, says Norman. You take a closer look as you're carrying it across the hall, barely noticing the floor markings. You're carrying a glass bathtub duck; neither you nor I can say anything else about that.

You're supposed to log a crate full of advent calendars into the system, but they're advent calendars filled with tea bags. Every tea bag has a drawing of a politician's face on it, intended to peep out over the edge of a cup once the calendar reaches the customer. You carry the crate of calendars over to the MHD department, where all foodstuffs are processed.

You come across a hairdryer with the name Alpine Hairdryer Grossglockner. You can't help laughing. You repeat the product name but Hans-Peter doesn't think there's anything funny about it, merely commenting that you are capable of laughing after all.

You rip up cardboard boxes; that's the hardest part. Norman comes over, takes a cardboard box, rips it into pieces, and throws it in with the used cardboard. You yawn inside as he does so.

Other than that, you're refreshing your old knowledge of the working world in here. You won't come across anything you don't already know from what your parents have told you.

You work, put the cut-resistant gloves on and take them off, you explain over and over to Hans-Peter how the computer works, you stare at the screen, sometimes you drop a product, and then you get a shock and hope it's not broken. You don't yet know the most important thing: Workers have to treat the products like a slave-driver treats slaves. After all, you're working here in a multilayered and complex system of dominances, and you always have to decide who you want to be. The question for every day is: Do you want the products to lead you around by the nose?

It's a matter of the prestige a person can obtain. It's a matter of the unpopular status of the lowest-ranking slave, which no one wants. So it's a matter of treating the products roughly, so that they don't rise up above the workers. You'll learn that soon enough, but you'll never be much good at it.

SEASONAL ASSOCIATE
[ASSOCIÉE SAISONNIÈRE]
Heike Geissler

Tote[1]
ASIN[2]
Scanner le tote
Scanner les ASIN
Scanner les ASIN jusqu'à ce que le tote soit plein
Tote plein
Tote suivant

Tote, quel drôle de mot, dit Hans-Peter. Vous l'ignorez peut-être mais en allemand, *Tote* signifie « morts ». On se croirait dans un crématorium. Vous rechignez encore à employer ces termes, mais Norman ne laisse pas de place au doute : vous pouvez l'appeler boîte si vous voulez, mais cela ne servira à rien, parce que le tote s'appelle *tote*, et s'appelle un *tote* partout. Vous feriez mieux de vous y habituer tout de suite.

Florian déboule. Norman ne dit rien, se plante devant lui, silencieux comme un père sévère qui peine à trouver les mots justes, mais dont le mutisme exprime tout le mal qu'il pense de Florian.

Vous vous répétez les nouveaux mots.

Tote
ASIN
Marquer défectueux
Cubi[3]
Problem solver[4]
Marchandise DDM[5]
Préparation

Rien ne semble réel, pas même le colis de marchandises qu'un conducteur de transpalette vient de déposer à côté de vous. Deux palettes sur lesquelles s'empilent des boîtes en carton entourées de film plastique. Vous voilà d'une part dans la vraie vie d'ouvrier, et d'autre part dans la continuation du jeu commencé lors de la mise à l'épreuve. Norman demande à Florian et à Hans-Peter de détacher le film plastique au moyen du couteau à poisson. Ils viennent à peine de commencer lorsqu'il intervient déjà parce qu'ils travaillent trop lentement et trop soigneusement à son goût. Par quelques mouvements rapides et brusques, il détache lui-même le film des cartons, le retire, le froisse et, d'un geste précis, le lance dans le conteneur à plastique. Il ouvre l'un des cartons et en sort une boîte sur laquelle figure une jante de voiture reluisante, la balance sur l'établi plutôt que de la poser et analyse la situation : bon, dit-il, on a un carton plein du même produit. Dans ce cas, on laisse le produit dedans, on ne sort pas tout, tout au plus un seul pour scanner le code-barres si on ne le trouve pas sur l'extérieur du carton. Sinon, ça prend trop de temps. Il retourne la boîte jusqu'à ce qu'il trouve le code-barres et le scanne. Regardez bien, dit-il, je ne fais pas ça pour moi, je sais déjà comment faire. Il renseigne le nombre de boîtes de jantes dans le carton marron. Puis, c'est comme si la table lui lançait la boîte pour qu'il puisse la remettre dans le carton marron avec entrain, sans se soucier d'abîmer les coins. Il n'y a rien de particulier dans ses mouvements, seule leur banalité attire l'attention : les mouvements de Norman suivent un rythme strict, il semble consacrer exactement le même laps de temps à chaque activité, tout est subordonné à la notion du temps, et chaque produit à manipuler n'est qu'un objet qui l'empêche de respecter plus ou moins le temps supposément imparti.

[...]

Vous avez tout juste encore l'impression de faire partie d'un groupe. Un groupe mis en débandade par un âne qui vient de détaler. Ou par le sérieux cynique d'une vie professionnelle incomprise.

Vous jouez avec les marchandises – sinon comment qualifier ce que vous faites ? Vous apprenez pas mal de choses sur les produits et comment les manier.

Vous devez sceller avec des bouts de ruban adhésif les trous dits « tactiles » percés dans l'emballage des housses de protection pour sièges-autos. Vous devez ensacher des valises non emballées et vous assurer que les sacs présentent des trous d'aération. Vous tombez sur un canard de bain en verre dont le code-barres n'est pas reconnu par l'ordinateur. Un nouveau produit, dit Norman. Vous l'examinez de plus près pendant que vous le portez à travers le hall en ignorant les marquages au sol. Vous portez un canard de bain en verre : que dire de plus ?

Vous êtes censé enregistrer une boîte pleine de calendriers de l'avent, mais ce sont des calendriers de l'avent remplis de sachets de thé. À chaque sachet est rattachée une étiquette avec le portrait d'un personnage politique, qui, lorsque le calendrier sera arrivé chez le client, doit dépasser du bord de la tasse. Vous portez la boîte avec les calendriers au département DDM, où sont traitées toutes les denrées alimentaires.

Vous tombez sur un sèche-cheveux appelé Alpenfön Groß Glockner. Vous ne pouvez pas vous empêcher de rire. Vous répétez le nom du produit, mais Hans-Peter ne lui trouve rien de drôle, constatant simplement que vous n'avez pas perdu l'envie de rire.

Vous déchiquetez des cartons, c'est la partie la plus difficile. Norman arrive, saisit un carton, le déchire en morceaux, le lance dans la benne à cartons usagés. Vous bâillez intérieurement en le regardant faire.

À part cela, vous remettez à jour vos connaissances sur le monde du travail. Vous ne rencontrerez rien dont vos parents ne vous auraient déjà parlé.

Vous travaillez, vous enfilez et vous enlevez les gants anticoupures, vous expliquez encore et encore à Hans-Peter comment fonctionne l'ordinateur, vous fixez l'écran, parfois vous laissez tomber un produit, ce qui vous fait sursauter, et vous espérez que rien ne se soit cassé. Vous ignorez encore la chose la plus importante : l'employé doit traiter les marchandises comme l'esclavagiste traite les esclaves. Après tout, vous travaillez ici dans un système de domination complexe et sophistiqué, et vous devez sans cesse décider de quel côté vous comptez vous retrouver. Chaque jour, vous devez vous poser la question suivante : allez-vous laisser les marchandises prendre le dessus ?

Il y va de votre réputation. Il y va du statut impopulaire de l'esclave au plus bas de l'échelle, dont personne ne veut hériter. Il s'agit donc de traiter les marchandises avec grossièreté afin qu'elles ne s'élèvent pas au-dessus des employés. Tout cela, vous finirez par l'apprendre, mais vous ne le maîtriserez jamais vraiment.

1 Dans les centres de distribution d'Amazon, le mot anglais *tote* désigne les caisses dans lesquelles les « collaborateurs » trient les marchandises selon leur destination.

2 Acronyme de « Amazon Standard Identification Number », un identifiant individuel composé de dix chiffres et lettres et attribué à chaque produit.

3 Abréviation pour *cubiscan*, qui désigne la saisie numérique des dimensions et du poids des marchandises pour générer l'ASIN correspondant.

4 Le « *problem solver* » est un néologisme qui désigne la personne habilitée à résoudre les problèmes pouvant intervenir dans la préparation des commandes que les employés ne sont pas en mesure de résoudre eux-mêmes.

5 Acronyme de « date de durabilité minimale », qui regroupe toutes les denrées périssables.

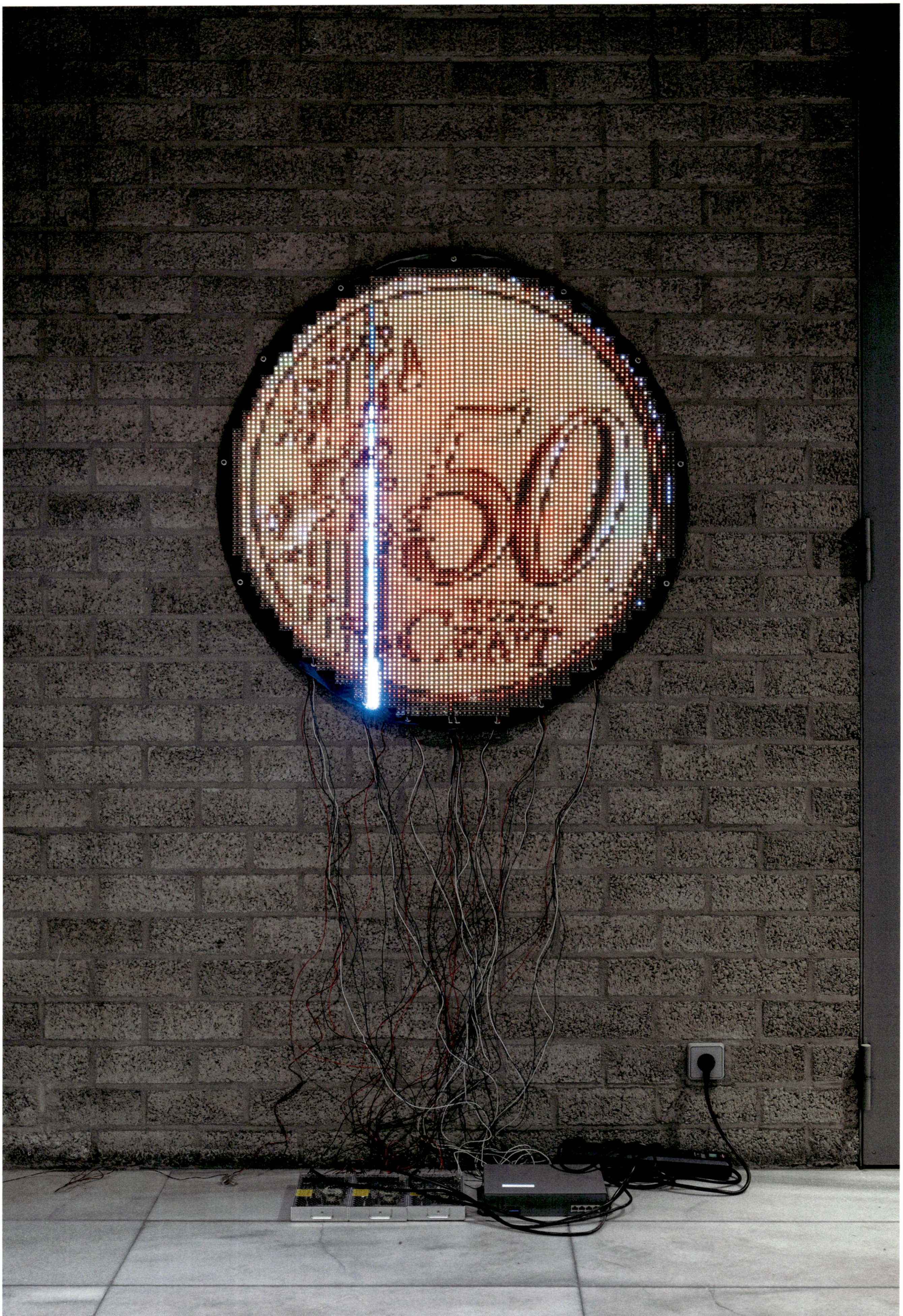

Ei Arakawa, *Family Dollar (Social Capital)*, 2020

Ei Arakawa

Made from fabric covered in light-emitting diodes (LEDs), *How to DISappear in America (Duration: multiple times in total of 9 hours, & approx. 60 hours on preparation, Honorarium: 3,500 EUR, 0.72 EUR per minute)*, belongs to a series of 2020 LED 'paintings' that display what Ei Arakawa was paid per minute for performances at various art institutions over the past fifteen years. To calculate the rate of 0.72 euros per minute, Arakawa divided his honorarium for this performance, which was staged as a part of the 9th Berlin Biennale, by the sum total of the work's approximate preparation time, length and number of times performed. As with the whole series these calculations, along with the performance's name, make up the title of the work. Created during a time when Covid-19-related measures left the artist unable to perform, *How to DISappear in America* not only brings attention to how value is measured and distributed in traditionally immaterial practices such as performance art, but also reflects the instability of these systems – particularly in times of crisis.

A second LED painting, entitled *YouTube Our Unemployment (Post-Capital)* (2021), is a new work acting as a 'performer' for a song, written by Arakawa in collaboration with writer Dan Poston, that reflects upon the economic fallout of the Coronavirus on performance artists, and the subsequent slow recovery of event culture from a more personal perspective. Collaborating with other artists and performers plays an important role in Arakawa's playful works, which can be seen to value collectivity over individuality. 'I'm not interested in the cult of personality or being alone on the stage', the artist has said of his approach. 'I always want to deal with other people'.[1]

Ei Arakawa was born in 1977 in Fukushima, Japan. He lives and works in Los Angeles, USA.

1 Andrew Maerkle, 'Pastoral Hide and Seek', *Art it*, 9 June 2017, https://www.art-it.asia/en/u/admin_ed_itv_e/towjzr5ibdps0hqrixce (accessed 9 April 2021).

How to DISappear in America (Duration: multiple times in total of 9 hours, & approx. 60 hours on preparation, Honorarium: 3,500 EUR, 0.72 EUR per minute) est une œuvre faite de tissu recouvert de diodes électroluminescentes (LED). Réalisée en 2020, elle s'inscrit dans une série de « peintures » LED évoquant la rémunération à la minute perçue par leur auteur, Ei Arakawa, pour ses performances dans diverses institutions artistiques au cours des quinze dernières années. Ce montant de 0,72 euro par minute a été obtenu en divisant les honoraires reçus pour cette performance réalisée dans le cadre de la neuvième Biennale de Berlin par la somme totale du temps de préparation, de la durée de l'œuvre et du nombre de fois où Ei Arakawa l'a exécutée. Comme pour le reste de la série, ces calculs et le nom de la performance constituent le titre de l'œuvre. Imaginée à une période où les mesures liées au Covid-19 empêchaient l'artiste de performer, *How to DISappear in America* met l'accent sur la manière dont la valeur est déterminée et répartie dans les pratiques traditionnellement immatérielles telles que l'art de la performance ; mais elle reflète aussi l'instabilité de ces systèmes – d'autant plus en temps de crise.

Une seconde peinture LED, *YouTube Our Unemployment (Post-Capital)* (2021), joue le rôle de « performeuse », interprétant une chanson écrite par Ei Arakawa en collaboration avec Dan Poston. Ce morceau fait allusion à l'impact économique du coronavirus sur les artistes qui réalisent des performances et, d'un point de vue plus personnel, à la lente reprise des événements culturels. On peut dire des œuvres d'Ei Arakawa qu'elles sont ludiques et qu'elles privilégient la collectivité sur l'individualité en favorisant les collaborations avec d'autres artistes et performeurs. « Le culte de la personnalité ou le fait d'être seul sur scène ne m'intéresse pas », a déclaré l'artiste au sujet de sa démarche. « J'ai toujours envie d'avoir affaire à d'autres personnes[1]. »

Ei Arakawa est né en 1977 à Fukushima, au Japon. Il vit et travaille à Los Angeles, aux États-Unis.

1 Andrew Maerkle, « Pastoral Hide and Seek », *Art it*, 9 juin 2017, https://www.art-it.asia/en/u/admin_ed_itv_e/towjzr5ibdps0hqrixce, (consulté le 9 avril 2021).

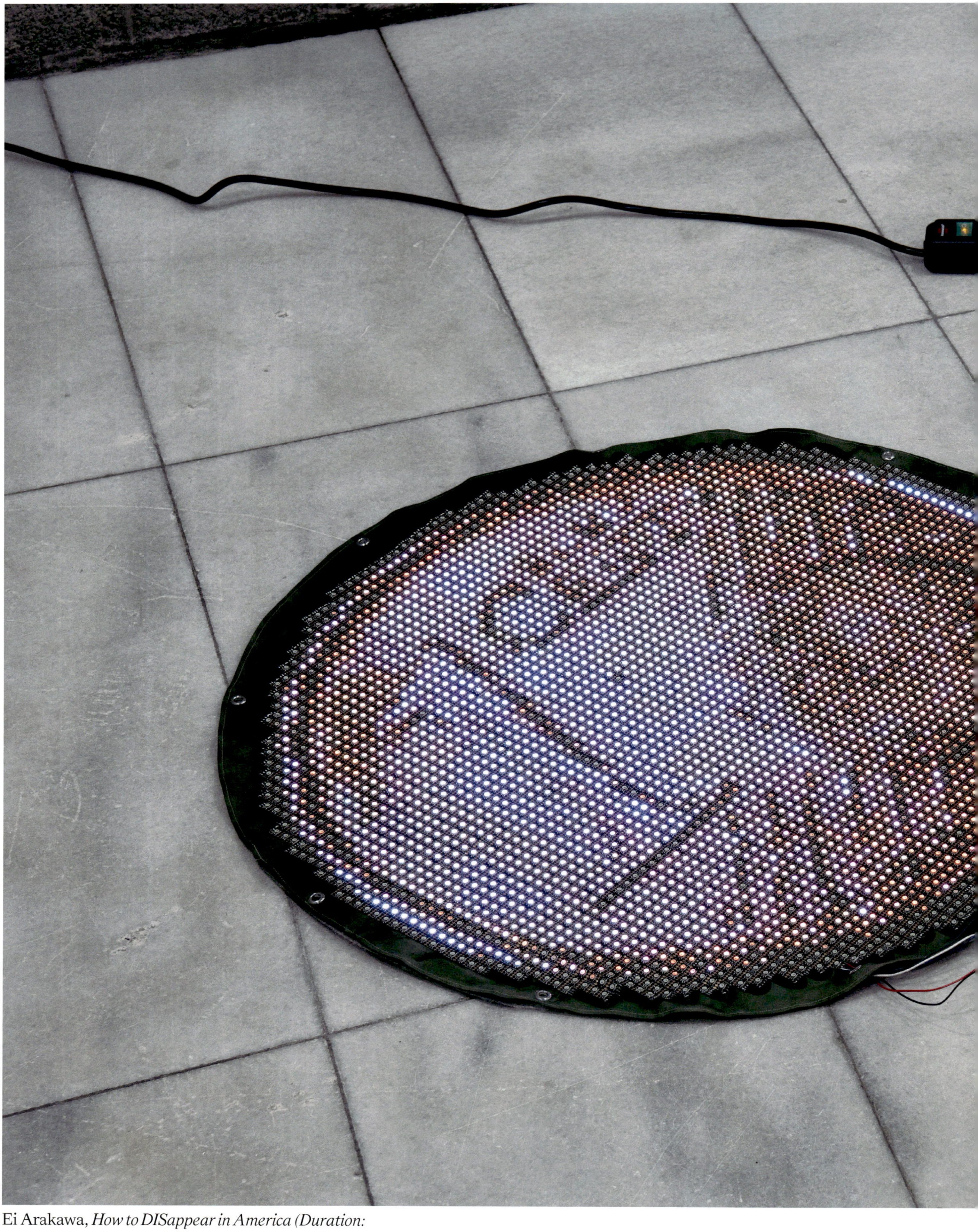

Ei Arakawa, *How to DISappear in America (Duration: multiple times in total of 9 hours, & approx. 60 hours on preparation, Honorarium: 3,500 EUR, 0.72 EUR per minute)*, 2020

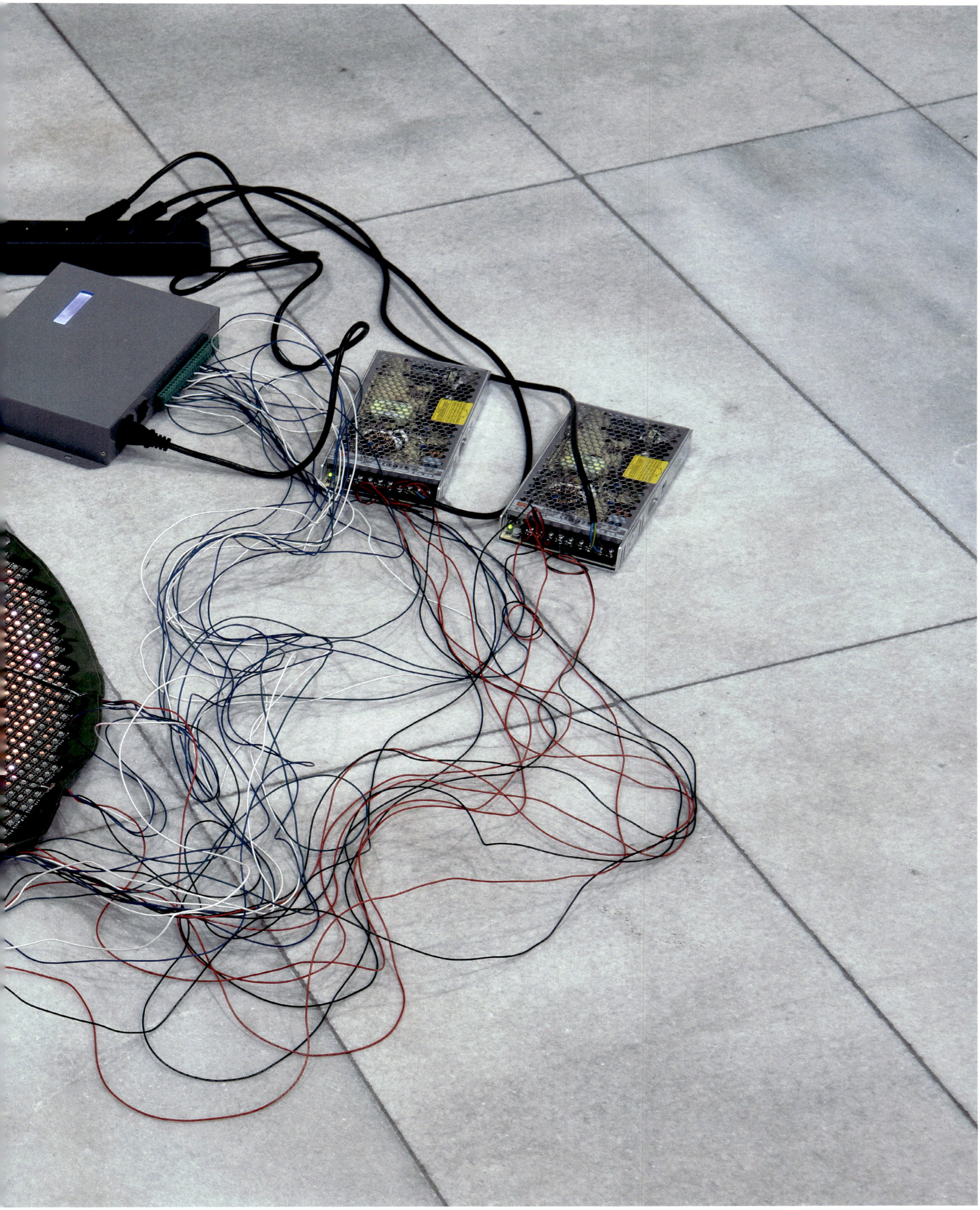

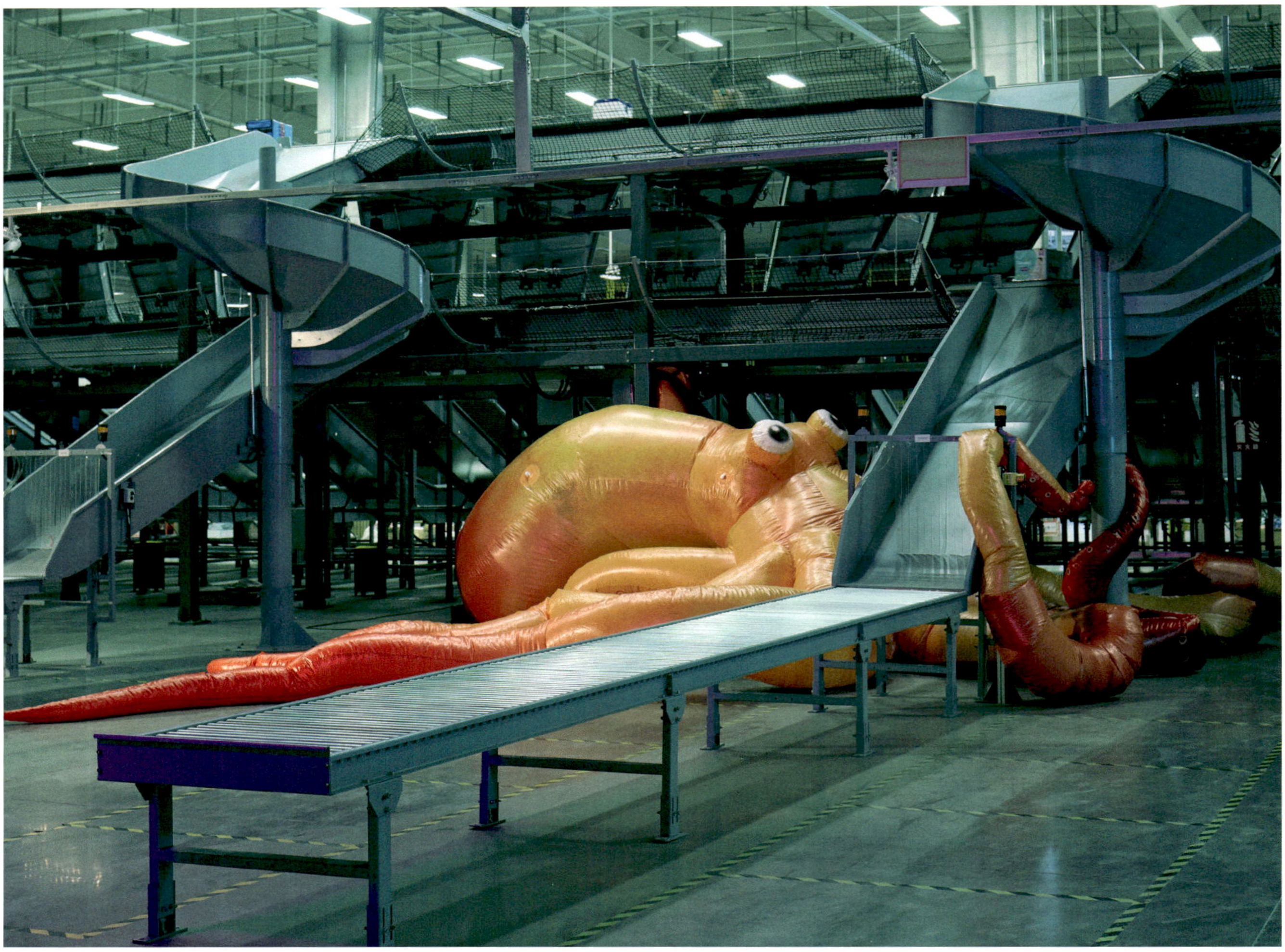

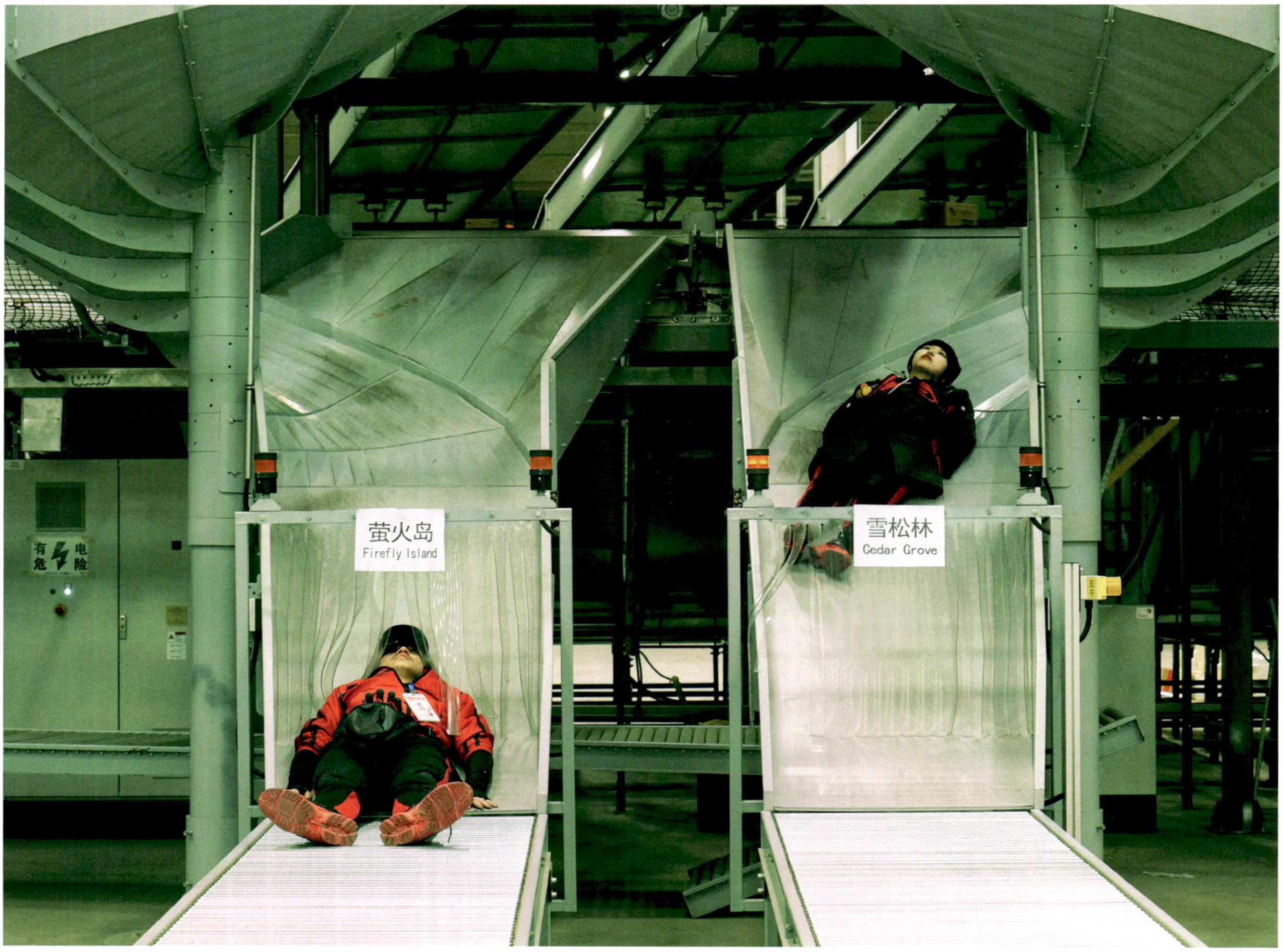

Film stills from Cao Fei, *Asia One*, 2018

Cao Fei

Part Sci-fi and part romance, Cao Fei's *Asia One* (2018) is a fictional film that addresses the physical and psychological effects of living in an increasingly automated society. Partly set in a highly automated warehouse belonging to JD.com, also known as the 'Amazon of China', it follows the plant's two lone human employees as they struggle to forge connections in a world that appears no longer built for them. Over the 63-minute film, Cao Fei's protagonists go from feeling more comfortable around robots to developing feelings for each other, leading them to question their roles in this highly regulated system. Their story is broken up by a series of dance sequences that recall the operas of the Chinese Cultural Revolution. The dancers' balletic movements stand in direct contrast to those of the lethargic workers, enhancing their appearance of isolation and detachment.

As is typical of the artist's practice, which encompasses video, performance and digital media, *Asia One* mixes reality with fiction. The human characters, for example, are tracked and evaluated by their robot co-workers in a process that could be seen to refer to China's social credit system. Unveiled in 2014, the governmental initiative judges citizens' behaviour and trustworthiness on a points-based system. The artist has said of this section of the film, 'I wanted to show that robots have their own simple and arbitrary procedures'. Cao Fei goes on to consider how this 'poses problems' when such technology is used within 'a social system that is based on these black and white mechanisms and on an electronic evaluation'.[1]

Labour has long been a thematic concern for Cao Fei, whose 2006 video and photo series *Whose Utopia* followed the lives of workers in a lightbulb factory in the Pearl River Delta to examine the role technology has played in the social and economic transformation of Modern China. '... my works, to varying degrees, relate to the relationship between technology and the development of human society today', the artist has said. 'They are strategic technologies developed by nationalism, unmanned technologies that accelerate the era, technological progress – also the loss of love and contradictions between technology and human nature. Technology brings order, progress and equal rights; it also fosters new chaos and restrictions. It has the power to destroy us'.[2]

Cao Fei was born in 1978 in Guangzhou, China. She lives and works in Beijing, China.

1 Artist profile: Cao Fei, guggenheim.org, video, posted 2 July 2018, https://www.guggenheim.org/video/one-hand-clapping-cao-fei (accessed 20 April 2021).
2 Noor Brara, '"Communication and Control Are Inextricably Linked": Artist Cao Fei on How Technology Both Serves and Suppresses Humanity', *Artnet*, 18 August 2020, https://news.artnet.com/art-world/cao-fei-blue-prints-1901957 (accessed 20 April 2021).

À mi-chemin entre la science-fiction et l'histoire d'amour, la vidéo *Asia One* (2018) de Cao Fei traite à travers la fiction des effets physiques et psychologiques d'une existence menée au sein d'une société de plus en plus automatisée. Le film, en partie situé dans un entrepôt automatisé appartenant à JD.com, surnommé « l'Amazon chinois », suit les deux seuls employés humains du lieu tentant tant bien que mal d'établir une relation dans un monde qui ne semble plus fait pour eux. Au cours des soixante-trois minutes du film, les protagonistes de Cao Fei – d'abord plus à l'aise en compagnie des robots – développent progressivement l'un pour l'autre des sentiments qui les conduisent à interroger leur rôle dans ce système fortement régulé. Leur histoire est entrecoupée d'une série de séquences dansées rappelant les opéras de la Révolution culturelle chinoise. Les mouvements chorégraphiques des danseurs, qui contrastent avec ceux des ouvriers léthargiques, renforcent l'apparence d'isolation et de détachement qui se dégage de ces derniers.

En mêlant réalité et fiction, *Asia One* s'inscrit dans la continuité de la pratique de l'artiste, qui se déploie à travers la vidéo, la performance et les médias numériques. Ainsi, dans cette œuvre, les personnages humains sont suivis et évalués par leurs collègues robots selon un processus qui pourrait faire référence au système chinois du crédit social. Cette initiative étatique, dévoilée en 2014, consiste à juger le comportement et la fiabilité des citoyens selon un système de points. L'artiste a par ailleurs déclaré, à propos de cette section du film : « Je voulais montrer que les robots ont des règles simples et arbitraires qui leur sont propres. » Lorsqu'une telle technologie est employée dans « un système social qui repose sur ces mécanismes binaires et sur une évaluation électronique », cela « pose problème », ajoute-t-elle[1].

Le travail est depuis longtemps un thème central de l'œuvre de Cao Fei. Dans sa série de photos et vidéos *Whose Utopia* (2006), elle suivait la vie des ouvriers d'une usine d'ampoules électriques du delta de la rivière des Perles pour examiner le rôle joué par la technologie dans la transformation sociale et économique de la Chine moderne. « [M]es œuvres se rapportent, à différents degrés, à la relation entre la technologie et le développement actuel de la société humaine, a expliqué l'artiste. Ce sont des technologies stratégiques développées par le nationalisme, des technologies qui se passent des humains et accélèrent l'époque, le progrès technologique – ainsi que la disparition de l'amour et les contradictions entre technologie et nature humaine. La technologie apporte ordre, progrès et égalité des droits ; elle nourrit aussi un chaos et des restrictions d'un genre nouveau. Elle a le pouvoir de nous détruire[2]. »

Cao Fei est née en 1978 à Guangzhou, en Chine. Elle vit et travaille à Pékin, en Chine.

1 « Artist Profile: Cao Fei », vidéo, guggenheim.org, 2 juillet 2018, https://www.guggenheim.org/video/one-hand-clapping-cao-fei, (consulté le 20 avril 2021).

2 Noor Brara, « "Communication and Control Are Inextricably Linked": Artist Cao Fei on How Technology Both Serves and Suppresses Humanity », *Artnet*, 18 août 2020, https://news.artnet.com/art-world/cao-fei-blueprints-1901957, (consulté le 20 avril 2021).

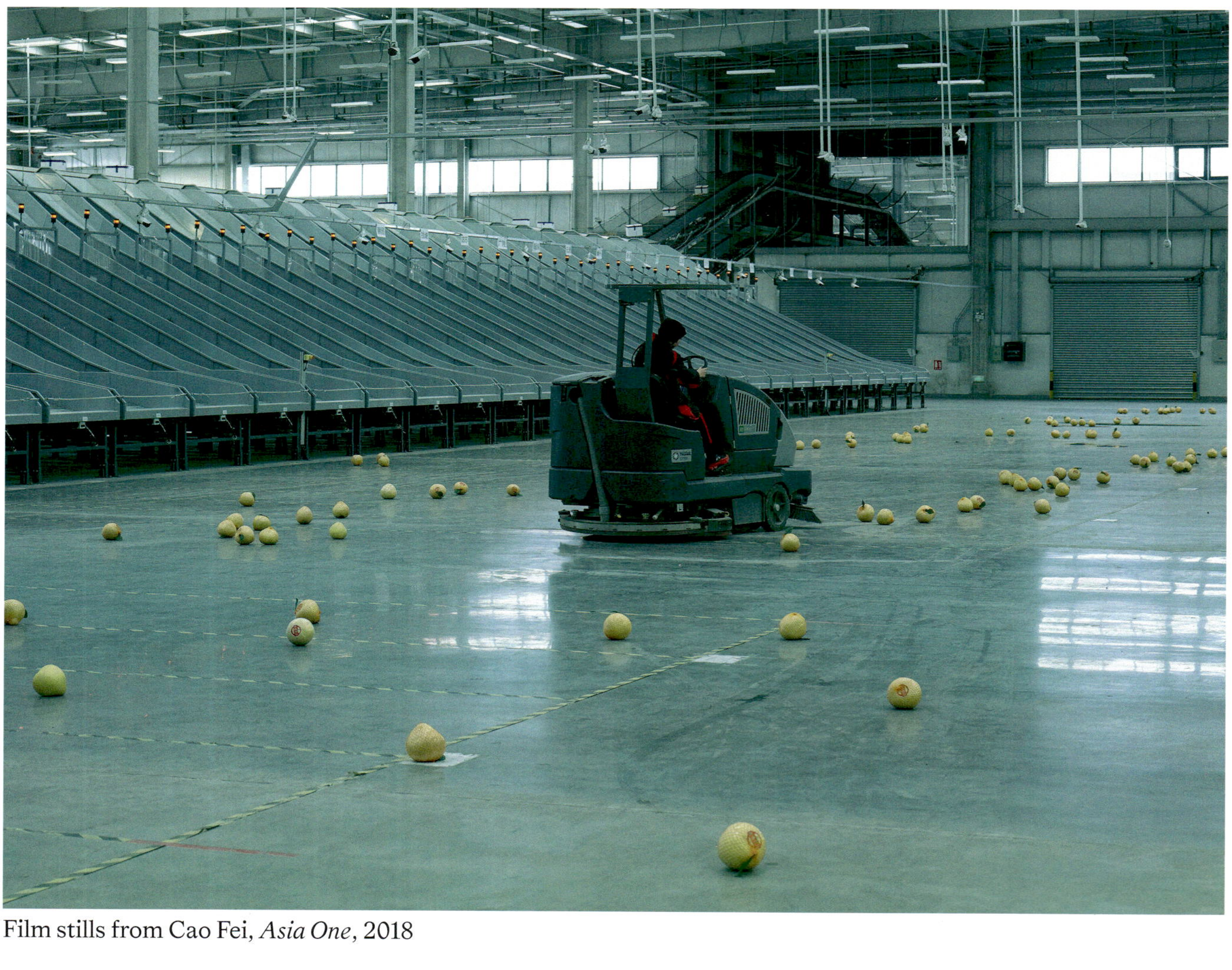

Film stills from Cao Fei, *Asia One*, 2018

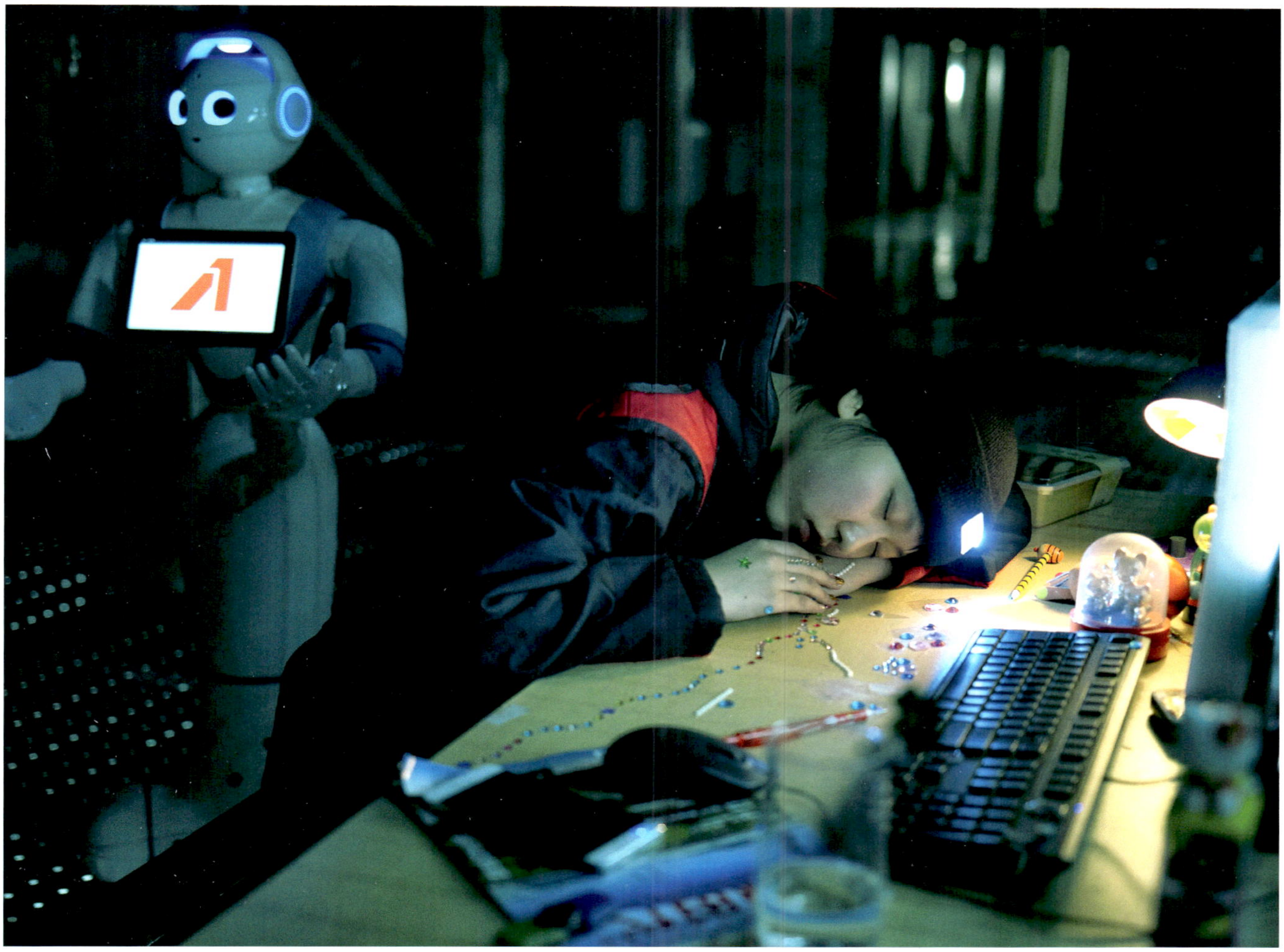

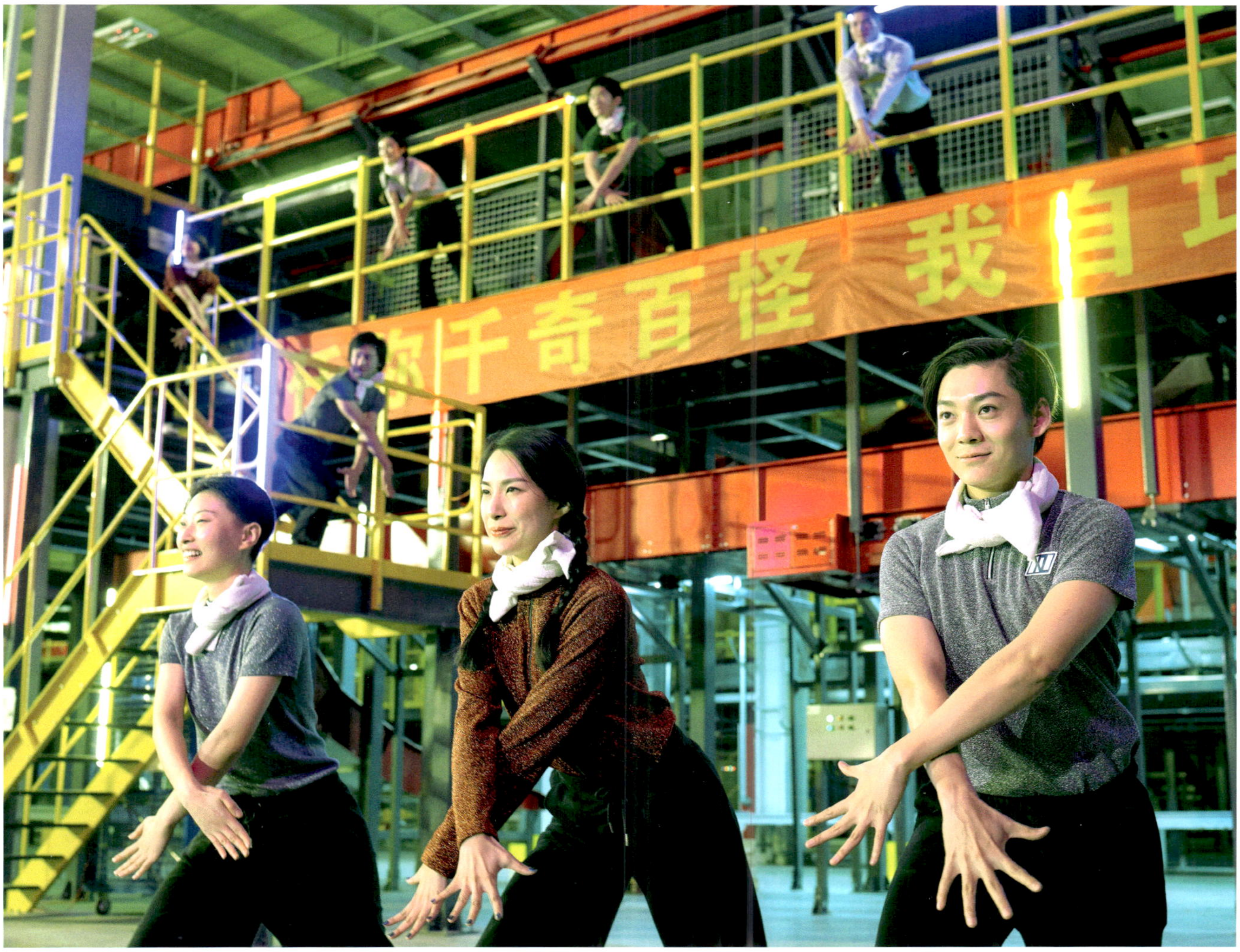
千奇百怪 我自

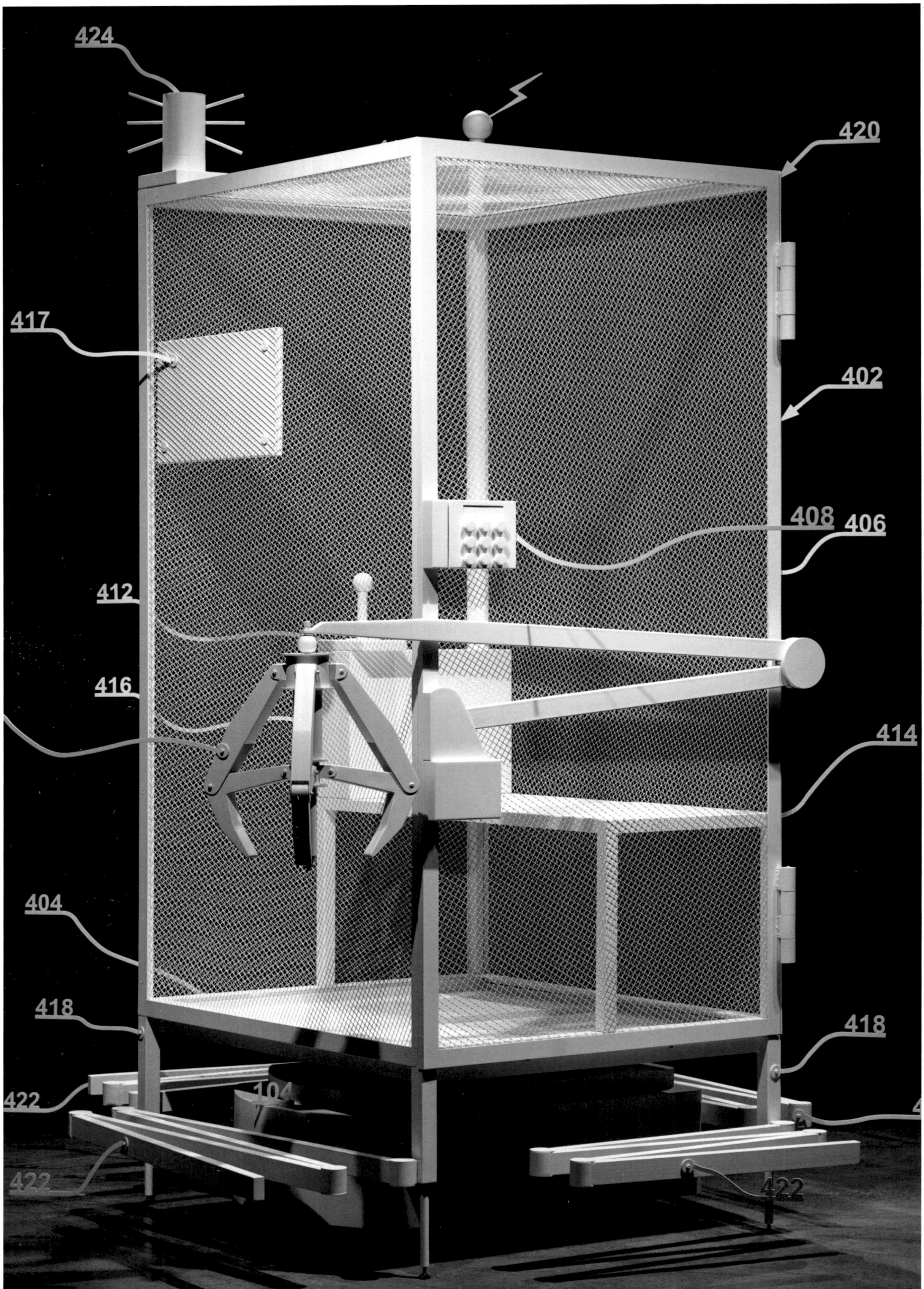

Simon Denny, *Amazon worker cage patent drawing as virtual Aquatic Warbler cage (US 9,280,157 B2: "System and method for transporting personnel within an active workspace", 2016)*, 2020

Simon Denny

Amazon worker cage patent drawing as virtual Aquatic Warbler cage (US 9,280,157 B2: "System for transporting personnel within an active workspace", 2016) (2020) is an installation by Simon Denny that references a patent filed in 2016 by the multinational technology corporation Amazon. Amazon proposed the production of an automated cage to 'protect' their workers as they moved around heavily-automated warehouses. Denny discovered the patent via the 2018 essay by Kate Crawford and Vladan Jones, 'Anatomy of an AI System: The Amazon Echo as an Anatomical Map of Human Labour, Data and Planetary Resources', which discusses the environmental, social and political implications of Amazon's Artificial Intelligence assistant Alexa, now installed in millions of homes around the world.

While the Amazon 'worker cage' was not adopted, Denny realised it as a sculpture, following the sketches included in the patent. The human-scale metal cage evokes the alienating conditions that are prevalent in the low-paid echelons of employment in the tech economy, in which workers' bodies are increasingly treated like machines. Exhibited alongside the sculpture and printed pages of the patent are a pair of 'document-reliefs', made from copies of the document. These carefully crafted objects imply a choreography between human and machine, employing an obsolete 3D printer to render shapes from the cage in cut and layered paper.

The sculpture also alludes to the exploitation of animals in industrial contexts, specifically referencing the historic practice of carrying caged birds into coal mines to test for the presence of toxic gases. Visitors are prompted to use an iPhone or iPad and scan a QR code to activate an augmented reality component of the work. An avatar of an Aquatic Warbler bird appears on screen, moving around in the cage when the device is pointed at it. This small bird, which is native to Europe, is a globally threatened species; its decline is believed to be linked to a loss of natural habitat and the industrialisation of agriculture. In Denny's work it can be seen as a symbol of an ongoing ecological disaster.

The work draws parallels between the physical extraction of minerals and the 21st century practice of data mining (the app used to view the bird also collects visitors' data). This practice, widely used in e-commerce, consists of drawing out patterns from users' datasets, for marketing and potentially other purposes. Crawford and Jones suggest that data mining activities, despite often being perceived as abstract and intangible, are as environmentally destructive as coal mining, due to the carbon emissions generated by the high levels of energy they

Amazon worker cage patent drawing as virtual Aquatic Warbler cage (US 9,280,157 B2: "System for transporting personnel within an active workspace", 2016) (2020) est une installation de Simon Denny qui fait référence à un brevet déposé par le géant des nouvelles technologies Amazon en 2016. La multinationale y proposait la production d'une cage automatisée destinée à « protéger » ses employés lors de leurs déplacements dans des entrepôts lourdement automatisés. Ce brevet, Simon Denny l'a découvert en lisant un article de Kate Crawford et Vladan Jones, « Anatomy of an AI System: The Amazon Echo as an Anatomical Map of Human Labour, Data and Planetary Resources », qui examine les implications environnementales, sociales et politiques de l'assistant d'Amazon, l'intelligence artificielle Alexa, aujourd'hui installée dans des millions de foyers à travers le monde.

Si Amazon n'a pas adopté la « cage pour travailleur », Simon Denny en a fait une sculpture en suivant les esquisses comprises dans le brevet. Reproduite à échelle humaine, la cage en métal évoque les conditions aliénantes qui prévalent dans les plus bas échelons de l'économie de la tech, où les corps des travailleurs sont de plus en plus considérés comme des machines. Les pages du brevet, imprimées, ainsi que deux « reliefs » réalisés à partir de copies de ce même document, sont exposés aux côtés de la sculpture. Les reliefs ont été réalisés avec soin, à l'aide d'un modèle obsolète d'imprimante 3D utilisée pour découper le bloc de papier de manière à restituer la forme de la cage. Ils impliquent ainsi une chorégraphie entre l'humain et la machine.

L'œuvre fait aussi allusion à l'exploitation des animaux par l'industrie, en particulier à ces canaris en cage que l'on emmenait tout au long du XXe siècle dans les mines de charbon pour y détecter la présence de gaz toxiques. Ainsi, les visiteurs sont incités à utiliser un smartphone ou une tablette et à scanner un QR code pour activer une partie de l'œuvre se manifestant en réalité augmentée. Un avatar de phragmite aquatique, un oiseau migrateur, apparaît alors à l'écran. En pointant l'appareil en direction de la cage, l'animal se déplace à l'intérieur. Ce petit oiseau natif d'Europe est une espèce menacée, dont le déclin est dû en partie à la disparition de son habitat naturel et à l'industrialisation de l'agriculture. Ici, il symbolise la catastrophe écologique en cours.

Cette sculpture établit un parallèle entre l'extraction physique de minerais et le *data mining* du XXIe siècle – l'application utilisée pour visualiser l'oiseau collectant aussi les données des visiteurs. Cette pratique, massivement employée dans le commerce en ligne, consiste à extraire

consume. The work is emblematic of the artist's long-standing research into the tech industry and its systems of extraction, highlighting processes that impact our daily lives and natural resources.

Simon Denny was born in 1982 in Auckland, New Zealand. He lives and works in Berlin, Germany.

des schémas à partir des données d'utilisateurs récoltées à des fins publicitaires et, potentiellement, dans d'autres buts. Crawford et Jones expliquent dans leur article que les activités de *data mining*, bien qu'elles soient souvent perçues comme abstraites et intangibles, détruisent tout autant l'environnement que les mines de charbon, à cause des émissions de carbone générées par la forte consommation d'énergie qu'elles impliquent. Cette œuvre, emblématique des recherches que l'artiste mène depuis plusieurs années sur l'industrie de la tech et ses systèmes d'extraction, met en lumière des processus qui affectent notre vie quotidienne tout comme les ressources naturelles.

Simon Denny est né en 1982 à Auckland, en Nouvelle-Zélande. Il vit et travaille à Berlin, en Allemagne.

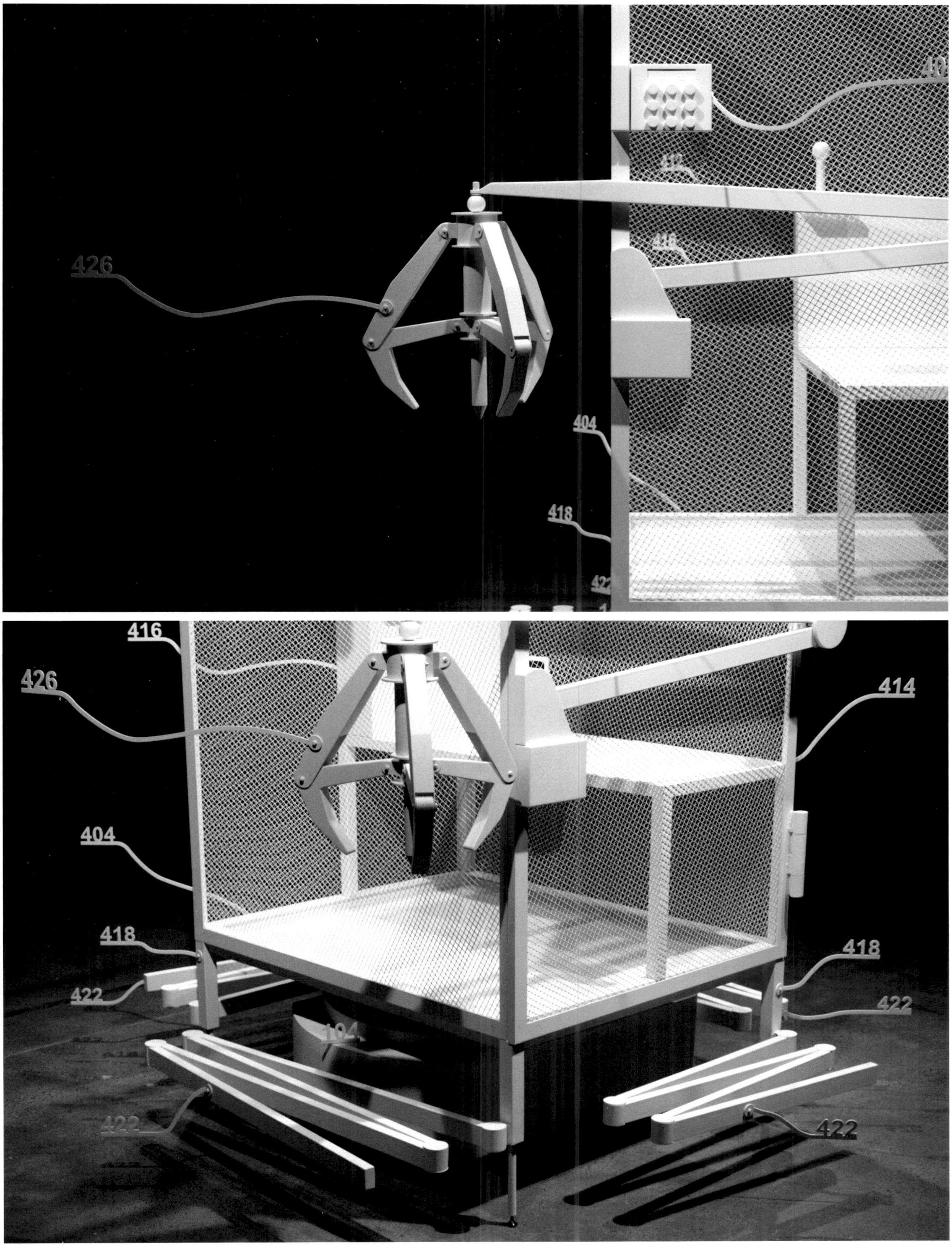

Simon Denny, *Amazon worker cage patent drawing as virtual Aquatic Warbler cage (US 9,280,157 B2: "System and method for transporting personnel within an active workspace", 2016)*, 2020 (details)

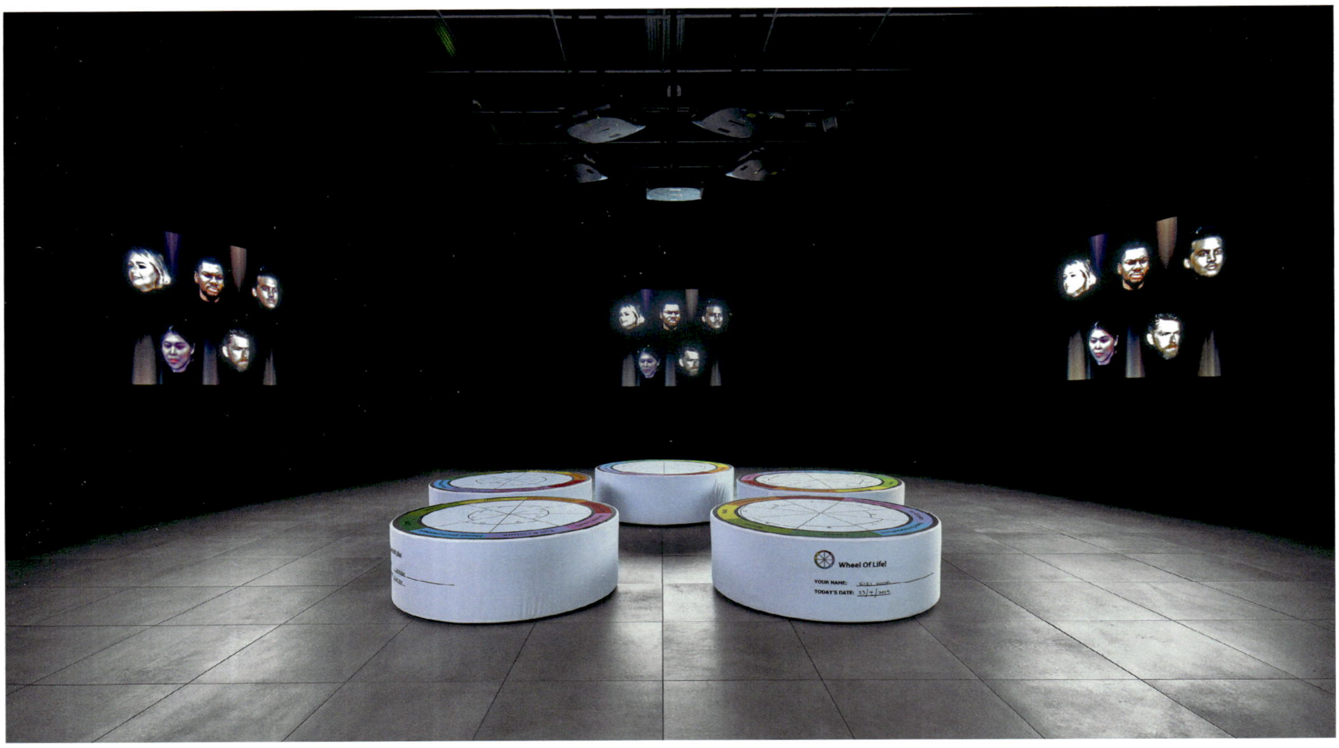

Liz Magic Laser, *In Real Life*, 2019 (installation view)

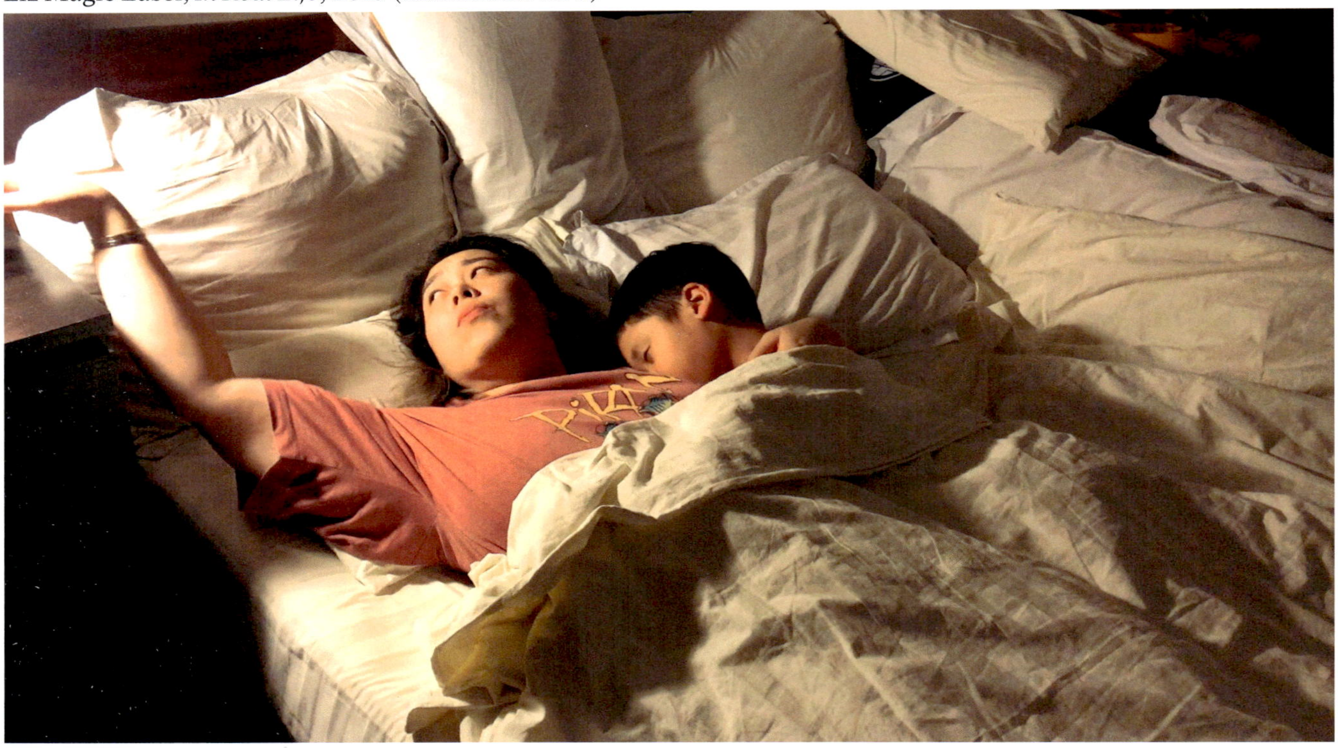
Film still from Liz Magic Laser, *In Real Life,* 2019

Liz Magic Laser

In Real Life (2019), a five-channel video installation comprising five separate episodes, follows freelancers from different parts of the world as they adopt a 30-day 'biohacking challenge'. Shot and edited in the style of a reality TV show, the subjects Cardy, Zahid, Alabi, Kiki and Nikki can be seen simultaneously from the installation's custom-made circular seating. Whilst each individual's episode plays sequentially, the four other screens show the other subjects as they work. The artist hired these individuals via online platforms such as PeoplePerHour, Upwork and Fiverr, and their skills as screenwriter, graphic designer, animator, voice-over artist and social media content creator, respectively, are integral to the production of the work.

Laser employs the very same economic strategies that disrupt the value of labour today. She also examines the world of 'biohacking', an emerging industry geared towards well-being and optimising productivity by deploying science and technology. Over the course of the challenge, the cast of *In Real Life* follow a programme that includes customised consultations with a life coach, tarot card readings and the use of apps and other digital tools intended to measure their progress. A voice-over tells us in the introduction that all this is intended to 'optimise their mind and body for success'. The episodes, shot with cell phones and computer webcams, fluctuate between moments of excitement and disenchantment as we follow the successes and failures of the participants, who appear unable to switch off from their work. Under the seemingly innocuous guise of a reality show, *In Real Life* illustrates the contradictory nature of 'platform capitalism', which is characterised by the dematerialisation of labour, constant connectivity and the logic of a gig economy, which can be seen as a vehicle of both emancipation and alienation.

Liz Magic Laser was born in 1981 in New York, USA. She lives and works in New York, USA.

In Real Life (2019) est une installation vidéo immersive, composée de cinq épisodes. On y suit des freelances de différentes nationalités qui se prêtent à un défi de *biohacking* de trente jours. Filmés à la manière d'un *reality show*, Cardy, Zahid, Alabi, Kiki et Nikki sont visibles simultanément depuis les sièges circulaires conçus spécifiquement pour l'installation. Les épisodes consacrés à chacun y sont présentés de manière consécutive sur un écran, tandis que les quatre écrans restants montrent les autres participants en train de travailler. Liz Magic Laser a engagé les participants pour leur savoir-faire respectif, qu'ils mettent habituellement à disposition sur des plateformes de travail à la demande telles que PeoplePerHour, Upwork ou Fiverr. Outre leur statut d'acteur au sein de *In Real Life*, ceux-ci en ont conçu le scénario, le design graphique, les animations, commenté le déroulé et assuré la communication sur les réseaux sociaux.

Liz Magic Laser emploie donc les mêmes stratégies économiques qui bousculent la valeur du travail aujourd'hui. Elle rend également compte de l'émergence simultanée du *biohacking*, un marché destiné au bien-être et à l'optimisation de la productivité qui allie la science et la technologie. Durant les trente jours du défi, les participants de *In Real Life* suivent en effet un programme élaboré par l'artiste, comprenant un échange personnalisé avec une coach, une lecture de l'avenir dans les cartes de tarot ou l'utilisation d'applications et autres outils digitaux destinés à mesurer l'évolution du bien-être. Ceci, afin « d'optimiser leur esprit et leur corps pour réussir », comme l'annonce Kiki, la voix off de l'émission. Les épisodes, filmés au moyen de téléphones et de webcams d'ordinateurs personnels, oscillent entre enthousiasme et désenchantement, au rythme des succès et des échecs de chacun, dans un mode de vie où le travail s'immisce dans chaque interstice du quotidien. Sous l'apparente légèreté d'un *reality show*, *In Real Life* illustre la réalité paradoxale du « capitalisme des plateformes » marqué par la dématérialisation du travail, son omniprésence dès lors qu'une connexion est possible et par une logique d'économie à la tâche (*gig economy*), à la fois vecteur d'émancipation et d'aliénation.

Liz Magic Laser est née en 1981 à New York, aux États-Unis, où elle vit et travaille.

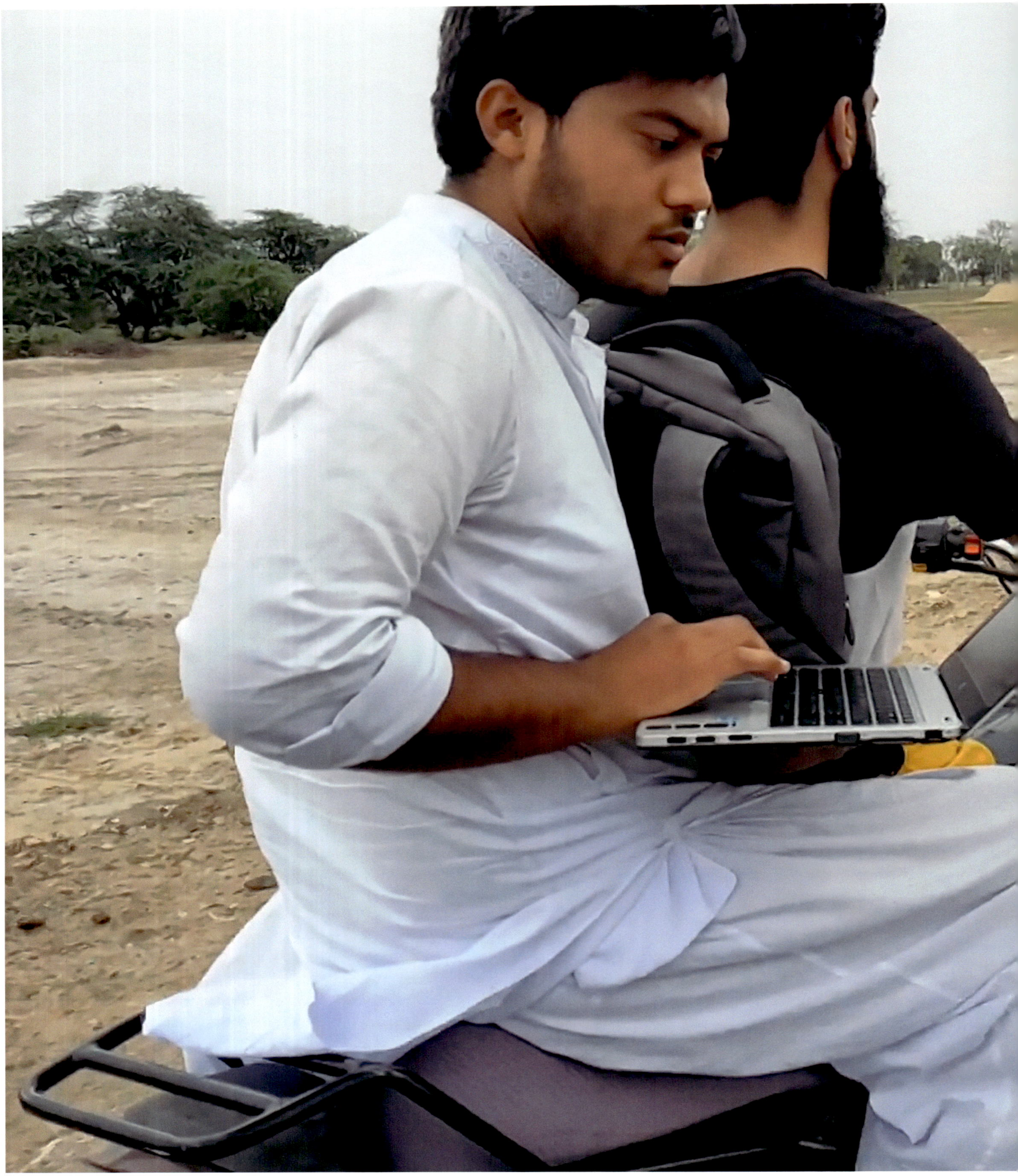

Film still from Liz Magic Laser, *In Real Life,* 2019

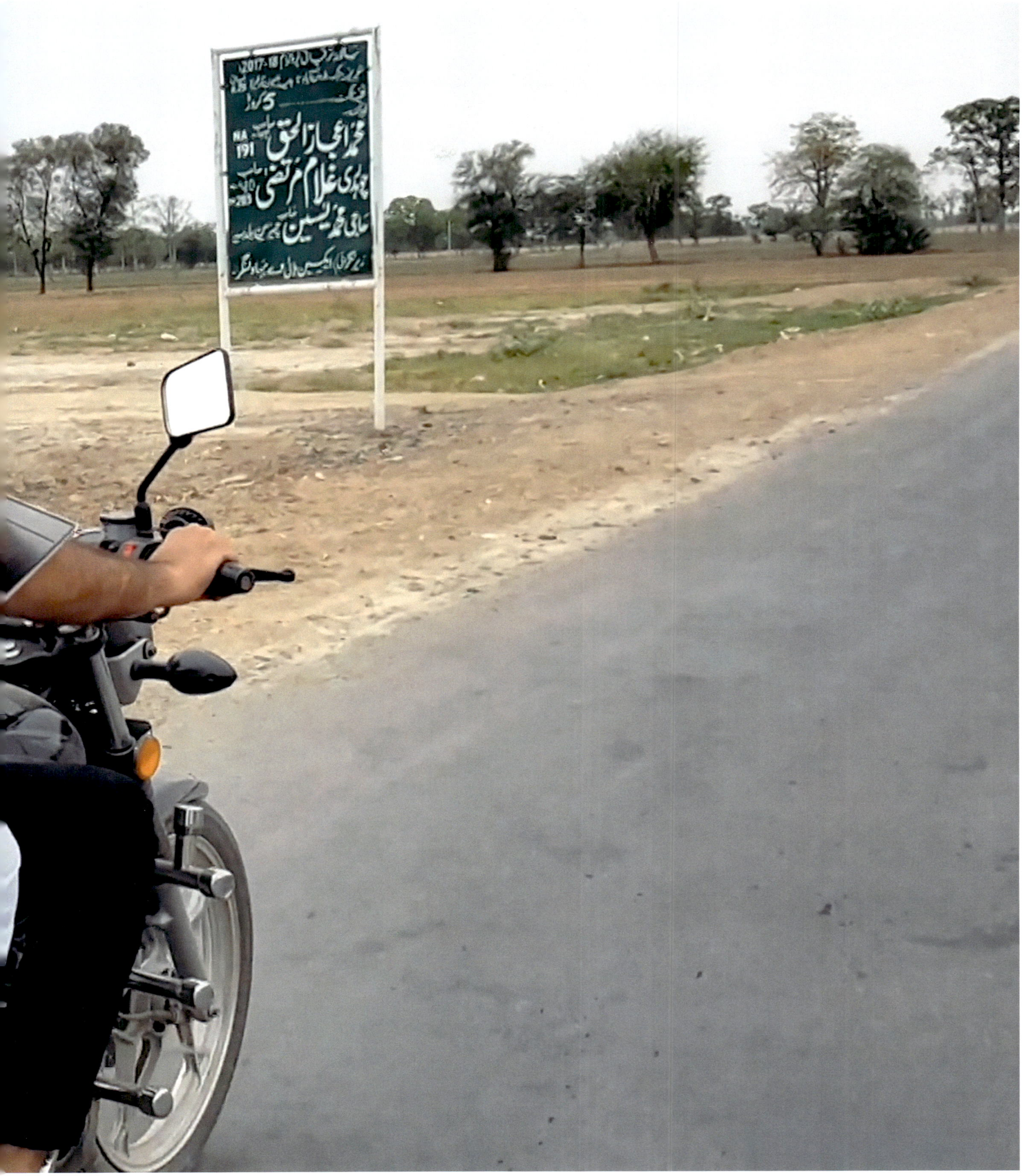
2017-18
5 کروڑ
NA 191
محمد اعجاز الحق
چوہدری غلام مرتضیٰ
حاجی محمد یٰسین

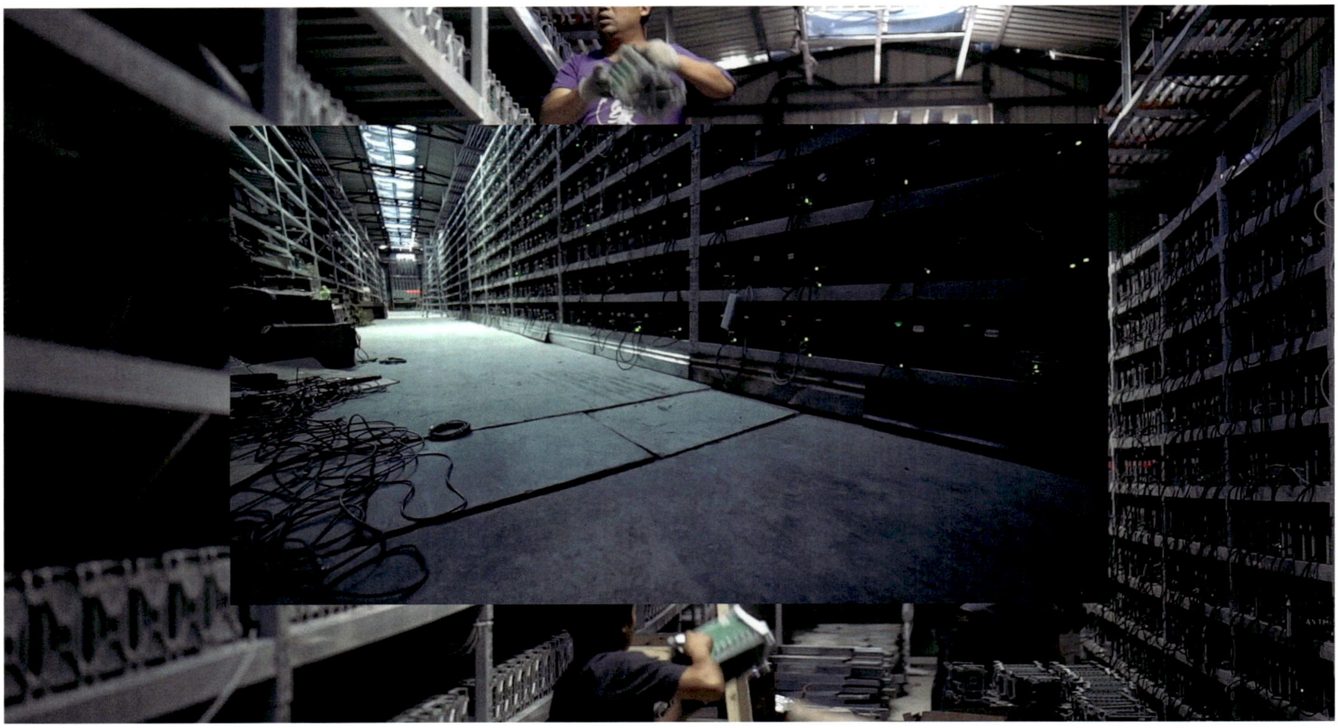

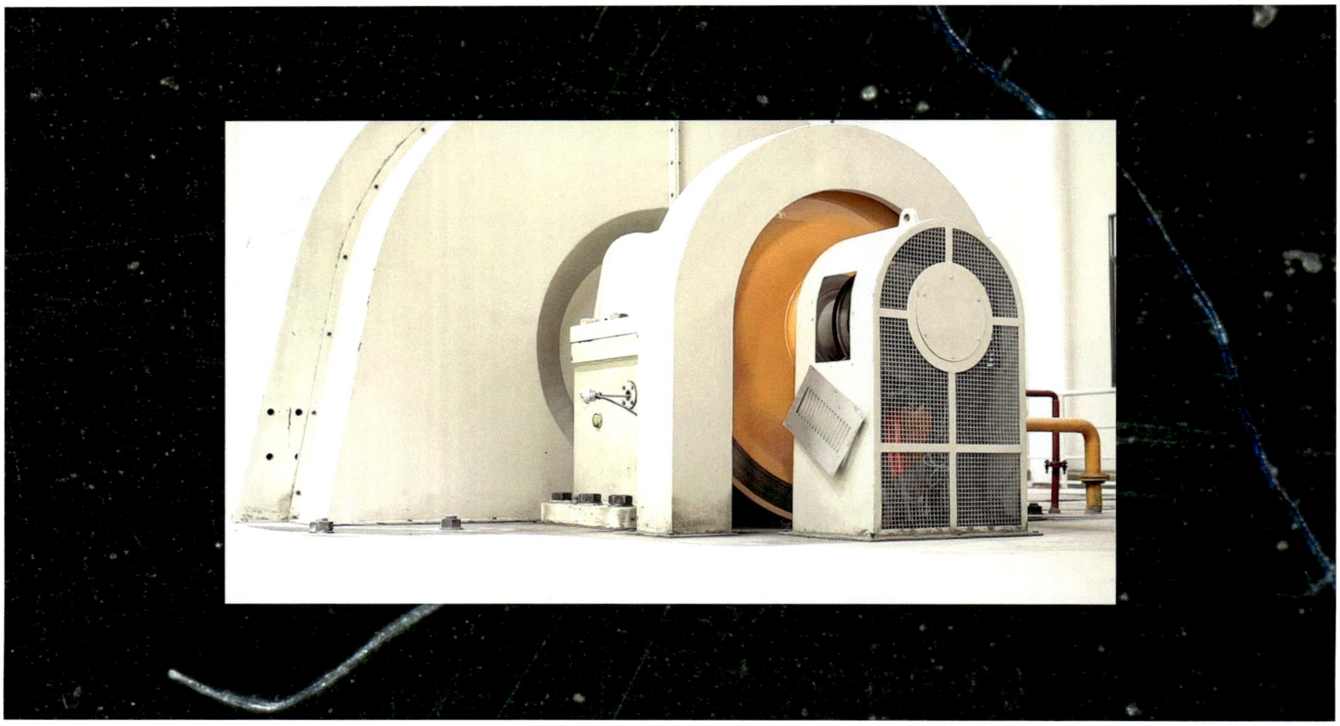

Film stills from Yuri Pattison, *the ideal*, 2015–ongoing

Yuri Pattison

The ideal (2015–ongoing) is a video installation by Yuri Pattison that features footage from a remote Bitcoin mine run by Beijing-based start-up HaoBTC in Kangding, Tibet / China. Made in close collaboration with Eric Mu, the company's then-Chief Marketing Officer, the video contrasts scenes of warehouses full of bitcoin mining rigs with views that showcase the natural beauty of the surrounding area. Although bitcoin is a digital currency, the mining process itself – in which powerful processors solve complex mathematical problems in exchange for bitcoins – is incredibly energy intensive. This has led companies such as HaoBTC to move their operations to places like Tibet, where hydroelectric power is cheap and plentiful. This undoubtedly offers employment opportunities for locals but is also seen by some as an exploitation of Tibetan natural resources by a colonial power. The work's title refers to 'Ideal Money', a theoretical notion put forward by the mathematician John Nash to stabilise international currencies.

As well as revealing the expansive physical apparatus behind bitcoin mining, *the ideal* also displays the invisible human labour necessary to keep these machines running. Through scenes in which workers are shown carrying out their duties, as well as resting, eating and playing cards within the compound, the video invites the viewer to reflect on the human aspect of this intangible process. The unseen labour behind digital networks is a recurring theme in Pattison's video and sculptural work. In *outsourced views, visual economies* (2014–15), for instance, the artist asked members of Amazon's Mechanical Turk workforce, who are banned from sharing personal information, to send him a photograph from the nearest window in their workspace.

Pattison's video plays on a monitor that is set within a structure made from industrial racking resembling the shelving used for the hardware in the warehouse in Kangding. The work also incorporates a working, although now outdated Bitcoin machine with a water-based cooling system. The latter is both a reference to the hydroelectric dam that powers the bitcoin mine and an allusion to the circulation of digital currency in general. In the time since the work was created bitcoin production has become more competitive, and therefore harder to mine, but in the first few years of the project Pattison was able to use the currency generated by this machine to self-fund subsequent versions of the work.

Yuri Pattison was born in 1986 in Dublin, Ireland. He lives and works in London, UK.

L'installation vidéo *the ideal* (2015-en cours) de Yuri Pattison montre des images d'une mine de bitcoins située dans un endroit reculé, à Kangding (Tibet, Chine), et exploitée par la start-up pékinoise HaoBTC. Réalisée en étroite collaboration avec Eric Mu, alors responsable du marketing, la vidéo oppose des images d'entrepôts remplis de mineurs de bitcoins à des vues de la beauté naturelle des environs. Bien que le bitcoin soit une monnaie numérique, le processus de minage – au cours duquel de puissants processeurs résolvent des problèmes mathématiques complexes en échange de bitcoins – nécessite une quantité d'énergie considérable. C'est ce qui a conduit des entreprises comme HaoBTC à déplacer leurs activités dans une région comme le Tibet, où l'énergie hydraulique est abondante et peu coûteuse. Si cela crée certes des emplois pour la population locale, certains y voient aussi une exploitation des ressources naturelles tibétaines par une puissance coloniale. Le titre de l'œuvre fait en outre référence au concept théorique de « monnaie idéale » développé par le mathématicien John Nash dans le but de stabiliser les devises internationales.

En plus de dévoiler le gigantesque appareillage matériel qui sous-tend le minage de bitcoins, *the ideal* expose le travail humain invisible indispensable au fonctionnement de ces machines. Au travers de scènes où l'on voit les travailleurs effectuer des tâches, mais aussi se reposer, manger et jouer aux cartes dans le complexe, la vidéo invite les spectateurs à réfléchir à l'aspect humain de ce processus intangible. Le travail dissimulé au regard qui constitue la toile de fond des réseaux numériques est un thème récurrent dans les vidéos et les sculptures de Pattison. Par exemple, dans *outsourced views, visual economies* [vues externalisées, économies visuelles] (2014-2015), l'artiste a demandé aux travailleurs d'Amazon Mechanical Turk, qui ont l'interdiction de communiquer des informations personnelles, de lui envoyer une photo prise depuis la fenêtre la plus proche de leur espace de travail.

La vidéo de *the ideal* est diffusée sur un écran monté sur une structure de type industriel ressemblant aux racks utilisés pour ranger le matériel informatique dans l'entrepôt de Kangding. L'œuvre incorpore aussi une machine à bitcoins, en état de marche mais désormais obsolète, accompagnée de son système de refroidissement hydraulique. Ce dernier fait à la fois référence au barrage hydroélectrique qui alimente la mine de bitcoins et à la circulation des cryptomonnaies en général. Depuis la création de cette œuvre, la production de bitcoins est devenue plus compétitive et le bitcoin plus difficile à extraire. Cependant, au cours des premières années du projet, Yuri Pattison a pu utiliser la monnaie générée par cette machine pour autofinancer les versions successives de cette œuvre.

Yuri Pattison est né en 1986 à Dublin, en Irlande. Il vit et travaille à Londres, au Royaume-Uni.

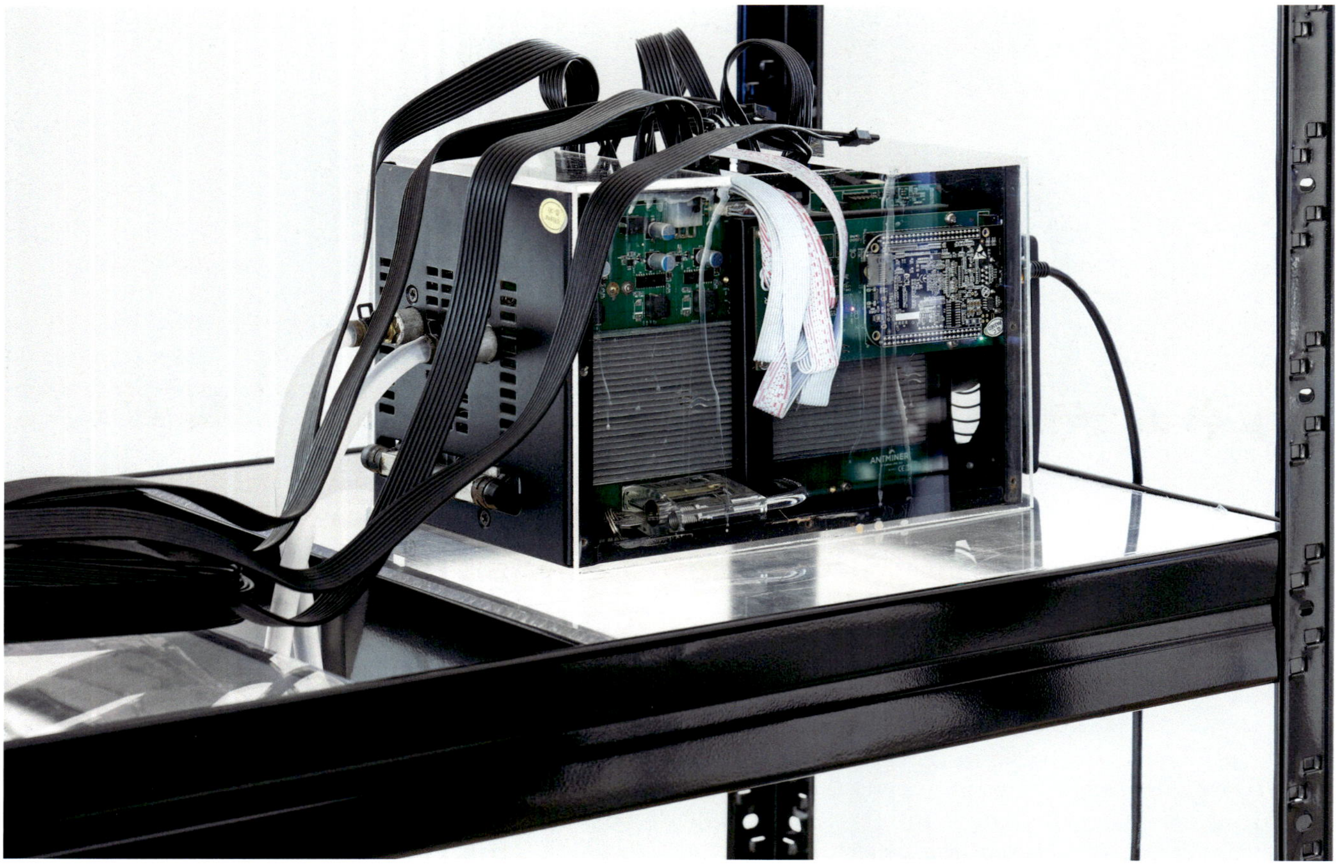

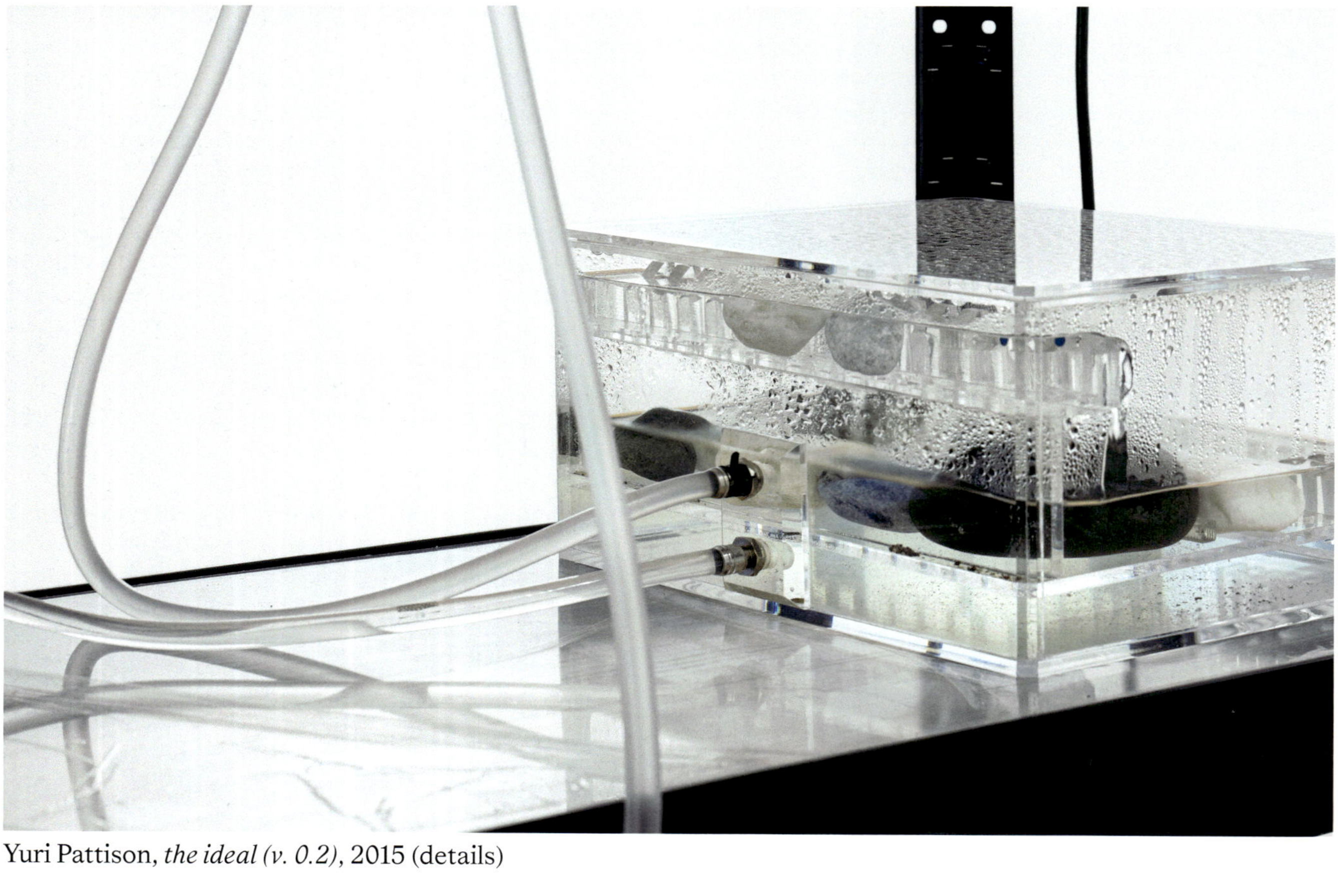

Yuri Pattison, *the ideal (v. 0.2)*, 2015 (details)

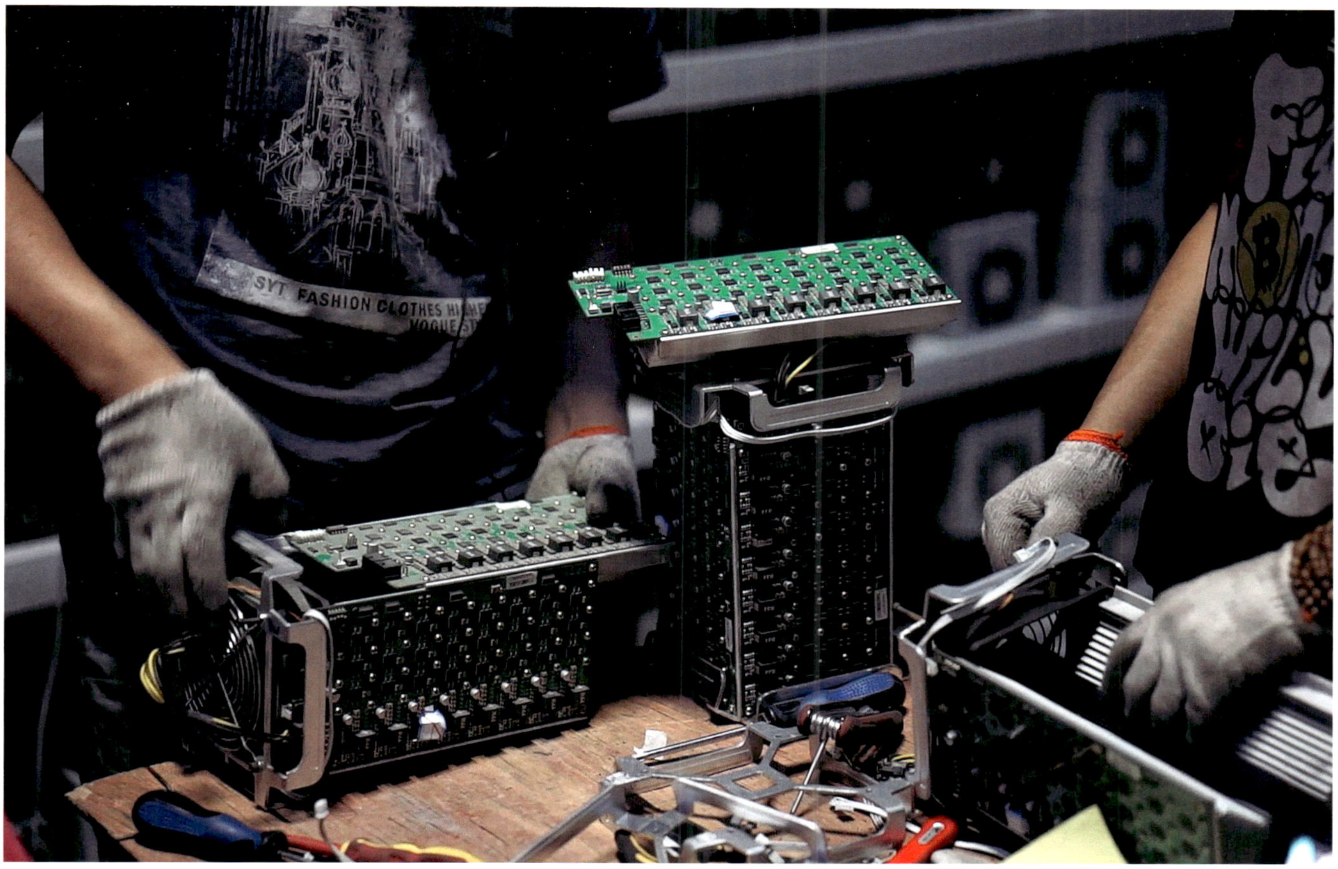

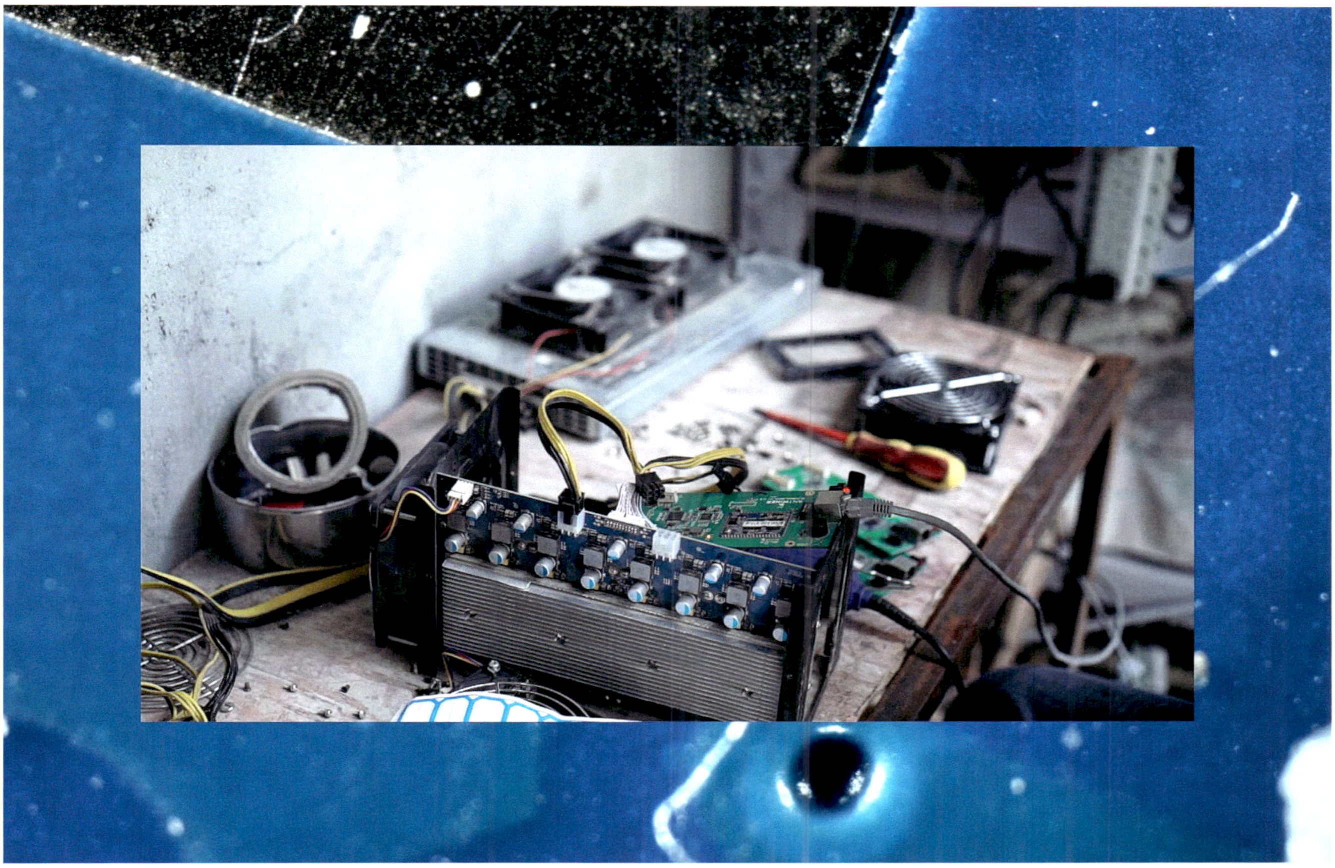

Film stills from Yuri Pattison, *the ideal*, 2015–ongoing

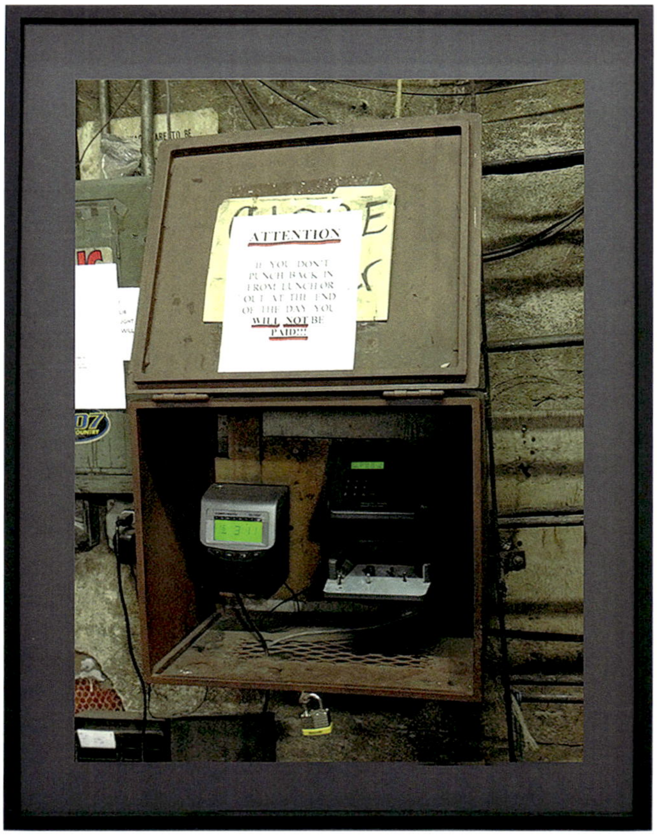

Cameron Rowland
Handpunch, 2014
Photograph
35.56 × 25.81 cm

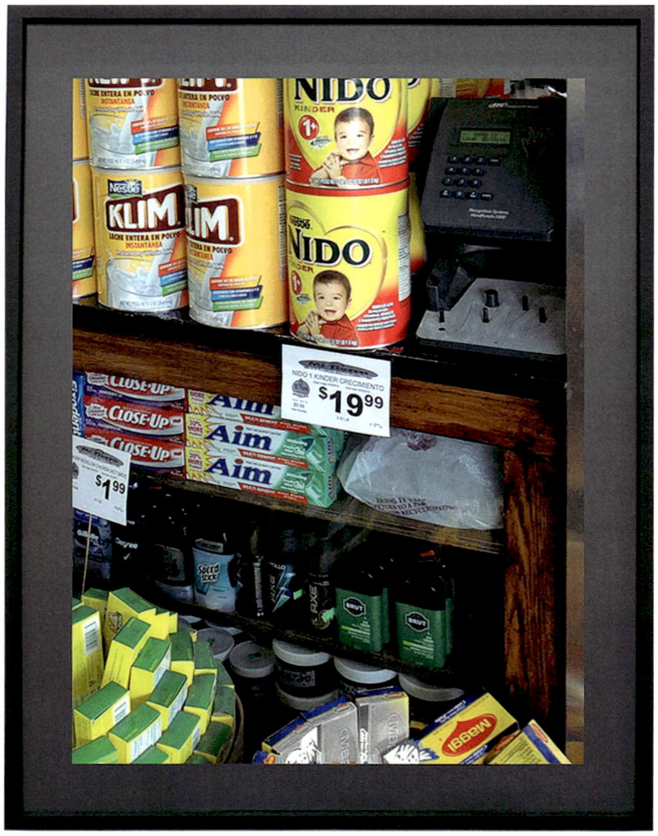

Cameron Rowland
Handpunch, 2014
Photograph
35.56 × 25.81 cm

In businesses where employees' time is one of the most valuable assets, the Handpunch time clock secures this time. Manufactured by Schlage (the American lock company) the Handpunch uses biometric readings of employees' right hands to inhibit false clock-ins and payment for false hours. Biometric recognition was developed to replace photography as a superior form of criminal indexing[1].

1 Dans les entreprises où le temps des employés est l'un des biens les plus précieux, la pointeuse « Handpunch » sécurise ce temps. Fabriquée par Schlage (fabricant américain de serrures), la pointeuse « Handpunch » utilise des lectures biométriques de la main droite des employés pour empêcher les pointages frauduleux et le paiement d'heures non travaillées. La reconnaissance biométrique a été développée pour remplacer la photographie et s'est imposée comme une forme plus fiable d'indexation criminelle.

Cameron Rowland

Handpunch (2014–15) by Cameron Rowland is a series of five photographs depicting the Handpunch time clock installed in various businesses across the US. Produced by an American lock company, the device uses biometric technology to identify workers, thereby preventing false clock-ins and payment for unworked hours. Rowland's interest in the machine originated in the artist's research on biometric systems that were initially developed as a form of criminal indexing. Before the widespread use of fingerprints, police used the Bertillon system, which consisted of five measurements: head length, head breadth, length of the middle finger, length of the left foot and length of the 'cubit' (the forearm from the elbow to the extremity of the middle finger), along with a photographic 'mug shot', to identify the accused. Fingerprint identification, which would go on to become the basis of biometric security, became standard practice in law enforcement after being proven more reliable than the Bertillon system and facial recognition alone (which sometimes resulted in cases of mistaken identity). Rowland, whose photographic and sculptural work often deals with the economic legacy of slavery and its relationship with the prison system, considers the use of this technology outside of law enforcement as 'indicative of attempts to limit criminal behaviour by regulating access: not generally like a lock, but specifically and individually'.[1] Seen in this light the widespread use of biometric security, which many accept as a minor invasion of personal privacy, takes on a more sinister air. Furthermore, the surroundings of the machines in Rowland's images – grocery stores and scrap metal yards – suggest that it may be low-waged and marginalised workers, rather than executives, whose time is policed by the Handpunch clocks.

Cameron Rowland was born in 1988 in Philadelphia, USA. Rowland lives and works in New York, USA.

1 Cameron Roland, quoted from a talk given at the Museum of Modern Art, New York, 22 November 2019.

Handpunch (2014-2015), de Cameron Rowland, est une série de cinq photographies représentant la pointeuse horaire (nommée « Handpunch ») installée dans de nombreuses entreprises des États-Unis. Produit par un fabricant américain de serrures, l'appareil identifie les travailleurs grâce à une technologie biométrique qui permet d'éviter les pointages frauduleux et le paiement d'heures non travaillées. Cameron Rowland s'est d'abord intéressé à cette machine dans le cadre d'une recherche sur les systèmes biométriques développés dans le but de répertorier les criminels. Avant que l'usage des empreintes digitales ne se généralise, la police employait le bertillonnage, méthode qui reposait sur cinq mesures : longueur et largeur de la tête, longueur du médius, longueur du pied gauche, longueur de la coudée (distance du coude à l'extrémité du majeur), ainsi que sur des photographies du visage, le tout permettant d'identifier l'accusé. L'identification fondée sur les empreintes digitales, qui deviendra la base de la sécurité biométrique, s'est imposée comme méthode policière standard après s'être révélée plus fiable que le bertillonnage et la reconnaissance faciale, qui conduisaient parfois à des erreurs d'identification. Les photographies et les sculptures de Cameron Rowland traitent souvent de l'héritage économique de l'esclavage et de son rapport au système carcéral. L'artiste estime que l'utilisation de cette technologie en dehors du cadre policier est « un signe des tentatives de limiter les conduites criminelles en régulant l'accès : pas en général, comme le fait une serrure, mais de façon spécifique et individuelle[1] ». Ainsi envisagé, l'emploi généralisé de la sécurité biométrique, que beaucoup acceptent comme une violation mineure de l'intégrité personnelle, revêt un aspect plus sinistre. En outre, si l'on en juge par le cadre où sont placées les machines photographiées par l'artiste – des épiceries et des déchetteries –, le temps que ces pointeuses surveillent n'est pas celui des cadres dirigeants, mais bien celui de travailleurs mal payés et marginalisés.

Cameron Rowland est né·e en 1988 à Philadelphie, aux États-Unis. L'artiste vit et travaille à New York, aux États-Unis.

1 Cameron Rowland, citation tirée d'une conférence donnée au Museum of Modern Art (MoMA), New York, 22 novembre 2019.

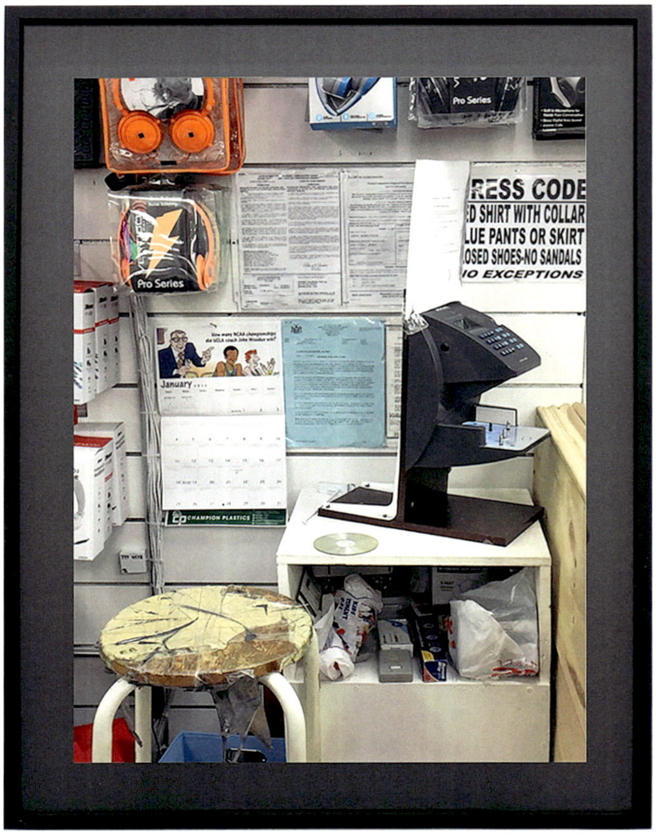

Cameron Rowland
Handpunch, 2015
Photograph
35.56 × 25.81 cm

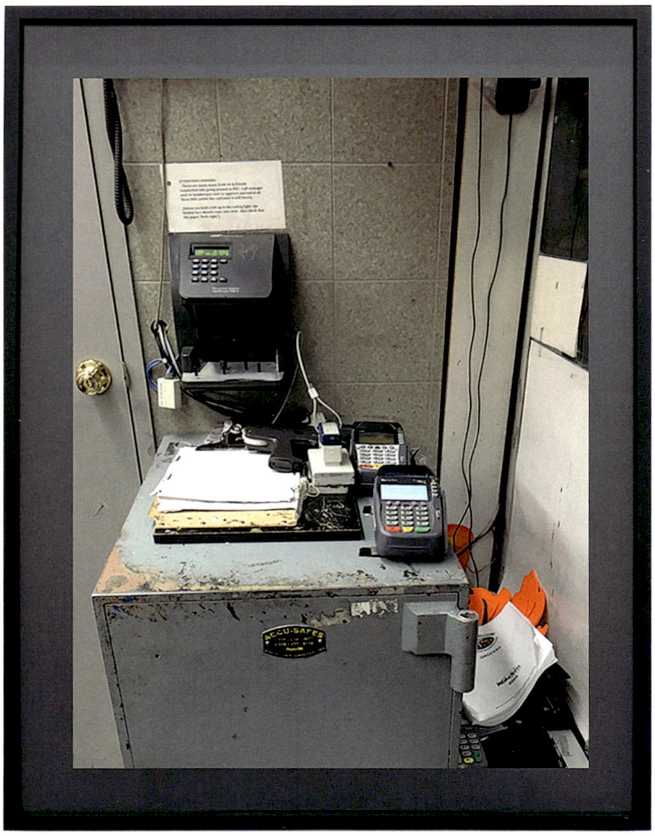

Cameron Rowland
Handpunch, 2015
Photograph
35.56 × 25.81 cm

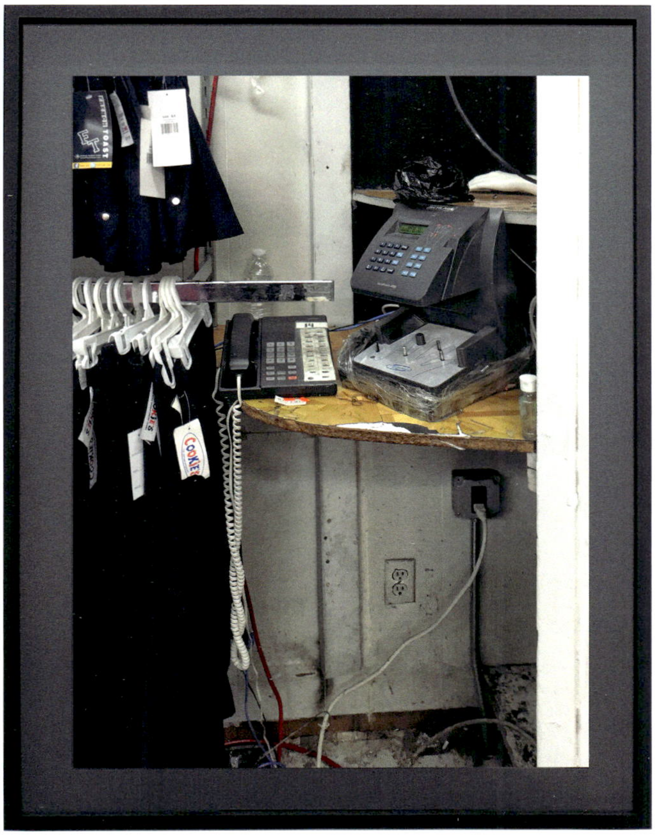

Cameron Rowland
Handpunch, 2015
Photograph
35.56 × 25.81 cm

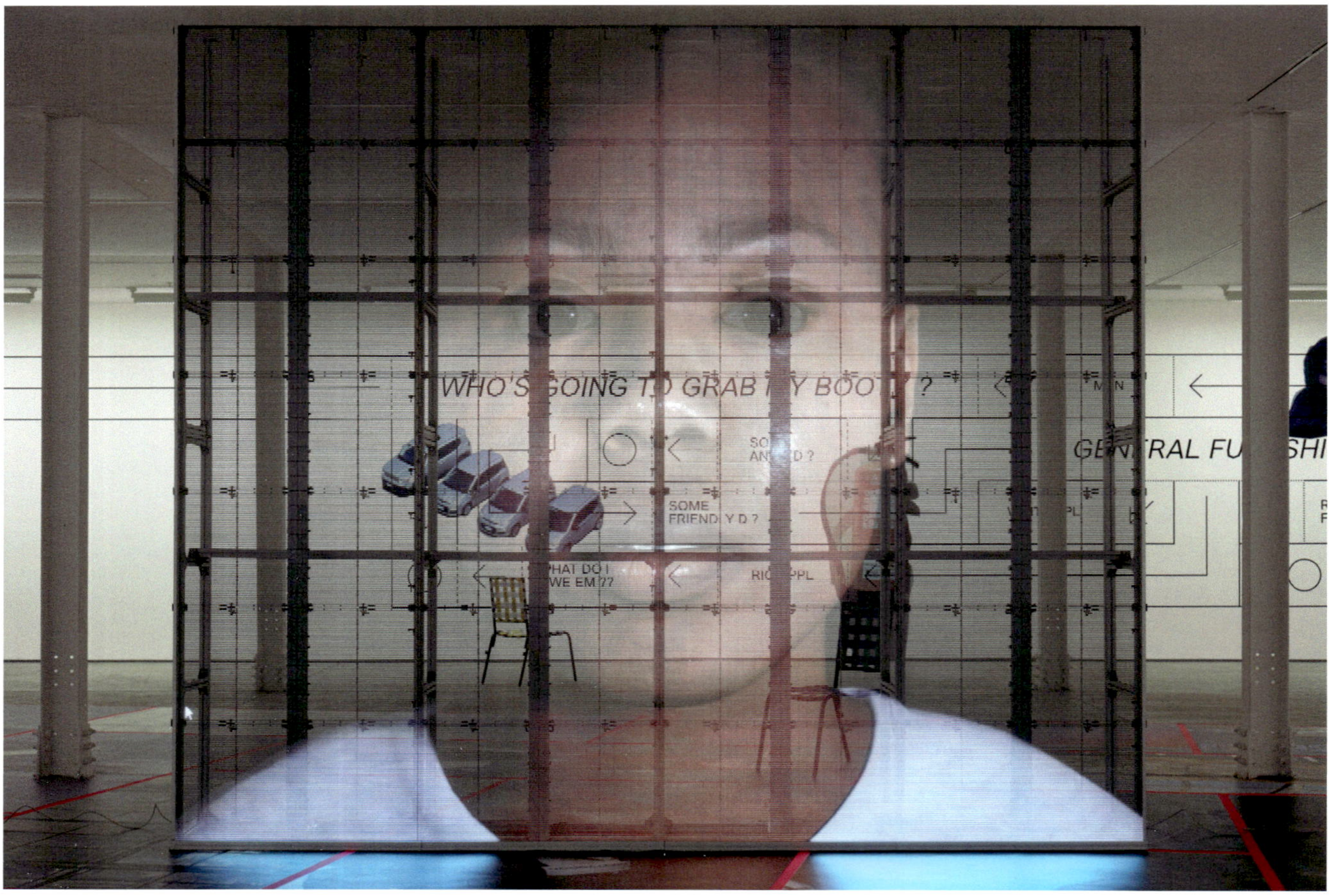

Martine Syms, *Mythiccbeing*, 2018 (installation view)

Martine Syms

Mythiccbeing (2018) is an interactive video installation featuring an SMS-activated chatbot that represents the artist's avatar, an apparently sentient intelligence that Syms describes as 'Black, upwardly mobile, violent, solipsistic, sociopathic, gender-neutral femme', or 'a bad Siri'.[1] The avatar appears on a monitor mounted over printed wallpaper, detailing a 'threat map': a modelling process used in cyber security to identify possible points of weakness – in this case, Syms' own vulnerabilities. Syms programmed the script for *Mythiccbeing* with over 200 hours of interactive content from three years of autobiographical material. This personal history becomes data activated by the chatbot, who both represents and then abstracts Syms' selfhood.[2]

Syms' work focuses on contemporary representations and self-conception of Blackness, as they manifest across media, entertainment and digital communication. Intervening in systems of representation that disenfranchise and deny the self-determination of Black people, technological systems are a point of focus for Syms. Programmed by the artist, with Syms' image, words and information, *Mythiccbeing* points to the ways that the self operates in contemporary society via surveillance and communication technologies, by asking 'What would it mean to make technology thicc?'[3] For Syms, making technology 'thicc' means designing an operating system that questions who is permitted to exist within these technologies and thinking about the development of artificial intelligence as a segregating process, of identifying and replicating human intelligence. In designing a chatbot that embodies Blackness, gender queerness and non-compliance, Syms makes visible the 'many different types of people that have, throughout history, been excluded from the notion of humanity'.[4]

Martine Syms was born in 1988 in Los Angeles, USA. She lives and works in Los Angeles, USA.

1 Martine Syms' website, https://martinesy.ms/projects/mythiccbeing (accessed 27 May 2021).

2 Although a direct reference was not intended the title and methodology bear a resemblance to Adrian Piper's performance *Mythic Being* (1973), in which Piper wanders the streets of New York dressed as a man, repeating mantras composed of lines from her diary. Piper's intention was to 'see what would happen if there was a being who had exactly my history, only a completely different visual appearance to the rest of society', Adrian Piper in *Other Than Art's Sake*, dir. Peter Kennedy, 1973, http://www.adrianpiper.com/vs/video_tmb.shtml (accessed 27 May 2021).

3 Martine Syms quoted in Kathryn O'Regan, '"Anything You Do on Camera is Like a Performance" – LA Artist Martine Syms on Being Seen in a Surveillance Society', *Sleek*, 7 January 2019, https://www.sleek-mag.com/article/martine-syms-2019 (accessed 27 May 2021).

4 Martine Syms, audio guide for *Shame Space*, Institute for Contemporary Art, Virginia Commonwealth University, 16 February–12 May 2019, https://icavcu.org/audio/syms (accessed 27 May 2021).

Mythiccbeing (2018) est une installation vidéo interactive reposant sur un chatbot activé par SMS représentant l'avatar de l'artiste, une intelligence apparemment sensible que Martine Syms décrit en ces termes: « Une femme noire, en pleine ascension sociale, violente, autocentrée, sociopathe, de genre neutre[1] ». L'avatar apparaît sur un moniteur monté sur un fond imprimé détaillant une « carte des menaces » : un processus de modélisation employé dans le domaine de la cybersécurité pour identifier d'éventuels points faibles – dans ce cas, les vulnérabilités de Martine Syms elle-même. L'artiste a programmé le script de *Mythiccbeing* à partir de 200 heures de contenu interactif tiré de trois ans de matériel autobiographique. Cet historique personnel devient un ensemble de données activées par le chatbot, qui constitue tout à la fois une représentation et une abstraction de l'identité de l'artiste[2].

Le travail de Martine Syms se concentre sur les (auto) représentations contemporaines de la *blackness*, telles qu'elles se manifestent dans les médias, le divertissement et la communication numérique. Son travail intervient dans les systèmes de représentation qui entravent, voire qui nient l'autodétermination des personnes noires. Les systèmes technologiques sont au centre de son œuvre. Programmé par l'artiste à partir de son image, de ses mots et de ses informations personnelles, *Mythiccbeing* interroge les modes de fonctionnement du soi dans la société contemporaine à travers les technologies de surveillance et de communication, en posant cette question: « Qu'est-ce que rendre la technologie "*thicc*" signifierait[3]? » Pour Martine Syms, « rendre la technologie "*thicc*" » signifie concevoir un système d'exploitation interrogeant qui a le droit d'exister au sein de ces technologies, mais aussi réfléchir au développement de l'intelligence artificielle en tant que processus ségrégatif identifiant et imitant l'intelligence humaine. À travers ce chatbot qui incarne la *blackness*, la *queerness* et l'indocilité, Martine Syms rend visibles les « nombreux et divers types de personnes qui, au cours de l'histoire, ont été exclus de la notion d'humanité[4] ».

Martine Syms est née en 1988 à Los Angeles, aux États-Unis. Elle vit et travaille à Los Angeles, aux États-Unis.

1 Site internet de Martine Syms, https://martinesy.ms/projects/mythiccbeing (consulté le 27 mai 2021).

2 Bien que l'artiste n'ait pas voulu y faire directement référence, le titre tout comme la méthodologie de cette œuvre rappellent la performance d'Adrian Piper, *Mythic Being* (1973), dans laquelle cette dernière errait dans les rues de New York habillée en homme, répétant des mantras formés à partir de phrases de son journal intime. Piper souhaitait « voir ce qu'il se passerait s'il existait un être ayant exactement la même histoire [qu'elle-même], mais une apparence visuelle totalement différente du reste de la société », Adrian Piper dans le film *Other than Art's Sake*, réal. par Peter Kennedy, 1973, http://www.adrianpiper.com/vs/video_tmb.shtml (consulté le 27 mai 2021).

3 Propos de Martine Syms, cités dans Kathryn O'Regan, « "Anything You Do on Camera Is like a Performance" – LA Artist Martine Syms on Being Seen in a Surveillance Society », *Sleek*, 7 janvier 2019, https://www.sleek-mag.com/article/martine-syms-2019/(consulté le 27 mai 2021).

4 Martine Syms, audioguide de *Shame Space*, Institute for Contemporary Art, Virginia Commonwealth University, 16 février–12 mai 2019, https://icavcu.org/audio/syms/(consulté le 27 mai 2021).

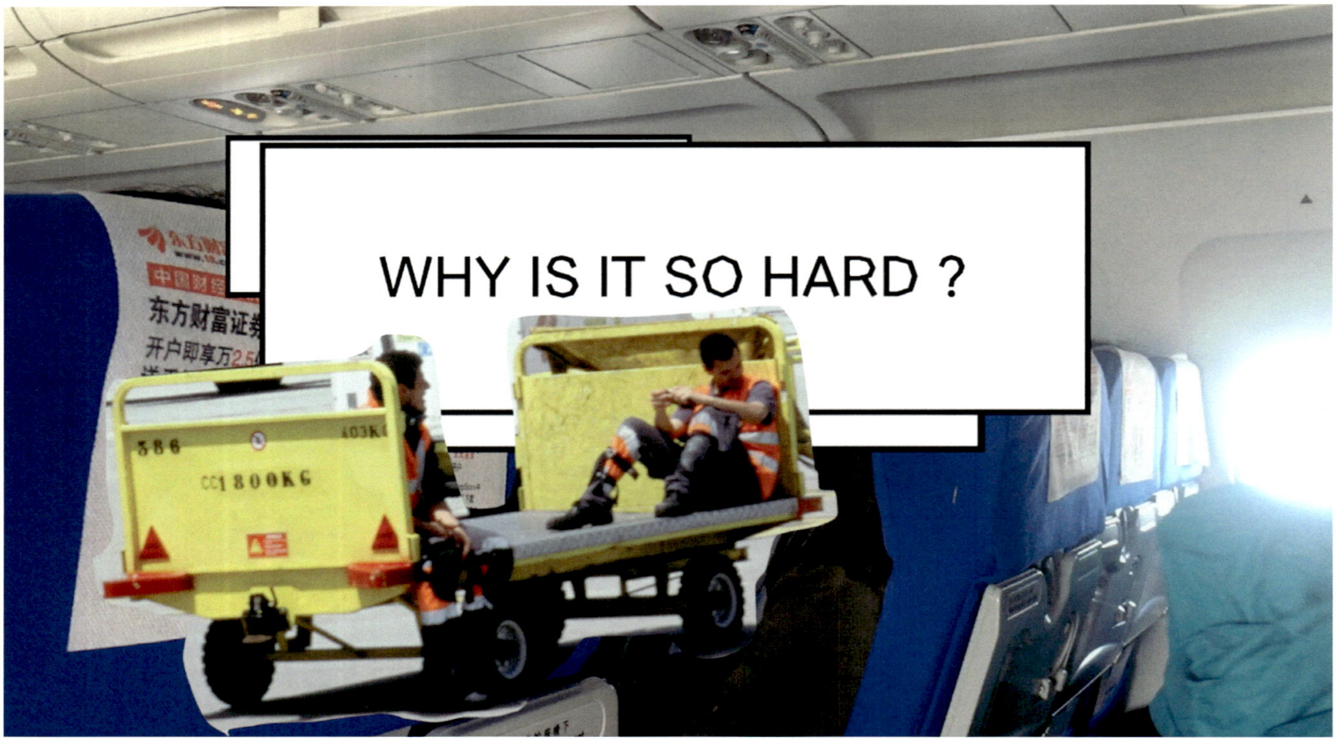

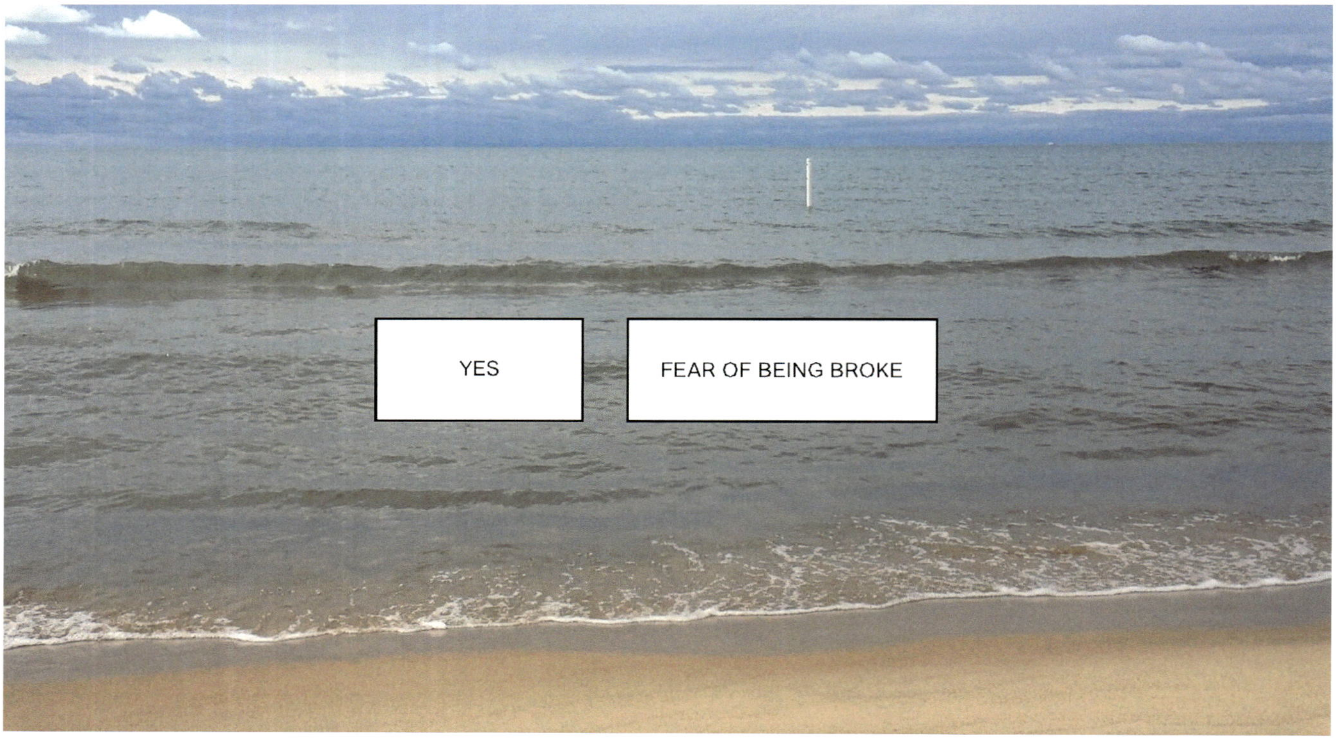

Film stills from Martine Syms, *Mythiccbeing*, 2018

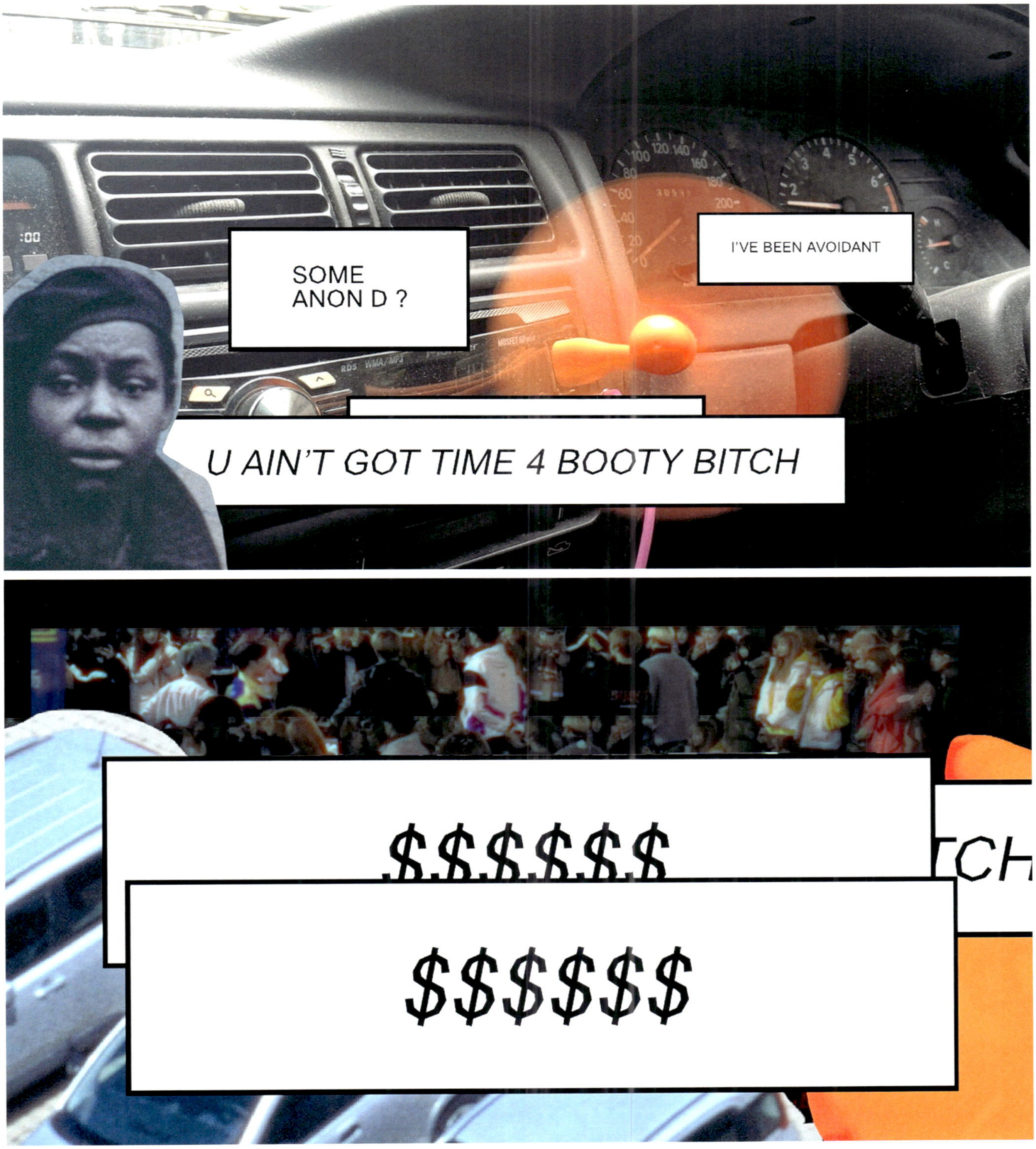
SOME
ANON D ?
I'VE BEEN AVOIDANT
U AIN'T GOT TIME 4 BOOTY BITCH
$$$$$$
$$$$$$

Consumption

THE AGE OF SURVEILLANCE CAPITALISM: THE FIGHT FOR A HUMAN FUTURE AT THE NEW FRONTIER OF POWER

Shoshana Zuboff

THE DEFINITION

Sur-veil-lance Cap-i-tal-ism, n.

1. A new economic order that claims human experience as free raw material for hidden commercial practices of extraction, prediction, and sales;
2. A parasitic economic logic in which the production of goods and services is subordinated to a new global architecture of behavioural modification;
3. A rogue mutation of capitalism marked by concentrations of wealth, knowledge, and power unprecedented in human history;
4. The foundational framework of a surveillance economy;
5. As significant a threat to human nature in the twenty-first century as industrial capitalism was to the natural world in the nineteenth and twentieth;
6. The origin of a new instrumentarian power that asserts dominance over society and presents startling challenges to market democracy;
7. A movement that aims to impose a new collective order based on total certainty;
8. An expropriation of critical human rights that is best understood as a coup from above: an overthrow of the people's sovereignty.

[...]

VIII. SUMMARISING THE LOGIC AND OPERATIONS OF SURVEILLANCE CAPITALISM

Behavioural surplus defines Google's earnings success. In 2016, 89 percent of the revenues of its parent company, Alphabet, derived from Google's targeted advertising programmes.[1] The scale of raw-material flows is reflected in Google's domination of the internet, processing over 40,000 search queries every second on average: more than 3.5 billion searches per day and 1.2 trillion searches per year worldwide in 2017.[2]

On the strength of its unprecedented inventions, Google's $400 billion market value edged out ExxonMobil for the number-two spot in market capitalisation in 2014, only sixteen years after its founding, making it the second-richest company in the world behind Apple.[3] By 2016, Alphabet/Google occasionally wrested the number-one position from Apple and was ranked number two globally as of September 20, 2017.[4]

It is useful to stand back from this complexity to grasp the overall pattern and how the puzzle pieces fit together:

1. *The logic*: Google and other surveillance platforms are sometimes described as 'two-sided' or 'multi-sided' markets, but the mechanisms of surveillance capitalism suggest something different.[5] Google had discovered a way to translate its nonmarket interactions with users into surplus raw material for the fabrication of products aimed at genuine market transactions with its real customers: advertisers.[6] The translation of behavioural surplus from outside to inside the market finally enabled Google to convert investment into revenue. The corporation thus created out of thin air and at zero marginal cost an asset class of vital raw materials derived from users' non-market online behaviour. At first those raw materials were simply 'found', a by-product of users' search actions. Later those assets were hunted aggressively and procured largely through surveillance. The corporation simultaneously created a new kind of marketplace in which its proprietary 'prediction products' manufactured from these raw materials could be bought and sold.
   The summary of these developments is that the behavioural surplus upon which Google's fortune rests can be considered as *surveillance assets.* These assets are critical raw materials in the pursuit of *surveillance revenues* and their translation into *surveillance capital.* The entire logic of this capital accumulation is most accurately understood as *surveillance capitalism*, which is the foundational framework for a surveillance-based economic order: a *surveillance economy*. The big pattern here is one of subordination and hierarchy, in which earlier reciprocities between the firm and its users are subordinated to the derivative project of our behavioural surplus captured for others' aims. We are no longer the *subjects* of value realisation. Nor are we, as some have insisted, the 'product' of Google's sales. Instead, we are the *objects* from which raw materials are extracted and expropriated for Google's prediction factories. Predictions about our behaviour are Google's products, and they are sold to its actual customers but not to us. *We are the means to others' ends.*
   Industrial capitalism transformed nature's raw materials into commodities, and surveillance capitalism lays its claims to the stuff of human nature for a new commodity invention. Now it is human nature that is scraped, torn, and taken for another century's market project. It is obscene to suppose that this harm can be reduced to the obvious fact that users receive no fee for the raw material they supply. That critique is a feat of misdirection that would use a pricing mechanism to institutionalise and therefore legitimate the extraction of human behaviour for manufacturing and sale. It ignores the key point that the essence of the exploitation here is the rendering of our lives as behavioural data for the sake of others' improved control of us. The remarkable questions here concern the facts that our lives are rendered as behavioural data in the first place; that ignorance is a condition of this ubiquitous rendition; that decision rights vanish before one even knows that there is a decision to make; that there are consequences to this diminishment of rights that we can neither see nor foretell; that there is no exit, no voice, and no loyalty, only helplessness, resignation, and psychic numbing; and that encryption is the only positive action left to discuss when we sit around the dinner table and casually ponder how to hide from the forces that hide from us.
2. The means of production: Google's internet-age manufacturing process is a critical component of the unprecedented. Its specific technologies and techniques, which I summarise as 'machine intelligence', are constantly evolving, and it is easy to be intimidated by their complexity. The same term may mean one thing today and something very different in one year or in five years. For example, Google has been described as developing and deploying 'artificial intelligence' since at least 2003, but the term itself is a moving target, as capabilities have evolved from primitive programmes that can play tic-tac-toe to systems that can operate whole fleets of driverless cars.
   Google's machine intelligence capabilities feed on behavioural surplus, and the more surplus they consume, the more accurate the prediction products that result. *Wired* magazine's founding editor, Kevin Kelly, once suggested that although it seems like Google is committed to developing its artificial intelligence capabilities to improve Search, it's more likely that Google develops Search as a means of continuously training its evolving AI capabilities.[7] This is the essence of the machine intelligence project. As the ultimate tapeworm, the machine's intelligence depends upon how much data it eats. In this important respect the new means of production differs fundamentally from the industrial model, in which there is a tension between

quantity and quality. Machine intelligence is the synthesis of this tension, for it reaches its full potential for quality only as it approximates totality.
As more companies chase Google-style surveillance profits, a significant fraction of global genius in data science and related fields is dedicated to the fabrication of prediction products that increase click-through rates for targeted advertising. For example, Chinese researchers employed by Microsoft's Bing's research unit in Beijing published breakthrough findings in 2017. 'Accurately estimating the click-through rate (CTR) of ads has a vital impact on the revenue of search businesses; even a 0.1% accuracy improvement in our production would yield hundreds of millions of dollars in additional earnings', they begin. They go on to demonstrate a new application of advanced neural networks that promises 0.9 percent improvement on one measure of identification and 'significant click yield gains in online traffic'.[8] Similarly, a team of Google researchers introduced a new deep-neural network model, for the sake of capturing 'predictive feature interactions' and delivering 'state-of-the-art performance' to improve click-through rates.[9] Thousands of contributions like these, some incremental and some dramatic, equate to an expensive, sophisticated, opaque, and exclusive *twenty-first-century 'means of production'*.

3. The products: Machine intelligence processes behavioural surplus into *prediction products* designed to forecast what we will feel, think, and do: now, soon, and later. These methodologies are among Google's most closely guarded secrets. The nature of its products explains why Google repeatedly claims that it does not sell personal data. What? Never! Google executives like to claim their privacy purity because they do not sell their raw material. Instead, the company sells the predictions that only it can fabricate from its world-historic private hoard of behavioural surplus. Prediction products reduce risks for customers, advising them where and when to place their bets. The quality and competitiveness of the product are a function of its approximation to certainty: the more predictive the product, the lower the risks for buyers and the greater the volume of sales. Google has learned to be a data-based fortune-teller that replaces intuition with science at scale in order to tell and sell our fortunes for profit to its customers, but not to us. Early on, Google's prediction products were largely aimed at sales of targeted advertising, but as we shall see, advertising was the beginning of the surveillance project, not the end.
4. The marketplace: Prediction products are sold into a new kind of market that trades exclusively in future behaviour. Surveillance capitalism's profits derive primarily from these *behavioural futures markets.* Although advertisers were the dominant players in the early history of this new kind of marketplace, there is no reason why such markets are limited to this group. The new prediction systems are only incidentally about ads, in the same way that Ford's new system of mass production was only incidentally about automobiles. In both cases the systems can be applied to many other domains. The already visible trend ... is that any actor with an interest in purchasing probabilistic information about our behaviour and/or influencing future behaviour can pay to play in markets where the behavioural fortunes of individuals, groups, bodies, and things are told and sold (see Figure 2).

IV. PROPHECY

Nearly seventy years ago, the economic historian Karl Polanyi reflected on the ways in which industrial capitalism's market dynamics would, if left unchecked, destroy the very things that it aimed to buy and sell: 'The commodity fiction disregarded the fact that leaving the fate of soil and people to the market would be tantamount to annihilating them'.[10] In the absence of synthetic declaration, Polanyi's prophecy appears headed for fulfilment, and this fact alone must put us on alert. What does Polanyi's prophecy augur for our time?

Industrial capitalism followed its own logic of shock and awe, taking aim at nature to conquer 'it' in the interests of capital; now surveillance capitalism has *human* nature in its sights. We have only gradually come to understand that the specific methods of domination employed by industrial capitalism for more than two centuries have fundamentally disoriented the conditions that support life on Earth, violating the most basic precepts of civilisation. Despite the many benefits and immense accomplishments of industrial capitalism, it has left us perilously close to repeating the fate of the Easter Islanders, who wrecked the ground that gave them life, then fashioned statues to scan the horizon for the aid and succour that would never come. *If industrial capitalism dangerously disrupted nature, what havoc might surveillance capitalism wreak on human nature?*

The answer to this question requires a return to imperatives. Industrial capitalism brought us to the brink of epic peril, but not as a consequence of an evil lust for

Figure 2: The Discovery of Behavioural Surplus

Surveillance capitalism begins with the discovery of behavioural surplus. More behavioural data are rendered than required for service improvements. This surplus feeds machine intelligence – the new means of production – that fabricates predictions of user behaviour. These products are sold to business customers in new behavioural futures markets. The Behavioural Value Reinvestment Cycle is subordinated to this new logic.

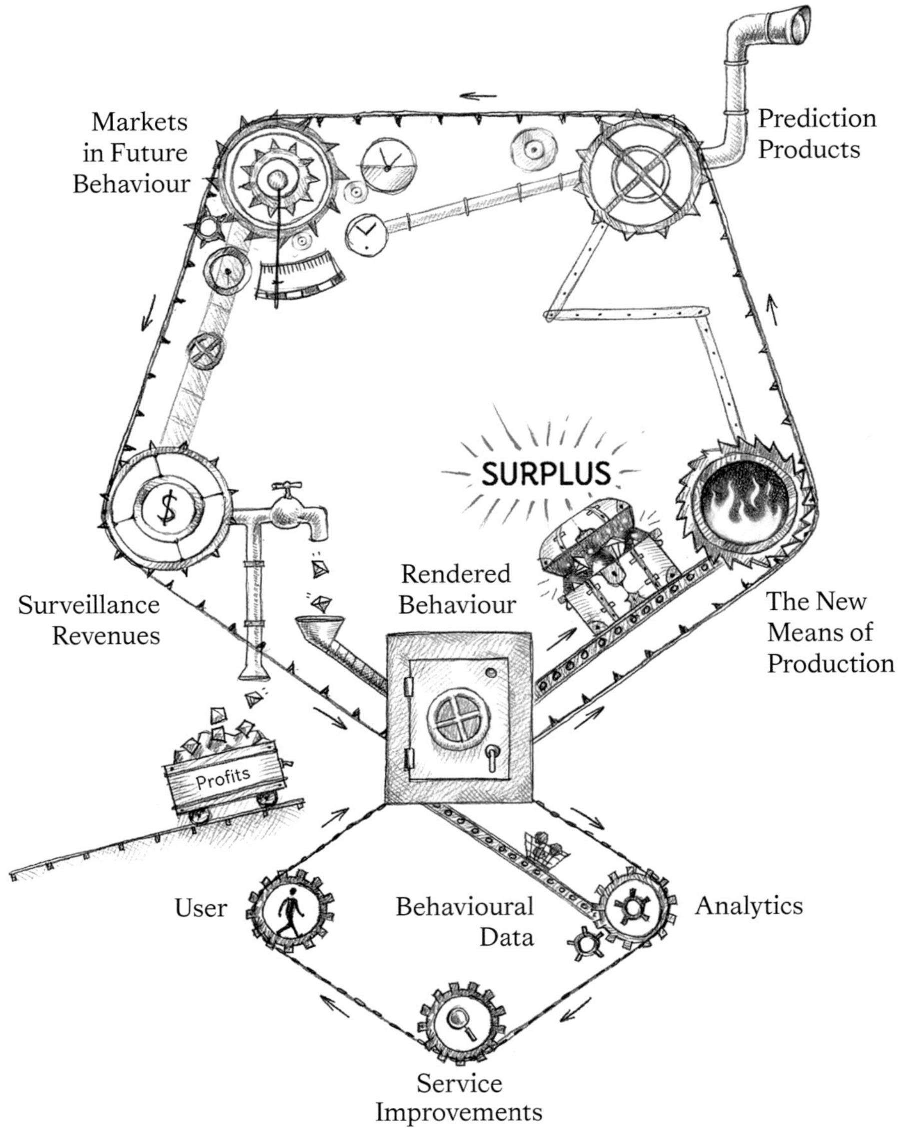

destruction or runaway technology. Rather, this result was ineluctably driven by its own inner logic of accumulation, with its imperatives of profit maximisation, competition, the relentless drive for labour productivity through the technological elaboration of production, and growth funded by the continuous reinvestment of surplus.[11] It is Weber's 'economic orientation' that matters, and how that orientation merges with the specific form of capitalism that rises to dominance in each age.

The logic of industrial capitalism exempted the enterprise from responsibility for its destructive consequences, unleashing the destabilisation of the climate system and the chaos it spells for all creatures. Polanyi understood that raw capitalism could not be cooked from within. He argued that it was up to society to impose those obligations on capitalism by insisting on measures that tether the capitalist project to the social, preserving and sustaining life and nature.

Similarly, the meaning of Polanyi's prophecy for us now can be grasped only through the lens of surveillance capitalism's economic imperatives as they frame its claim to human experience. If we are to rediscover our sense of astonishment, then let it be here: *if industrial civilisation flourished at the expense of nature and now threatens to cost us the Earth, an information civilisation shaped by surveillance capitalism will thrive at the expense of human nature and threatens to cost us our humanity.* Polanyi's prophecy requires us to ask if we may yet avert this fate with our own synthetic declarations.

[...]

Industrial capitalism was marked by the specialised division of labour, with its historically specific characteristics: the conversion of craft work to mass production based on standardisation, rationalisation, and the interchangeability of parts; the moving assembly line; volume production; large populations of wage earners concentrated in factory settings; professionalised administrative hierarchies; managerial authority; functional specialisation; and the distinction between white-collar work and blue-collar work.

The list is illustrative, not exhaustive, but enough to remind us that industrial civilisation was drawn from these expressions of the economic imperatives that ruled industrial expansion. The division of labour shaped culture, psychology, and social experience. The shift from craft to hourly wages created new populations of employees and consumers, men and women wholly dependent on the means of production owned and operated by private firms.

This was the crucible of mass society, its hierarchical authority, and its centralised bureaucratic forms of public and private power, all of it haunted by the spectres of conformity, obedience, and human standardisation. Lives were defined by institutions that mirrored industrial organisation: schools, hospitals, and even aspects of family and domestic life, in which ages and stages were understood as functions of the industrial system, from training to retirement.

At a time when surveillance capitalism has emerged as the dominant form of information capitalism, we must ask the question: what kind of civilisation does it foretell? ... I have said that there can be no commitment to 'guaranteed outcomes' without the power to make it so. What is the nature of this new power? How will it transform our societies? What solution for a third modernity does it proffer? What novel struggles will haunt these new days, and what do they portend for a digital future that we can call home?

1 'Selected Financial Data for Alphabet Inc'., Form 10-K, Commission File, United States Securities and Exchange Commission, 31 December 2016, https://www.sec.gov/Archives/edgar/data/1652044/000165204417000008/goog10-kq42016.htm#s58C60B74D56A630AD6EA2B64F53BD90C. According to Alphabet's account in 2016, its revenues were $90,272,000,000. This included 'Google segment revenues of $89.5 billion with revenue growth of 20% year over year and Other Bets revenues of $0.8 billion with revenue growth of 82% year over year'. Google Segment advertising revenues were $79,383,000,000, or 88.73% of Google Segment revenues.

2 'Google Search Statistics – Internet Live Stats', Internet Live Stats, 20 September 2017, http://www.internetlivestats.com/google-search-statistics; Greg Sterling, 'Data: Google Monthly Search Volume Dwarfs Rivals Because of Mobile Advantage', *Search Engine Land*, 9 February 2017, http://searchengineland.com/data-google-monthly-search-volume-dwarfs-rivals-mobile-advantage-269120. This translated into 76% of all desktop searches and 96% of mobile searches in the US and corresponding shares of 87% and 95% worldwide.

3 Roben Farzad, 'Google at $400 Billion: A New No. 2 in Market Cap', *BusinessWeek*, 12 February 2014, http://www.businessweek.com/articles/2014-02-12/google-at-400-billion-a-new-no-dot-2-in-market-cap.

4 'Largest Companies by Market Cap Today', *Dogs of the Dow*, 2017, https://web.archive.org/web/20180701094340/http://dogsofthedow.com/largest-companies-by-market-cap.htm.

5 Jean-Charles Rochet and Jean Tirole, 'Two-Sided Markets: A Progress Report', *RAND Journal of Economics 37*, no. 3 (2006), pp. 645–67.

6 For a discussion on this point and its relation to online target advertising, see Katherine J. Strandburg, 'Free Fall: The Online Market's Consumer Preference Disconnect' (working paper, New York University Law and Economics, 1 October 2013).

7 Kevin Kelly, 'The Three Breakthroughs that Have Finally Unleashed AI on the World', *Wired*, 27 October 2014, https://www.wired.com/2014/10/future-of-artificial-intelligence.

8 Xiaoliang Ling et al., 'Model Ensemble for Click Prediction in Bing Search Ads', in *Proceedings of the 26th International Conference on World Wide Web Companion*, pp. 689–98, https://doi.org/10.1145/3041021.3054192.

9 Ruoxi Wang et al., 'Deep & Cross Network for Ad Click Predictions', *ArXiv:1708.05123 [Computer Science. Learning]*, 16 August 2017, http://arxiv.org/abs/1708.05123.

10 Karl Polanyi, *The Great Transformation: The Political and Economic Origins of Our Time*, 2nd ed., Boston: Beacon, 2001, p. 137.

11 Ellen Meiksins Wood, *The Origin of Capitalism: A Longer View*, London: Verso, 2002.

L'ÂGE DU CAPITALISME DE SURVEILLANCE. LE COMBAT POUR UN AVENIR HUMAIN FACE AUX NOUVELLES FRONTIÈRES DU POUVOIR

Shoshana Zuboff

DÉFINITION

Capitalisme de surveillance, n.

1. Un nouvel ordre économique qui revendique l'expérience humaine comme matière première gratuite à des fins de pratiques commerciales dissimulées d'extraction, de prédiction et de vente ;
2. Une logique économique parasite selon laquelle la production des biens et des services est subordonnée à une nouvelle architecture globale de modification des comportements ;
3. Une mutation dévoyée du capitalisme marquée par des concentrations de richesse, de savoir et de pouvoir sans précédent dans l'histoire humaine ;
4. La structure fondatrice d'une économie de surveillance ;
5. Une menace pour la nature humaine, au XXIe siècle, aussi cruciale que l'a été le capitalisme industriel pour le monde naturel aux XIXe et XXe siècles ;
6. L'origine d'un nouveau pouvoir instrumentarien qui affirme sa domination sur la société et lance des défis inédits à la démocratie de marché ;
7. Un mouvement qui vise à imposer un nouvel ordre collectif fondé sur la certitude absolue ;
8. Une dépossession des droits humains essentiels mieux comprise comme *coup* d'en haut : un renversement de la souveraineté du peuple.

[...]

VIII. RÉSUMER LA LOGIQUE ET LES OPÉRATIONS DU CAPITALISME DE SURVEILLANCE

Le surplus comportemental définit les profits extraordinaires de Google. En 2016, 89% des revenus de la société mère Alphabet provenaient des campagnes de publicité ciblée de Google[1]. L'échelle des flux de matière première se reflète dans la souveraineté de Google sur Internet qui, en 2017, a traité en moyenne 40 000 requêtes de recherche par seconde, soit plus de 3,5 milliards par jour et 1,2 milliard de milliards par an dans le monde[2]. En vertu de ses inventions sans précédent, dès 2014, c'est-à-dire seulement seize ans après sa fondation, Google a vu sa valeur de marché, soit 400 milliards de dollars, surpasser celle d'ExxonMobil et conquis ainsi la deuxième place en termes de capitalisation boursière, ce qui en a fait la plus riche entreprise du monde derrière Apple[3]. Et dès 2016, Alphabet / Google a de temps à autre arraché la première place à Apple pour être classé globalement numéro deux à partir du 20 septembre 2017[4].

Il est utile de prendre du recul par rapport à cette complexité afin de saisir le modèle global et la manière dont les pièces du puzzle s'assemblent.

1. *La logique*. Google ainsi que d'autres plateformes de surveillance sont parfois décrites comme des marchés « bifaces » ou « multifaces », mais les mécanismes du capitalisme de surveillance suggèrent quelque chose de différent[5]. Google avait découvert une manière de convertir ses interactions non commerciales avec les utilisateurs en surplus de matière première pour fabriquer des produits destinés à de véritables transactions commerciales avec ses véritables clients : les annonceurs[6]. La transposition du surplus comportemental de l'extérieur à l'intérieur du marché a finalement permis à Google de convertir l'investissement en chiffre d'affaires. L'entreprise a ainsi créé de toutes pièces et à un coût marginal nul une catégorie d'actifs composés de matières premières essentielles provenant du comportement en ligne non marchand des utilisateurs. Au départ, il s'agissait simplement de « trouver » ces matières premières ; c'était un sous-produit des requêtes de recherche des utilisateurs – lequel donna lieu, par la suite, à une traque agressive et fut fourni en abondance par le biais du capitalisme de surveillance. L'entreprise créa simultanément un nouveau type de marché où l'on pouvait acheter et vendre des « produits de prédiction » fabriqués à partir de ces matières premières.
   On pourrait résumer ces développements en disant que le surplus comportemental sur lequel repose la fortune de Google peut être considéré comme *des actifs de surveillance*. Ces actifs sont des matières premières décisives en quête des *revenus de surveillance* et de leur conversion en *capital de surveillance*. La logique entière de cette accumulation de capital s'entend plus exactement au sens de *capitalisme de surveillance*, lequel constitue le cadre fondateur d'un ordre économique basé sur la surveillance, soit une *économie de surveillance*. Le grand modèle ici est un modèle de subordination et de hiérarchie où les relations de réciprocité antérieures entre l'entreprise et ses utilisateurs sont subordonnées à un projet dérivé, celui de la captation de notre surplus comportemental pour atteindre les objectifs d'autres que nous. Nous ne sommes plus les *sujets* de la réalisation de la valeur. Nous ne sommes pas non plus, comme quelques-uns l'ont répété, le « produit » des ventes de Google. Bien au contraire, nous sommes les *objets* d'où sont extraites les matières premières et que s'approprient les usines de prédiction de Google. Les prédictions relatives à notre comportement sont les produits de Google, et ces produits sont vendus à ses véritables clients et non à nous. *Nous sommes les moyens permettant à d'autres d'atteindre leurs objectifs.*
   Le capitalisme industriel a transformé les matières premières de la nature en marchandises, et le capitalisme de surveillance revendique la nature humaine comme matériau pour créer une nouvelle marchandise. Aujourd'hui, c'est la nature humaine qui est raclée, lacérée, et dont on s'empare pour le nouveau projet de marché du siècle. Il est choquant de supposer que ce préjudice peut être réduit au fait évident que les utilisateurs ne reçoivent aucune rétribution pour la matière première qu'ils fournissent. C'est un formidable fourvoiement que de recourir au mécanisme de fixation des prix pour institutionnaliser et donc légitimer l'extraction du comportement humain dans un objectif de fabrication et de vente. C'est aussi ignorer le point-clé de l'affaire, à savoir que l'essence de l'exploitation ici est la restitution de nos vies sous forme de données comportementales destinées à améliorer le contrôle que d'autres ont sur nous. Les questions les plus remarquables qui se posent ici concernent d'abord le fait que nos existences sont restituées sous forme de données comportementales ; ensuite, le fait que l'ignorance est une condition de cette restitution omniprésente et que le droit de décider s'évanouit avant même que l'utilisateur ait eu connaissance qu'il y avait une décision à prendre ; enfin, le fait que cette réduction de nos droits entraîne des conséquences que nous ne pouvons ni voir, ni prévoir ; qu'il n'y a aucune issue, aucune voix, aucune loyauté à attendre et que seuls l'impuissance, la résignation et l'engourdissement psychique sont notre lot. Ajoutons que le cryptage est l'unique action positive dont nous pouvons encore discuter quand nous sommes assis autour d'une table à réfléchir négligemment à la manière dont nous pourrions nous dissimuler aux forces qui se soustraient à notre regard.
2. *Les moyens de production*. Le processus de fabrication de Google à l'âge d'Internet est un élément crucial du sans-précédent. Ses technologies et ses techniques spécifiques,

que je résume sous le nom d'*intelligence machine* (intelligence artificielle), ne cessent d'évoluer, et l'on est facilement intimidé par leur complexité. Le même terme peut signifier une chose aujourd'hui et quelque chose de très différent dans un an ou dans cinq ans. Ainsi, Google a été décrit comme développant et déployant une « intelligence artificielle » depuis au moins 2003, mais le terme lui-même est une cible mouvante, ses capacités étant passées des premiers programmes permettant de jouer au morpion (*tic-tac-toe*) à des systèmes susceptibles de faire fonctionner des parcs entiers de voitures sans conducteur.

Les capacités d'intelligence artificielle de Google se nourrissent du surplus comportemental : plus elles consomment de surplus comportemental, plus les produits de prédiction qui en résultent sont exacts. Le fondateur et rédacteur en chef du magazine *Wired*, Kevin Kelly, a laissé entendre un jour que, même si Google semble engagé à développer ses capacités d'intelligence artificielle pour améliorer Search, il est plus vraisemblable qu'il développe Search comme moyen d'exercer continuellement ses capacités d'IA en constante évolution[7]. Telle est l'essence du projet d'intelligence artificielle. Comme un ultime ver solitaire, l'intelligence artificielle dépend du nombre de données qu'elle dévore. Dans cette perspective décisive, les nouveaux moyens de production diffèrent fondamentalement du modèle industriel dans lequel il y a une tension entre qualité et quantité. L'intelligence artificielle est la synthèse de cette tension, car elle atteint son plein potentiel de qualité seulement quand elle approche la totalité.

Tandis qu'un nombre accru d'entreprises recherchent les profits de surveillance à la manière de Google, une fraction importante du génie mondial de la science des données et les domaines qui lui sont liés se consacre à la fabrication de produits de prédiction qui augmentent les taux de clics pour la publicité ciblée. Ainsi, les chercheurs chinois employés par l'unité de recherche de Bing (Microsoft) à Pékin ont publié des conclusions capitales en 2017. « Estimer exactement le taux de clics (TDC) des annonces publicitaires a un impact important sur le chiffre d'affaires des moteurs de recherche ; même une amélioration d'exactitude de 1% dans notre production rapporterait des centaines de millions de dollars supplémentaires », commencent-ils. Puis ils font la démonstration d'une nouvelle application de réseaux de neurones artificiels qui promet 0,9% d'amélioration sur une seule mesure d'identification et des « gains importants de clics dans le trafic web[8] ». De même, une équipe de chercheurs de Google a introduit un nouveau modèle de réseau de neurones profonds, aux fins de capter des « interactions de fonctions prédictives » et d'offrir une « performance de pointe » pour améliorer les taux de clics[9]. Des milliers de contributions comme celles-ci, certaines graduelles et certaines spectaculaires, équivalent à un *« moyen de production » du XXIe siècle* coûteux, sophistiqué, opaque et exclusif.

3. *Les produits*. L'intelligence artificielle transforme le surplus comportemental en *produits de prédiction* destinés à prédire ce que nous sentirons, penserons et ferons – aujourd'hui, prochainement et par la suite. Ces méthodologies sont parmi les secrets les mieux gardés de Google. La nature de ses produits explique la raison pour laquelle Google ne cesse de proclamer qu'il ne vend pas de données personnelles. Quoi ? Jamais ! Les dirigeants de Google aiment clamer leur pureté en matière de confidentialité, car ils ne vendent pas leur matière première. Par contre, l'entreprise vend les prédictions qu'elle peut seulement fabriquer à partir de sa réserve privée de surplus comportemental, unique au monde. Les produits de prédiction réduisent les risques pour les clients en leur conseillant où et quand placer leurs mises. La qualité et la compétitivité du produit constituent une fonction de son approche de la certitude : plus le produit est prédictif, plus le risque couru est bas et plus le volume des ventes est important. Google a appris à être une voyante des bases de données en remplaçant l'intuition par la science à grande échelle afin de prédire et de vendre notre avenir à ses clients pour leur plus grand profit, mais non le nôtre. Initialement, les produits de prédiction de Google avaient en grande partie pour objectif la publicité ciblée, mais comme nous le verrons, si la publicité était au commencement du projet de surveillance, elle n'en était pas la fin.
4. *Le marché*. Les produits de prédiction sont vendus sur un nouveau genre de marché qui négocie exclusivement des comportements futurs. Les profits du capitalisme de surveillance proviennent principalement de ces *marchés des comportements futurs*. Bien que les annonceurs aient été les acteurs dominants dans les premières années de ce nouveau genre de marché, il n'y a aucune raison pour que de tels marchés se limitent à ce groupe. Les nouveaux systèmes de prédiction ne sont appliqués qu'accessoirement aux annonces publicitaires, tout comme le nouveau système de production de masse de Ford n'était appliqué qu'accessoirement aux automobiles. Dans

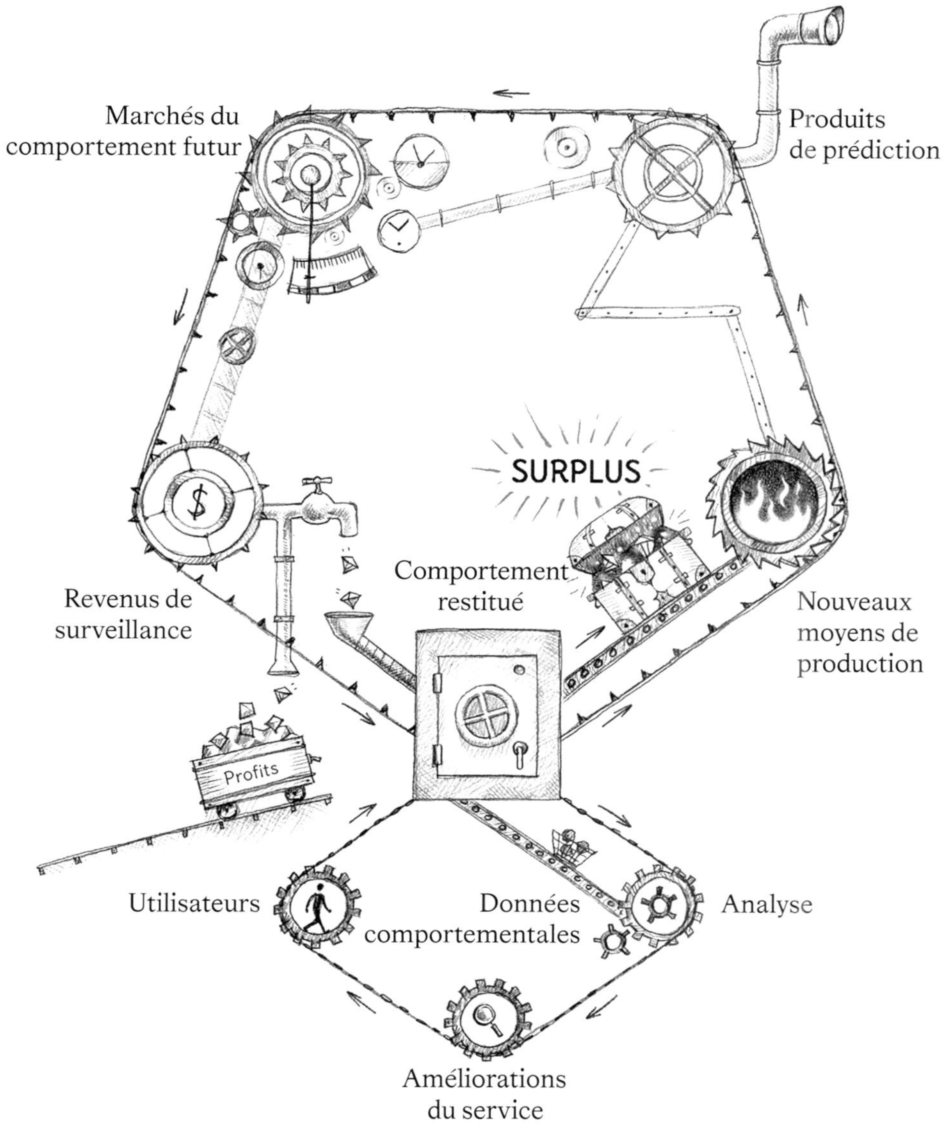

Figure 2 : La découverte du surplus comportemental

Le capitalisme de surveillance commence par la découverte du surplus comportemental. Il y a plus de données restituées que de données requises pour l'amélioration des services. Ce surplus alimente l'intelligence artificielle – les nouveaux moyens de production – qui fabrique les prédictions du comportement de l'utilisateur. Ces produits sont vendus à des entreprises clientes sur de nouveaux marchés des comportements futurs. Le cycle de réinvestissement de la valeur comportementale est subordonné à cette nouvelle logique.

les deux cas, les systèmes peuvent être adoptés dans beaucoup d'autres domaines. La tendance déjà visible [...] est que tout acteur ayant intérêt à acheter des informations probabilistes à propos de notre comportement et / ou à influencer les futurs comportements peut payer pour jouer dans des marchés où les données comportementales des individus, des groupes ou des organismes sont énoncées et vendues (voir Figure 2).

IV. PROPHÉTIE

Il y a soixante-dix ans, l'économiste Karl Polanyi réfléchissait sur la manière dont la dynamique de marché du capitalisme industriel finirait, en l'absence de tout contrôle, par détruire ce qu'elle était censé acheter et vendre. « La marchandise fictive ignorait le fait que confier le sort de la terre et des gens au marché équivalait peu ou prou à les anéantir[10]. » En l'absence d'une déclaration synthétique, la prophétie de Polanyi semble se diriger vers sa réalisation, ce qui devrait nous mettre sur le qui-vive. Que signifie cet augure pour notre époque ?

Le capitalisme industriel a suivi sa propre logique de « choc et stupeur », s'emparant de la nature pour « la » conquérir au nom des intérêts du capital ; ce que le capitalisme de surveillance a désormais en ligne de mire, c'est la nature *humaine*. Ce n'est que progressivement que nous avons compris que les méthodes de domination adoptées par le capitalisme industriel pendant plus de deux siècles ont perturbé de manière fondamentale les conditions qui entretiennent la vie sur terre – ce qui est une violation des principes les plus essentiels de la civilisation. En dépit des bénéfices nombreux et des accomplissements considérables du capitalisme industriel, nous nous trouvons dans une passe dangereuse ; notre sort pourrait bien ressembler rapidement à celui du peuple de l'île de Pâques qui dévasta la terre qui l'avait nourri puis érigea des statues qui devaient chercher à l'horizon un secours qui ne vint jamais. *Si le capitalisme industriel a mis en péril l'équilibre de la nature, quel peut être l'effroyable effet du capitalisme de surveillance sur la nature humaine ?*

La réponse à cette question exige un retour aux impératifs. Le capitalisme industriel nous a conduits au bord d'une catastrophe aux proportions épiques ; pour autant, ce n'est pas la conséquence d'un appétit pervers pour la destruction ou les technologies galopantes. Ce résultat est l'inéluctable produit de la logique interne d'accumulation, avec ses impératifs de maximisation des profits, sa concurrence, sa poussée incessante à la productivité du travail par le biais de l'élaboration technique de la production, et sa croissance fondée sur un réinvestissement permanent des surplus[11]. C'est l'« orientation économique » de Weber qui compte, et la manière dont cette orientation se fond dans la forme spécifique de capitalisme qui établit sa domination à chaque époque.

Dans la logique du capitalisme industriel, ses acteurs n'étaient pas tenus responsables des dommages qu'ils provoquaient, d'où la déstabilisation du système climatique de la planète et le chaos dans lequel elle plonge toutes les espèces. Polanyi avait compris que le capitalisme, dans toute sa crudité, ne pouvait pas être cuit de l'intérieur. Pour lui, il incombait à la société d'imposer ces obligations au capitalisme en imposant des mesures qui attachaient le projet capitaliste au poteau social, préservant la vie, la nature et restaurant leurs forces.

De la même manière, nous ne pouvons comprendre le sens de la prophétie de Polanyi pour notre époque qu'en la considérant à la lumière des impératifs économiques du capitalisme de surveillance, charpentes de sa prise de possession de l'expérience humaine. Si nous voulons redécouvrir notre sens de la stupéfaction, que ce soit devant ce constat : *si la civilisation industrielle a prospéré aux dépens de la nature et menace à présent de nous coûter la Terre, une civilisation de l'information modelée par le capitalisme de surveillance prospérera aux dépens de la nature humaine et menacera de nous coûter notre humanité.* La prophétie de Polanyi nous pousse à nous demander si nous pouvons encore éviter ce sort par la grâce de nos propres déclarations synthétiques.

[...]

Le capitalisme industriel se démarquait par la division spécialisée du travail et ses caractéristiques historiquement spécifiques : passage de l'artisanat à la production de masse rendu possible par la standardisation, par la rationalisation et l'interchangeabilité des parties ; les chaînes de montage ; la production en série ; la concentration de populations importantes de salariés sur le lieu de travail ; la professionnalisation de la hiérarchie ; les pouvoirs de décision ; la spécialisation fonctionnelle et la distinction entre le travail des cols bleus et celui des cols blancs.

Liste non exhaustive mais suffisamment détaillée pour que nous nous souvenions que la civilisation industrielle est née de ces expressions des impératifs économiques qui régirent l'expansion industrielle. La division du travail transforma la culture, la psychologie, les expériences sociales. Le passage de l'artisanat au salaire horaire créa de nouvelles populations d'employés et de consommateurs, hommes et femmes entièrement dépendants des moyens de production que possédaient et pilotaient les entreprises privées.

Ce fut le creuset de la société de masse, de sa hiérarchisation et de ses formes centralisées et bureaucratiques de pouvoir public et privé – et flottaient sur tout cela les spectres de la conformité, de l'obéissance, de la standardisation des individus. Les vies étaient définies par des institutions qui reflétaient l'organisation industrielle : écoles, hôpitaux, et même en certains aspects la vie familiale – où les âges et les phases de développement étaient envisagés comme des fonctions du système industriel, de l'apprentissage à la retraite.

Au moment où le capitalisme de surveillance s'impose comme forme dominante du capitalisme de l'information, nous devons nous poser cette question : de quelle sorte de civilisation est-il l'augure ? J'ai conçu les chapitres de la partie III comme un début de contribution à ce débat qui ne peut attendre. J'ai dit qu'il ne pouvait y avoir d'engagement pour des « résultats garantis » sans le pouvoir de les rendre tels. Quel est la nature de ce nouveau pouvoir ? Comment va-t-il transformer nos sociétés ? Quelle solution propose-t-il pour une troisième modernité ? Quels combats nouveaux vont faire trembler ces temps à venir et que laissent-ils présager d'un futur numérique que nous puissions habiter ?

1 « Selected Financial Data for Alphabet Inc. », Form 10-K, Commission File, United States Securities and Exchange Commission, 31 décembre 2016. D'après les rapports d'activité d'Alphabet portant sur l'année 2016, ses revenus se montaient à 90 272 000 000 dollars. Ce qui comprend « les revenus de Google Segment, soit 89,5 milliards de dollars – et une croissance de 20% d'une année sur l'autre ; et 0,8 milliard de dollars pour Other Bets – et une croissance de 82% d'une année sur l'autre ». La part des revenus de Google Segment imputable à la publicité était de 70 383 000 000 dollars, soit 88,73% des revenus de Google Segment.

2 « Google Search Statistics – Internet Live Stats », Internet Live Stats, 20 septembre 2017 ; Greg Sterling, « Data : Google Monthly Search Volume Dwarfs Rivals Because of Mobile Advantage », *Search Engine Land*, 9 février 2017. Ce qui correspond à 76% des recherches sur ordinateur fixe et 96% des recherches sur appareils mobiles aux États-Unis ; pourcentages qui s'établissent respectivement à 87 et à 95 pour le monde entier.

3 Roben Farzad, « Google at $400 Billion: A New No 2 in Market Cap », *BusinessWeek*, 12 février 2014.

4 « Largest Companies by Market Cap Today », *Dogs of the Dow*, 2017.

5 Jean-Charles Rochet et Jean Tirole, « Two-Sided Markets: A Progress Report », *RAND Journal of Economics* 37, n° 3, 2006, p. 645-667.

6 Pour une discussion sur ce point et son rapport avec la publicité ciblée sur Internet, voir Katherine J. Strandburg, « Free Fall: The Online Market's Consumer Preference Disconnect », document de travail, New York University Law and Economics, 1er octobre 2013.

7 Kevin Kelly, « The Three Breakthroughs that Have Finally Unleashed AI on the World », *Wired*, 27 octobre 2014.

8 Xiaoliang Ling et al., « Model Ensemble for Click Prediction in Bing

Search Ads », dans *Proceedings of the 26th International Conference on World Wide Web Companion*, p. 689-698.

9 Ruoxi Wang et al., « Deep & Cross Network for Ad Click Predictions », *ArXiv:1708.05123 [Computer Science. Learning]*, 16 août 2017.

10 Karl Polanyi, *La Grande Transformation. Aux origines politiques et économiques de notre temps*, trad. Maurice Angeno et Catherine Malamoud, Gallimard, coll. Tel, 2009.

11 Ellen Meiksins Wood, *L'Origine du capitalisme*, trad. François Tétreau, Lux, coll. Humanités, 2009.

THE TWITTERING MACHINE

Richard Seymour

Addiction is all about attention. For the social industry bosses, this is axiomatic. We attend to what feels good, to 'rewards'. And, in an attention economy, the social industry platforms are waging a constant battle to manipulate our attention in real time.

Facebook's founding president Sean Parker echoed a raft of research in claiming that social media platforms achieve this by exploiting the craving for a 'dopamine hit'. Their machinery generates regular hits in the form of 'likes', with flashing red notifications administering the same high that a slot-machine addict gets when three bells line up. The anthropologist Natasha Dow Schüll argues, based on her study of gambling, that once these unnaturally large dopamine rewards flood into the brain, 'we lose our willpower'. Our brains, not prepared by evolution for such a flood, 'become overwhelmed and screwed up'. Nora Volkow, director of the US National Institute on Drug Abuse, insists: 'Addiction is all about the dopamine'.

And, whether or not the theory is true, techniques based on the dopamine theory seem to work. Adam Alter, a psychologist who studies online addiction, has sifted through the data collected by the app Moment, which tracks smartphone usage. Some eighty-eight per cent of users spent 'an average of a quarter of their waking lives on their phones'. His own data showed, to his astonishment, that he had spent three hours a day on his phone, picking it up an average of forty times a day. And his behaviour may be relatively moderate: a 2013 study found that the average user checks their phone 150 times a day, which other research suggests includes 2,617 touches, taps or swipes. One recent survey even found that one in ten users has checked their phone during sex. But for Alter, as for most of us, the bait was so subtle and seductive that the catch didn't even notice his mouth clamping around the hook.

Not everyone accepts the dopamine consensus, however. Marc Lewis, a former heroin addict and neuroscientist, has written movingly about his own escape from addiction, and contributed enormously to the science of addiction. In his book, *The Biology of Desire*, he argues that addiction is not about taking this or that substance. It is the 'motivated repetition' of a thought or behaviour. The thought or behaviour might initially be motivated by the prospect of a high, or by the wish to avoid depression. But once it has been repeated often enough, it acquires its own motivation.

This is possible, Lewis says, because of the way the brain works. The billions upon billions of nerve cells that organise thoughts and emotions undergo constant change. Cells die, new cells are born. Some synapses become more efficient through practice, enabling better connections, others less so. By repeating a thought or a behaviour, we ensure the synapses and cells associated with it flourish, while underused cells die or become less effective. We change the 'brain's wiring', the 'neural circuitry' of wanting. The more we repeat an action, the more we train our brains for further repetition. We create an attention tunnel. As Lewis puts it, 'what fires together, wires together'.

At another level, that of meaning, one could say that addiction is a thwarted form of love. It is a passionate attachment to something that, slowly, occupies a larger and larger part of one's mind. It exercises a veto over other loves, aspirations and dreams. It occupies attention, when attention is subject to economic scarcity. It usurps our ingenuity, when the goal in life becomes maintaining access to the object, staying close to it. For the Twittering Machine, this is good: it keeps us writing. In an attention economy, addiction is not so much a scourge as a mode of production.

Anything that so captures our attention must be the object of intense fantasies. In the history of junkie literature, for example, drugs are magical, fairy-tale objects, summoning abundance from nothing, defying the laws of physics. Or so it seems at first. Thomas De Quincey's famous *Confessions of an English Opium-Eater*, for example, stands out for its utopian air. With the first hit, he had discovered 'the secret of happiness', 'a resurrection, from the lowest depth', an 'abyss of divine enjoyment', 'an apocalypse of the world within', 'portable ecstasies ... corked up in a pint bottle'. He had discovered the magic beans, the goose that laid the golden egg, the flax spun into gold: emotional plenitude. A bounty comparable only to the oceanic bliss in pursuit of which mystics of all faiths have undergone extraordinary physical and mental rigours.

As the high diminishes, however, the fantasies become darker. When the Catholic mystic and poet Francis Thompson sang of 'The Poppy', the source of his 'withered dreams', it was as though he had become a hapless husk for the magical substance:

> The sleep-flower sways in the wheat its head,
> Heavy with dreams, as that with bread.
> [...]
> I hang 'mid men my needless head,
> And my fruit is dreams, as theirs is bread.
> [...]
> Love! I fall into the claws of Time:
> But lasts within a leavèd rhyme
> All that the world of me esteems –
> My wither'd dreams, my wither'd dreams.

His head, the actual source of his dreams, was, just like the flower, a 'needless' drooping cocoon for the opium. He credited his remaining creative power to the drug. Addicts tend to *fetishise* the object of their addiction. They attribute to it their own agency and imagine that it holds great powers that it really doesn't. At the same time, they suffer a profound subjective impoverishment: the addict is as poor as the object is rich.

The Twittering Machine appears to have a similar magical quality. Technology has never been just technology. It is always a world of intense emotional attachments. The Twittering Machine promises to give us access to everything, limitlessly, allowing us to transcend the limitations of mere flesh. This is how the telecommunications firm, MCI, sold the internet two decades ago. People could communicate 'mind to mind'. No race, no gender, no age, no infirmity. 'There are only minds', the advertising breathlessly suggested. 'Utopia? No ... The internet. Where minds, doors and lives open up'. This was digital Clintonism, a kind of thin liberal utopianism. Standing in a weak shadow of the opiate sublime, it promised an abundance of being, ageless immortality, protean plasticity beyond the bedrock of the body. The name of this abundance was *connectivity*, a truly magical substance.

The social platforms give concentrated expression to this idea, turning it into a business model and raison d'être. Facebook's first video advertisement reminded us that the universe 'is vast and dark and makes us wonder if we are alone'. We build connections, it said, to 'remind ourselves that we are not'. Connection was the basis for 'a great nation', 'something people build so they can have a place where they belong'. By implication, the platforms would be nation-builders, through the power of connectivity. At the outset of the 'Twitter revolutions', this same magical substance was supposed to outflank the old regimes and engender democratic upheaval.

But as the cyberpunk writer Bruce Sterling points out, connectivity is not necessarily a symbol of affluence and plenty. It is, in a sense, the poor who most prize connectivity. Not in the sense of the old classist stereotype that 'the poor love their cellphones': no powerful group would turn down the opportunities that smartphones and social media offer. The powerful simply engage differently with the machine. But any culture that values connectivity so highly must be as impoverished in its social life as a culture obsessed with happiness is bitterly depressed. What Bruce Alexander calls the state of permanent 'psychosocial dislocation' in late capitalism, with life overrun by the law of markets and competition, is the context for soaring addiction rates. It is as if the addictive relationship stands in for the social relationships that have been upended by the turbulence of capitalism.

The nature of this social poverty can be recognised in a situation typical of a social industry addict. We often use our smartphones to take us away from a social situation, *without actually leaving that situation*. It is as though we are both lonely and threatened by intimacy. We develop ways of simulating conversational awareness while attending to our phones, a technique known as 'phubbing'. We experience this weirdly detached 'uniform distancelessness', as Christopher Bollas calls it. We become nodes in the network, equivalent to 'smart' devices, mere points of relay for fragments of information; as much extensions of the tablet or smartphone as they are of us. We prefer the machine when human relationships have become disappointing.

THE TWITTERING MACHINE [LA MACHINE À TWEETER]
Richard Seymour

La dépendance est avant tout affaire d'attention. Pour les patrons de l'industrie des réseaux sociaux, c'est là un axiome. Nous accordons notre attention à ce qui est agréable, aux « récompenses ». Et dans l'économie de l'attention, les plateformes sociales mènent un combat de tous les instants pour manipuler notre attention en temps réel.

Le président fondateur de Facebook, Sean Parker, s'est fait l'écho de toute une volée d'études en déclarant que pour parvenir à leurs fins les plateformes sociales exploitaient notre envie irrépressible de « shots de dopamine ». Leurs machines dispensent des doses régulières sous la forme de *likes*, le clignotement des notifications ayant un effet similaire à celui que ressent un joueur accro aux machines à sous quand trois cloches s'alignent. En s'appuyant sur les résultats de son étude sur le jeu, l'anthropologue Natasha Dow Schüll soutient que lorsque ces récompenses – des quantités anormalement élevées de dopamine – inondent le cerveau, « nous perdons toute volonté ». Le cerveau, que l'évolution n'a pas préparé à une telle inondation, « est dépassé et complètement détraqué ». Nora Volkow, directrice du National Institute on Drug Abuse aux États-Unis, abonde dans ce sens : « L'addiction repose avant tout sur la dopamine. »

Que cette hypothèse se vérifie ou non, les techniques dérivées de la théorie de la dopamine semblent fonctionner. Adam Alter, psychologue spécialiste de la cyberdépendance, a passé au crible les données collectées par l'application Moment, qui permet un suivi du temps passé sur un smartphone. Près de 88% des utilisateurs restaient « en moyenne un quart de leur temps d'éveil sur leur téléphone ». À son grand étonnement, les chiffres sur sa propre utilisation indiquaient qu'il avait passé trois heures par jour sur son téléphone et l'avait pris en main en moyenne quarante fois. Mais il faut croire que son comportement est plutôt mesuré : une étude de 2013 a ainsi révélé que l'utilisateur moyen consulte son téléphone 150 fois par jour, ce qui, selon d'autres études, implique 2 617 touchers, pressions ou balayages. Une enquête récente a même montré qu'un utilisateur sur dix avait consulté son téléphone lors d'un rapport sexuel. Mais dans le cas d'Alter, comme pour la plupart d'entre nous, l'appât était si subtil et alléchant que la proie n'a même pas remarqué quand sa gueule s'est refermée sur l'hameçon.

Cependant, tout le monde n'adhère pas à l'hypothèse de la dopamine. Marc Lewis, ancien héroïnomane et neuroscientifique qui décrit de manière émouvante comment il a vaincu sa propre dépendance, a énormément contribué à faire avancer les connaissances sur l'addiction. Dans son livre *The Biology of Desire* [La Biologie du désir], il affirme que la dépendance ne consiste pas à abuser de telle ou telle substance. Il s'agit de la « répétition motivée » d'une pensée ou d'un comportement donnés. Cette pensée ou ce comportement peuvent initialement être motivés par la perspective du sentiment d'euphorie ressenti lors d'un trip, ou par le désir d'éviter la dépression. Mais lorsqu'ils sont répétés assez souvent, ils acquièrent leur propre motivation.

Ceci est possible, selon Lewis, en raison de la façon dont fonctionne le cerveau. Les milliards de cellules nerveuses qui organisent nos pensées et nos émotions se transforment sans cesse. Les cellules meurent, de nouvelles cellules naissent. Certaines synapses deviennent plus efficaces à force de répétitions et permettent de meilleures connexions, d'autres moins. En répétant une pensée ou un comportement, nous faisons en sorte que les synapses et les cellules qui leur sont associées s'épanouissent, tandis que les cellules sous-utilisées meurent ou perdent de leur efficacité. Nous modifions le « câblage du cerveau », le « circuit neuronal » du désir. Plus nous répétons une action, plus nous entraînons le cerveau à être réceptif à la répétition. Nous ne portons plus notre attention que sur un nombre très limité de choses. Comme l'écrit Lewis, « ce qui se déclenche ensemble s'enclenche ensemble ».

À un autre niveau, celui du sens, on pourrait dire que la dépendance est une forme d'amour contrarié. C'est un attachement passionnel à quelque chose qui, progressivement, occupe une place grandissante dans notre cerveau. Il exerce un droit de veto sur d'autres amours, désirs et rêves. Il occupe l'attention alors que l'attention est une denrée rare. Il usurpe notre ingéniosité lorsque le but de la vie est de s'assurer l'accès à l'objet, de rester proche de lui. Cette caractéristique arrange bien les affaires de la « Machine à tweeter » [*The Twittering Machine*[1]], puisque c'est elle qui nous pousse à écrire. Dans l'économie de l'attention, la dépendance n'est pas tant un fléau qu'un mode de production.

Quelque chose qui capte notre attention à ce point doit faire l'objet de fantasmes intenses. Dans l'histoire de la littérature junkie, par exemple, les drogues sont des objets magiques tout droit sortis d'un conte de fées, qui créent de l'abondance à partir de rien en défiant les lois de la physique. Ou, du moins, c'est ce qui semble à première vue. Les célèbres *Confessions d'un mangeur d'opium anglais* de Thomas De Quincey, par exemple, se distinguent par leurs airs utopiques. À la première prise de drogue, l'auteur découvre « le secret du bonheur », une « surrection de l'esprit intérieur du tréfonds de ses abîmes », un « abîme de plaisirs divins », une « apocalypse du monde que je portais en moi », « des extases portatives... bouchées en bouteilles d'une pinte[2] ». Il découvre les haricots magiques, la poule aux œufs d'or, le moyen de changer la paille de lin en or : bref, la plénitude émotionnelle. Une abondance comparable tout au plus au sentiment de béatitude absolue, dans la poursuite duquel les mystiques de toutes confessions ont affronté de prodigieuses rigueurs physiques et mentales.

Mais au fur et à mesure que l'euphorie s'évanouit, les fantasmes s'assombrissent. Lorsque le mystique et poète catholique Francis Thompson chante « Le Coquelicot » comme source de ses « rêves flétris », on dirait qu'il n'est plus qu'une malheureuse cosse vide en attente de la substance magique :

> La fleur de sommeil, dans le froment, hoche la tête,
> Lourde de rêves, comme il est lourd de pain ;
> [...]
> Parmi les hommes je porte ma tête inutile,
> Et mon fruit est de rêves comme le leur est de pain :
> [...]
> Mon amour ! Je tomberai, moi, dans les griffes du Temps :
> Mais il restera parmi les feuilles de ces rimes
> Tout ce que le monde estimera de moi,
> Mes rêves flétris, mes rêves flétris[3].

À l'image de la fleur, sa tête, véritable source de ses rêves, n'était qu'un cocon « inutile » et affaissé en attente d'opium. Il a attribué à la drogue ce qui restait de sa force créatrice. Les toxicomanes ont tendance à *fétichiser* l'objet de leur dépendance. Ils lui attribuent leur propre pouvoir et une influence qu'il ne possède pas. En même temps, ils souffrent d'un profond appauvrissement subjectif : plus l'objet est riche, plus le toxicomane est pauvre.

La Machine à tweeter semble posséder une qualité magique similaire. La technologie ne s'est jamais suffi d'elle-même. C'est toujours un monde fait d'intenses attaches émotionnelles. La Machine à tweeter promet de nous donner accès à tout, sans limites, de nous permettre de transcender les limites de la simple chair. C'est sous cet angle que la société de télécommunications MCI fit la publicité d'Internet il y a une vingtaine d'années. Les individus pourraient communiquer « d'esprit à esprit ». Pas de race, pas de sexe, pas d'âge, pas d'infirmité. « Il n'y a que des esprits », s'époumonait la publicité. « Une utopie ? Non… Internet. Là où s'ouvrent les esprits, les portes et les vies. » C'était du clintonisme numérique, une sorte d'utopisme libéral allégé. Tapi dans l'ombre ténue du sublime opiacé, il promettait une abondance d'existence, une immortalité sans âge, une plasticité protéiforme au-delà du substrat physique du corps. Cette abondance avait pour nom la *connectivité*, une substance véritablement magique.

Les réseaux sociaux sont un concentré de cette idée, qu'ils transforment en un modèle commercial et une raison d'être. La première publicité vidéo de Facebook nous rappela que l'univers « est vaste et sombre et nous incite à nous demander si nous sommes seuls » ; si nous nous connectons à d'autres, c'est pour « nous rappeler que nous ne le sommes pas ». La connexion allait devenir le fondement d'une « grande nation », « quelque chose que les gens construisent pour avoir leur place à eux ». Ceci impliquait que les réseaux sociaux étaient des bâtisseurs de nations, grâce au pouvoir de la connectivité. Au début des « révolutions Twitter », cette même substance magique était censée nous débarrasser des anciens régimes et engendrer des bouleversements démocratiques.

Mais comme le souligne l'écrivain cyberpunk Bruce Sterling, la connectivité n'est pas nécessairement un symbole de richesse et d'abondance. D'une certaine manière, ce sont les pauvres qui tiennent le plus à la connectivité. Non pas au sens du vieux stéréotype classiste selon lequel « les pauvres aiment leurs téléphones portables » : aucun groupe social puissant ne renoncerait aux possibilités offertes par les smartphones et les réseaux sociaux ; simplement, les puissants interagissent différemment avec la machine. Mais toute culture qui attache autant d'importance à la connectivité doit être en proie à un appauvrissement de la vie sociale, de la même manière qu'une culture obsédée par le bonheur sera forcément amère et déprimée. C'est dans le contexte de ce que Bruce Alexander qualifie d'état de « dislocation psychosociale » permanente dans le capitalisme tardif, où la vie est régie par les lois du marché et de la concurrence, que s'inscrit la flambée des taux de dépendance – comme si celle-ci se substituait aux relations sociales chamboulées par les turbulences du capitalisme.

La nature de cet appauvrissement social se manifeste dans la situation type de la dépendance aux réseaux sociaux. Nous utilisons volontiers le smartphone pour nous tenir à l'écart d'une situation sociale, *sans pour autant quitter cette situation*. C'est comme si nous étions à la fois seuls et menacés par l'intimité. Nous développons des astuces pour faire semblant de prêter attention à une conversation tout en consultant notre téléphone, une technique connue sous le nom de *phubbing*[4]. Nous faisons l'expérience d'une « absence de distance uniforme » étrangement détachée, comme l'explique Christopher Bollas. Nous devenons des nœuds dans le réseau, équivalents à des appareils « intelligents », de simples points de relais pour des fragments d'information ; des extensions de la tablette ou du smartphone autant que ceux-ci sont des extensions de nous-mêmes. Nous préférons la machine à la déception des rapports humains.

1 Le titre anglais de l'ouvrage de Richard Seymour, *The Twittering Machine*, reprend la traduction anglaise du titre d'une œuvre de Paul Klee, *Die Zwitscher-Maschine* (1922), communément appelée *La Machine à gazouiller* en français. Il évoque à la fois le « gazouillis » (*tweet*) des utilisateurs des réseaux sociaux et les incessants signaux sonores émis par nos smartphones. Pour rester au plus près du raisonnement déployé par l'auteur, nous avons choisi de traduire par *La Machine à tweeter*.

2 Thomas De Quincey, *Les Confessions d'un mangeur d'opium anglais* [1822], trad. Pierre Leyris, Gallimard, Paris, 1990, p. 93.

3 Traduction citée dans Pierre Danchin, *Francis Thompson. La vie et l'œuvre d'un poète*, Faculté des lettres, Université de Paris, Paris, 1955.

4 Mot-valise anglais formé à partir de *phone* [téléphone] et de *snubbing* [« snober » ou « ignorer »].

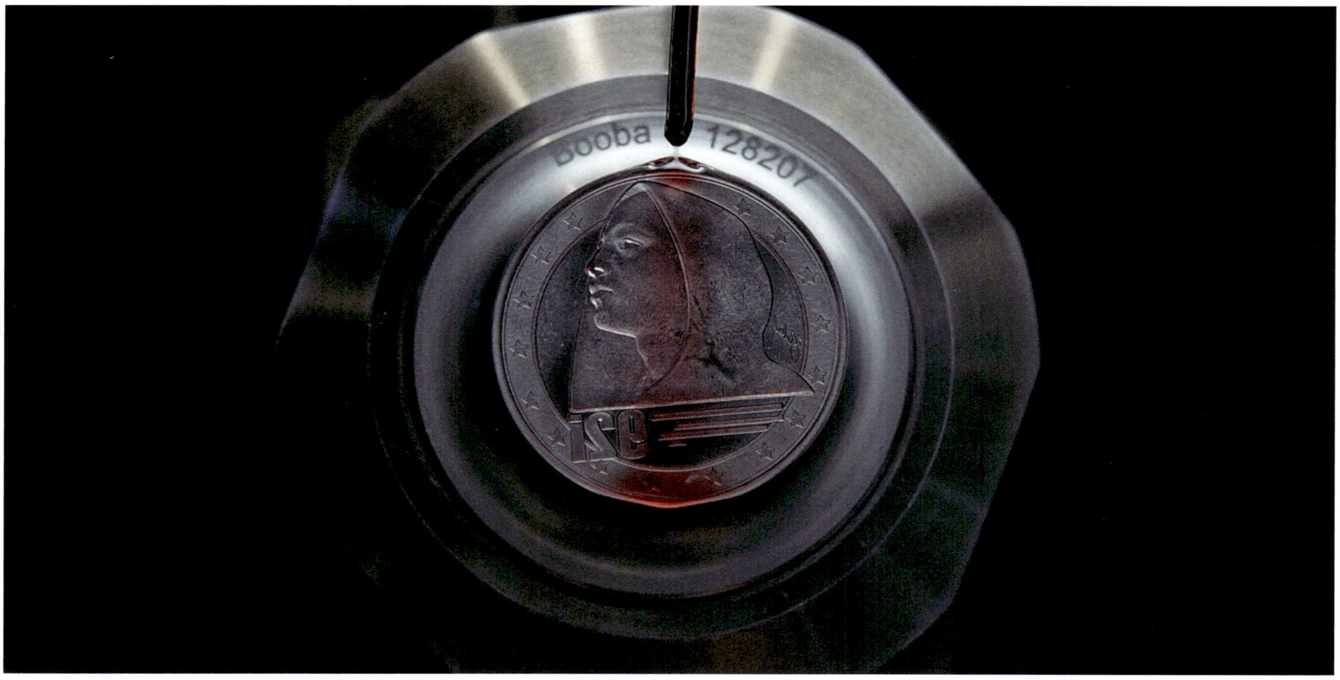

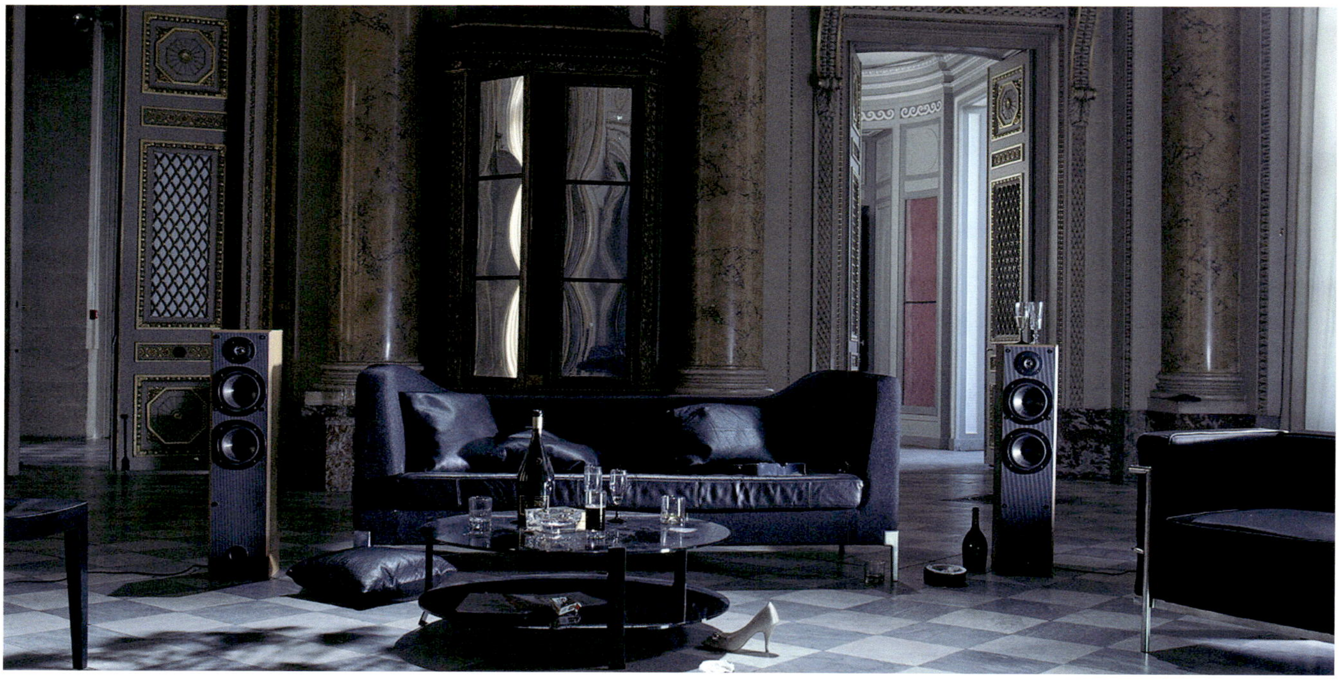

Film stills from Mohamed Bourouissa, *All-In*, 2012

Mohamed Bourouissa

Mohamed Bourouissa's film *All-in* (2012) playfully appropriates the genre of the music video to question symbols of power and capitalism.

The video shows the different stages of production of a coin bearing the likeness of the French rapper Booba. His song 'Foetus', which recounts his life story, forms the soundtrack to the work. Its narrative describes his ascendency from '*petit lionceau*' [lion cub] to 'Black entrepreneur', alluding to his struggle as a Black man born and raised in France. The rapper's rhythmic delivery and antagonistic language synchronises with the movements of the coin minting machine at the Monnaie de Paris factory in Pessac, in the southwestern part of France, where euros are manufactured. Shots of the factory offer a glimpse into the intricacies of our global economy via its industrial architecture.

Bourouissa splices this footage with images of the lavish interiors of the Monnaie de Paris headquarters on the Quai de Conti in Paris, creating a contrast between symbols of institutional power and the street culture that permeates his work. By placing Booba's image on a coin – a symbol of state sovereignty – the artist upends hierarchical tradition, elevating a figure from popular culture to the status of a national icon.

The sleek aesthetic of *All-in* recalls the mainstream, commercial appeal of rap videos, supporting the claim in Booba's lyrics that money is the way to power in capitalist society. The video's title, a reference drawn from the card game poker, alludes to this: in the absence of privilege or family wealth, one must be willing to take risks in order to 'win'. When he proudly recounts his past as a drug dealer, the rapper implies that circumventing the rules is sometimes necessary to pave one's way. Economic power

Dans la vidéo *All-in* (2012), Mohamed Bourouissa emprunte et joue avec les codes du clip musical pour questionner les symboles du pouvoir et du capitalisme.

La vidéo suit les différentes étapes de la confection d'une pièce de monnaie à l'effigie du rappeur français Booba, au son de son morceau « Fœtus », qui retrace sa vie. Le récit de son ascension sociale, de « petit lionceau » à « *black entrepreneur* », évoque aussi les obstacles auxquels il a dû faire face en évoluant en France en tant qu'homme noir. La diction rythmée et le lexique belliqueux du rappeur s'accordent avec la chorégraphie de la machine gravant la pièce, filmée à l'usine de production de la Monnaie de Paris à Pessac, en Gironde, où les euros sont fabriqués. Les vues de l'architecture industrielle imposante de l'usine et de ses entrepôts sont une plongée dans les arcanes de notre économie mondialisée.

Entrecoupant ces séquences d'images des intérieurs fastueux du siège historique de la Monnaie de Paris, situé quai de Conti à Paris, Mohamed Bourouissa met en tension les symboles du pouvoir institutionnel et la culture *street*, qui imprègne son travail. En apposant le visage de Booba sur une pièce de monnaie, symbole de la souveraineté de l'État, l'artiste élève une icône populaire au rang de figure nationale et défie ainsi une certaine tradition hiérarchique.

L'esthétique léchée de la photographie de *All-in* rappelle les clips de rap et leur portée commerciale. Comme les paroles de la chanson de Booba le suggèrent, l'argent est, dans notre société capitaliste, la voie d'accès au pouvoir. Le titre de la vidéo y fait référence, en invoquant le vocabulaire du poker : en l'absence de privilège ou de patrimoine, il s'agit de prendre des risques pour « gagner ». Lorsqu'il souligne avec fierté son passé de dealer, le

relations and the way they intersect with racial and social issues are recurrent subjects in Bourouissa's work.

In the last scene, shot in a *salon* of the Monnaie de Paris, coins rain down in slow motion onto the remains of a party, ostentatiously symbolising a cultural clash between the subculture of rap and the dominance of state authority. Two seemingly antithetical worlds, united under capitalism, bound by money.

Mohamed Bourouissa was born in 1978 in Blida, Algeria. He lives and works in Gennevilliers and Pantin, France.

rappeur sous-entend que contourner les règles est parfois nécessaire pour tracer sa voie. Les rapports de force économiques et leur intersection avec les questions raciales et sociales sont ainsi un sujet récurrent dans l'œuvre de Mohamed Bourouissa.

Dans la dernière scène, une pluie de pièces s'abat au ralenti sur les restes d'une fête dans un salon de la Monnaie de Paris, donnant à voir avec éclat le choc culturel entre le monde du rap et celui, dominant, de l'autorité étatique. Deux milieux que tout semble séparer, mais qui sont unis, sous les auspices du capitalisme, par l'argent.

Mohamed Bourouissa est né en 1978 à Blida, en Algérie. Il vit et travaille à Gennevilliers et Pantin, en France.

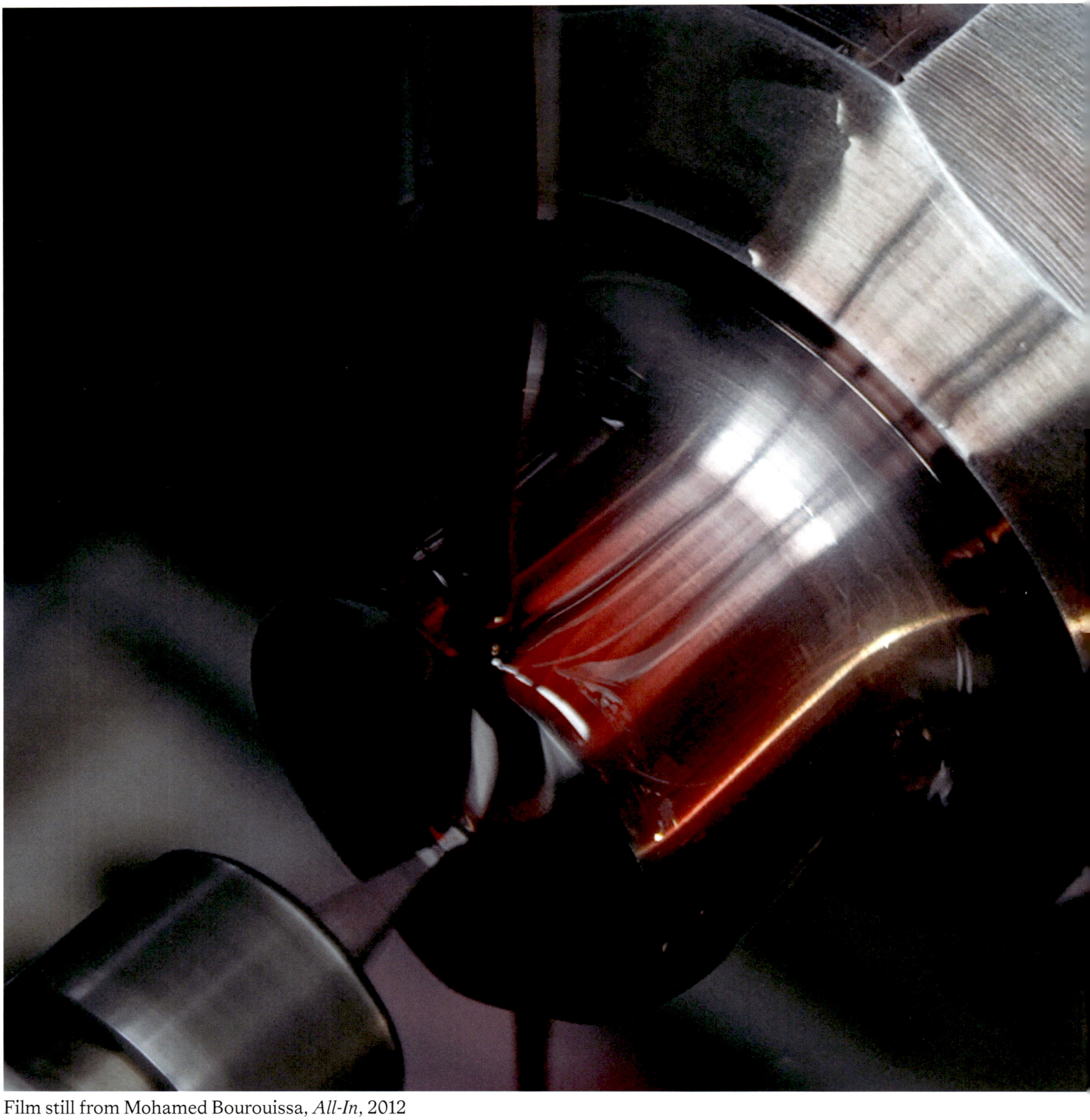

Film still from Mohamed Bourouissa, *All-In*, 2012

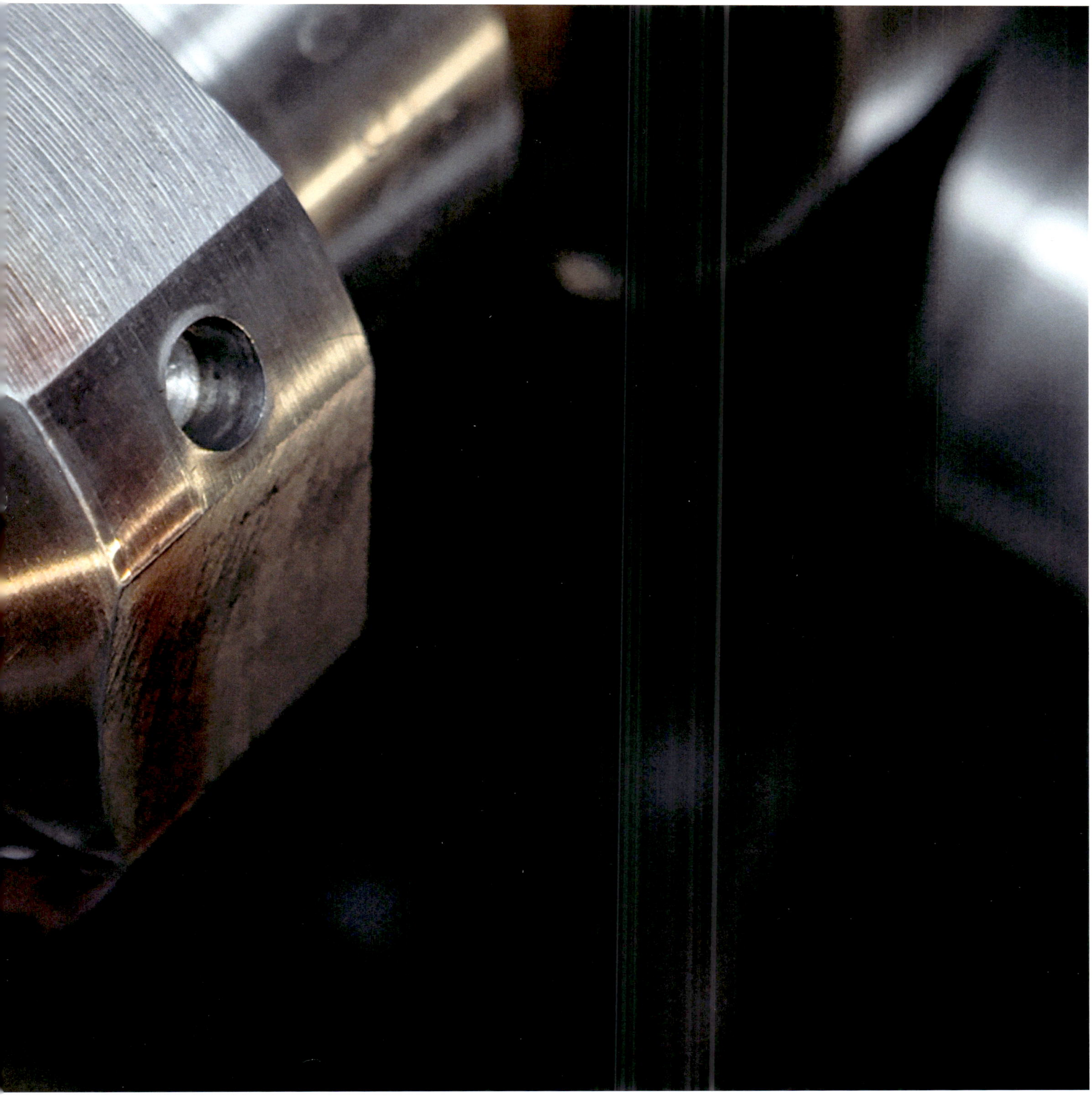

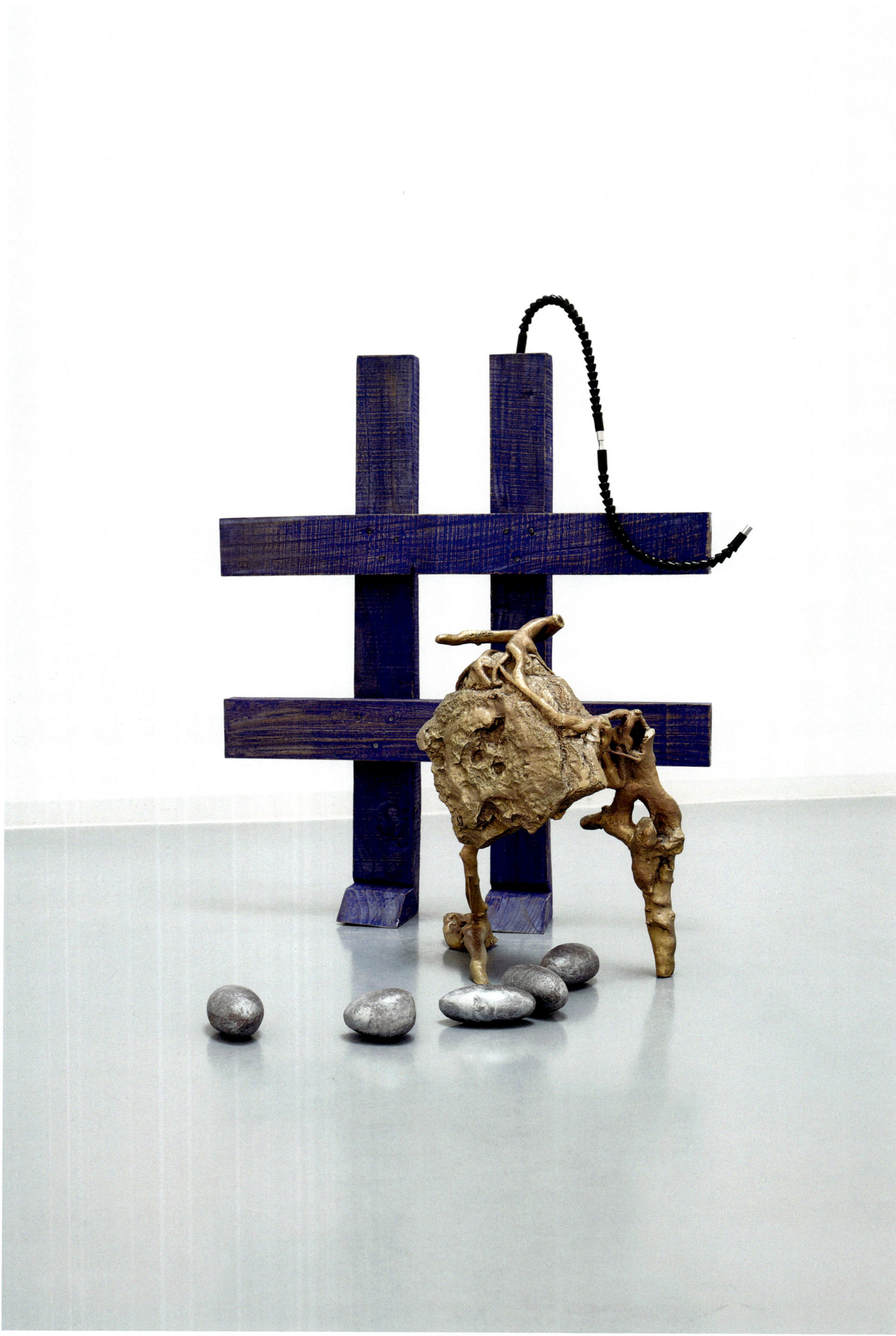

Guan Xiao, *Chicken House,* 2019

Guan Xiao

'Agriculture is the most sci-fi of things to me... The more that we think about the future, and manufacture the so-called civilised world, the further we distance ourselves from nature, the land and ourselves'.[1]

« L'agriculture est à mes yeux ce qui relève le plus de la science-fiction. […] Plus nous pensons à l'avenir, plus nous fabriquons le monde dit civilisé, plus nous nous éloignons de la nature, de la terre et de nous-mêmes[1]. »

Guan Xiao's expansive installations and sculptural assemblages combine readymade and crafted elements, often assimilating traditional media or artisanal techniques within works that are designed on the computer and produced with the aid of digital models and technologies such as 3D printing. Her work negotiates the disjuncture between the physical world of objects and the virtual experience on screen.

The Daughter of Tree; *Chicken House* and *A Sinking Blue Field* (all 2019) belong to a series of works inspired by industrial agriculture and the application of science and technology to intervene in natural processes. Each of these anthropomorphic works is organised around a bronze cast of a tree root, a reference to the ancient Chinese tradition of carving and polishing roots for ornamental purposes. Guan Xiao has described the twisted and gnarled wooden forms as representing a 'perfect' sculptural object: readymade, natural entities, shaped by their genetic and environmental conditions. Appended to these casts are lengths of dyed rope and a combination of mass-produced found objects and abstract graphic characters cast in fibreglass.

Stretching out over the floor or extending upwards, antenna-like, into space, they imply an idea of transmission or communication, with one another and with the viewer. This theme is underpinned by a selection of objects that serve visual or aural senses: for instance, microphones,

Les vastes installations et assemblages sculpturaux réalisés par Guan Xiao mêlent *ready-mades* et éléments fabriqués, en intégrant souvent des mediums traditionnels ou des techniques artisanales à des œuvres conçues par ordinateur et produites à l'aide de modèles et technologies numériques tels que l'impression 3D. Son œuvre traite de la disjonction entre le monde physique des objets et l'expérience virtuelle sur écran.

The Daughter of Tree [La fille de l'arbre], *Chicken House* [Poulailler] et *A Sinking Blue Field* [Un champ bleu qui sombre] (toutes réalisées en 2019) s'inscrivent dans une série d'œuvres inspirées de l'agriculture industrielle et de l'utilisation de la science et de la technologie dans le but d'intervenir sur des processus naturels. Chacune de ces œuvres anthropomorphiques est agencée autour du moulage en bronze de la racine d'un arbre, référence à une très ancienne tradition chinoise consistant à sculpter et à polir des racines à des fins ornementales. Selon Guan Xiao, ces formes en bois tordues et noueuses représentent un objet sculptural « parfait » : des entités naturelles préexistantes, façonnées par leurs propres conditions génétiques et environnementales. Elle ajoute à ces moulages des morceaux de cordes teintes, mais aussi un mélange d'objets produits en masse qu'elle glâne et de caractères graphiques abstraits en fibre de verre.

S'étendant au sol ou s'étirant vers le haut comme des antennes à travers l'espace, ces éléments suggèrent la

LED reading lamps or camera equipment such as tripods. Other objects make visual analogies, such as the paper parasol perched on top of *The Daughter of Tree*, which resembles a satellite dish. Iconographic fibreglass elements are strewn like discarded graphic design characters, recalling contemporary logos or familiar symbols (such as #). Despite their material and process of fabrication (they are modelled on a computer and cast from a 3D-printed mould), these elements are often based upon ancient artefacts, such as ornamental clasps, amulets, weaponry or tools.

Moving back and forth between ancient crafts and contemporary modes of production; traditional Chinese cultural symbols and the products of global capitalism; Guan Xiao's sculptures can also be seen to reflect upon the transition from an agrarian to a high-tech manufacturing economy.

Guan Xiao was born in 1983 in Chongqing China. She lives and works in Beijing, China.

1 Guan Xiao, quote from the exhibition text for *Products Farming*, 2 February–20 April 2019, Bonner Kunstverein, Bonn.

transmission ou la communication, les uns avec les autres et avec les visiteurs. Ce thème est sous-tendu par une sélection d'objets mis au service des sens de la vue ou de l'ouïe, tels que des micros, des lampes de lecture à LED ou des trépieds pour caméra. D'autres objets établissent des analogies visuelles, comme ce parasol en papier placé au sommet de *The Daughter of Tree*, qui s'apparente à une antenne satellite. Les éléments iconographiques en fibre de verre, dispersés comme des caractères graphiques abandonnés, rappellent les logos contemporains ou des symboles familiers (tels que « # »). Malgré les matériaux qui les composent et leur processus de fabrication (ils sont modélisés par ordinateur et produits à partir d'un moule imprimé en 3D), ces éléments s'inspirent souvent d'artefacts anciens – fermoirs ornementaux, amulettes, armes ou outils.

Oscillant entre artisanats anciens et modes de production contemporains, entre symboles traditionnels de la culture chinoise et produits du capitalisme global, les sculptures de Guan Xiao peuvent aussi évoquer une réflexion sur la transition d'une économie agraire à une économie de manufacture de pointe.

Guan Xiao est née en 1983 à Chongqing, en Chine. Elle vit et travaille à Pékin, en Chine.

1 Guan Xiao, citation du texte de présentation de l'exposition *Products Farming*, 2 février–20 avril 2019, Bonner Kunstverein, Bonn.

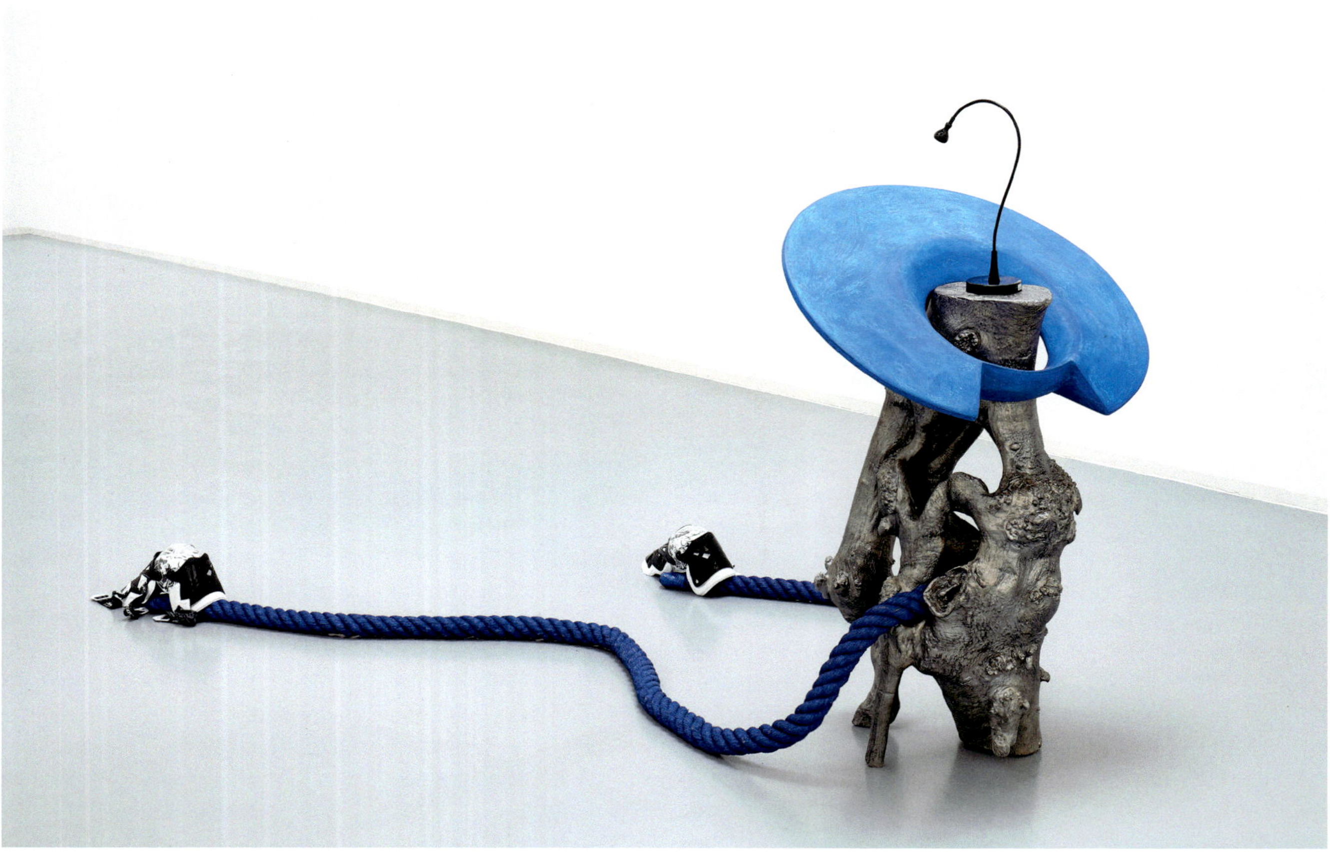

Guan Xiao, *A Sinking Blue Field*, 2019

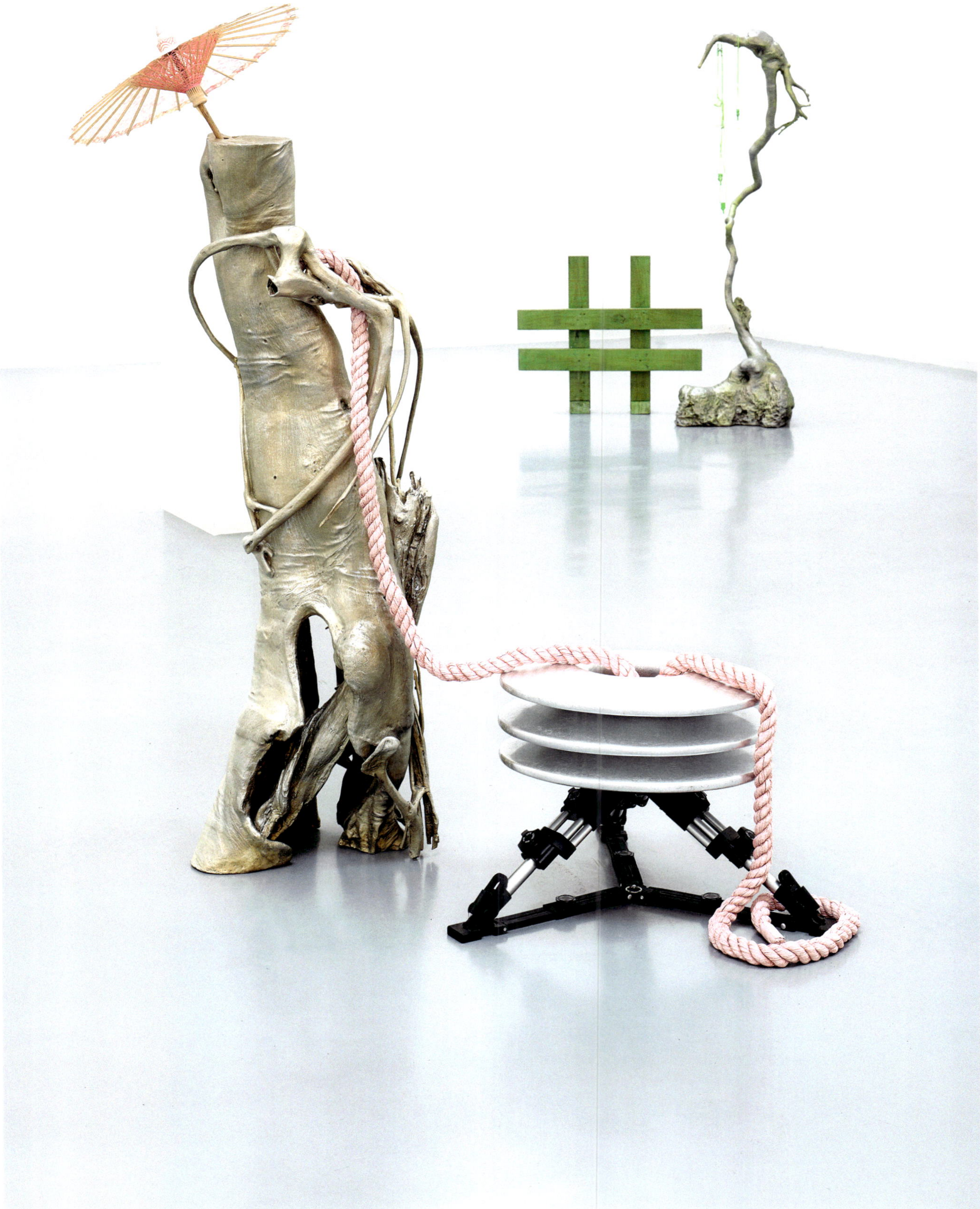

Guan Xiao, *The Daughter of Tree,* 2019 (installation view)

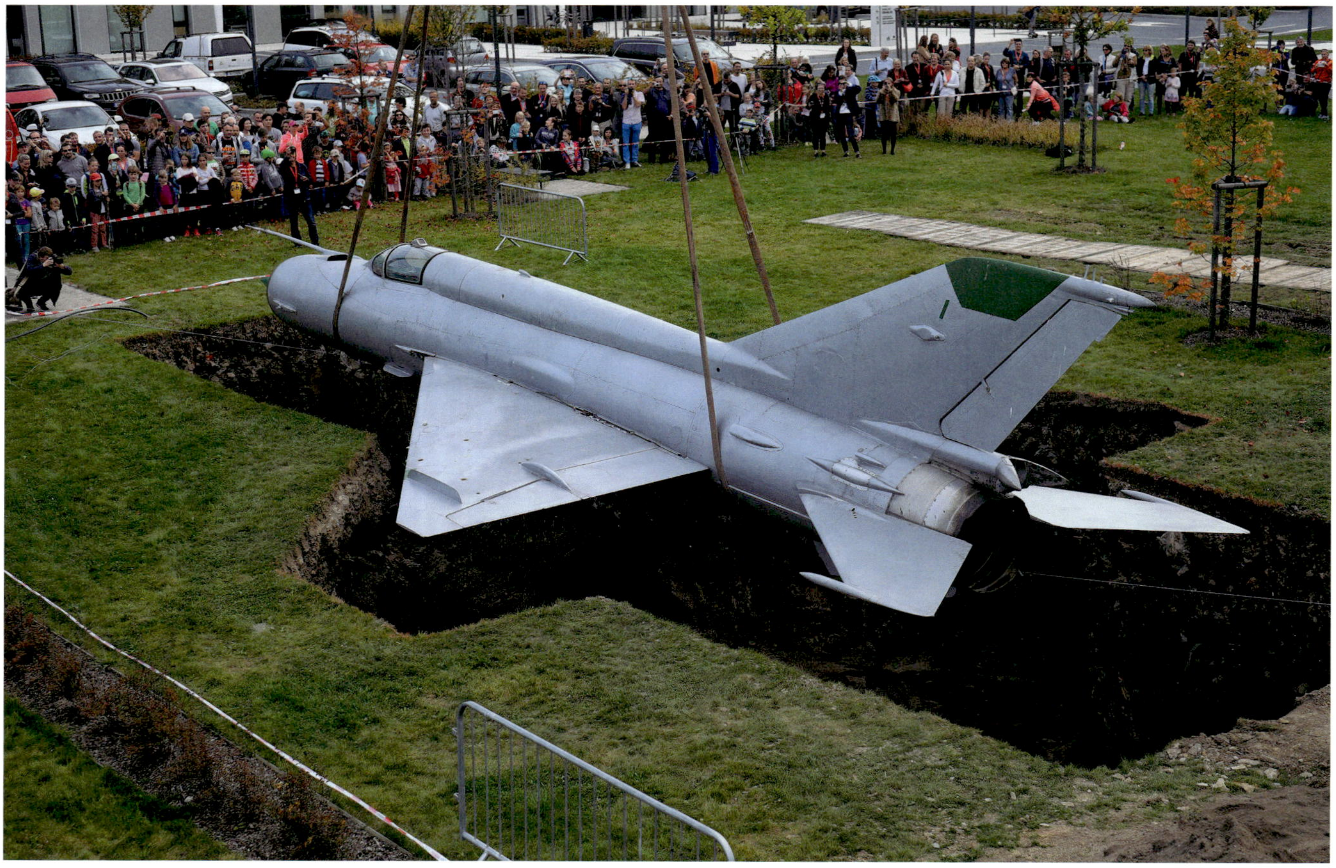

Roger Hiorns, *The retrospective view of the pathway,* 2017–ongoing

Roger Hiorns

The retrospective view of the pathway (2017–ongoing) is a large-scale installation by Roger Hiorns. It employs a Soviet-made MiG-21 jet plane that the artist previously buried in Prague as a temporary public artwork. At Mudam, this history is present in the layers of dirt, dents and rust that cover the surface of the 16-metre-long aircraft, installed in the Great Hall on the ground floor of the museum. Hiorns' choice of plane is highly significant: in service since the early 1960s, it is the most-produced supersonic jet aircraft in aviation history. An object that Hiorns has referred to as 'a piece of discarded power', the MiG-21 is seen by many as an icon of the Cold War.

The work is part of an ongoing project that has seen Hiorns bury a number of planes at various locations across Europe, including sites in the UK and The Netherlands. Beginning with a single aircraft, it has evolved into an international network of subterranean planes. 'It's got something to do with taking something out of the air, and putting it under the skin of the land',[1] he has said of the burials, which he sees as a 'proposal' for the 'next stage' of an aircraft's life. As a piece of global technology and a symbol of power, the MiG-21 and its burial can also be seen to refer to the often-unseen global systems, both political and economic, that structure our day-to-day lives.

Exhumed and displaced in the museum, the aircraft is supplemented by a 'digestive system' comprising a peristaltic pump, and approximately fifty metres of silicone tubing and a suspension of liquified pizza materials, which is pumped in loops around the aircraft. The apparatus extends Hiorns' treatment of the object as a corpus whilst also referring to the interconnectedness between mankind and machine, a common theme in Hiorns'

The retrospective view of the pathway [La vue rétrospective du chemin] (2017-en cours) est une installation à grande échelle de Roger Hiorns. Elle utilise un jet soviétique MiG-21 que l'artiste avait auparavant enterré à Prague en tant qu'œuvre d'art publique temporaire. Au Mudam, cette histoire est présente au travers des couches de terre, des bosses et de la rouille qui couvrent la surface de cet avion long de seize mètres, installé dans le Grand Hall, au rez-de-chaussée du musée. Le choix de cet appareil est lourd de sens : mis en service au début des années 1960, c'est le jet supersonique le plus produit de l'histoire de l'aviation. Le MiG-21, qui constitue pour l'artiste un « morceau de puissance abandonnée », est considéré par beaucoup comme une icône de la guerre froide.

Cette œuvre fait partie d'un projet en cours : ces dernières années, Roger Hiorns a enterré un certain nombre d'avions dans divers endroits d'Europe, notamment au Royaume-Uni et aux Pays-Bas. Il a commencé avec un seul appareil avant de développer un réseau international d'avions souterrains. « Cela a trait au fait d'arracher quelque chose aux airs pour l'enfouir sous la peau de la terre[1] », a-t-il dit à propos de ces enterrements, qu'il considère comme une « proposition » concernant la « prochaine étape » de la vie de l'appareil. En tant qu'exemple de technologie globale et symbole de puissance, le MiG-21 et son enfouissement peuvent aussi faire référence aux systèmes globaux – politiques et économiques – souvent invisibles qui structurent nos existences quotidiennes.

Exhumé et déplacé dans le musée, l'avion est supplémenté par un « système digestif » comprenant une pompe péristaltique, des tubes en silicone d'une cinquantaine de mètres et une solution faite à partir de pizzas liquéfiées qui circule le long de l'appareil. Ce dispositif prolonge le

sculptural work. As a food that is eaten around the world, pizza is symbolic of his interest in global systems.

Roger Hiorns was born in 1975 in Birmingham, UK. He lives and works in London, UK.

1 Roger Hiorns, 'The Man Who Buries Planes', *Seriously...* (podcast), 27 April 2018.

traitement de l'objet comme un corps tout en faisant référence à l'interconnexion entre humanité et machine, thème récurrent dans l'œuvre sculpturale de Roger Hiorns. La pizza, plat consommé partout dans le monde, symbolise l'intérêt de l'artiste pour les systèmes globaux.

Roger Hiorns est né en 1975 à Birmingham, au Royaume-Uni. Il vit et travaille à Londres, au Royaume-Uni.

1 Roger Hiorns, « The Man Who Buries Planes », podcast *Seriously...*, 27 avril 2018.

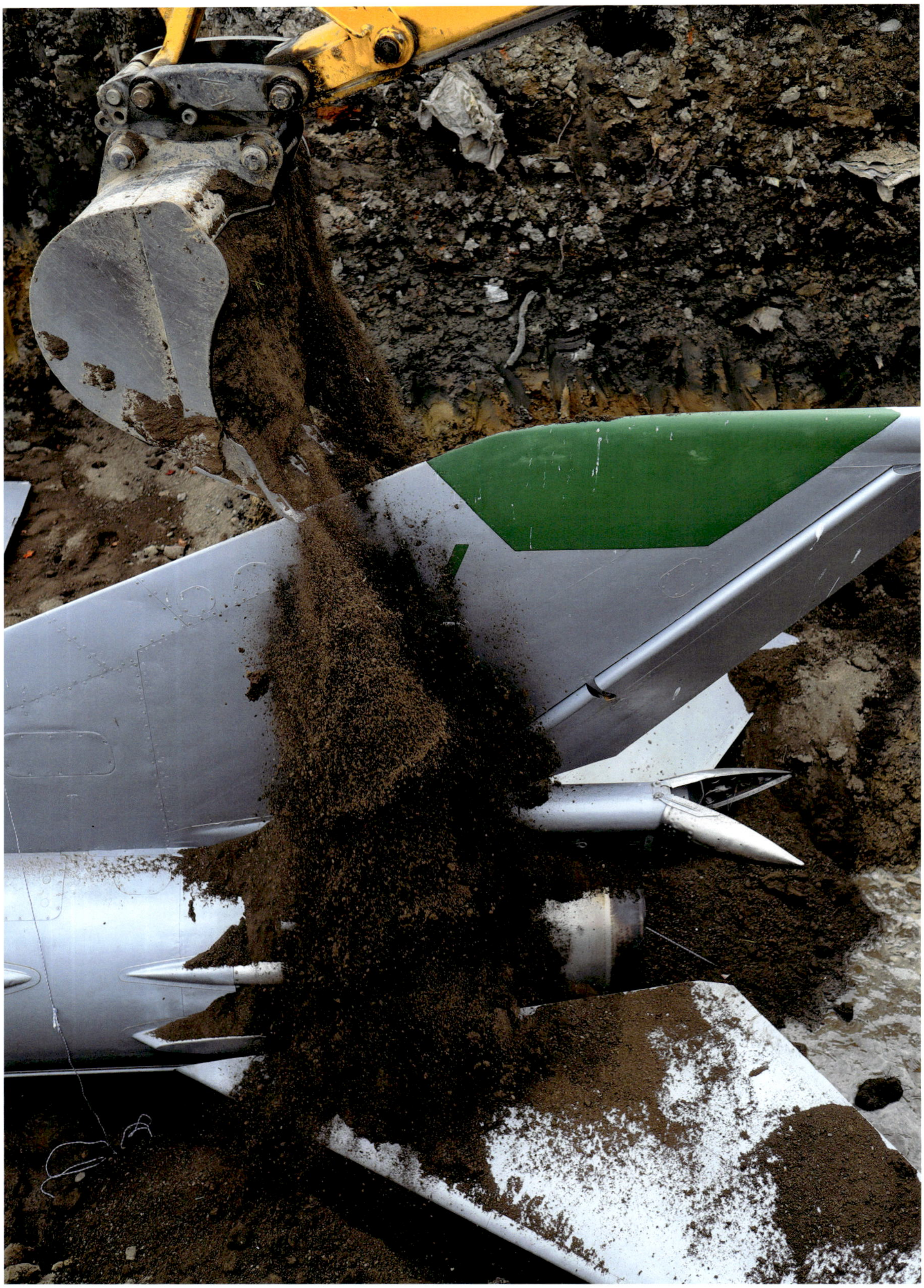

Roger Hiorns, *The retrospective view of the pathway*, 2017–ongoing (detail)

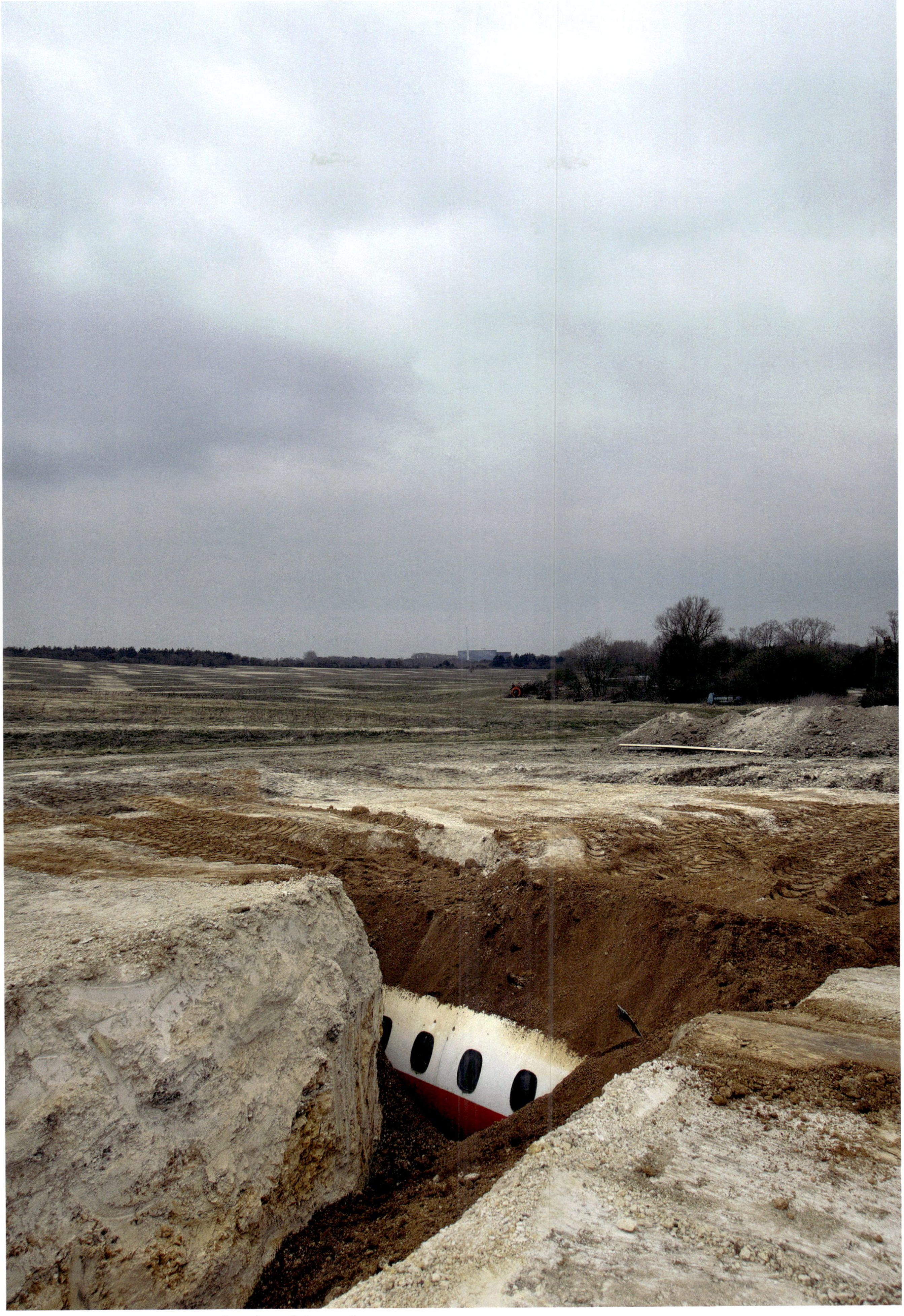

Roger Hiorns, *The retrospective view of the pathway,* 1990–2016

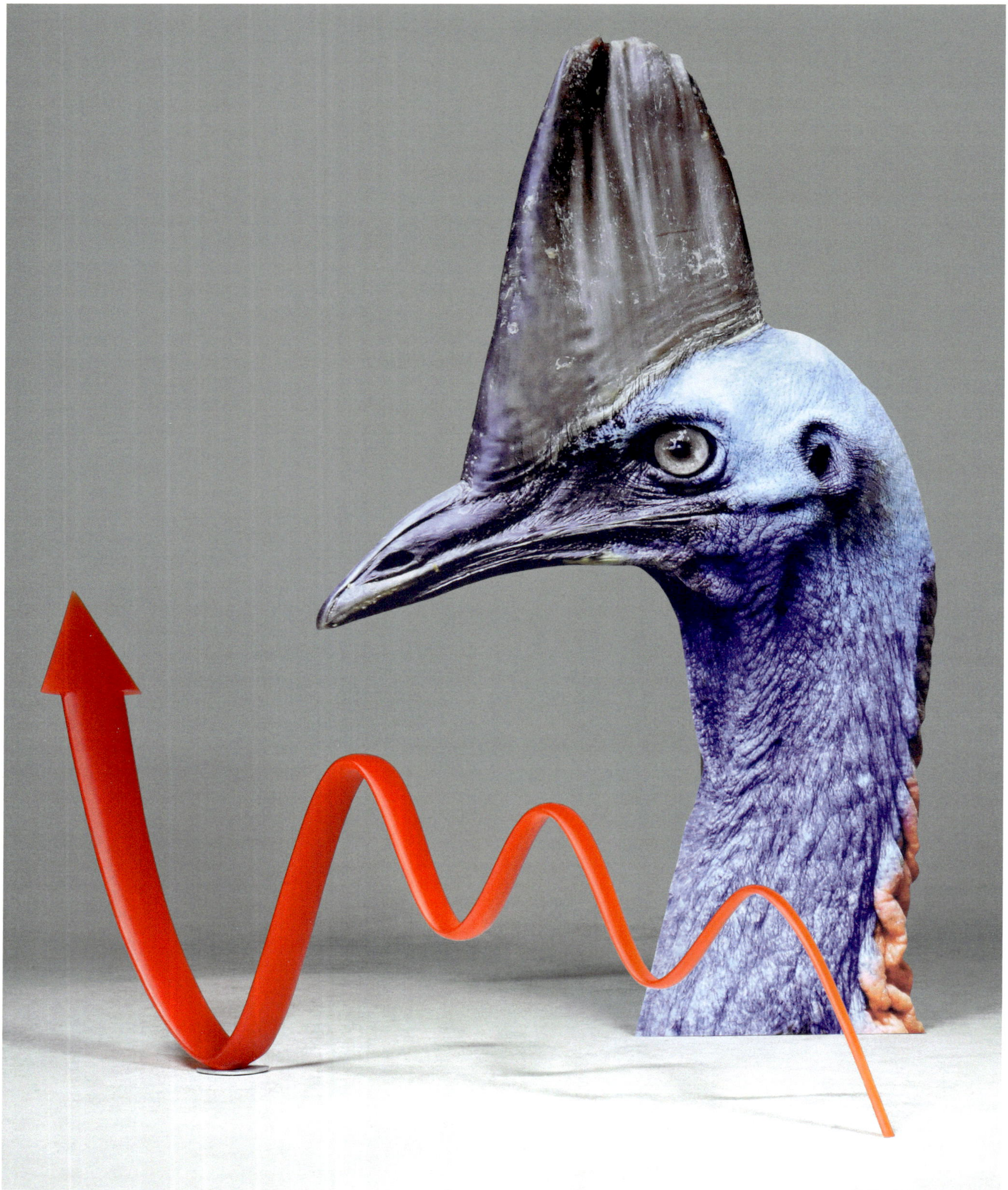

Katja Novitskova, *Pattern of Activation (emu)*, 2014

Katja Novitskova

Pattern of Activation (emu) (2014) and *Pattern of Activation (jumping spider, termite cathedral mounds, growth potential)* (2015) are two sculptural installations by Katja Novitskova. Part of the series *Approximations* (2014–ongoing), these free-standing cut-outs employ visual materials appropriated from the internet to explore circulation and distribution in the digital era. Novitskova's use of 'cute' images of animals – in this instance an emu and a spider – reflect their popularity on algorithm-driven social media platforms, which must compete for viewers' attention to make profits. 'Animal forms', the artist has explained, 'especially ones with eyes and facial expressions, display visual patterns that activate certain primal reactions in the viewer, charge them emotionally, whether they know it's an artwork or not'.[1] Printed in high resolution and inherently two-dimensional, these works are intentionally made by the artist to be easy to photograph and share: 'For me the work is not just the sculpture but the smiles and stares, the nearly automatic smartphone snapping, the archaic "posing with a trophy" photo-op behaviour that often coincides with the work being exhibited. The sculpture triggers all these behaviour patterns'.[2]

These larger-than-life sculptures, that the viewer must negotiate in space, can also be seen to physically manifest the real-world effects created through the circulation of these ostensibly ephemeral images. Alongside images of non-human entities, Novitskova also presents brightly coloured clip-art growth curves, which are commonly associated with corporate presentations. This combination of two seemingly contradictory fields can be considered in connection with the artist's long-held interest in acknowledging the environmental impact of data and the so-called 'attention economy': 'Digital images

Pattern of Activation (emu) [Schéma d'activation (émeu)] (2014) et *Pattern of Activation (jumping spider, termite cathedral mounds, growth potential)* [Schéma d'activation (araignée sauteuse, termitières cathédrales, potentiel de croissance)] (2015) sont deux installations sculpturales de Katja Novitskova. Ces silhouettes découpées font partie de la série *Approximations* (2014-en cours) et emploient des visuels glanés sur internet pour explorer leur circulation et leur distribution à l'ère du digital. L'utilisation d'images « mignonnes » d'animaux, en l'occurrence un émeu et une araignée, reflète leur popularité dans les algorithmes des réseaux sociaux, qui sont en concurrence pour capter l'attention des utilisateurs, source de leurs profits. « Les silhouettes d'animaux, explique l'artiste, surtout celles avec des yeux et des expressions, présentent des motifs visuels qui activent des réactions primales, émotionnelles, chez le spectateur, qu'il sache ou non s'il s'agit d'une œuvre d'art[1]. » Imprimées en haute résolution, intrinsèquement bidimensionnelles, ces œuvres sont délibérément réalisées pour être faciles à photographier et à partager : « Pour moi, l'œuvre, ce n'est pas seulement la sculpture, mais aussi les sourires et les regards, le déclenchement quasi automatique du smartphone, le comportement archaïque consistant à "poser avec un trophée" pour la photo, qui coïncide souvent avec l'œuvre exposée. La sculpture suscite tous ces types de comportements[2]. »

On peut en outre considérer que ces sculptures, plus grandes que nature et entre lesquelles le spectateur doit naviguer, manifestent concrètement les effets produits dans le monde réel par la circulation de ces images apparemment éphémères. En parallèle de ces images d'êtres non-humains, Katja Novitskova présente des courbes de croissance de couleurs vives généralement associées aux

need our attention to exist', she has said, 'but they also require carbon-based fuel: a palette of rare minerals has to be mined in order to assemble the simplest of smartphones'.[3]

Katja Novitskova was born in 1984 in Tallinn, Estonia. She lives and works in Berlin, Germany and Amsterdam, The Netherlands.

1 'Post Internet, Katja Novitskova, in Conversation with Gene McHugh', *Garage Magazine*, no. 7, 2014, pp. 208–209.
2 *Ibid.*
3 Katja Novitskova, 'Beginnings + Ends', *Frieze*, 21 November 2013, https://www.frieze.com/article/beginnings-ends (accessed 13 April 2021).

présentations professionnelles en entreprise. Cette combinaison de deux domaines en apparence antithétiques peut être rattachée à l'intérêt que porte l'artiste à souligner l'impact environnemental des données et de l'« économie de l'attention ». « Les images numériques ont besoin de notre attention pour exister, mais elles nécessitent aussi des combustibles carbonés : pour fabriquer le smartphone le plus élémentaire, il faut extraire toute une palette de minerais rares[3]. »

Katja Novitskova est née en 1984 à Tallinn, en Estonie. Elle vit et travaille à Berlin, en Allemagne, et à Amsterdam, aux Pays-Bas.

1 « Post Internet, Katja Novitskova, in Conversation with Gene McHugh », *Garage Magazine*, n° 7, 2014, p. 208-209.
2 *Ibid.*
3 Katja Novitskova, « Beginnings + Ends », *Frieze* 21, novembre 2013, https://www.frieze.com/article/beginnings-ends (consulté le 13 avril 2021).

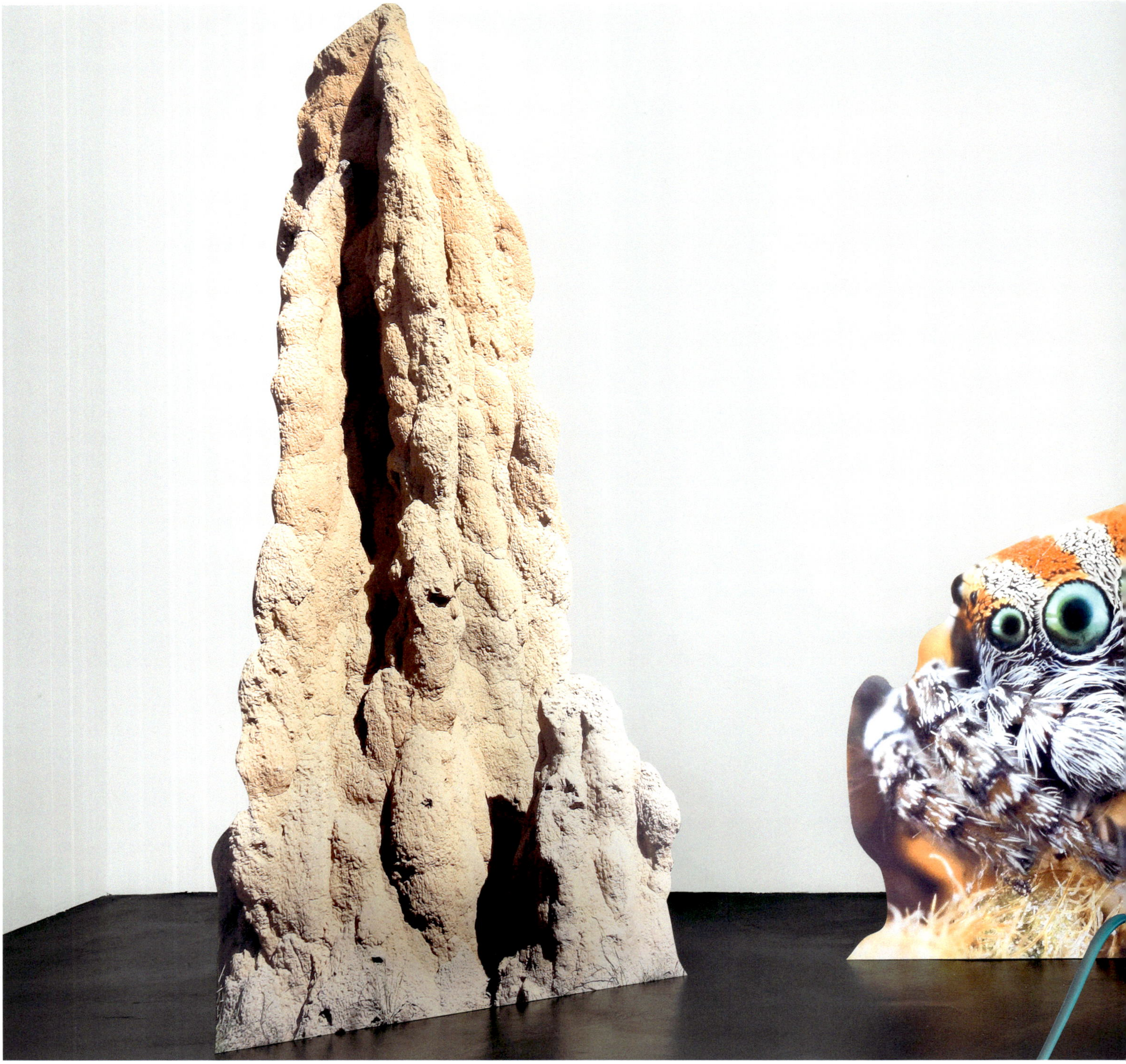

Katja Novitskova, *Pattern of Activation (jumping spider, termite cathedral mounds, growth potential)*, 2015

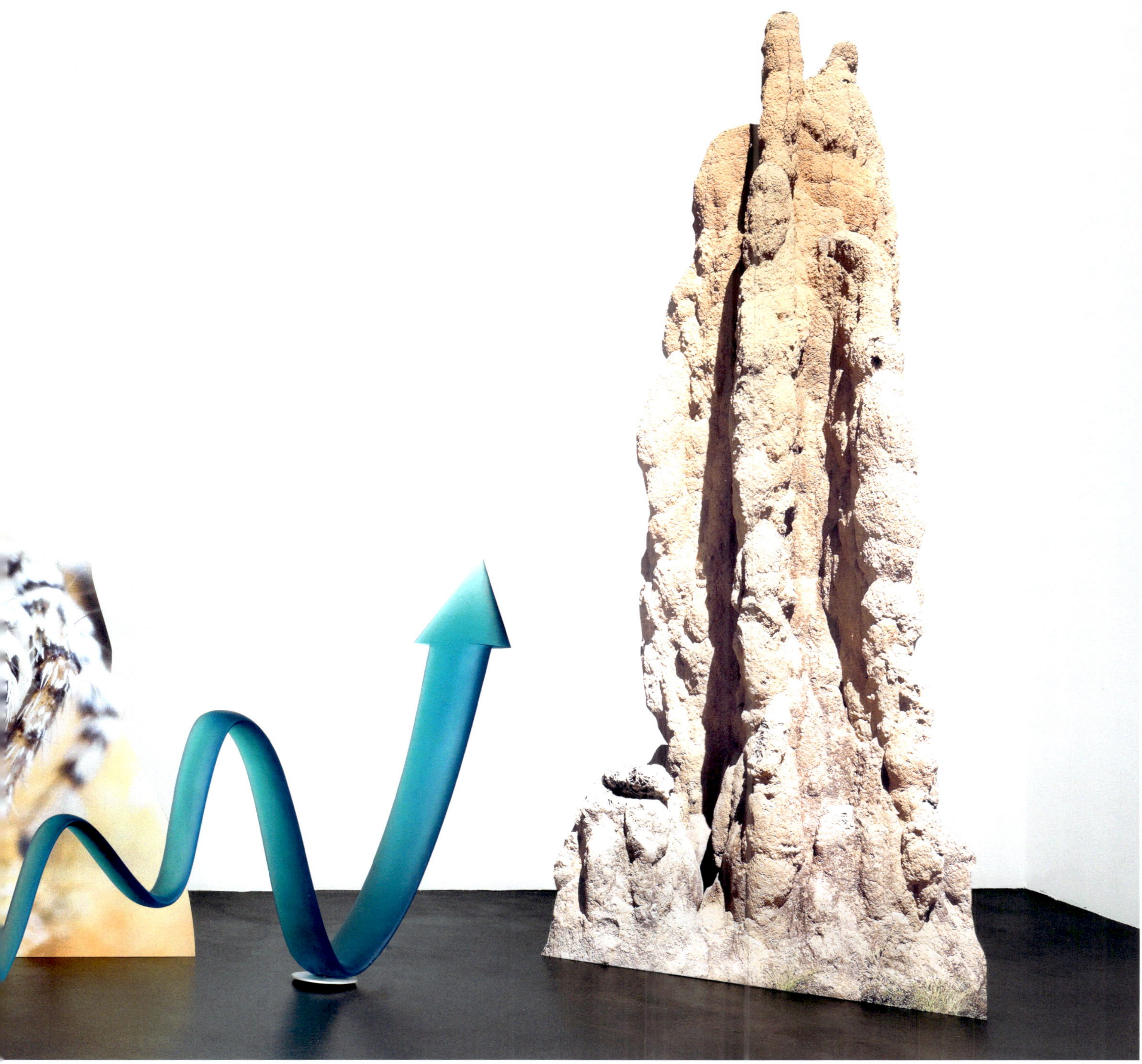

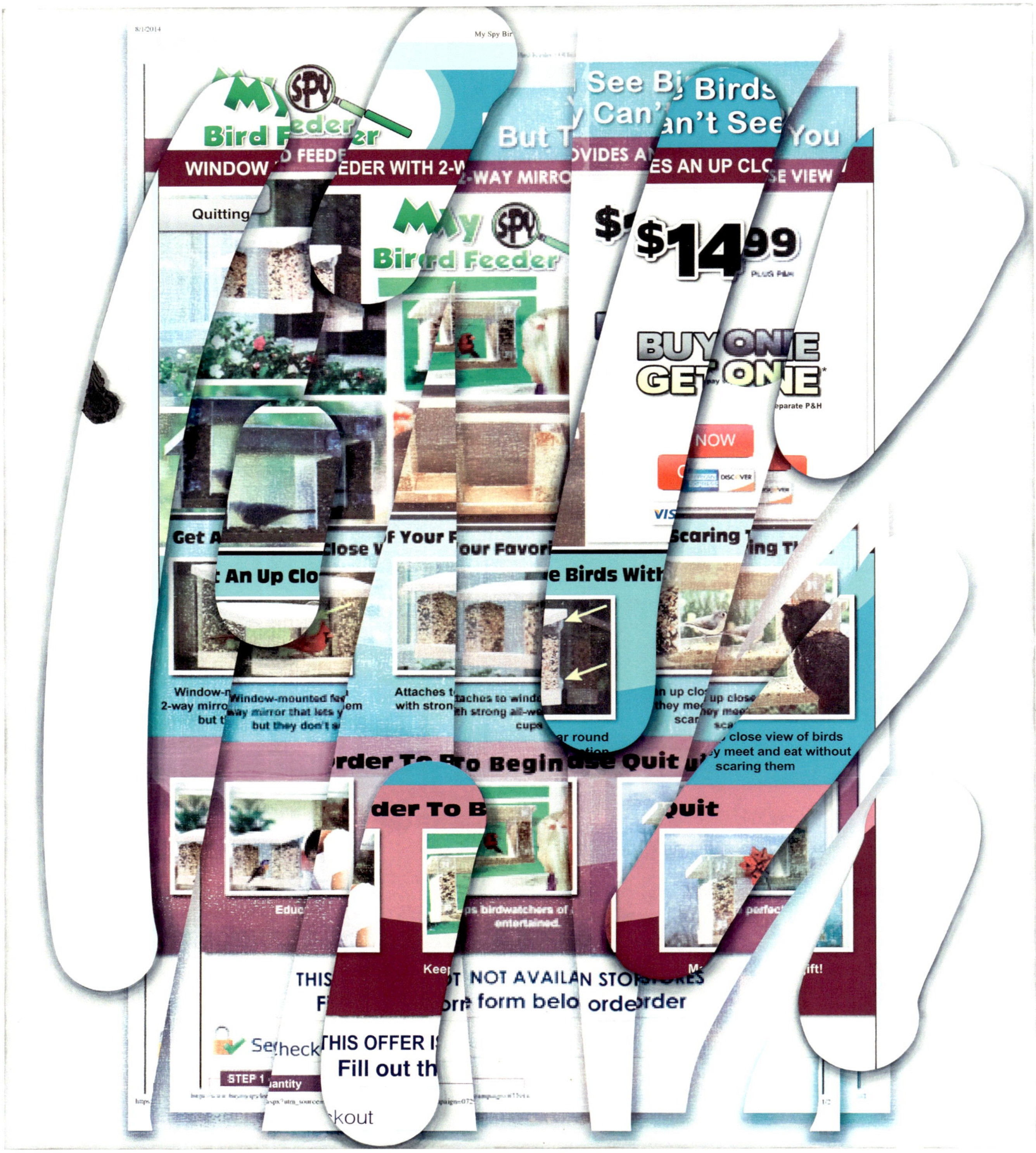

Laura Owens, *Untitled*, 2014

Laura Owens

This untitled 2014 painting by Laura Owens depicts an internet advertisement for My Spy Bird Feeder, a bird feeder with a two-way mirror. Owens is known for her use of non-hierarchical and heterogeneous source imagery, including paintings by Henri Matisse, Édouard Vuillard, Henri de Toulouse-Lautrec and Vincent van Gogh, motivational posters and drawings by her children. An earlier series quoted pages from the classified section of 1960s editions of *The Berkeley Barb* newspaper. This work is one of several paintings and artist books featuring spam emails she received for products that sometimes turned out to be unavailable or non-existent. 'I am certainly influenced by different forms of art and non-art', the artist has said of her approach. 'I was getting spam emails that you would normally delete, but I decided this was free material and started using the messages in my paintings. You try to bring up what's being repressed'.[1]

Like much of the artist's work since the mid-1990s, this composition was made with the aid of a computer programme, alongside analogue techniques. Its curved lines, for instance, are a screen-printed representation of marks made in Photoshop combining a four-colour printing process based on halftone patterns with hand-mixed colours. The composition is formed of three layers that reproduce the advertisement at different resolutions and with progressive definition. The first two layers, which appear more pixelated are printed using a process based on halftone patterns in standard CMYK colours. These are overlaid by a top layer of 'brushstrokes': flat areas of colour with crisp edges that combine CMYK printing with hand-mixed paint. These differences in image quality add to the illusion of spatial depth. By adding illusionistic drop shadows to these forms, Owens can be seen to push

Cette peinture sans titre réalisée en 2014 par Laura Owens représente une publicité en ligne pour My Spy Bird Feeder, un distributeur de graines pour oiseau doté d'un miroir sans tain. Laura Owens est connue pour son utilisation non hiérarchisée d'images tirées de sources disparates, qui vont de la peinture (Henri Matisse, Édouard Vuillard, Henri de Toulouse-Lautrec, Vincent van Gogh) aux affiches aux slogans motivants, en passant par les dessins de ses propres enfants. Une de ses séries antérieures citait des pages de la rubrique « petites annonces » de numéros des années 1960 du journal *Berkeley Barb*. L'œuvre exposée compte parmi les tableaux et les livres d'artiste réalisés à partir des spams reçus par Laura Owens et faisant parfois la promotion de produits indisponibles ou inexistants. « Je suis sans aucun doute influencée par différentes formes d'art et de *non-art* », a-t-elle déclaré à propos de sa démarche. « Je recevais des spams que l'on supprimerait en temps normal, mais je me suis dit que c'était du contenu gratuit et je me suis mise à utiliser ces messages dans mes tableaux. On essaie de mettre en avant ce qui est refoulé[1]. »

Comme une bonne partie des œuvres de l'artiste depuis les années 1990, cette composition a été réalisée avec l'aide d'un programme informatique, employé en parallèle de techniques analogiques. Ses lignes courbes, par exemple, sont une représentation sérigraphiée de marques réalisées dans Photoshop et mêlant l'impression de demi-teintes en quadrichromie avec des couleurs mélangées manuellement. La composition est constituée de trois couches superposées, qui reproduisent la publicité en différentes résolutions et avec une définition de plus en plus nette. Les deux premières, qui apparaissent plus pixélisées, sont imprimées en demi-teintes dans les couleurs CMJN standard. Elles sont recouvertes d'une couche

these sections of the composition out towards the viewer while also creating a relationship between the illusionistic shadows printed on the surface and the real shadow cast by the thick black impasto mark within the 'Photoshop brushstroke' on the left side of the composition.

Laura Owens was born in 1970 in Euclid, USA. She lives and works in Los Angeles, USA.

1 'Laura Owens, a Mid-Career Interview', Paul Laster, *Conceptual Fine Arts*, 14 March 2020, https://www.conceptualfinearts.com/cfa/2017/11/21/laura-owens (accessed 3 May 2021).

de « coups de pinceau », des zones de couleur planes, aux bords nets et qui combinent impression CMJN et peinture mélangée manuellement. Ces différences de qualités d'image ajoutent à l'illusion de profondeur spatiale. En ajoutant à ces formes des ombres de gouttes en trompe-l'œil, Laura Owens projette ces parties vers le visiteur et met en relation les ombres en trompe-l'œil imprimées sur la surface avec l'ombre réelle portée par l'épais empattement noir contenu dans le « coup de pinceau Photoshop », à gauche de la composition.

Laura Owens est née en 1970 à Euclid, aux États-Unis. Elle vit et travaille à Los Angeles, aux États-Unis.

1 Paul Laster, « Laura Owens, a Mid-Career Interview », *Conceptual Fine Arts*, 14 mars 2020, https://www.conceptualfinearts.com/cfa/2017/11/21/laura-owens (consulté le 3 mai 2021).

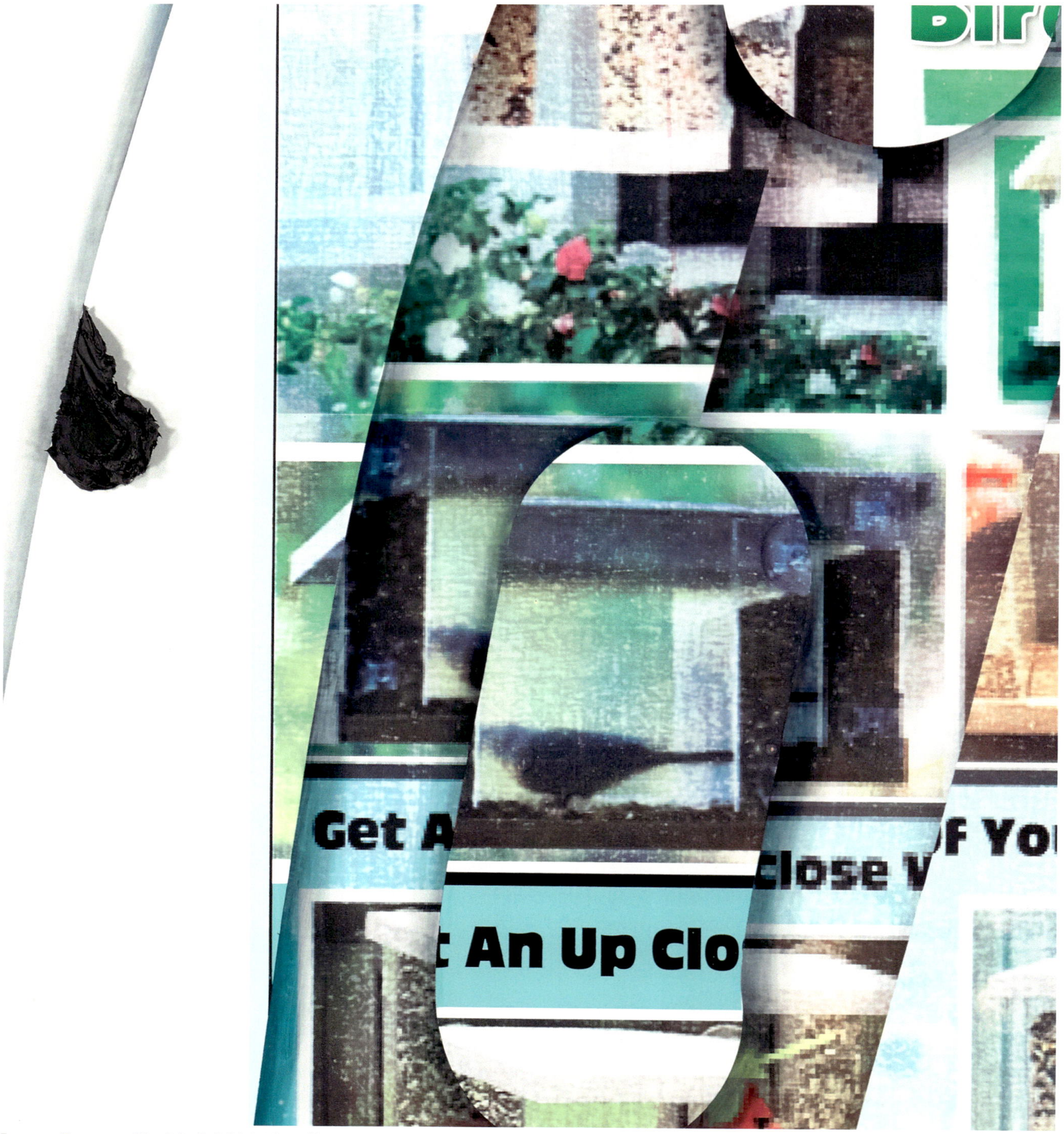

Laura Owens, *Untitled*, 2014 (details)

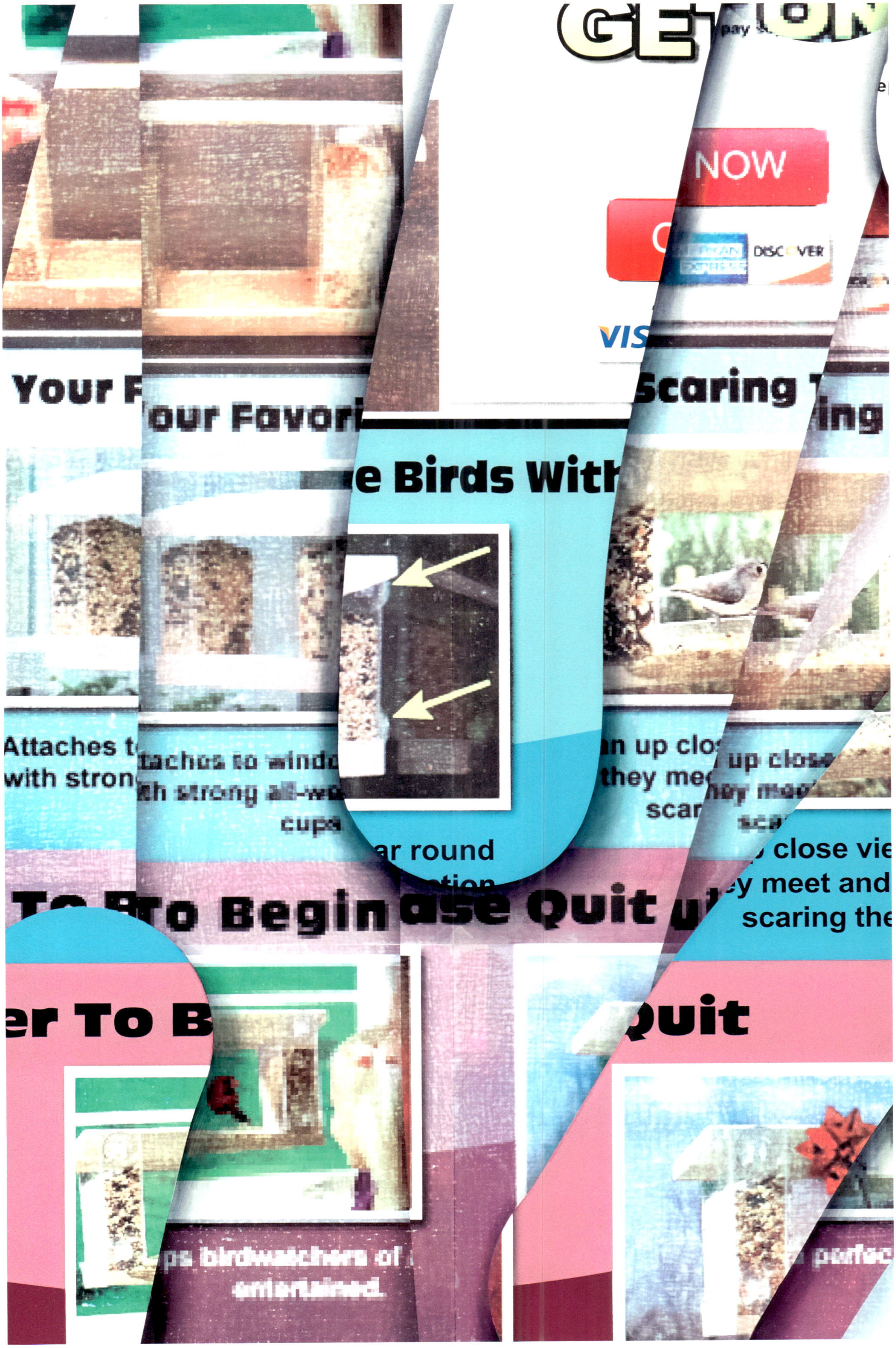
GET
pay
NOW
DISCOVER
VIS
Your F
our Favori
e Birds With
Scaring
ing
Attaches t
with stron
taches to windo
th strong all-we
cups
n up clo
they me
scar
up close
ar round
To Begin
ase Quit
close vie
y meet and
scaring the
er To B
Quit
ps birdwatchers of
entertained.
perfec

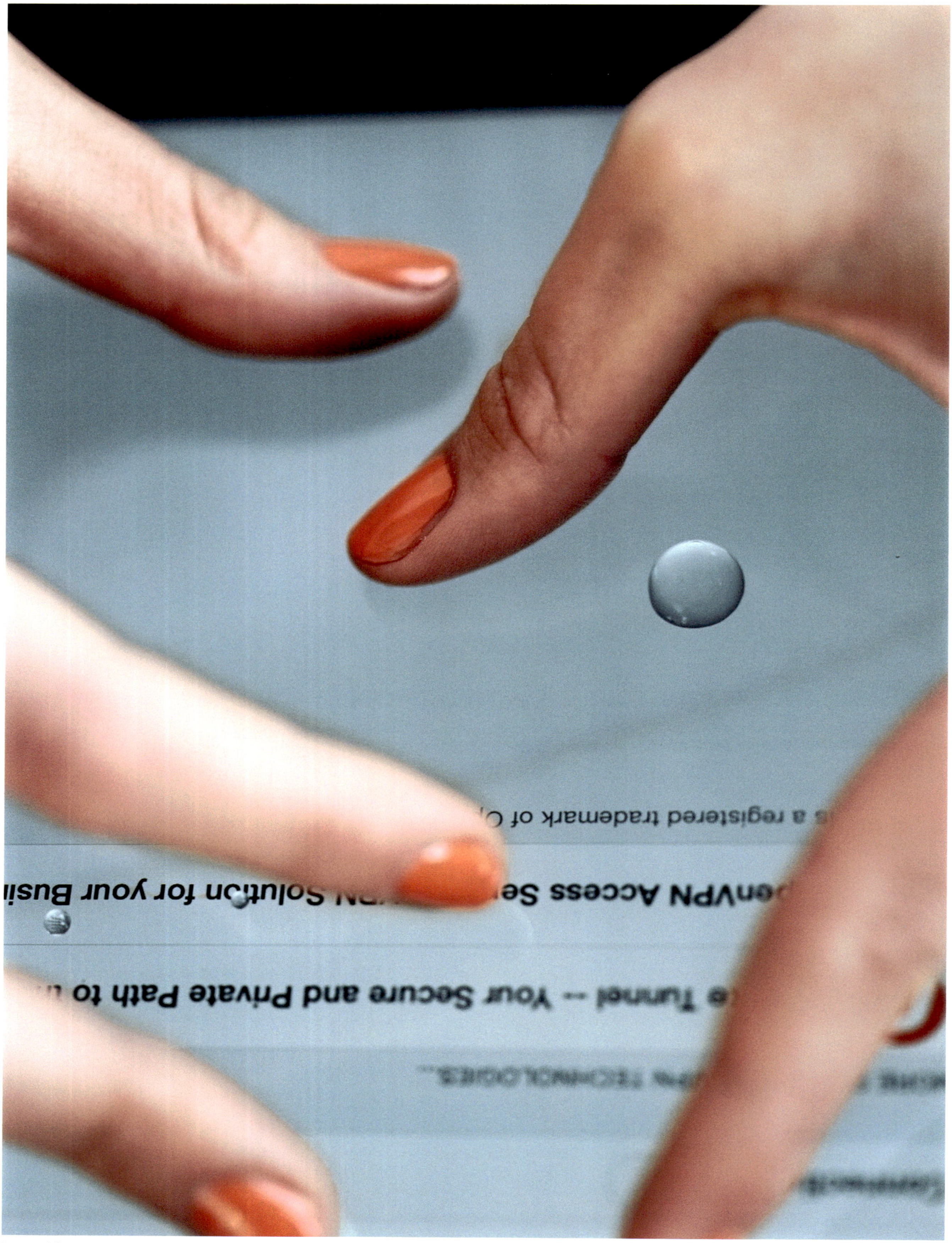

Josephine Pryde, *Your Secure and Private Path,* 2015

Josephine Pryde

These six photographs by Josephine Pryde belong to the 2012–16 series *Für mich* [For me], which comprises closely cropped images of hands interacting with touch-sensitive objects or being placed on the chests of their owners. *Küsse sind das* [Kisses are that] (2014), for instance, depicts a pair of hands wearing purple nail polish and holding an inexpensive dimmable light (controlled by touching its surface). By not including the heads of her sitters, Pryde highlights touch as a sense that, in a digital world, we increasingly use to create connections with others. Likewise, the brightly coloured nail polish evident throughout the series draws the viewer's attention to the point of contact between hand and object. Other works in the series, including *Sorry Not Sorry* (2016), *Your Secure and Private Path* (2015) and *Here Do You Want To* (2014), show hands using tablet computers and smart phones. Reminiscent of commercial photography, these images depict the point of engagement between the hand or digit and the screen. In doing so, they can be seen to highlight our increasingly intimate and dependent relationships with these technologies, which have, in many ways, become extensions of our bodies.

Für mich was partly inspired by Pryde's experience on examination boards in her capacity as a professor at the University of the Arts Berlin: 'When the commission asks, "Why do you want to study art?" the candidate responds with, "I want to do it for me", and in some cases, puts their hand on their chest to identify themselves as the "me" in question. I became interested in examining my own pre-conceptions about this answer... I suppose I was curious why "for me" would be an answer, and not something along the lines of "I am curious to experiment in a field that compels me..." or simply, "who cares?"'[1]

Ces six photographies de Josephine Pryde font partie de la série *Für mich* [Pour moi] (2012-2016), composée de plans rapprochés de mains interagissant avec des objets tactiles ou placées sur la poitrine de leur propriétaire. Par exemple, *Küsse sind das* [Des baisers, c'est cela] (2014) montre deux mains aux ongles vernis de violet et tenant une lampe modulable bon marché (dont l'intensité est contrôlée par contact avec sa surface). En choisissant de ne pas montrer la tête de ses modèles, Josephine Pryde met en avant le toucher comme sens que nous utilisons de plus en plus pour créer des liens avec autrui dans un monde numérique. De la même façon, le vernis à ongles de couleur vive, récurrent dans la série, attire l'attention des visiteurs sur le point de contact entre la main et l'objet. D'autres œuvres de cette série, telles que *Sorry Not Sorry* [Désolé pas désolé] (2016), *Your Secure and Private Path* [Ton chemin sécurisé et privé] (2015) ou *Here Do You Want To* [Ici veux-tu] (2014) montrent des mains utilisant respectivement des tablettes numériques et des smartphones. Ces images, qui rappellent la photographie commerciale, représentent le point où la main ou le doigt rencontre l'écran. Dès lors, on peut considérer qu'elles soulignent l'intimité et la dépendance croissantes que nous entretenons avec ces technologies, qui sont devenues, à bien des égards, des prolongements de notre corps.

Für mich s'inspire en partie des jurys où Josephine Pryde a siégé en sa qualité de professeure à l'Université des arts de Berlin : « Quand la commission demande : "Pourquoi voulez-vous étudier l'art ?", les candidats répondent : "Je veux le faire pour moi", en mettant parfois la main sur leur poitrine pour s'identifier comme le "moi" en question. J'ai voulu examiner mes propres préjugés au sujet de cette réponse. [...] J'imagine que je voulais découvrir pourquoi

Josephine Pryde was born in 1967 in Alnwick, UK. She lives and works in Berlin, Germany and London, UK.

1 Josephine Pryde, 'Josephine Pryde: In Case My Mind Is Changing', summer 2019.

la réponse était "Pour moi" et non pas quelque chose comme : "Je suis curieux d'expérimenter dans un domaine qui me passionne". Ou, tout simplement, "Qu'est-ce que ça peut faire[1] ?" »

Josephine Pryde est née en 1967 à Alnwick, au Royaume-Uni. Elle vit et travaille à Berlin, en Allemagne et à Londres, au Royaume-Uni.

1 Josephine Pryde, « Josephine Pryde: In Case My Mind Is Changing », été 2019.

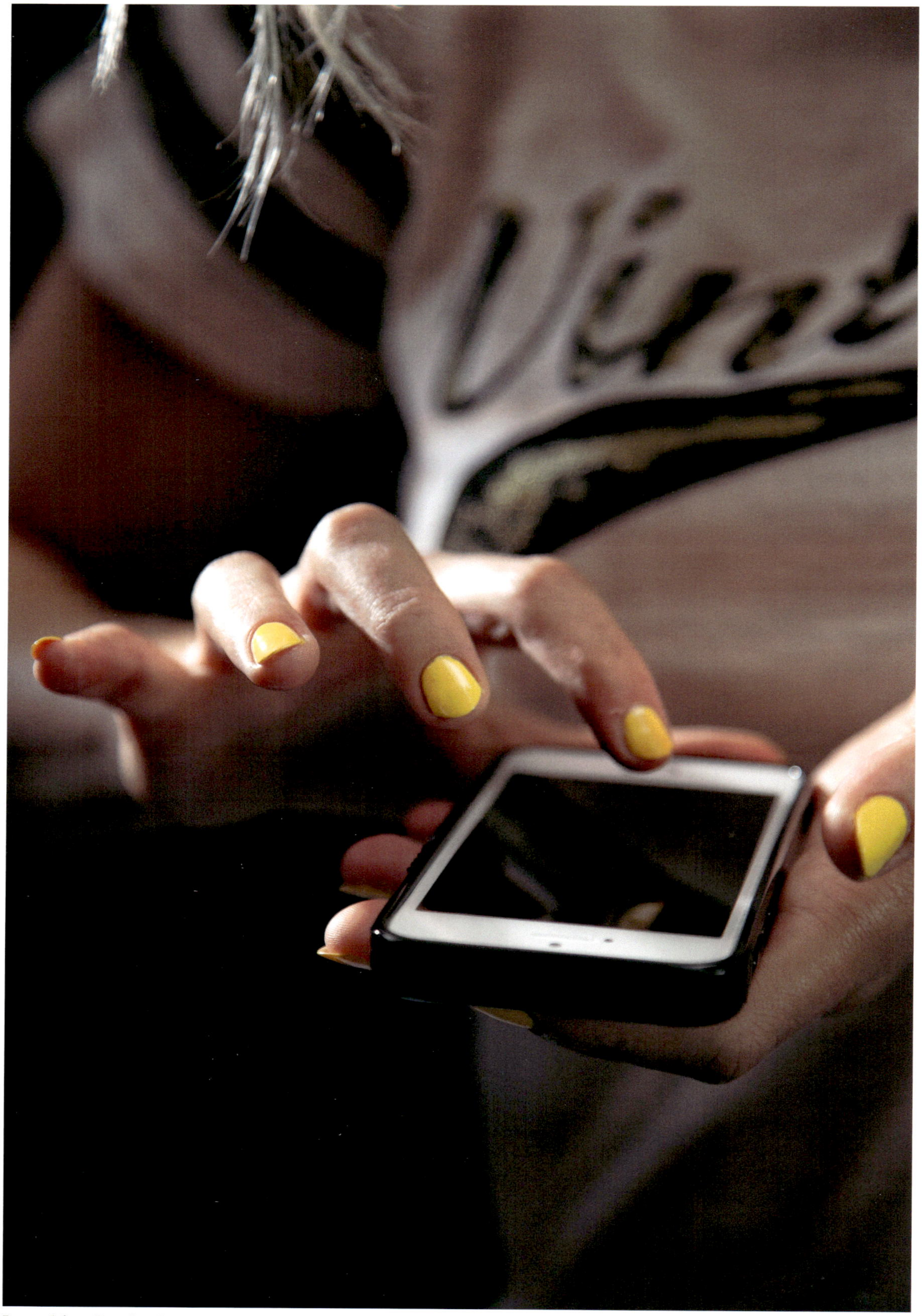

Josephine Pryde, *Here Do You Want To*, 2014

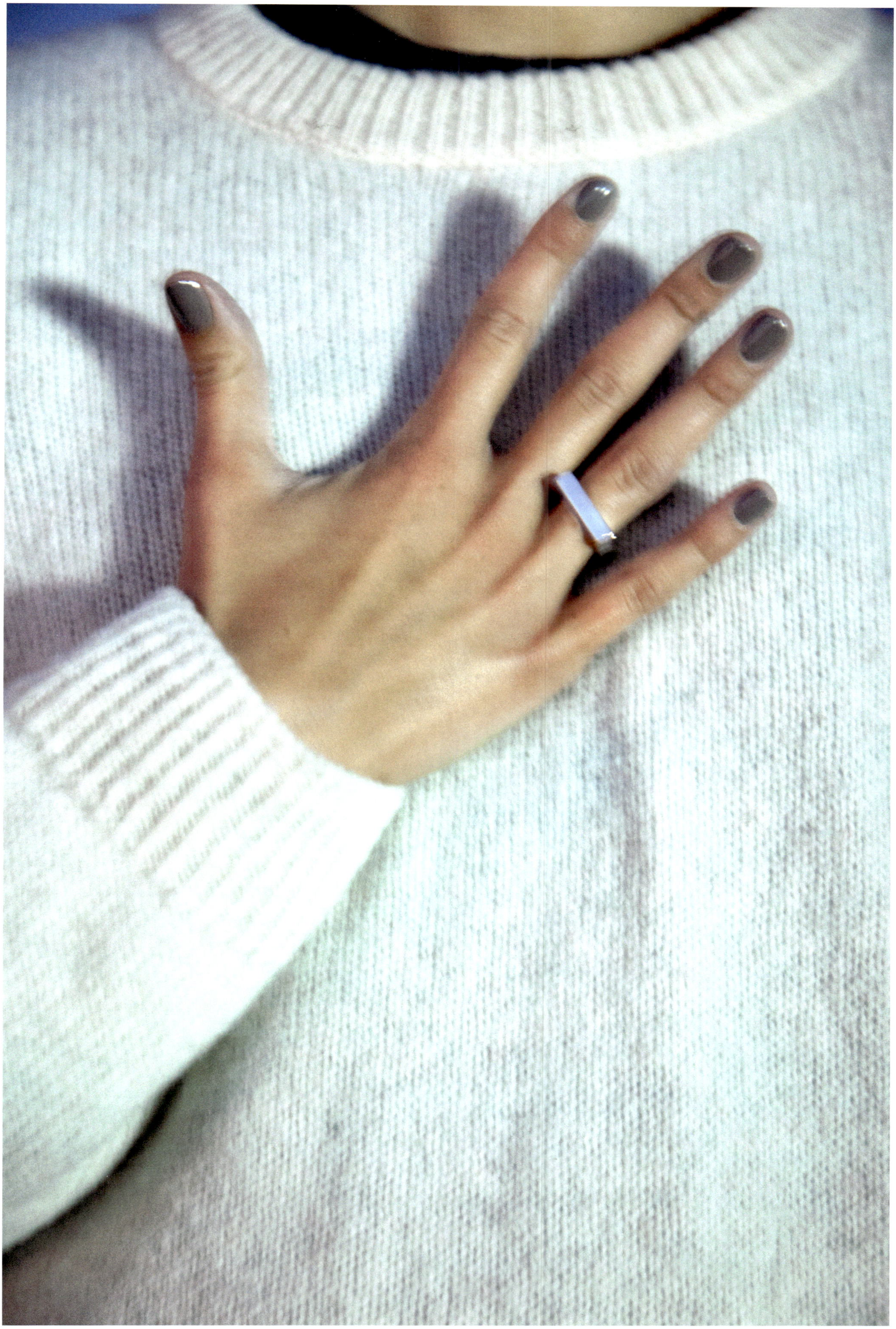

Josephine Pryde, *Für Mich*, 2014

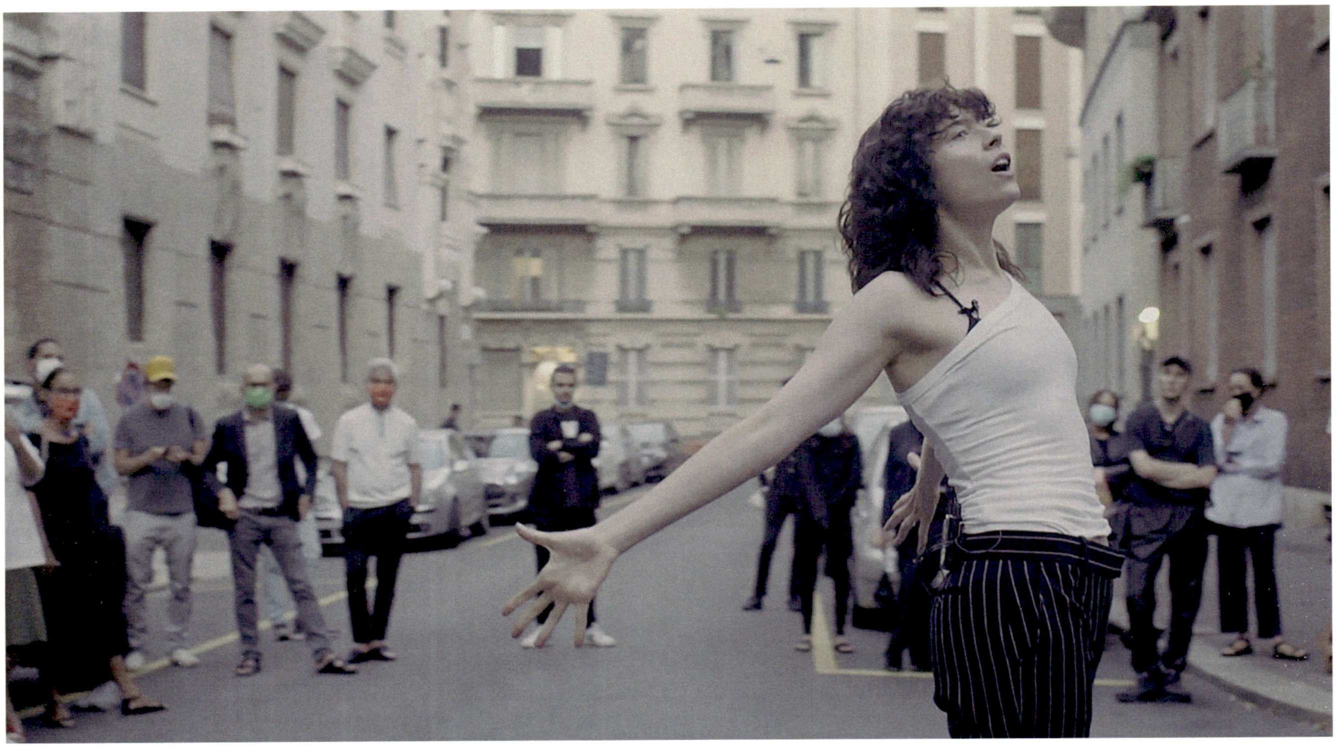

Nora Turato, *wow this huge wooden horse is great!*, 2020

Nora Turato

Nora Turato's work considers the volatility of language, translating information from her daily intake of articles, conversations, subtitles and advertising slogans into scripts for videos, artist books, murals, text-based installations and spoken word performances. The work reflects the multifarious nature of its sources, playing with the semantic and visual qualities of language.

Words and phrases employed by Turato reflect the ready-made vocabulary of the Internet. Political statements merge with conversations from reality TV shows, revealing subtle overlaps between social interactions, marketing strategies, consumer behaviour and introspection. To quote the artist: 'No matter how random, many of these interests can be catalysed into something of a more political and topical meaning, that can resonate with an audience not necessarily interested in these subjects to begin with'.[1]

A trained graphic designer, the works combine references to the International Typographic Style, cigarette packaging design, graffiti tags and commercial advertisements, alluding to a life lived amidst typesetting, hyphenation, grids and Venn diagrams. In addition to the bold typography that predominates, Turato's own handwriting often appears in a sprawling script, alluding to the more private register of the artist's notebook. The latter also refers to artist's daily diaristic practice of note-writing, a somewhat anachronistic ritual in an era of digital correspondence. Scaled up and writ large on a wall or billboard poster, these hand-drawn marks also begin to resemble the gestural lines of abstract painting.

Turato's presentation in *Post-Capital* comprises a large-scale mural, *eeeexactlyyy my point.* (2021), a new performance *pool 5* (2021) and a poster campaign for sites

Le travail de Nora Turato examine la volatilité du langage et traduit les informations délivrées quotidiennement dans des articles, des conversations, des sous-titres et des slogans publicitaires en script pour des vidéos, en livres d'artistes, en œuvres murales, en installations et en performances. Son travail reflète la diversité de ses sources et joue sur les propriétés sémantiques et visuelles du langage.

Les mots et expressions employés par Nora Turato sont le reflet du vocabulaire propre à internet. Les déclarations politiques se confondent avec des conversations tirées d'émissions de téléréalité, révélant des chevauchements subtils entre interactions sociales, stratégies marketing, comportement des consommateurs et introspection. Pour citer l'artiste : « Un grand nombre de ces thèmes, malgré leur caractère parfois aléatoire, peuvent se cristalliser dans une signification plus politique, liée à l'actualité, qui peut parler à un public qui n'est a priori pas nécessairement intéressé par ces sujets[1]. »

Les œuvres de cette graphiste de formation mêlent des références au style typographique international, au design de paquets de cigarettes, au graffiti et à la publicité ; allusion à une vie menée dans la typographie, les césures, les grilles et les diagrammes de Venn. Outre les lettrages épais qui prédominent, l'écriture manuscrite de Nora Turato apparaît sous la forme d'un texte proliférant, référence au registre plus intime du carnet d'artiste. Chaque jour, Nora Turato prend des notes et tient son journal, rituel assez anachronique à l'époque de la correspondance numérique. Agrandies sur un mur ou une affiche, ces marques manuscrites se mettent aussi à ressembler aux lignes gestuelles de la peinture abstraite.

Pour *Post-Capital*, Nora Turato propose une grande peinture murale intitulée *eeeexactlyyy my point.* (2021),

across the city of Luxembourg. The mural will see the text 'eeeexactlyyy my point.' superimposed over a psychedelic background of orange and blue concentric circles, painted on a wall that runs approximately eighteen metres in length and up to eight metres high. Conceived especially for the exhibition, the affirmative content can be interpreted in a variety of ways. Firstly, in reference to an ostensibly post-capital situation, but also in agreement with the other works installed in the space. Turato describes it as a 'hypnotic, rollercoaster luna park of points... like a circus halo of opinions spinning on top of our heads'. She elaborates, 'Everyone [is] a protagonist in a post-capital world. Corruption for everyone, grinding and grifting; everyone is the main character... capital as myself to me, me as an asset... MY points and opinions as my assets'.[2]

Nora Turato was born in 1991 in Zagreb, Croatia. She lives and works in Amsterdam, The Netherlands.

1 Stefano Pirovano, 'Nora Turato: Proustian Interview with Afterword', https://www.conceptualfinearts.com/cfa/2019/11/12/nora-turato-interview (accessed 28 June 2021).
2 Email to the author, 28 June 2021.

une nouvelle performance *pool 5* (2021) et une campagne d'affichage dans plusieurs lieux de la ville de Luxembourg. Dans l'œuvre murale, le texte « *eeeexactlyyy my point.* » se superpose à un fond psychédélique, constitué de cercles concentriques orange et bleu peints sur un mur d'environ dix-huit mètres de long sur huit mètres de haut. Le contenu affirmatif de cette œuvre conçue spécialement pour l'exposition peut s'interpréter de diverses manières. Tout d'abord, en référence à une situation visiblement post-capitaliste, mais aussi en accord avec les autres œuvres installées dans l'espace. Selon Nora Turato, il s'agit d'un « parcours hypnotique, de montages russes d'idées [...], comme un halo d'opinions tournant au-dessus de nos têtes dans une grande parade ». Car, développe-t-elle, « tout le monde [est] un protagoniste dans un monde postcapitaliste. La corruption pour tous, la galère et la persévérance, chacun est le personnage principal... le capital est ce que je suis à moi-même, moi-même comme actif... MES idées et opinions sont mes actifs[2] ».

Nora Turato est née en 1991 à Zagreb, en Croatie. Elle vit et travaille à Amsterdam, aux Pays-Bas.

1 Stefano Pirovano, « Nora Turato: Proustian Interview with Afterword », Conceptual Fine Arts, https://www.conceptualfinearts.com/cfa/2019/11/12/nora-turato-interview (consulté le 28 juin 2021).
2 Correspondance par e-mail avec l'artiste, 28 juin 2021.

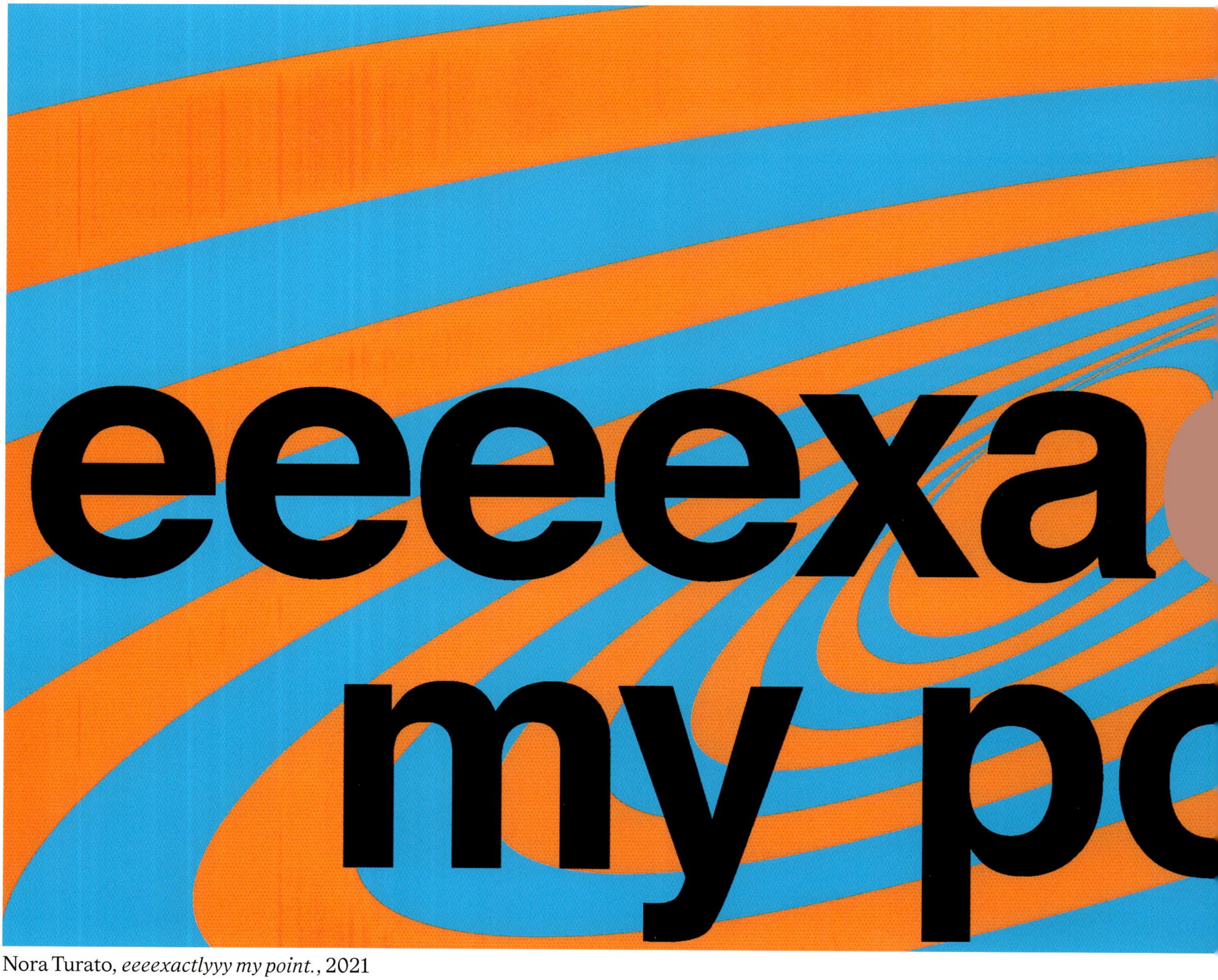

Nora Turato, *eeeexactlyyy my point.*, 2021

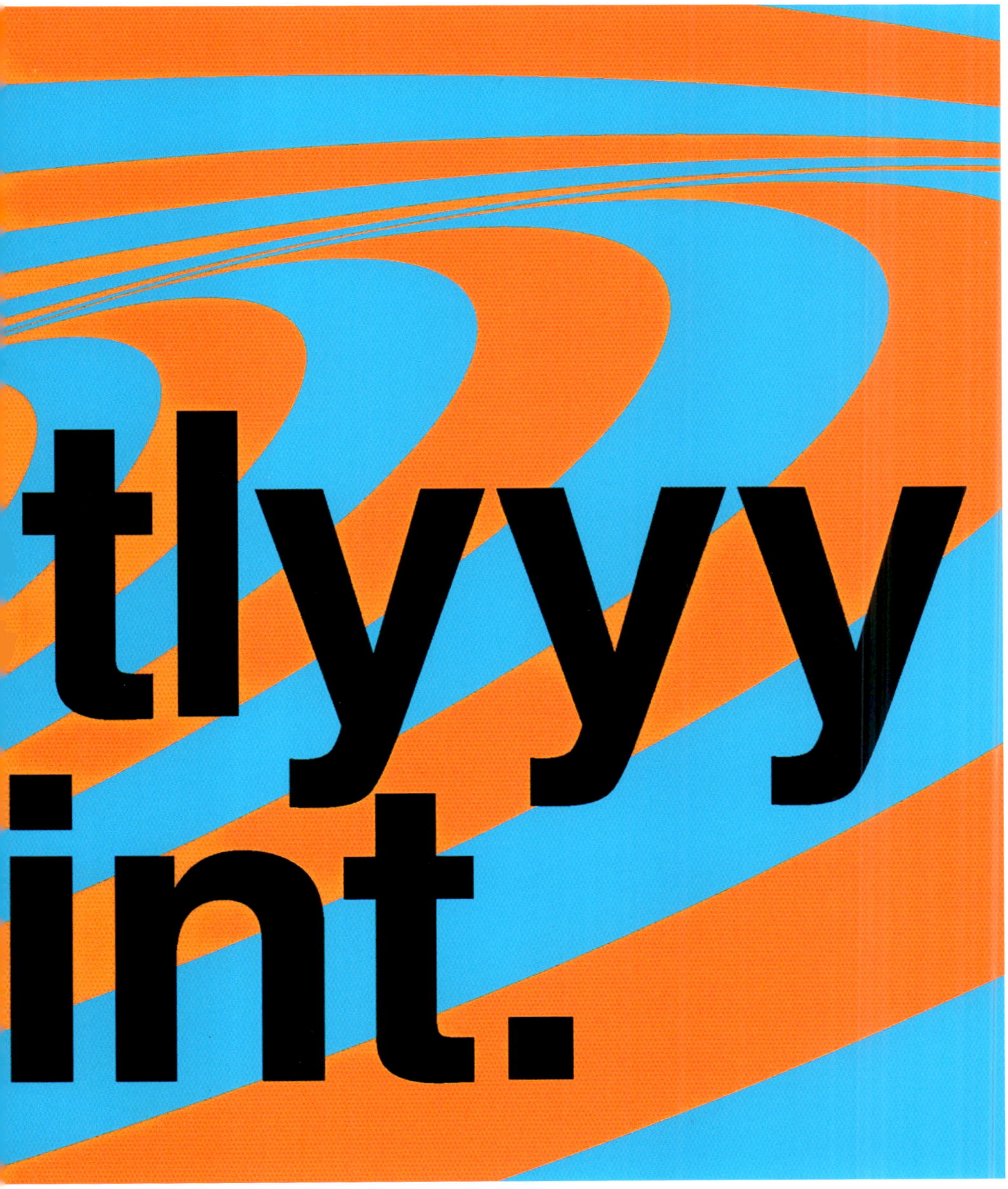
tlyyy
int.

Wealth

DUTY FREE ART: ART IN THE AGE OF PLANETARY CIVIL WAR

Hito Steyerl

THIRD CHAPTER: CONDITIONS OF POSSIBILITY

According to the Google Ngram viewer,[1] usage of the word 'impossible' has dropped steeply since around the mid-twentieth century. But what does this tell us? Does it mean that fewer and fewer things are impossible? Does it mean that impossibility 'as such' is in historical decline? Perhaps it just means that the conditions for possibilities as such are subject to change over time? Are both the possible and the impossible defined by historical and external conditions?

According to Immanuel Kant, time and space are necessary conditions for us to perceive or understand anything. Without time and space, knowledge, experience, and vision cannot unfold. Kant calls this perspective 'criticism'. With this in mind, what kind of time and space is necessary for contemporary art to become manifest? Or rather: What does criticism about contemporary art say about time and space today?

To brutally summarise a lot of scholarly texts: contemporary art is made possible by neoliberal capital plus the internet, biennials, art fairs, parallel pop-up histories, growing income inequality. Let's add asymmetric warfare – as one of the reasons for the vast redistribution of wealth – real estate speculation, tax evasion, money laundering, and deregulated financial markets to this list.

To paraphrase the philosopher Peter Osborne's illuminating insights on this topic: contemporary art shows us the lack of a (global) time and space. Moreover, it projects a fictional unity onto a variety of different ideas of time and space, thus providing a common surface where there is none.[2]

Contemporary art thus becomes a proxy for the global commons, for the lack of any common ground, temporality, or space. It is defined by a proliferation of locations, and a lack of accountability. It works by way of major real estate operations transforming cities worldwide as they reorganise urban space. It is even a space of civil wars that trigger art-market booms a decade or so later through the redistribution of wealth by warfare. It takes place on servers and by means of fibre-optic infrastructure, and whenever public debt miraculously transforms into private wealth. Contemporary art happens when taxpayers are deluded into believing they are bailing out other sovereign states when in fact they are subsidising international banks that thus get compensated for pushing high-risk debt onto vulnerable nations.[3] Or when this or that regime decides it needs the PR equivalent of a nip and tuck procedure.

But contemporary art also creates new physical spaces that bypass national sovereignty. Let me give you a contemporary example: freeport art storage.

This is the mother of all freeport art storage spaces: Geneva freeport, a tax-free zone in Geneva that includes parts of an old freight station and an industrial storage building. The free-trade zone takes up the backyard and the fourth floor of the old storage building, so that different jurisdictions run through one and the same building, as the other floors are set outside the freeport zone. A new art storage space was opened in 2014. Up until just a few years before, the freeport wasn't even officially considered part of Switzerland.

This building is rumoured to house thousands of Picassos, but no one knows the exact number since documentation is rather opaque. There is little doubt though that its contents could compete with any very large museum.[4]

Let's assume that this is one of the most important art spaces in the world right now. It is not only not public, but it is also sitting inside a very interesting geography.

From a legal standpoint, freeport art storage spaces are somewhat extraterritorial. Some are located in the transit zones of airports or in tax-free zones. Keller Easterling describes the free zone as a 'fenced enclave for warehousing'.[5] It has now become a primary organ of global urbanism copied and pasted to locations worldwide. It is an example of 'extra-statecraft', as Easterling terms it, within a 'mongrel state of exception', beyond the laws of the nation-state. In this deregulatory state of exemption, corporations are privileged at the expense of common citizens, 'investors' replace taxpayers, and modules supplant buildings: '[Freeports'] attractions are similar to those offered by offshore financial centres: security and confidentiality, not much scrutiny ... and an array of tax advantages ... Goods in freeports are technically in transit, even if in reality the ports are used more and more as permanent homes for accumulated wealth'.[6]

The freeport is thus a zone for permanent transit.

Although it is fixed, does the freeport also define perpetual ephemerality? Is it simply an extraterritorial zone, or is it also a rogue sector carefully settled for financial profitability?[7]

The freeport contains multiple contradictions: it is a zone of terminal impermanence; it is also a zone of legalised extra-legality maintained by nation-states trying to emulate failed states as closely as possible – by selectively losing control. Thomas Elsaesser once used the term 'constructive instability' to describe the aerodynamic properties of fighter jets that gain decisive advantages by navigating at the brink of system failure.[8] They would more or less 'fall' or 'fail' in the desired direction. This constructive instability is implemented within nation-states by incorporating zones where they 'fail' on purpose. Switzerland for example contains '245 open customs warehouses',[9] enclosing zones of legal and administrative exception. Are this state and others a container for different types of jurisdictions that get applied, or rather do not get applied, in relation to the wealth of corporations or individuals? Does this kind of state become a package for opportunistic statelessness? As Elsaesser pointed out, his whole idea of 'constructive instability' originated with a discussion of Swiss artists Fischli and Weiss's work *Der Lauf der Dinge* (1987). Here all sorts of things are knocked off balance in celebratory collapse. The film's glorious motto is:

> *Am schönsten ist das Gleichgewicht, kurz bevor's zusammenbricht.*
> [Balance is most beautiful just at the point when it is about to collapse.]

Among many other things, freeports also become a zone for duty free art, a zone where control and failure are calibrated according to 'constructive instability' so that things cheerfully hang in a permanently frozen failing balance.

FOURTH CHAPTER: DUTY FREE ART

Huge art storage spaces are being created worldwide in what could essentially be called a luxury no man's land, tax havens where artworks are shuffled around from one storage room to another once they get traded. This is also one of the prime spaces for contemporary art: an offshore or extraterritorial museum. In September 2014, Luxembourg opened its own freeport. The country is not alone in trying to replicate the success of the Geneva freeport: 'A freeport that opened at Changi Airport in Singapore in 2010 is already close to full. Monaco has one, too. A planned "freeport of culture" in Beijing would be the world's largest art-storage facility'.[10] A major player in setting up many of these facilities is the art-handling company Natural Le Coultre, run by Swiss national Yves Bouvier.

Freeport art storage facilities are secret museums. Their spatial conditions are reflected in their designs. In contrast to the rather perfunctory Swiss facility, designers stepped up their game at the freeport art storage facility in Singapore:

> Designed by Swiss architects, Swiss engineers and Swiss security experts, the 270,000-square-foot facility is part bunker, part gallery. Unlike the freeport facilities in Switzerland, which are staid yet secure warehouses, the Singapore FreePort sought to combine security and style. The lobby, showrooms and furniture were designed by contemporary designers Ron Arad and Johanna Grawunder. A gigantic arcing sculpture by Mr. Arad, titled *Cage sans Frontières* [Cage Without Borders], spans the entire lobby. Paintings that line the exposed concrete walls lend the facility the air of a gallery. Private rooms and vaults, barricaded by seven-ton doors, line the corridors. Near the lobby, private galleries give collectors a chance to view or show potential buyers their art under museum-quality spotlights. A planned second phase will double the size of the facility to 538,000 square feet. Collectors are picked up by FreePort staff at their plane and whisked by limousine, any time of day or night, to the facility. If the client is packing valuables, an armed escort will be provided.[11]

The title 'Cage Without Borders' has a double meaning. It not only means that the cage has no limits, but also that the prison is now everywhere, in an extrastatecraft art withdrawal facility that seeps through the cracks of national sovereignty and establishes its own logistic network. In this ubiquitous prison, rules still apply, though it might be difficult to specify exactly which ones, to whom or what they apply, and how they are implemented. Whatever they are, their grip seems to considerably loosen in inverse proportion to the value of the assets in question. But this construction is not only a device realised in one particular location in 3D space. It is also basically a stack of juridical, logistical, economic, and data-based operations, a pile of platforms mediating between clouds and users via state laws, communication protocols, corporate standards, etc., that interconnect not only via fibre-optic connections but aviation routes as well.[12]

Freeport art storage is to this 'stack' as the national museum traditionally was to the nation. It sits in between countries in pockets of superimposing sovereignties where national jurisdiction has either voluntarily retreated or been demolished. If biennials, art fairs, 3D renderings of gentrified real estate, starchitect museums decorating various regimes, etc., are the corporate surfaces of these areas, the secret museums are their dark web, their Silk Road into which things disappear, as into an abyss of withdrawal.[13]

Think of the artworks and their movement. They travel inside a network of tax-free zones and also inside the storage spaces themselves. Perhaps as they do, they never get uncrated. They move from one storage room to the next without being seen. They stay inside boxes and travel outside national territories with a minimum of tracking or registration, like insurgents, drugs, derivative financial products, and other so-called investment vehicles. For all we know, the crates could even be empty. It is a museum of the internet era, but a museum of the dark net, where movement is obscured and data-space is clouded.

1 From Wikipedia: 'The Google "Ngram" Viewer is an online viewer, initially based on Google Books, that charts frequencies of any word or short sentence using yearly count of n-grams found in the sources printed since 1800 up to 2012 in any of the following eight languages: American English, British English, French, German, Spanish, Russian, Hebrew, and Chinese'.

2 Osborne argues that contemporary art expresses the 'disjunctive unity of present times… As a historical concept, the contemporary thus involves a projection of unity onto the differential totality of the times of human lives'. Peter Osborne, *Anywhere or Not At All: Philosophy of Contemporary Art*, London: Verso, 2013, p. 22.

3 As in the case of the relation between Germany (or EU taxpayers) and Greece. 89% of the so-called bailout funds have gone to international banks. Only the remaining 11% has reached the Greek national budget. Even if only a fraction of this money ends up at auction, how would auctions nowadays fare without the constant subsidies from public funds that mysteriously end up as private assets?

4 'Suffice it to say, there is wide belief among art dealers, advisers and

insurers that there is enough art tucked away here to create one of the world's great museums'. David Segal, 'Swiss Freeports Are Home for a Growing Treasury of Art', *New York Times*, 21 July 2012.

5 Keller Easterling, *Extrastatecraft: The Power of Infrastructure Space*, London: Verso, 2014.

6 'Freeports: Über-warehouses for the Ultra-rich', *The Economist*, 23 November 2013.

7 'According to a confidential document, Geneva freeport in total would generate no less than 300 million Swiss francs of revenue for the canton'. Marie Maurisse, 'La "caverne d'Ali Baba" de Genève, plus grand port franc du monde, ignore la crise', *Le Figaro*, 20 September 2014.

8 Thomas Elsaesser, '"Constructive Instability", or: The life of Things as the Cinema's Afterlife?' (2008), at pure.uva.nl. This notion's manifold implications for contemporary political thought and its relation to managed collapse cannot be underestimated in regard not only to technology but also political usage: 'Its engineering provenance has been overlaid by a neo-con political usage, for instance, by Condoleezza Rice when she called the deaths among the civilian population and the resulting chaos during the Lebanon-Israel war in the summer of 2006 the consequence of "constructive instability"' (19).

9 Cynthia O'Murchu, 'Swiss Businessman Arrested in Art Market Probe', *Financial Times*, 26 February 2015.

10 'Freeports', *The Economist*.

11 Cris Prystay, 'Singapore Bling', *Wall Street Journal*, 21 May 2010.

12 Benjamin Bratton, 'On the Nomos of the Cloud: The Stack, Deep Address, Integral Geography', November 2011, at bratton.info: 'The Stack, the megastructure, can be understood as a confluence of interoperable standards-based complex material-information system of systems, organised according to a vertical section, topographic model of layers and protocols. The Stack is a standardised universal section. The Stack, as we encounter it and as I prototype it, is composed equally of social, human and "analogue" layers (chthonic energy sources, gestures, affects, user-actants, interfaces, cities and streets, rooms and buildings, organic and inorganic envelopes) and informational, non-human computational and "digital" layers (multiplexed fibre-optic cables, datacentres, databases, data standards and protocols, urban-scale networks, embedded systems, universal addressing tables). Its hard and soft systems intermingle and swap phase states, some becoming "harder" or "softer" according to occult conditions. (Serres, hard soft). As a social cybernetics, The Stack that we know and design composes both equilibrium and emergence, one oscillating into the other in indecipherable and unaccountable rhythm, territorialising and deterritorialising the same component for diagonal purposes'.

13 An audience member in Moscow made the extremely intelligent remark that this was to be seen as a huge benefit, as a lot of shoddy 'market art' would get safely quarantined without anyone having to see it. I sympathise very much with her point of view.

DE L'ART EN DUTY FREE – L'ART À L'ÉPOQUE DE LA GUERRE CIVILE PLANÉTAIRE

Hito Steyerl

TROISIÈME CHAPITRE : CONDITIONS DE POSSIBILITÉ

Selon la visionneuse Google Ngram[1], l'emploi du mot « impossible » a fortement diminué depuis le milieu du vingtième siècle. Qu'est-ce que cela nous apprend ? Cela signifie-t-il que de moins en moins de choses sont impossibles ? Cela signifie-t-il que l'impossibilité « en tant que telle » est entrée dans une phase de déclin historique ? Cela pourrait-il signifier que les conditions de possibilité sont en tant que telles soumises au changement dans le temps ? Le possible et l'impossible sont-ils définis par des conditions historiques extérieures ?

Pour Emmanuel Kant, le temps et l'espace sont les conditions nécessaires de toute perception et compréhension. Hors du temps et de l'espace, le savoir, l'expérience et la vision ne peuvent se déployer. Kant qualifie cette perspective de « critique ». Dans ce contexte, quel est le type de temps et d'espace nécessaire à la manifestation de l'art contemporain ? Ou plutôt : que nous apprend la critique de l'art contemporain du temps et de l'espace actuels ?

Pour résumer grossièrement un paquet de textes savants : l'art contemporain est rendu possible par le capital néolibéral plus Internet, les biennales, les foires d'art, l'apparition d'histoires parallèles artificielles et l'accroissement des inégalités de revenu. Ajoutons encore à cette liste l'asymétrie des guerres – l'une des raisons derrière la redistribution des richesses –, la spéculation immobilière, l'évasion fiscale, le blanchiment d'argent et la dérégulation des marchés financiers.

Pour paraphraser les intuitions lumineuses du philosophe Peter Osborne : l'art contemporain donne à voir l'absence d'espace-temps (global). Il projette en outre une unité fictionnelle sur une grande variété de conceptions du temps et de l'espace, produisant une surface commune là où il n'en existe pas[2].

L'art contemporain devient de sorte un substitut [*proxy*] pour les biens communs planétaires [*global commons*] : pour l'absence de terrain, de temporalité ou d'espace communs. Il se caractérise par une prolifération de ses sites et par un manque de traçabilité. Il repose sur des opérations immobilières de grande ampleur qui transforment des villes autour du monde en réorganisant l'espace urbain. C'est aussi un espace de guerres civiles, capables de déclencher à dix ans d'intervalle un boom du marché de l'art porté par la redistribution des richesses dans le sillage des guerres. Il se déploie sur les serveurs et par fibre optique, et partout où la dette publique est miraculeusement transformée en richesse privée. L'art contemporain fleurit dès que les contribuables sont poussés à croire qu'ils participent au sauvetage d'autres États souverains alors qu'ils subventionnent en réalité des banques internationales récompensées pour avoir poussé des nations vulnérables à racheter de la dette à haut-risque[3]. Ou lorsque tel ou tel régime décide qu'il lui faut l'équivalent com' d'un bon lifting.

Mais l'art contemporain crée aussi de nouveaux espaces physiques qui court-circuitent les souverainetés nationales. C'est le cas du stockage d'art en zone franche.

C'est la mère de tous les entrepôts d'art en zone franche : le port franc de Genève, une zone de Genève exempte de taxes qui comprend une partie d'une ancienne gare de fret et d'un entrepôt industriel. La zone franche occupe la cour et le quatrième étage de l'ancien entrepôt, de sorte que différentes juridictions parcourent le même bâtiment, les autres étages se trouvant en-dehors de la zone franche. Un nouvel espace de stockage d'art a été inauguré en 2014. Quelques années plus tôt, le port franc n'était même pas officiellement considéré comme faisant partie de la Suisse.

La rumeur veut que ce bâtiment abrite des milliers de Picasso, mais personne n'en connaît le nombre exact car les documents sont assez opaques. Il fait toutefois peu de doute que son contenu serait capable de concurrencer celui de n'importe quel grand musée[4].

Partons du principe qu'il s'agit de l'un des espaces artistiques les plus importants au monde à l'heure actuelle. Non seulement il n'est pas public, mais il s'inscrit au sein d'une géographie profondément intéressante.

D'un point de vue juridique, les espaces de stockage d'art en port franc sont plus ou moins extraterritoriaux. Certains sont situés dans des zones de transit d'aéroports ou dans des zones franches. Keller Easterling décrit la zone franche comme une « enclave clôturée de stockage[5] ». Elle représente aujourd'hui une entité essentielle de l'urbanisme mondial, copiée-collée partout dans le monde. C'est un exemple d'« infrastructure extra-étatique » [*extrastatecraft*], pour reprendre Easterling, au sein d'un « état d'exception hybride » [*mongrel state of exception*] étranger aux lois de l'État-nation. Dans cet état d'exonération dérèglementé, les entreprises sont privilégiées aux dépens des simples citoyens, les « investisseurs » remplacent les contribuables et les préfabriqués détrônent les immeubles : « Les atouts [des ports francs] rejoignent ceux offerts par les centres financiers *offshore* : sécurité et confidentialité, faible niveau de vérification [...] et un vaste éventail d'avantages fiscaux [...]. Les biens dans les ports francs sont techniquement en transit, même si en réalité les ports sont de plus en plus utilisés comme des résidences permanentes pour de riches patrimoines[6]. »

Le port franc est donc une zone de transit permanent.

Le port franc, en dépit de sa fixité, définirait-il une éphémérité perpétuelle ? S'agit-il uniquement d'une zone extraterritoriale, ou bien également d'un secteur informel soigneusement instauré dans une optique de rentabilité financière[7] ?

Le port franc renferme de nombreuses contradictions : c'est une zone d'impermanence extrême ; c'est aussi une zone extralégale légalisée entretenue par des États-nations qui tentent d'imiter des États défaillants à travers une perte de contrôle sélective. Thomas Elsaesser a employé le terme d'« instabilité constructive » pour décrire les propriétés aérodynamiques d'avions de chasse susceptibles d'acquérir des avantages décisifs en pilotant à la limite de la défaillance de système[8]. Ils « chutent » ou « échouent » plus ou moins dans la direction voulue. Cette instabilité constructive est mise en œuvre par des États-nations moyennant l'incorporation de zones au sein desquelles ils « échouent » volontairement. La Suisse accueille ainsi « 245 entrepôts douaniers ouverts[9] » qui renferment des zones d'exception juridique et administrative. Cet État et d'autres du même type sont-ils des réceptacles pour différentes sortes de juridictions appliquées – ou plutôt non appliquées – en fonction de la richesse des entreprises et des individus ? Ces États se transforment-t-ils en emballages pour une apatridie opportuniste ? Comme le souligne Elsaesser, l'idée même d'une « instabilité constructive » est née d'un débat autour de l'œuvre des artistes suisses Fischli et Weiss, *Der Lauf der Dinge* (1987). L'œuvre met en scène toutes sortes de choses perdant leur équilibre dans un effondrement jubilatoire. La magnifique devise du film est la suivante :

> *Am schönsten ist das Gleichgewicht, kurz bevor's zusammenbricht.*
> [Le plus bel équilibre est celui qui s'apprête à se rompre.]

Les ports francs sont devenus, entre autres choses, une zone d'art en duty-free, une zone où le contrôle et l'échec sont calibrés en fonction d'une « instabilité constructive », de sorte que tout est joyeusement suspendu dans un équilibre sans cesse au bord de la rupture.

QUATRIÈME CHAPITRE : DUTY FREE ART

Aujourd'hui et partout dans le monde, de gigantesques espaces de stockage d'art sortent de terre dans ce que l'on pourrait qualifier de no man's land du luxe, des paradis fiscaux dans lesquels les œuvres sont déplacées d'un entrepôt à l'autre au gré des transactions. C'est également l'un des espaces privilégiés de l'art contemporain : un musée offshore ou extraterritorial. En septembre 2014, le Luxembourg a inauguré son propre port franc. Le pays n'est pas le seul à tenter d'imiter le succès du port franc de Genève. « Le port franc inauguré en 2010 à l'aéroport Changi de Singapour arrive déjà à saturation. Monaco aussi a le sien. Le "port franc de la culture" prévu à Pékin constituerait le plus grand espace de stockage d'art au monde[10]. » Parmi les principaux acteurs du développement de ces infrastructures se trouve la société de transport d'œuvres Natural Le Coultre, dirigée par le Suisse Yves Bouvier.

Les espaces de stockage d'art en port franc sont des musées secrets. Leurs conditions spatiales se reflètent dans leur design. À la différence de l'infrastructure suisse, plutôt sommaire, les designers semblent être passés pour l'entrepôt d'art en port franc de Singapour à la vitesse supérieure :

> Conçu par des architectes suisses, des ingénieurs suisses et des experts en sécurité suisses, le complexe de 25 000 mètres carrés est moitié bunker, moitié galerie. À la différence du port franc suisse, composé d'entrepôts simples mais sûrs, le FreePort de Singapour a cherché à marier style et sécurité. L'accueil, les espaces d'exposition et l'ameublement ont été conçus par les designers contemporains Ron Arad et Johanna Grawunder. Une gigantesque sculpture arquée réalisée par M. Arad et intitulée *Cage sans frontières* occupe tout l'accueil. Les tableaux accrochés le long des murs en béton brut confèrent au complexe un air de galerie. Les salles privées et les coffres-forts, barricadés derrière des portes de sept tonnes, se succèdent le long des couloirs. Près de l'accueil, les galeries privées donnent aux collectionneurs l'occasion de contempler leurs œuvres ou de les montrer à de potentiels acheteurs sous un éclairage digne d'un musée. Une seconde phase en cours de préparation projette de doubler la taille du complexe, la portant à 50 000 mètres carrés. Les collectionneurs sont accueillis à la descente de l'avion par le personnel du FreePort et conduits en limousine, à toute heure du jour ou de la nuit, jusqu'au complexe. Si le client transporte des objets de valeur, une escorte armée sera mise à sa disposition[11].

Le titre « Cage sans frontières » renferme un double sens. Il ne signifie pas seulement que la cage n'a pas de limites, mais suggère aussi que la prison est désormais partout, dans une infrastructure extra-étatique de mise en retrait d'art [*art withdrawal*] qui s'infiltre par les failles de la souveraineté nationale pour établir son propre réseau logistique. Dans cette prison omniprésente, des règles s'appliquent toujours, quoiqu'il puisse être difficile de dire exactement lesquelles, pour qui ou pour quoi elles s'appliquent, ou même comment elles sont appliquées. Quelles qu'elles soient, leur emprise semble se relâcher en proportion inverse de la valeur du patrimoine. Cette construction n'est par ailleurs pas uniquement un dispositif réalisé dans un endroit particulier au sein de l'espace tridimensionnel. Il s'agit également d'un ensemble d'opérations juridiques, logistiques, économiques et informatiques, un empilement de plateformes qui sert de médiateur entre *clouds* et utilisateurs par l'exploitation de lois nationales, de protocoles de communications, de normes d'entreprise, etc., reliées entre elles via fibre optique et voie aérienne[12].

Le stockage d'art en port franc est à cette « pile » [*stack*] ce que le musée national est traditionnellement à la nation. Il occupe un espace entre les pays, dans des poches de superposition de souverainetés d'où la juridiction nationale s'est soit volontairement retirée, soit a été détruite. Si les biennales, les foires, les rendus 3D de projets de gentrification immobilière, les musées de starchitectes qui décorent différents régimes et ainsi de suite sont les surfaces entrepreneuriales de ces secteurs, les musées secrets en sont le *dark web*, la route de la soie dans laquelle les choses disparaissent comme dans un abîme de mise en retrait[13].

Prenez les œuvres et leurs déplacements. Elles se meuvent au sein d'un réseau de zones franches et au sein des entrepôts mêmes. Peut-être ce faisant ne sont-elles jamais déballées. Elles passent d'un entrepôt à l'autre sans être vues. Elles restent dans leurs caisses et sortent des territoires nationaux avec un minimum de suivi et de documents officiels, comme les insurgés, les drogues, les produits financiers dérivés et d'autres supports d'investissement. Pour autant que l'on sache, ces caisses pourraient être vides. C'est un musée à l'ère d'Internet – mais un musée du *dark net* dans lequel les déplacements sont dissimulés et l'espace des données brouillé.

1 Sur Wikipedia : « L'outil "Ngram" de Google est une visionneuse en ligne initialement basée sur Google Books qui permet d'observer l'évolution de la fréquence d'un mot ou d'une phrase courte grâce au décompte du nombre de n-grammes par an au sein de sources imprimées de 1800 jusqu'à 2012 dans les huit langues suivantes : anglais-américain, anglais-britannique, français, allemand, espagnol, russe, hébreu et chinois. »

2 Osborne défend l'idée selon laquelle l'art contemporain exprime « l'unité disjonctive des temps présents. [...] En tant que concept historique, le contemporain implique ainsi la projection d'une unité sur la totalité différentielle des temporalités des vies humaines ». Peter Osborne, *Anywhere or Not At All: Philosophy of Contemporary Art*, Londres, Verso, 2013, p. 22.

3 Comme c'est le cas pour les rapports entre l'Allemagne (ou les contribuables de l'UE) et la Grèce. 89% des fonds dits de sauvetage ont été versés à des banques internationales. Seuls les 11% restants sont parvenus jusqu'au budget national grec. Même si seule une fraction de cet argent finit aux enchères, comment les ventes aux enchères se dérouleraient-elles aujourd'hui sans les subventions continues de fonds publics qui se retrouvent mystérieusement transformées en actifs privés ?

4 « On se contentera de dire que la conviction largement répandue chez les marchands d'arts, les conseillers et les assureurs, veut qu'il existe suffisamment d'œuvres enfermées ici pour créer l'un des plus grands musées du monde. » David Segal, « Swiss Freeports Are Home for a Growing Treasury of Art », *New York Times*, 21 juillet 2012.

5 Keller Easterling, *Extrastatecraft: The Power of Infrastructure Space*, Londres, Verso, 2014.

6 « Freeports: Über-warehouses for the Ultra-rich », *The Economist*, 23 novembre 2013.

7 « Selon un document confidentiel, le port franc de Genève générerait à lui seul non moins de 300 millions de francs suisses de revenu pour le canton. » Marie Maurisse, « La "caverne d'Ali Baba" de Genève, plus grand port franc du monde, ignore la crise », *Le Figaro*, 20 septembre 2014.

8 Thomas Elsaesser, « "Constructive Instability", or: The Life of Things as the Cinema's Afterlife? », pure.uva.nl, 2008. Les nombreuses implications de cette notion pour la pensée politique contemporaine et ses rapports avec un effondrement contrôlé ne peuvent être sous-estimées au regard non seulement de la technologie mais aussi de l'usage politique : « Son origine dans l'ingénierie a été recouverte par un emploi politique néo-conservateur, par exemple lorsque Condoleezza Rice a décrit la mort de civils et le chaos consécutif au cours de la guerre entre le Liban et Israël à l'été 2006 comme la conséquence d'une "instabilité constructive" », p. 19.

9 Cynthia O'Murchu, « Swiss Businessman Arrested in Art Market Probe », *Financial Times*, 26 février 2015.

10 « Freeports: Über-warehouses for the Ultra-rich », art. cit.

11 Cris Prystay, « Singapore Bling », *Wall Street Journal*, 21 mai 2010.

12 Benjamin Bratton, « On the Nomos of the Cloud: The Stack, Deep Address, Integral Geography », novembre 2011, abratton.info: « La Pile [*the Stack*], la méga-structure, peut être comprise comme un système à la confluence de systèmes informationnels-matériels complexes et interopérables basés sur des normes, organisée en fonction d'un modèle de strates et de protocoles topographique en coupe verticale. La Pile est une section universelle standardisée. La Pile, telle que nous la rencontrons et telle que je la modélise, se compose aussi bien de strates sociales, humaines et "analogiques" (sources d'énergie chthonique, gestes, affects, usagers-actants, interfaces, villes et rues, pièces et bâtiments, enveloppes organiques et non organiques) et de strates informationnelles, non humaines, informatiques et "numériques" (câbles de fibre optique multiplexes, centres de traitement des données, bases de données, normes et protocoles de données, réseaux à échelle urbaine, systèmes intégrés, systèmes d'adresse universels). Ses systèmes "durs" et "doux" s'entremêlent et troquent leurs changements états, certains devenant plus "durs" ou plus "doux" en fonction de conditions opaques (Serres, le dur, le doux). En tant que cybernétique sociale, la Pile telle que nous la connaissons et que nous la construisons se présente à la fois comme un équilibre et une émergence, l'un oscillant vers l'autre à un rythme indéchiffrable et inexplicable, territorialisant et déterritorialisant la même composante à des fins diagonales. »

13 Un membre du public à Moscou m'a fait remarquer, de manière extrêmement intelligente, que cela devrait être perçu comme un immense avantage, une grande partie de l'« art marchand » médiocre étant soigneusement tenu à l'écart sans que personne n'ait à le regarder. J'ai beaucoup de sympathie pour ce point de vue.

NEW DARK AGE: TECHNOLOGY AND THE END OF THE FUTURE
James Bridle

When most people picture a stock exchange, they imagine a vast hall or pit filled with screaming traders, clutching fistfuls of paper, making deals and making money. But over the last few decades, most of the trading floors around the world have fallen silent. First they were replaced with more mundane offices: men (almost always men) clutching phones and staring at lines on computer screens. Only when something went badly wrong – bad enough to be assigned a colour, like Black Monday or Silver Thursday – did the screaming appear again. Most recently, even the men have been replaced with banks of computers that trade automatically, following fixed – but highly complex – strategies developed by banks and hedge funds. As computing power has increased and networks have gotten faster and faster, the speed of the exchanges has accelerated, giving this technique its sobriquet: high-frequency trading.

High-frequency trading on stock markets evolved in response to two closely related pressures, which were actually the result of a single technological shift. These pressures were latency, and visibility. As stock exchanges deregulated and digitised through the

1980s and 1990s – what was called, on the London Stock Exchange, the 'big bang' – it became possible to trade on them ever faster, and at ever-greater distances. This produced a series of weird effects. While profits have long been made by being the first to leverage the difference between prices on different markets – Paul Reuter famously arranged for ships arriving from America to toss canisters containing news overboard off the Irish coast so their contents could be telegraphed to London ahead of the ship's arrival – digital communications hyperaccelerate the process.

Financial information now travels at the speed of light; but the speed of light is different in different places. It's different in glass and air, and it encounters limitations, as fibre-optic cables are bundled together, pass through complex exchanges, and route around natural obstacles and under oceans. The greatest prizes go to those with the lowest latency: the shortest travel time between two points. This is where private fibre-optic lines and microwave towers come into the picture. In 2009–10, one company spent $300 million to build a private fibre link between the Chicago Mercantile Exchange and Carteret, New Jersey, home of the NASDAQ exchange.[1] They closed roads, they dug trenches, they bored through mountains, and they did it all in secret, so that no competitors discovered their plan. By shortening the physical distance between the sites, Spread Networks reduced the time it took a message to get between the two data centres from seventeen milliseconds to thirteen – resulting in a saving of about $75 million per millisecond.

In 2012, another firm, McKay Brothers, opened a second dedicated New York-Chicago connection. This time it used microwaves, which travel through the air faster than light through glass fibre. One of their partners stated that 'a single millisecond advantage could equate to an additional $100 million a year to a large high-frequency trading firm'.[2] McKay's link gained them four – a vast advantage over any of their competitors, many of whom were also taking advantage of another effect of the fallout from the big bang: visibility.

Digitisation meant that trades within, as well as between, stock exchanges could happen faster and faster. As the actual trading passed into the hands of machines, it became possible to react almost instantaneously to any price change or new offer. But being able to react meant both understanding what was happening, and being able to buy a place at the table. Thus, as in everything else, digitisation made the markets both more opaque to non-initiates, and radically visible to those in the know. In this case, the latter were those with the funding and the expertise to keep up with light-speed information flows: the private banks and hedge funds employing high-frequency traders. Algorithms designed by former physics PhDs to take advantage of millisecond advantages in access entered the market, and the traders gave them names like Ninja, Sniper, and The Knife. These algorithms were capable of eking out fractions of a cent on every trade, and they could do it millions of times a day. Seen within the turmoil of the markets, it was rarely clear who actually operated these algorithms; and it is no more so today, because their primary tactic is stealth: masking their intentions and their origins while capturing a vast portion of all traded value. The result was an arms race: whoever could build the fastest software, reduce the latency of their connection to the exchanges, and best hide their true objective, made bank.

Operating on stock exchanges became a matter of dark dealing, and of dark fibre. The darkness goes deeper too: many traders today opt to deal not in the relatively well-regulated public exchanges, but in what are called 'dark pools'. Dark pools are private forums for trading securities, derivatives, and other financial instruments. A 2015 report by the US Securities and Exchange Commission (SEC) estimated that dark pool trading accounted for one-fifth of all trades in stocks that also traded on the public exchanges – a figure that doesn't account for many other popular forms of financial instrument.[3] The dark pools allow traders to move large volumes of stock without tipping off the wider market, thus protecting their trades from other predators. But they're also shady places, where conflicts of interest run rampant. Initially advertised as places to trade securely, many dark pool operators have been censured for quietly inviting in the same high-frequency traders their clients were trying to avoid – either to provide liquidity to the market, or for their own profit. The 2015 SEC report lists numerous such deals, in what it calls 'a dismal litany of misconduct'. In 2016, Barclays and Credit Suisse were fined $154 million for secretly allowing high-frequency traders as well as their own staff access to their supposedly private dark pool.[4] Because the pool is dark, it's impossible to know how much their clients lost to these unseen predators, but many of their largest customers were pension funds, charged with managing the retirement plans of ordinary people.[5] What is lost in the dark pools, unknown to their members, is lifetime savings, future security, and livelihoods.

[...]

Technology is in fact a key driver of inequality across many sectors. The relentless progress of automation – from supermarket checkouts to trading algorithms, factory robots to self-driving cars – increasingly threatens human employment across the board. There is no safety net for those whose skills are rendered obsolete by machines; and even those who programme the machines are not immune. As the capabilities of machines increase, more and more professions are under attack, with artificial intelligence augmenting the process. The internet itself helps shape this path to inequality, as network effects and the global availability of services produces a winner-takes-all marketplace, from social networks and search engines to grocery stores and taxi companies. The complaint of the Right against communism – that we'd all have to buy our goods from a single state supplier – has been supplanted by the necessity of buying everything from Amazon. And one of the keys to this augmented inequality is the opacity of technological systems themselves.

In March of 2017, Amazon acquired Quidsi, a company that had built a huge business on the back of low-cost, high-volume goods such as infant supplies and cosmetics. They did so by pioneering automation at every level of the distribution chain, and removing the human in the process. The centre of Quidsi's operations is a vast warehouse in Goldsboro, Pennsylvania, and in the centre of that is a 200,000-square-foot area marked out with bright yellow paint and ringed with signs. This space is filled with racks of shelving, each unit six feet high and several feet deep, packed with goods – in this case, nappies and other childcare items. The signs are warning signs. Humans cannot enter this space to get to those goods, because this is where the robots work.

Within the robot zone, 260 bright orange, quarter-ton lozenges spin and lift, sliding under different shelving units and carrying them to the edges of the zone, where human pickers wait to add or remove packages. These are Kiva robots: warehouse automatons that trundle tirelessly around the merchandise, following computer-readable marks on the floor. Faster and more accurate than human handlers, they do the heavy lifting, allowing Quidsi, the owner of Diapers.com, to ship thousands of orders every day from this warehouse alone.

Amazon had its eye on Quidsi's use of Kiva robots for some time, but it was already working on its own forms of automation long before the acquisition. In Rugeley, England, inside a sky-blue warehouse the size of nine football pitches on the site of an old colliery, Amazon employs hundreds of people wearing orange tabards who push trolleys down deep aisles of shelving, stacking them with books, DVDs, electronics and other goods. Each worker walks quickly, following the directions on a hand-held device that pings constantly with new locations to be visited. It also tracks the worker's progress, ensuring that they cover enough ground – up to fifteen miles a day – and pick enough items to enable their employer to send out one fully loaded truck from one of its eight UK facilities every three minutes.

The reason Amazon's workers need hand-held devices to navigate around the warehouse is because it is otherwise impenetrable to humans. Humans would expect goods to be stored in human-type ways: the books over here, DVDs over there, racks of stationery to the left, and so on. But to a rational machine intelligence, such an arrangement is deeply inefficient. Consumers don't order goods alphabetically or by type; rather they fill a basket with goods from all over the store – or, in this case, the warehouse. As a result, Amazon employs a logistics technique called 'chaotic storage' – chaotic, that is, from a human point of view. By locating products by need and association rather than by type, it's possible to construct much shorter paths between items. Books are stacked on shelves next to saucepans; televisions share space with children's toys. Like data stored on a computer's hard drive, goods are distributed across the entirety of the warehouse space, each uniquely addressable by barcodes, but impossible to find without the help of a computer. Arranging the world from the perspective of the machine renders it computationally efficient, but makes it completely incomprehensible to humans. And moreover, it accelerates their oppression.

The hand-held devices carried by Amazon's workers and mandated by its logistics are also tracking devices, recording their every movement and keeping score of their efficiency. Workers are docked points – meaning money – for failing to keep up with the machine, for toilet breaks, for late arrival from home or meals, while constant movement prevents association with fellow employees. They have nothing to do but follow the instructions on the screen, pack and carry. They are intended to act like robots, impersonating machines while remaining, for now, slightly cheaper than them.

Reducing workers to meat algorithms, useful only for their ability to move and follow orders, makes them easier to hire, fire, and abuse. Workers who go where their wrist-mounted terminal tells them to don't even need to understand the local language, and they don't need an education. Both of these factors, together with the atomisation produced by technological augmentation, also prevent effective organisation. Whether you're a bone-tired, constantly moving picker on the Amazon shop floor getting your instructions from a Wi-Fi-enabled barcode scanner, or a late-night, individually contracted mini-cab driver following the bright line of a GPS system from red dot to red dot, the technology effectively precludes you from working with your colleagues for the advancement of working conditions. (This hasn't stopped Uber, for example, from requiring that its drivers listen to a set number of anti-union podcasts every week, all controlled by their app, to drive the message home.)[6]

[...]

Whatever one might think of the morals of executives at Uber, Amazon, and many, many companies like them, few set out to actively create such conditions for their workers. Nor is this a simple return to the robber barons and industrial tyrants of the nineteenth century. To the capitalist ideology of maximum profit has been added the possibilities of technological opacity, with which naked greed can be clothed in the inhuman logic of the machine.

Both Amazon and Uber wield technological obscurity as a weapon. Behind a few pixels on Amazon's homepage are hidden the labour of thousands of exploited workers: every time the buy button is pressed, electronic signals direct a real human to set off in motion, to perform their efficient duty. The app is a remote control device for other people, but one whose real-world effects are almost impossible to see.

This aesthetic and technological obscurity breeds political unease, and corporate contempt. At Uber, a deliberate ambiguity starts in the user interface and pervades the entire operation. In order to convince users that the system is more successful, more active, and more responsive than it actually is, the map sometimes displays 'ghost cars': circling potential drivers who do not actually exist.[7] Rides are tracked, without the user's knowledge, and this God's-eye view is used to stalk high-profile clients.[8] A programme called Greyball is used to deny rides to government employees investigating the company's numerous transgressions.[9]

But the thing that seems to bother us most about Uber is the social atomisation and reduction in agency that it produces. Company workers are no longer employees but precarious contractors. Instead of studying for years to gain 'the knowledge', as London's black cab drivers call their intimate familiarity with the city's streets, they simply follow the on-screen arrows from turn to turn, directed by distant satellites and unseen data. Their customers are in turn further alienated; the whole system contributing to the offshoring of tax revenues, the decline of public transport services, and the class divisions and congestion of city streets. And, like Amazon and most other digitally driven businesses, Uber's ultimate goal is to replace its human workers entirely with machines. It has its own self-driving car programme, and its chief product officer, asked about the company's long-term viability when so many of its employees were dissatisfied, responded simply, 'Well, we're just going to replace them all with robots'. What happens to the Amazon workers eventually happens to everyone.

1 Christopher Steiner, 'Wall Street's Speed War', *Forbes*, 9 September 2010, forbes.com.
2 Kevin Fitchard, 'Wall Street Gains an Edge by Trading over Microwaves', *GigaOM*, 10 February 2012, gigaom.com.
3 Luis A. Aguilar, 'Shedding Light on Dark Pools', US Securities and Exchange Commission, 18 November 2015, www.sec.gov.
4 'Barclays and Credit Suisse are Fined over US "dark pools"', *BBC*, 1 February 2016, bbc.com.
5 Martin Arnold, et al., 'Banks Start to Drain Barclays Dark Pool', *Financial Times*, 26 June 2014, ft.com.
6 Jordan Golson, 'Uber is Using in-app Podcasts to Dissuade Seattle Drivers from Unionising', *Verge*, 14 March 2017, theverge.com.
7 Kate Knibbs, 'Uber Is Faking Us Out with "Ghost Cabs" on its Passenger Map', *Gizmodo*, 28 July 2015, gizmodo.com.
8 Kashmir Hill, '"God View": Uber Allegedly Stalked Users for Party-Goers' Viewing Pleasure', *Forbes*, 3 October 2014, forbes.com.
9 Julia Carrie Wong, 'Greyball: how Uber Used Secret Software to Dodge the Law', *Guardian*, 4 March 2017, theguardian.com.

UN NOUVEL ÂGE DE TÉNÈBRES. LA TECHNOLOGIE ET LA FIN DU FUTUR
James Bridle

Lorsque la plupart des gens se représentent la Bourse, ils imaginent un vaste hall ou une fosse remplie de *traders* hurlant, le poing crispé sur des papiers, en train de conclure des transactions et de gagner de l'argent. Mais au cours des dernières décennies, la plupart des salles de marché du monde entier se sont tues. Elles ont d'abord été remplacées par des bureaux plus banals, où l'on trouvait (presque exclusivement) des hommes, un téléphone à la main, le regard fixé sur les lignes affichées par des écrans d'ordinateur. C'est seulement lorsque quelque chose tournait mal – suffisamment mal pour qu'on lui attribue une couleur, comme le lundi noir ou le jeudi de l'argent – que les hurlements se faisaient de nouveau entendre. Plus récemment, les hommes eux-mêmes ont été remplacés par des rangées d'ordinateurs qui négocient automatiquement, en suivant des stratégies fixes – mais très complexes – élaborées par les banques et les fonds spéculatifs. À mesure que la puissance de calcul augmentait et que les réseaux devenaient de plus en plus rapides, la vitesse des échanges s'est accélérée, ce qui a donné à cette technique son sobriquet : le *trading* à haute fréquence.

Celui-ci est apparu sur les marchés boursiers en réponse à deux pressions étroitement liées, qui sont en fait le résultat d'un seul et même virage technologique : la latence et la visibilité. Suite à la déréglementation et à la numérisation des marchés boursiers dans les années 1980 et 1990 – ce que l'on a appelé, à la Bourse de Londres, le « big bang » –, il est devenu possible d'y négocier toujours plus rapidement et à des distances toujours plus grandes. Une série d'effets étranges s'est alors produite. Bien que les profits soient depuis longtemps réalisés en étant les premiers à exploiter la différence entre les prix sur plusieurs marchés – on sait que Paul Reuter s'est arrangé pour que les navires arrivant d'Amérique jettent par-dessus bord des bidons contenant des dépêches au large des côtes irlandaises, afin que leur contenu puisse être télégraphié à Londres avant l'arrivée du navire –, les communications numériques accélèrent le processus exponentiellement.

Les informations financières voyagent désormais à la vitesse de la lumière, qui n'est d'ailleurs pas la même selon les endroits. Elle ne traverse pas le verre comme l'air et se heurte à des limites : les câbles en fibre optique sont attachés ensemble, transitent par des centraux complexes, contournent des obstacles naturels et passent sous les océans. Les grands vainqueurs sont ceux qui ont la latence la plus faible, c'est-à-dire le temps de trajet le plus court entre deux points. C'est là que les lignes en fibre optique et les tours à micro-ondes privées entrent en jeu. Entre 2009 et 2010, une entreprise a dépensé 300 millions de dollars pour construire une connexion privée par fibre entre le Chicago Mercantile Exchange et Carteret, dans le New Jersey, où se trouve la bourse NASDAQ[1]. Ils ont fermé des routes, creusé des tranchées, percé des montagnes, tout cela en secret pour qu'aucun concurrent ne découvre leurs plans. En raccourcissant la distance physique entre les sites, Spread Networks a réduit le temps nécessaire à un message pour passer d'un *data center* à l'autre de dix-sept millisecondes à treize, ce qui a permis d'économiser environ 75 millions de dollars par milliseconde.

En 2012, une autre entreprise, McKay Brothers, a établi une deuxième connexion spécialisée entre New York et Chicago. Cette fois, ce sont les micro-ondes qui ont été utilisées, car elles se déplacent dans l'air plus rapidement que la lumière dans la fibre de verre. L'un de leurs partenaires a déclaré qu'« un avantage d'une seule milliseconde pourrait représenter 100 millions de dollars supplémentaires par an pour une grande entreprise pratiquant le *trading* à haute fréquence[2] ». La liaison de McKay Brothers lui a permis d'en gagner quatre, soit un avantage considérable sur tous ses concurrents, dont beaucoup ont également profité d'un autre effet du big bang : la visibilité.

Avec l'arrivée de la numérisation, les transactions pouvaient se faire de plus en plus rapidement, que ce soit au sein des marchés ou entre eux. Le négoce proprement dit étant passé aux mains des machines, il est devenu possible de réagir presque instantanément à tout changement de prix ou à toute nouvelle offre. Mais pour pouvoir réagir, il fallait aussi bien être en mesure de comprendre ce qui se passait que d'acheter une place à la table des négociations. Ainsi, et comme partout ailleurs, la numérisation a rendu les marchés à la fois plus opaques pour les non-initiés et radicalement visibles pour les connaisseurs, ces derniers étant, en l'occurrence, ceux qui disposaient des fonds et de l'expertise nécessaires pour suivre les flux d'informations à la vitesse de la lumière : les banques privées et les fonds spéculatifs ayant recours aux transactions à haute fréquence. Des algorithmes conçus par d'anciens docteurs en physique pour profiter d'avantages de l'ordre de la milliseconde sont entrés sur le marché ; les *traders* leur ont donné des noms comme Ninja, Sniper et The Knife [« le couteau »]. Ces algorithmes étaient capables de grignoter quelques fractions de centime sur chaque transaction, et ce des millions de fois par jour. Au milieu du tumulte des marchés, il était rarement évident de savoir qui contrôlait réellement ces algorithmes ; ça ne l'est pas davantage aujourd'hui, car leur tactique repose principalement sur la furtivité : ils déguisent leurs intentions et leurs origines tout en captant une grande partie de la valeur échangée. Ainsi commença une course aux armements : quiconque développerait le logiciel le plus rapide, réduirait la latence de sa connexion aux marchés boursiers et dissimulerait au mieux son véritable objectif, toucherait le pactole.

Depuis lors, opérer sur les marchés boursiers, c'est mener de sombres affaires par de sombres fibres. Cette obscurité est plus profonde encore : de nombreux *traders* choisissent aujourd'hui de négocier non pas sur les marchés publics, relativement bien réglementés, mais dans ce que l'on appelle les « *dark pools* ». Ce sont des forums privés où s'échangent des valeurs mobilières, des produits dérivés et d'autres instruments financiers. Selon un rapport publié en 2015 par la Securities and Exchange Commission (SEC) des États-Unis, les *dark pools* représentent un cinquième de toutes les transactions en actions, parmi celles qui se négocient également sur les marchés publics ; ce chiffre ne tient pas compte de nombreux autres types répandus d'instruments financiers[3]. Les *dark pools* permettent aux *traders* de déplacer de gros volumes d'actions sans alerter le marché dans son ensemble ; ils protègent ainsi leurs transactions des autres prédateurs. Mais ce sont aussi des lieux interlopes, où les conflits d'intérêts sont monnaie courante. Alors que les *dark pools* ont été présentés à l'origine comme des endroits où l'on peut négocier en toute sécurité, beaucoup de leurs organisateurs ont été blâmés pour avoir discrètement invité les mêmes *traders* à haute fréquence que leurs clients cherchaient à éviter, soit pour fournir des liquidités au marché, soit pour leur profit personnel. Le rapport de la SEC de 2015 énumère de nombreuses transactions de ce type, une liste qu'il qualifie de « lamentable litanie de fautes ». En 2016, Barclays et le Credit Suisse ont été condamnés à une amende de 154 millions de dollars pour avoir secrètement permis à des *traders* à haute fréquence, ainsi qu'à leur propre personnel, d'accéder à leur *dark pool* prétendument privé[4]. Puisque le bassin [*pool*] est obscur [*dark*], il est impossible de savoir combien leurs clients ont perdu au profit de ces prédateurs invisibles, mais beaucoup de leurs plus gros clients étaient des fonds de pension chargés de gérer les projets de retraite de gens ordinaires[5]. Ce qui est perdu dans les *dark pools*, à l'insu de leurs participants, ce sont les épargnes de toute une vie, l'assurance d'un avenir et les moyens de subsister.

[...]

La technologie est en fait un facteur clé d'inégalité dans de nombreux secteurs. Les progrès incessants de l'automatisation – des caisses de supermarché jusqu'aux algorithmes boursiers, des robots d'usine jusqu'aux voitures autonomes – menacent de plus en plus l'emploi humain dans tous les domaines. Il n'existe aucun filet de sécurité pour ceux dont les compétences sont rendues obsolètes par les machines ; même ceux qui les programment ne sont pas à l'abri. À mesure que les capacités des machines augmentent, de plus en plus de professions sont menacées, l'intelligence artificielle venant renforcer le processus. Même Internet contribue à tracer ce chemin vers l'inégalité, car les effets de réseau et la disponibilité des services à l'échelle mondiale engendrent un marché où le vainqueur emporte tout, que ce soit pour les réseaux sociaux, les moteurs de recherche, les épiceries ou les compagnies de taxi. La critique de la droite envers le communisme – à savoir que nous serions tous contraints d'acheter nos produits auprès d'un unique fournisseur tenu par l'État – est rendue caduque par la nécessité de tout acheter sur Amazon. Et l'une des clés de cette inégalité accrue est l'opacité des systèmes technologiques eux-mêmes.

En mars 2017, Amazon a racheté Quidsi, une entreprise qui a monté une énorme affaire basée sur la vente de produits à faible coût et en grandes quantités, comme les fournitures pour bébés et les cosmétiques. Pour ce faire, elle a été l'une des premières à automatiser l'ensemble de la chaîne de distribution en supprimant l'élément humain du processus. Le centre des opérations de Quidsi est situé dans un vaste entrepôt à Goldsboro, en Pennsylvanie ; au cœur de celui-ci se trouve une zone de 18 500 mètres carrés balisée par une peinture jaune vif et entourée de panneaux. Cet espace est rempli de rayonnages, chaque module mesurant un mètre quatre-vingt de haut et plusieurs dizaines de centimètres de profondeur, bourrés de marchandises, en l'occurrence de couches et d'autres articles de puériculture. Les panneaux servent d'avertissement. Les humains ne peuvent pas entrer dans cet espace pour accéder à ces marchandises, car c'est là que les robots travaillent.

À l'intérieur de la zone des robots, 260 losanges orange vif d'un quart de tonne pivotent et soulèvent différents rayons, sous lesquels ils se glissent, pour les transporter jusqu'aux bords de la zone, où des préparateurs de commandes humains attendent pour ajouter ou retirer des colis. Ce sont des robots Kiva : des automates d'entrepôt qui trottinent inlassablement autour de la marchandise, en suivant des marques au sol lisibles par ordinateur. Plus rapides et plus précis que les manutentionnaires, ils font le gros du travail, permettant à Quidsi, le propriétaire de Diapers.com, d'expédier des milliers de commandes chaque jour depuis ce seul entrepôt.

Depuis un certain temps, Amazon avait l'œil sur Quidsi et son utilisation des robots Kiva, mais l'entreprise travaillait déjà sur ses propres techniques d'automatisation bien avant cette acquisition. À Rugeley, en Angleterre, dans un entrepôt bleu ciel de la taille de neuf terrains de football situé sur une ancienne houillère, Amazon emploie des centaines de personnes vêtues de tabliers orange qui poussent des chariots le long de grandes allées de rayonnages pour y empiler des livres, des DVD, des appareils électroniques et d'autres produits. Chaque travailleur marche rapidement, en suivant les indications d'un appareil portatif qui signale en permanence les nouveaux emplacements à visiter. De plus, l'appareil suit la progression du travailleur, s'assurant que celui-ci couvre suffisamment de terrain – jusqu'à 25 km par jour – et qu'il ramasse assez d'articles pour permettre à son employeur de faire partir un camion entièrement chargé toutes les trois minutes depuis l'un de ses huit sites britanniques.

Si les travailleurs d'Amazon ont besoin d'appareils portatifs pour se déplacer dans l'entrepôt, c'est parce que celui-ci est sinon incompréhensible pour les humains. On s'attendrait à ce que les marchandises soient stockées selon un ordre humain : les livres par ici, les DVD par là, la papeterie à gauche, etc. Mais pour l'intelligence rationnelle d'une machine, une telle organisation est complètement inefficace. Les consommateurs ne commandent pas les articles par ordre alphabétique ou par type; ils ont plutôt tendance à remplir leur panier avec des produits provenant de tout le magasin, ou, dans le cas présent, de tout l'entrepôt. C'est pourquoi Amazon utilise une technique logistique appelée « stockage chaotique », le chaos n'étant, en fait, que celui perçu par les humains. En plaçant les produits par besoin et par association plutôt que par type, il est possible d'établir des chemins beaucoup plus courts entre les articles. Les livres sont empilés à côté des casseroles, les téléviseurs se partagent l'espace avec les jouets pour enfants. À l'instar des données stockées sur un disque dur, les produits sont répartis sur l'ensemble de l'entrepôt; chacun d'entre eux reçoit sous la forme d'un code-barres une adresse unique qui est impossible à trouver sans l'aide d'un ordinateur. Le fait d'organiser le monde du point de vue de la machine le rend efficace sur le plan informatique, mais totalement incompréhensible pour les humains. En outre, cela précipite leur oppression.

Les appareils électroniques portés par les travailleurs d'Amazon et imposés par sa logistique sont également des dispositifs de suivi, qui enregistrent le moindre de leurs mouvements et évaluent leur efficacité. Les travailleurs se voient retirer des points – autrement dit de l'argent – s'ils ne parviennent pas à suivre le rythme de la machine, s'ils font des pauses toilettes, s'ils arrivent en retard de leur domicile ou de leurs déjeuners, tandis que le mouvement constant empêche toute association entre collègues. Ils n'ont rien d'autre à faire que suivre les instructions affichées à l'écran, emballer et transporter. Ils sont censés agir comme des robots, se faire passer pour des machines, tout en restant, pour l'heure, légèrement moins chers qu'elles.

Réduire les travailleurs à des algorithmes de chair et d'os, seulement utiles pour leur capacité à se déplacer et à suivre les ordres, les rend plus faciles à embaucher, à licencier et à maltraiter. Comme ils vont là où l'appareil qu'ils portent au poignet leur dit d'aller, ils n'ont pas besoin d'être formés ni même de comprendre la langue du pays. Ces deux facteurs, ainsi que le fractionnement produit par la surcouche technologique, empêchent également une organisation efficace. Que vous soyez un préparateur de commandes épuisé, en perpétuel mouvement dans un entrepôt d'Amazon, qui reçoit ses instructions d'un lecteur de codes-barres connecté en Wi-Fi, ou bien un chauffeur de minicab[6] sous contrat d'indépendant qui suit, tard le soir, la ligne lumineuse d'un GPS d'un point rouge à un autre, la technologie vous empêche en effet de travailler avec vos collègues à l'amélioration des conditions de travail. (Cela n'a pas empêché Uber, par exemple, d'exiger que ses chauffeurs écoutent chaque semaine un nombre déterminé de podcasts anti-syndicaux, tous contrôlés par leur application, pour faire passer le message[7]).

[...]

Quoi que l'on puisse penser de la moralité des dirigeants d'Uber, d'Amazon et d'un très grand nombre d'entreprises similaires, peu d'entre eux ont entrepris de créer activement de telles conditions pour leurs travailleurs. Il ne s'agit pas non plus d'un simple retour aux barons voleurs et aux tyrans industriels du XIXe siècle. À l'idéologie capitaliste du profit maximum se sont ajoutées les possibilités offertes par l'opacité technologique, au moyen de laquelle la cupidité nue peut être revêtue de la logique inhumaine de la machine.

Amazon et Uber manient tous deux l'opacité technologique comme une arme. Derrière quelques pixels sur la page d'accueil d'Amazon se cache le travail de milliers d'ouvriers exploités : chaque fois que l'on appuie sur le bouton d'achat, des signaux électroniques ordonnent à un véritable être humain de se mettre en mouvement, d'accomplir sa tâche avec diligence. L'application est une télécommande pour certains, mais dont les effets réels sont presque impossibles à voir.

Cette obscurité esthétique et technologique engendre un malaise politique et un mépris de la part des entreprises. Chez Uber, l'ambiguïté commence délibérément dès l'interface utilisateur et imprègne l'ensemble du processus. Afin de convaincre les utilisateurs que le système est plus performant, plus actif et plus réactif qu'il ne l'est en réalité, la carte affiche parfois des « voitures fantômes » : des conducteurs présents dans leur secteur qui, en fait, n'existent pas[8]. Les trajets sont suivis, à l'insu de l'utilisateur, et cette omniscience est mise à profit pour traquer les clients importants[9]. Un programme appelé Greyball est utilisé pour refuser un chauffeur aux fonctionnaires qui enquêtent sur les nombreuses transgressions de l'entreprise[10].

Mais ce qui semble nous déranger le plus avec Uber, c'est le fractionnement social et la restriction des libertés qu'il produit. Ceux qui travaillent pour l'entreprise ne sont plus des employés mais des indépendants en situation précaire. Au lieu d'étudier pendant des années pour acquérir « *the knowledge* » [« le savoir »], comme disent à Londres les chauffeurs des taxis noirs en parlant de leur connaissance intime des rues de la ville, ils se contentent de suivre les flèches à l'écran d'un virage à l'autre, dirigés par des satellites lointains et des données invisibles. Leurs clients sont eux-mêmes d'autant plus aliénés : le système dans son ensemble contribue à la délocalisation des recettes fiscales, au déclin des services de transport public, aux clivages sociaux et à la congestion urbaine. À l'image d'Amazon et de la plupart des autres entreprises du numérique, l'objectif ultime d'Uber est de remplacer entièrement ses travailleurs humains par des machines. L'entreprise développe son propre programme de voitures autonomes ; son chef de produit, lorsqu'on l'a interrogé sur la viabilité à long terme d'Uber au vu du mécontentement d'un grand nombre de ses employés, s'est contenté de répondre : « Eh bien, nous allons tout simplement les remplacer par des robots ». Ce qui arrive aux travailleurs d'Amazon finira par arriver à tout le monde.

1 Christopher Steiner, « Wall Street's Speed War », *Forbes*, 9 septembre 2010, forbes.com.
2 Kevin Fitchard, « Wall Street Gains an Edge by Trading over Microwaves », *GigaOM*, 10 février 2012, gigaom.com.
3 Luis A. Aguilar, « Shedding Light on Dark Pools », *US Securities and Exchange Commission*, 18 novembre 2015, www.sec.gov.
4 « Barclays and Credit Suisse are Fined over US "Dark Pools" », *BBC*, 1er février 2016, bbc.com.
5 Martin Arnold *et al.*, « Banks Start to Drain Barclays Dark Pool », *The Financial Times*, 26 juin 2014, ft.com.
6 Au Royaume-Uni, taxi disponible uniquement sur pré-réservation (NdT).
7 Jordan Golson, « Uber is Using In-app Podcasts to Dissuade Seattle Drivers from Unionizing », *The Verge*, 14 mars 2017, theverge.com.
8 Kate Knibbs, « Uber Is Faking Us Out with "Ghost Cabs" on its Passenger Map », *Gizmodo*, 28 juillet 2015, gizmodo.com.
9 Kashmir Hill, « "God View": Uber Allegedly Stalked Users for Party-Goers' Viewing Pleasure », *Forbes*, 3 octobre 2014, forbes.com.
10 Julia Carrie Wong, « Greyball: how Uber Used Secret Software to Dodge the Law », *The Guardian*, 4 mars 2017, theguardian.com.

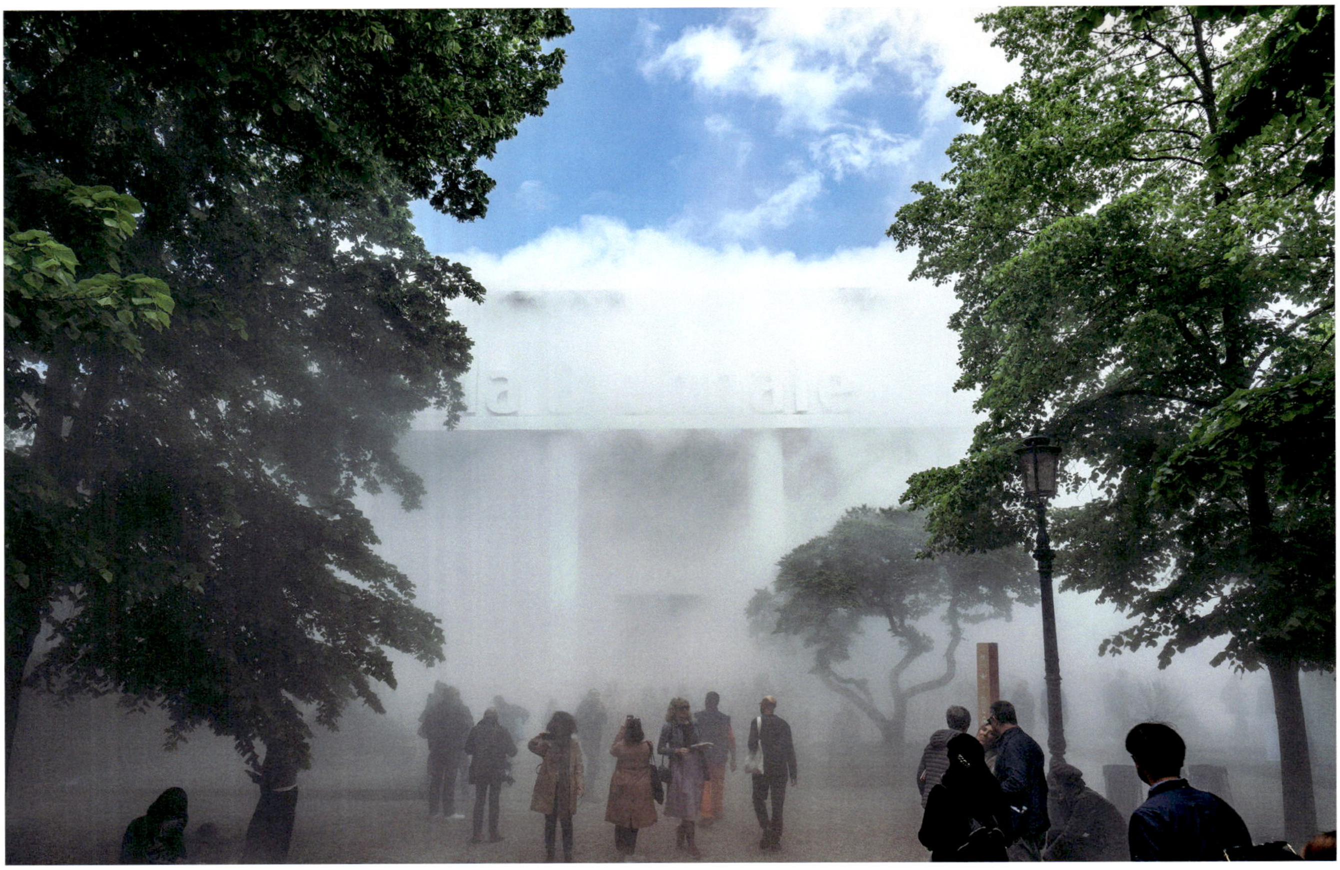

Lara Favaretto, *Thinking Head*, 2017–ongoing
(installation view)

Lara Favaretto

Lara Favaretto employs a variety of media to explore social, economic and cultural issues in our contemporary society, often with a degree of dark humour and irreverence. *Thinking Head* (2017–ongoing), originally commissioned for a solo exhibition at Nottingham Contemporary, was developed into a three-part work in 2019 and presented in the Central Pavilion at the 58th Venice Biennale. Collectively, the three distinct elements mirror the functioning of the human brain as if it were a machine, a generator of thoughts. First, a selection of objects that the artist has collected over the past twenty-five years were displayed in the Central Pavilion. Second, a series of 'clandestine talks' on single-word subjects inspired by these objects took place. Finally, a vapour emitted from the roof of the Pavilion partially obscured its façade. The latter is a nod to Alighiero Boetti's final sculpture *Autoritratto (Mi Fuma Il Cervello)*, (1993–94), an electrically-heated bronze

Lara Favaretto utilise différents médiums pour explorer des questions sociales, économiques et culturelles qui touchent la société contemporaine, avec bien souvent une touche d'humour noir et d'impertinence. *Thinking Head* (2017-en cours), initialement commandée dans le cadre d'une exposition personnelle de l'artiste à Nottingham Contemporary, est devenue en 2019 une œuvre en trois parties présentée dans le pavillon central de la 58e Biennale de Venise. Collectivement, ces trois éléments distincts reflètent le fonctionnement du cerveau humain, comme s'il s'agissait d'une machine ou d'un générateur de pensées. En premier lieu, une sélection d'objets rassemblés par l'artiste au cours des vingt-cinq dernières années était exposée dans le pavillon central. Puis une série de « discussions clandestines » sur des sujets inspirés par ces objets eurent lieu. Enfin, une vapeur était émise depuis le toit du pavillon, en en occultant partiellement la façade –

self-portrait in which the head literally fumes to suggest an overactive mind. Favaretto has said she wanted to turn a museum into a 'thinking machine'. Furthermore, this intervention functions as a form of institutional critique, obscuring the institution's architecture and dissolving its cultural authority from our view.

Favaretto's series of 'clandestine talks' are intended to deconstruct fifty 'key words' via a hidden discourse that takes place – according to the artist's instructions – in a 'bunker-like' environment (an undisclosed, protected, and soundproof location within or close to the institution). These 'key words' are described by the artist as 'vital and relevant to dissecting and redefining our present moment'. Each discussion involves three to seven participants, meeting behind closed doors and without a public audience for an undefined period of time during one day. The speakers are rigorously selected by the artist, connecting a variety of disciplines and areas of expertise to bring together different perspectives on the subjects. Each talk is broadcast as a live audio stream, as well as being transcribed and published on the website thinking-head.net.

For *Post-Capital,* Favaretto has selected three words, *surplus, power* and *hacker.* Each will form the subject of a new clandestine talk, which will take place at a secret location within the museum during the exhibition.

Lara Favaretto was born in 1973 in Treviso, Italy. She lives and works in Turin, Italy.

clin d'œil à l'ultime sculpture de Alighiero Boetti, *Autoritratto (Mi Fuma Il Cervello),* (1993-1994*)* autoportrait en bronze chauffé à l'électricité et dont la tête dégage de la fumée pour suggérer un esprit hyperactif. Lara Favaretto a dit vouloir faire du musée une « machine pensante ». Son intervention constitue en outre une forme de critique institutionnelle, qui, en occultant l'architecture de l'institution, dissout l'autorité qu'elle a à nos yeux.

Quant à la série de « discussions clandestines », elle vise à déconstruire cinquante « mots-clés » en s'appuyant sur un discours caché qui se déploie, selon les instructions de l'artiste, dans un cadre « semblable à un bunker » (un endroit secret, protégé et insonorisé, à l'intérieur ou à l'extérieur de l'institution). Ces « mots-clés » sont, selon l'artiste, « essentiels et pertinents pour disséquer et redéfinir notre présent ». Chaque discussion implique trois à sept participants qui se rencontrent à huis clos, sans public, pour une durée indéfinie mais au cours d'une seule journée. Les intervenants, rigoureusement choisis par l'artiste, couvrent différentes disciplines et divers domaines d'expertise de manière à apporter des points de vue différents sur les sujets traités. Chaque discussion est diffusée en direct, en streaming audio, mais aussi retranscrite et publiée sur le site internet : thinking-head.net

Pour *Post-Capital,* Lara Favaretto a choisi trois mots : *surplus, pouvoir* et *hacker.* Chacun d'entre eux sera l'objet d'une nouvelle discussion clandestine, qui se tiendra dans un endroit secret du musée, au cours de l'exposition.

Lara Favaretto est née en 1973 à Trévise, en Italie. Elle vit et travaille à Turin, en Italie.

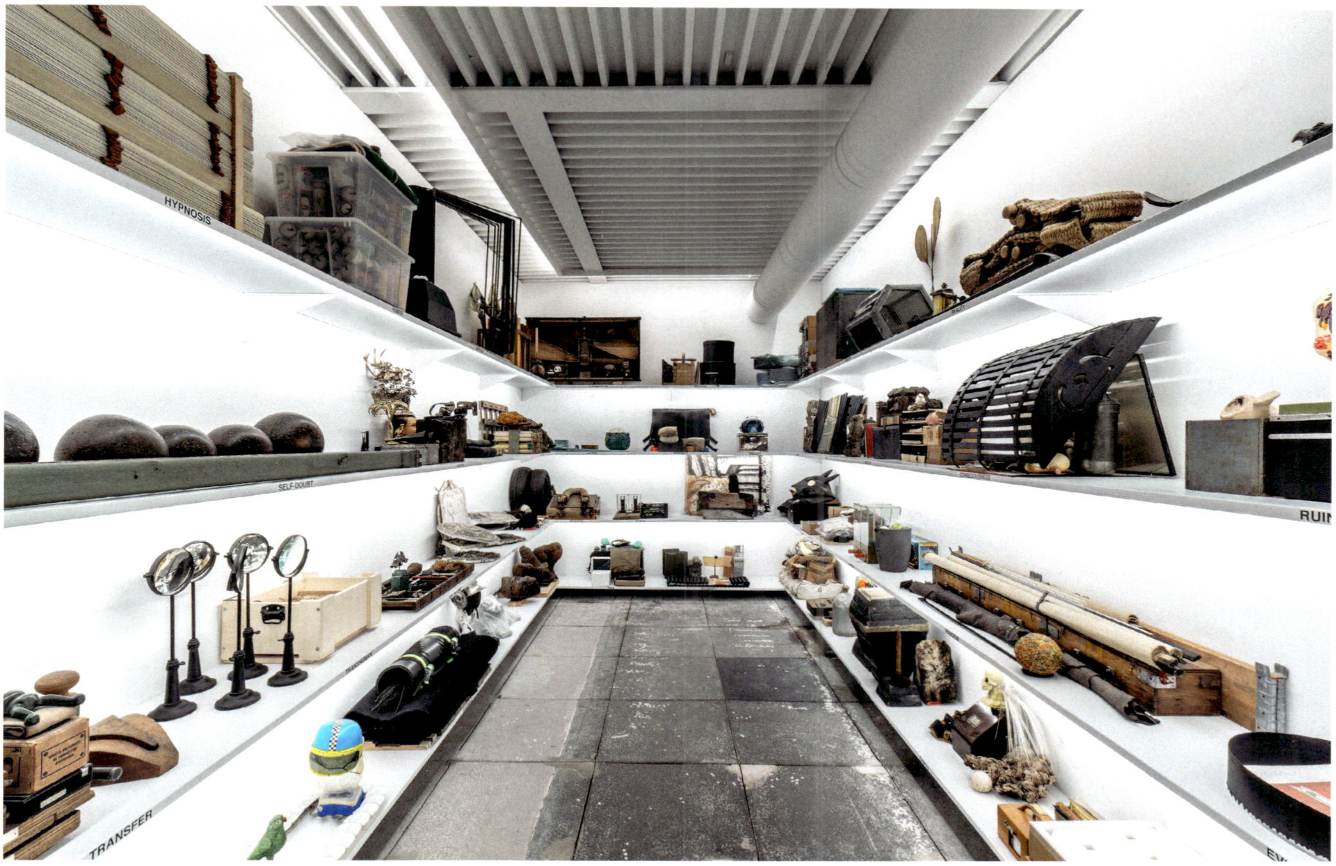

Lara Favaretto, *Thinking Head*, 2017–ongoing (installation view)

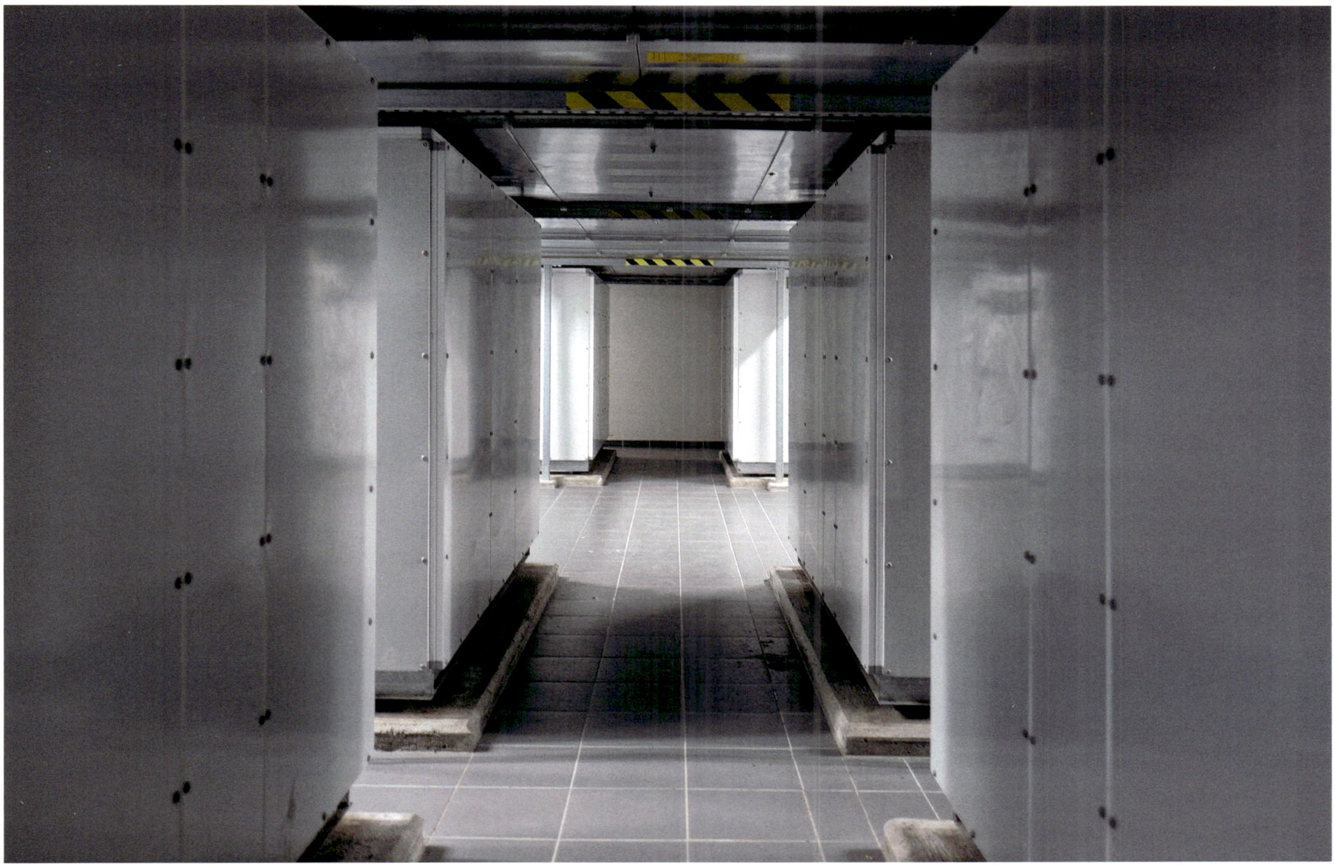

Location for Lara Favaretto, *Clandestine Talks [Thinking Head]*, 2017–ongoing

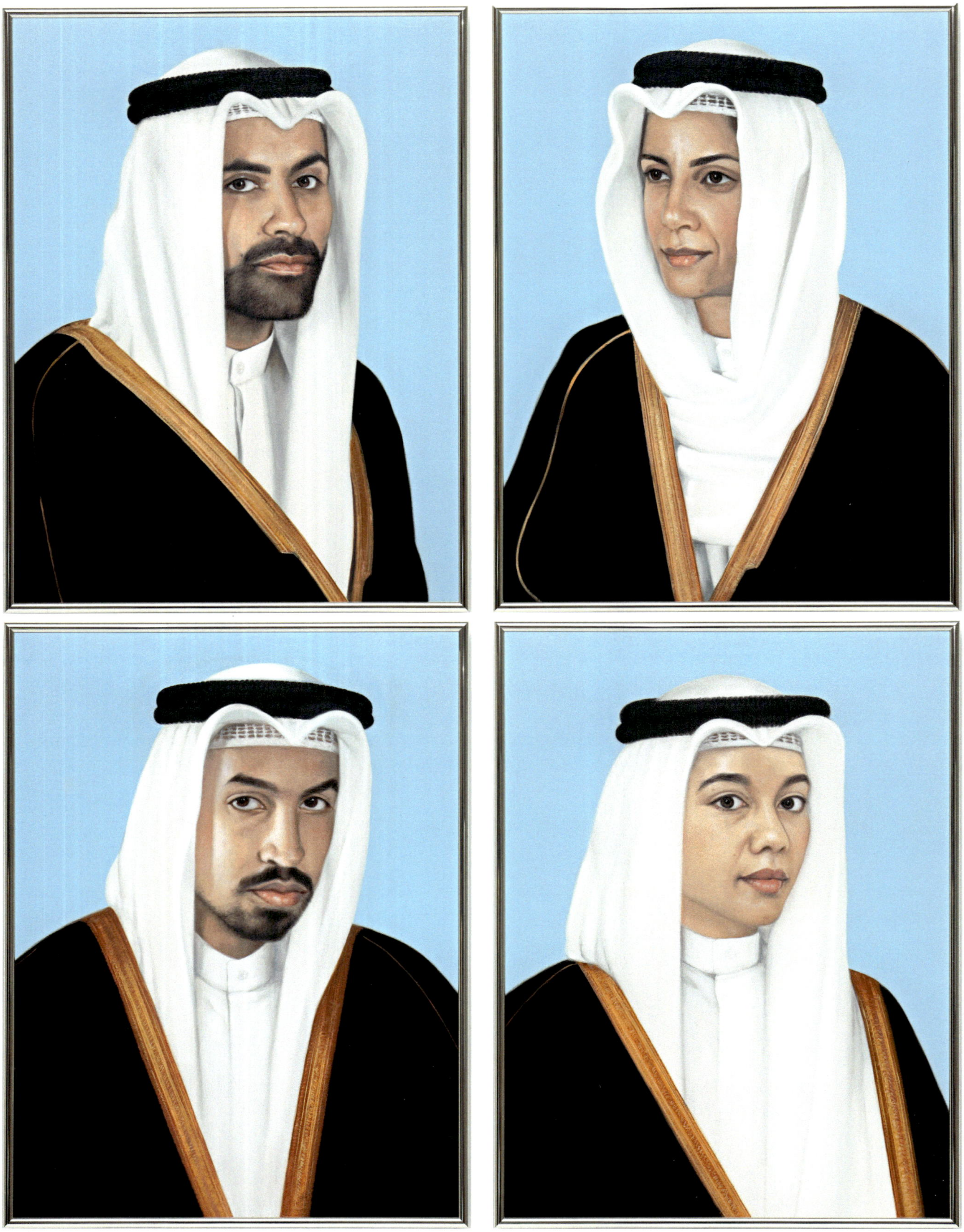

GCC, *Royal Mirage*, 2014
(details, left to right, top to bottom: *Royal Mirage III*,
Royal Mirage VII, *Royal Mirage I*, *Royal Mirage II*)

GCC

GCC is a collective or 'delegation' of artists, curators and writers with close ties to the Arabian Gulf. Their work examines how visual and rhetorical languages of power manifest across the Arab world and beyond. The name 'GCC' refers to the Gulf Cooperation Council, an intergovernmental political and economic union established between six countries, which has the present-day objective of maintaining a common economic market in the region. The adoption of this acronym is part of the collective's strategy of 'using the aesthetics of governmental bodies and global diplomacy to explore the way labour and business are performed in the Gulf'.

Motifs of ceremony – the rituals and objects associated with the public celebration of success – are recurrent in GCC's work. Their 2014 video *CO-OP* exemplifies this, presenting images that signify conspicuous wealth, technological progress and hyper-global connectivity in the

GCC est un collectif ou « délégation » d'artistes, de commissaires d'exposition et d'écrivains entretenant des liens étroits avec le golfe Arabique. Leur travail examine la manière dont les langages visuels et rhétoriques du pouvoir se manifestent dans le monde arabe et au-delà. Le nom « GCC » renvoie au Gulf Cooperation Council (Conseil de coopération du Golfe), union politique et économique entre les gouvernements de six pays qui se donne aujourd'hui pour objectif de maintenir un marché économique commun au sein de la région. Si le collectif a adopté cet acronyme, c'est parce que sa stratégie consiste à « utiliser l'esthétique des corps étatiques et de la diplomatie mondiale pour explorer la manière dont le travail et les affaires sont menés dans le Golfe ».

Les motifs cérémoniels – les rituels et objets associés à la célébration publique de la réussite – sont récurrents dans le travail de GCC. Leur vidéo intitulée *CO-OP* (2014)

Gulf as acontextual non sequiturs. *CO-OP* appears to be a promotional video for GCC, though it is not immediately clear which GCC, and this ambiguity permeates the work such that, though success is signified with generic images such as trophies and fireworks, we are not clear about what is being celebrated.

In the installation *Royal Mirage* (2014), the members of GCC insert themselves into the image economy of royal portraiture. The 'sheikh portraits', picturing each of the GCC members, were painted by an artist who often produces such likenesses for members of the Gulf monarchy. As objects, they replicate the signs and symbols of authority, but are subtextually undermined by the artists' individual identities (variously representing different heritages, genders and sexualities). The portraits are displayed on a wallpaper montage of photographs showing the lobby of a luxury hotel in Abu Dhabi, appearing virtually-situated within the grandiose elements of modern Islamic architecture. Presented within this disorienting space that describes unambiguous power, the portraits represent the uneasy relationship between political strength and significations of wealth.

GCC was founded in 2013 in Dubai, United Arab Emirates. The members live and work in Asia, Europe, and the United States.

en est une illustration, présentant des images associées à la richesse ostentatoire, au progrès technologique et à l'hyperconnexion globale comme des *non sequitur* dénués de tout contexte. *CO-OP* semble être une vidéo promotionnelle pour GCC, mais on ne saisit pas immédiatement de quel GCC il s'agit. Cette ambiguïté imprègne l'ensemble de l'œuvre : ainsi, bien que la réussite soit signifiée par des images génériques de trophées et de feux d'artifice, l'objet de la célébration demeure flou.

Dans l'installation *Royal Mirage* (2014), les membres de GCC s'inscrivent dans l'économie iconographique du portrait royal. Les « portraits de cheikhs », dont chacun représente un membre de GCC, ont été réalisés par un artiste qui effectue régulièrement ce genre de portraits pour les membres de la monarchie du Golfe. En tant qu'objets, ils reproduisent les signes et symboles de l'autorité, mais sont contredits par le sous-texte que constituent les identités individuelles des artistes (qui ensemble représentent différents héritages, genres et sexualités). Les portraits, accrochés sur un papier peint fait d'un montage de photographies du hall d'un luxueux hôtel d'Abou Dhabi, semblent prendre virtuellement place au sein d'une architecture islamique grandiose. Présentés dans cet espace qui désoriente, tout en décrivant un pouvoir pleinement assumé, les portraits révèlent le rapport complexe entre puissance politique et signes de richesse.

GCC a été formé en 2013 à Dubaï, aux Émirats arabes unis. Ses membres vivent et travaillent en Asie, en Europe et aux États-Unis.

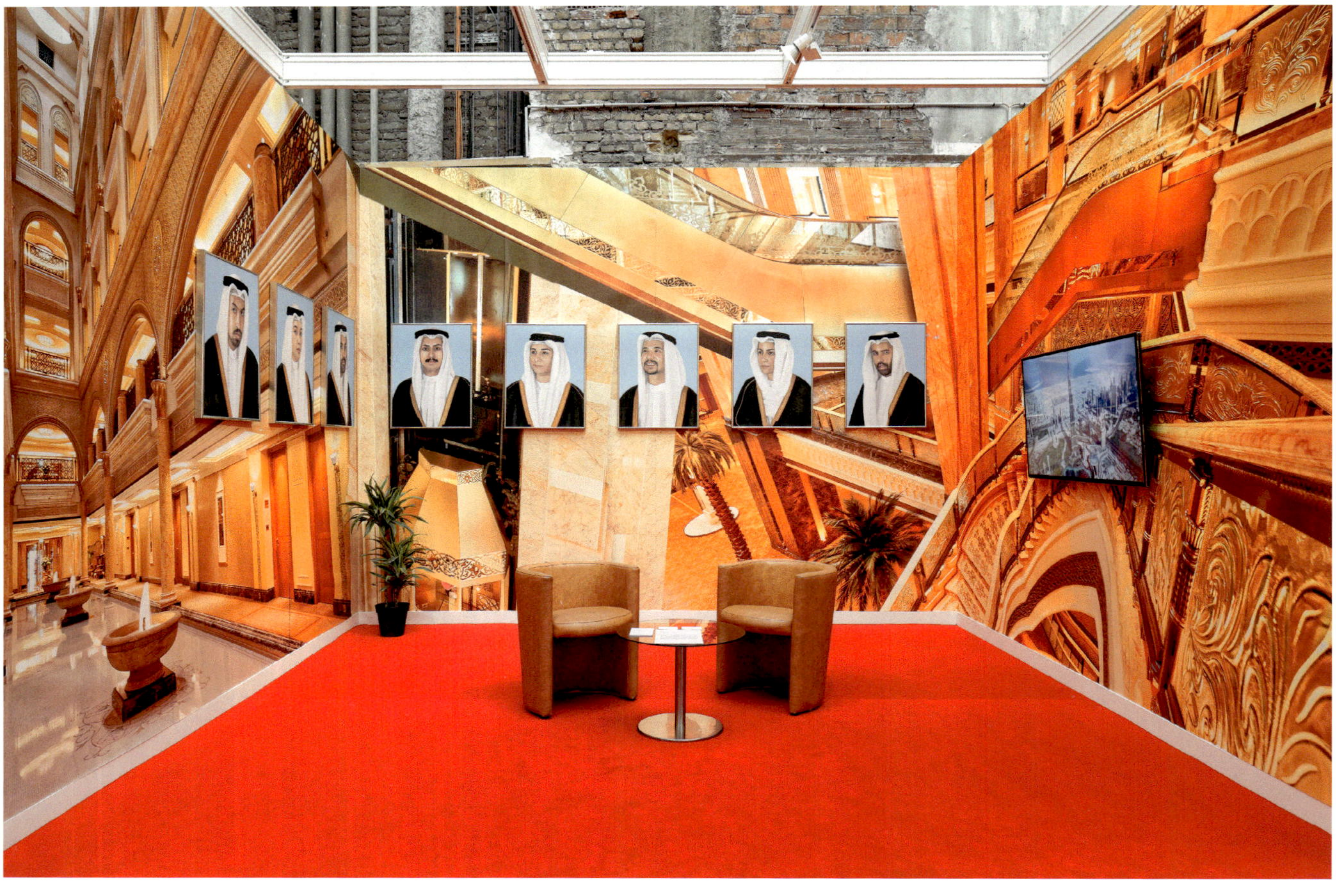

GCC, *Royal Mirage,* 2014 (installation view)

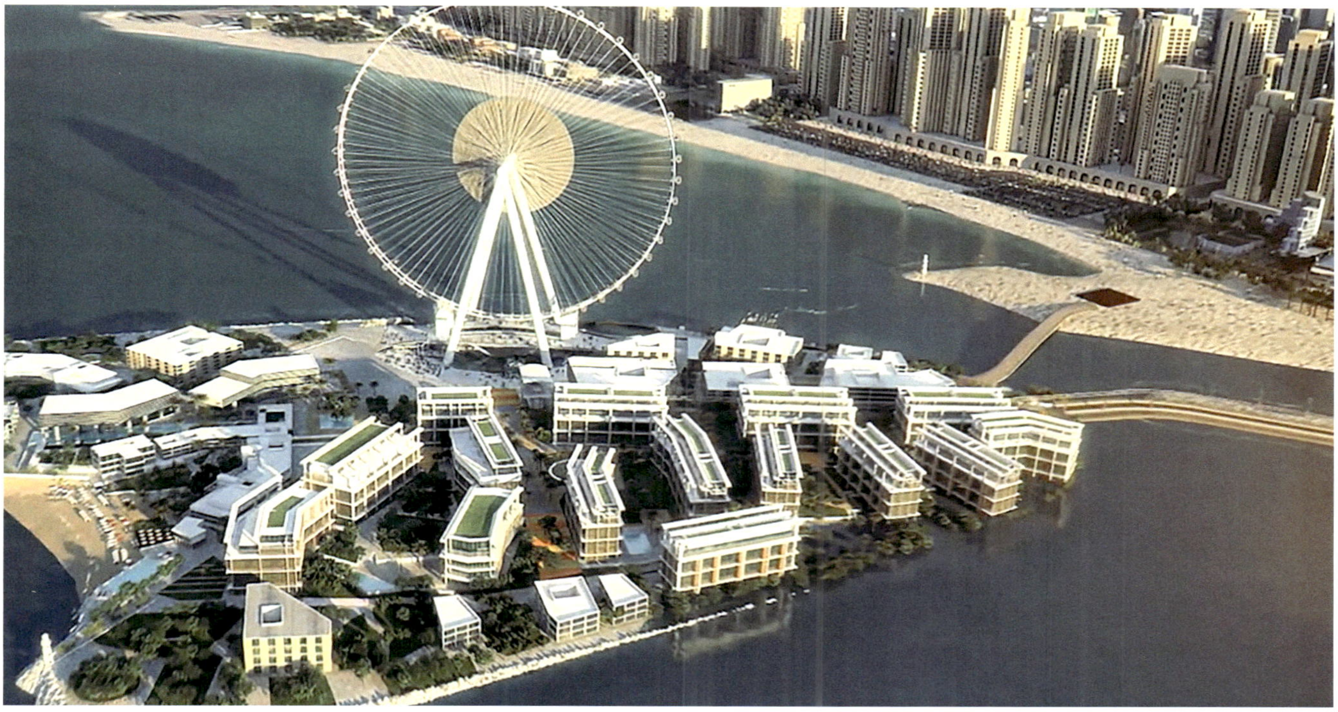

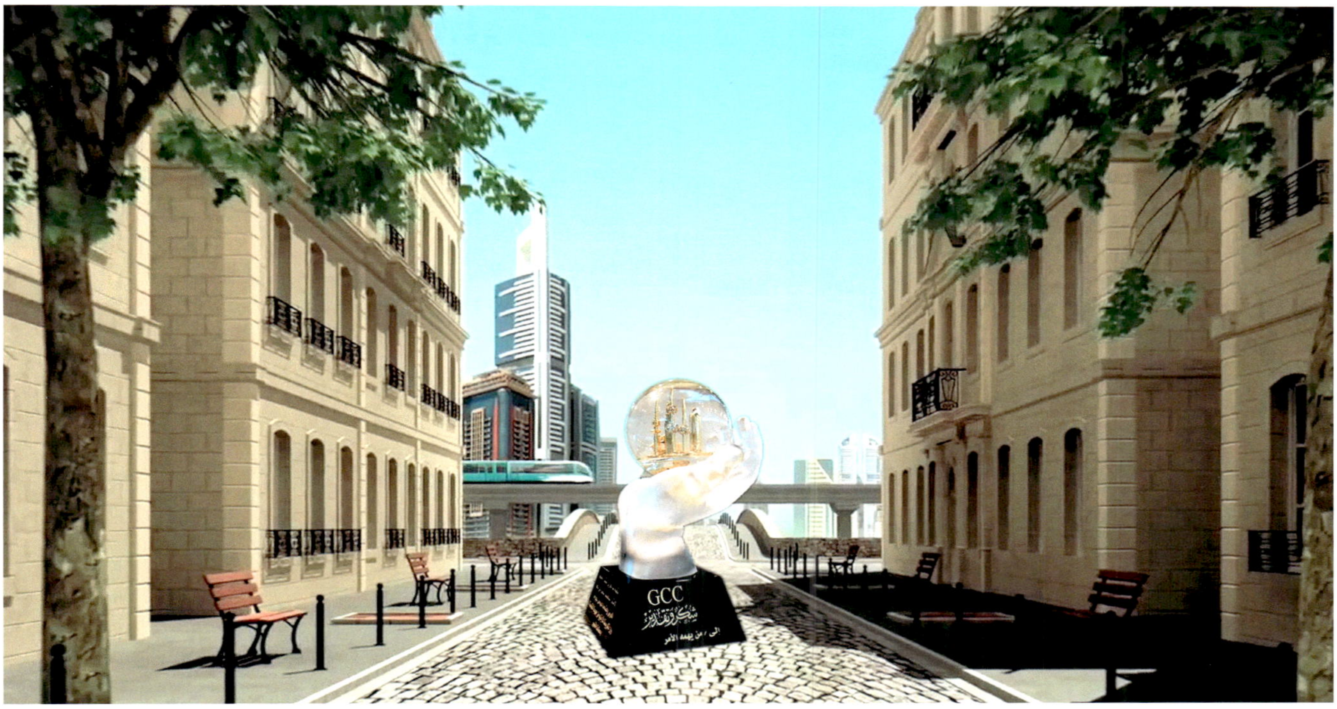

Film stills from GCC, *CO-OP*, 2014

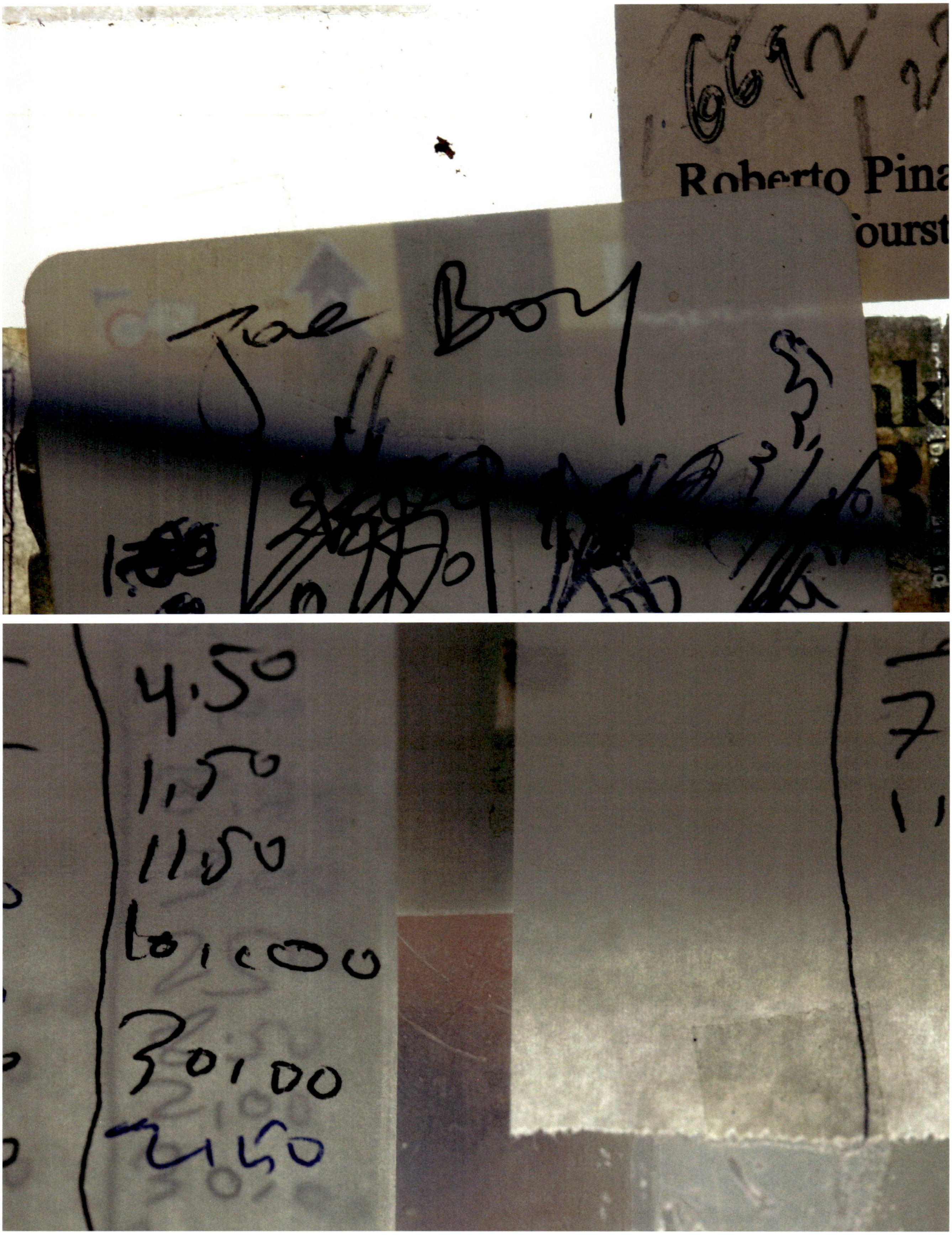

Shadi Habib Allah, *Dropping the 10th Digit*, 2018 (details)

Shadi Habib Allah

The United States government administrates a federal aid programme called the Supplemental Nutrition Assistance Program (SNAP) to provide low- and no-income citizens with access to food through a monthly budget for groceries. Initiated in 1939 as the 'Food Stamp Program (FSP)', SNAP serves approximately forty million people annually, assessing the eligibility of beneficiaries according to a complex and often preclusive matrix of poverty, health, citizenship and employment status. In the state of Florida, the payments are deposited once a month into an Electronic Benefit Transfer (EBT) card and made 'available between the 1st and 28th of every month, based on the 9th and 8th digits of the Florida case number, read backwards, dropping the 10th digit'.[1]

Shadi Habib Allah adopted this phrase, *Dropping the 10th Digit,* as the title for a series of photographs representing an informal economy that has developed alongside

Le gouvernement américain administre un programme fédéral d'aide sociale intitulé « Supplemental Nutrition Assistance Program » [programme d'aide alimentaire supplémentaire] (SNAP), destiné à fournir aux personnes ayant des revenus faibles ou inexistants un accès à des repas sous la forme d'une aide mensuelle à l'achat de denrées alimentaires. Ce programme, lancé en 1939 sous le nom de « Food Stamp Program » [programme de bons alimentaires] (FSP) et qui vient en aide à environ quarante millions de personnes chaque année, évalue l'éligibilité des bénéficiaires en fonction d'une matrice complexe et souvent très sélective, comprenant des facteurs comme la pauvreté, la santé, la nationalité et la situation professionnelle. Dans l'État de Floride, l'allocation est versée mensuellement sur une carte électronique (Electronic Benefit Transfer [EBT] card) et rendue « disponible entre le 1er et le 28 de chaque mois, en fonction

the technological evolution of the SNAP programme. During his time living in Liberty City, Miami, Habib Allah became acquainted with the owners of several local convenience stores. Once the sole source of consumable goods in the area, these businesses had suffered a loss of income following the arrival of large chain stores in the area. Habib Allah observed a nexus of supply and demand between the struggling independent retailers and their customers, whose basic needs were not being met by the SNAP benefits. Habib Allah explains that 'some stores will exchange food stamps for cash ... and a lot of the beneficiaries need cash: to take a bus to go look for a job, to pay a phone bill and so on. The storeowners keep the card for seven or ten days and they keep charging it in sums that correspond to merchandise'.[2]

Displayed as lightboxes, the images depict the handwritten notes that convenience store owners use to keep track of the exchange of benefits for cash and merchandise ineligible for purchase through SNAP. The images document 'under the counter' tabs describing the financial lives of customers such as 'Mamagirl', 'David's Wife' and 'Darleen', representing what Habib Allah describes as 'the continual calibration between the technological organisation of social life and community techniques coordinated to feed that system the proper data'.[3] The presentation of the images as lightboxes alludes to the ubiquitous illuminated signs of the stores in which they were taken. Although *Dropping the 10th Digit* functions as a portrait of a parallel economic system and a federal aid programme particular to the United States, part of Habib Allah's practice engages with the global phenomenon of communities who calibrate their own economic needs and realities to those imposed upon them by legal and political infrastructures.

Shadi Habib Allah was born in 1977 in Jerusalem, Palestine. He lives and works in New York, USA and Palestine.

1 *Supplemental Nutrition Assistance Program (SNAP): Monthly Issuance Schedule for All States and Territories*, United States Department of Agriculture, Food and Nutrition Service, 2020, p. 8.
2 Shadi Habib Allah interviewed by Michael McCanne, 'Everyday Undergrounds: A Conversation with Shadi Habib Allah', *Art in America*, 3 October 2018, https://www.artnews.com/art-in-america/interviews/everyday-undergrounds-conversation-shadi-habib-allah-56487 (accessed 21 May 2021).
3 Shadi Habib Allah, email correspondence with the author, 3 March 2021.

des neuvième et huitième chiffres du numéro d'allocataire, en partant de la fin et en laissant de côté le dixième chiffre[1] ».

Shadi Habib Allah a fait de cette expression, *Dropping the 10th Digit* [Laisser de côté le dixième chiffre], le titre d'une série de photographies représentant l'économie informelle qui s'est développée en parallèle de l'évolution technologique du SNAP. Lorsqu'il vivait à Miami, dans le quartier de Liberty City, Shadi Habib Allah a fait connaissance avec les propriétaires de plusieurs épiceries locales. Ces commerces, qui étaient auparavant les seules sources d'approvisionnement du quartier, ont subi avec l'implantation des grandes chaînes de supermarché une importante perte de chiffre d'affaires. L'artiste a observé les liens entre l'offre et la demande formés par les commerçants indépendants en difficulté et leurs clients, dont les besoins élémentaires n'étaient pas assurés par l'allocation du SNAP. Shadi Habib Allah explique que « certains commerces échangent des bons alimentaires contre de l'argent liquide [...] et [que] beaucoup de bénéficiaires ont besoin d'argent en liquide : pour prendre le bus afin de chercher du travail, pour régler une facture de téléphone, etc. Les propriétaires des magasins conservent la carte pendant sept à dix jours, en en déduisant des sommes correspondant à l'achat de produits[2] ».

Les images, montées sur des caissons lumineux, montrent les notes manuscrites utilisées par les commerçants pour conserver une trace du troc d'allocations contre du liquide et des produits inéligibles dans le cadre du SNAP. Elles documentent les notes officieuses qui décrivent l'existence financière de clients comme « la fille à sa maman », « la femme de David », « Darleen », et représentent, selon Shadi Habib Allah, « le calibrage permanent entre l'organisation technologique de la vie sociale et les techniques développées au sein des communautés coordonnées afin de fournir à ce système les données adéquates[3] ». L'exposition des photographies sur des caissons lumineux fait allusion aux omniprésentes enseignes lumineuses des magasins où elles ont été prises. Bien que *Dropping the 10th Digit* fonctionne comme le portrait d'un système économique parallèle et d'un programme d'aide fédérale propres aux États-Unis, la pratique de Shadi Habib Allah traite notamment du phénomène global des communautés qui calibrent leurs besoins et leurs réalités économiques en fonction de ceux que leur imposent les infrastructures juridiques et politiques.

Shadi Habib Allah est né en 1977 à Jérusalem, en Palestine. Il vit et travaille à New York, aux États-Unis et en Palestine.

1 *Supplemental Nutrition Assistance Program (SNAP): Monthly Issuance Schedule for All States and Territories*, United States Department of Agriculture, Food and Nutrition Service, 2020, p. 8.
2 Shadi Habib Allah, entretien réalisé par Michael McCanne, « Everyday Undergrounds: A Conversation with Shadi Habib Allah », *Art in America*, 3 Octobre 2018, https://www.artnews.com/art-in-america/interviews/everyday-undergrounds-conversation-shadi-habib-allah-56487, (consulté le 21 mai 2021).
3 Shadi Habib Allah, dans une correspondance par e-mail avec l'auteure, 3 mars 2021.

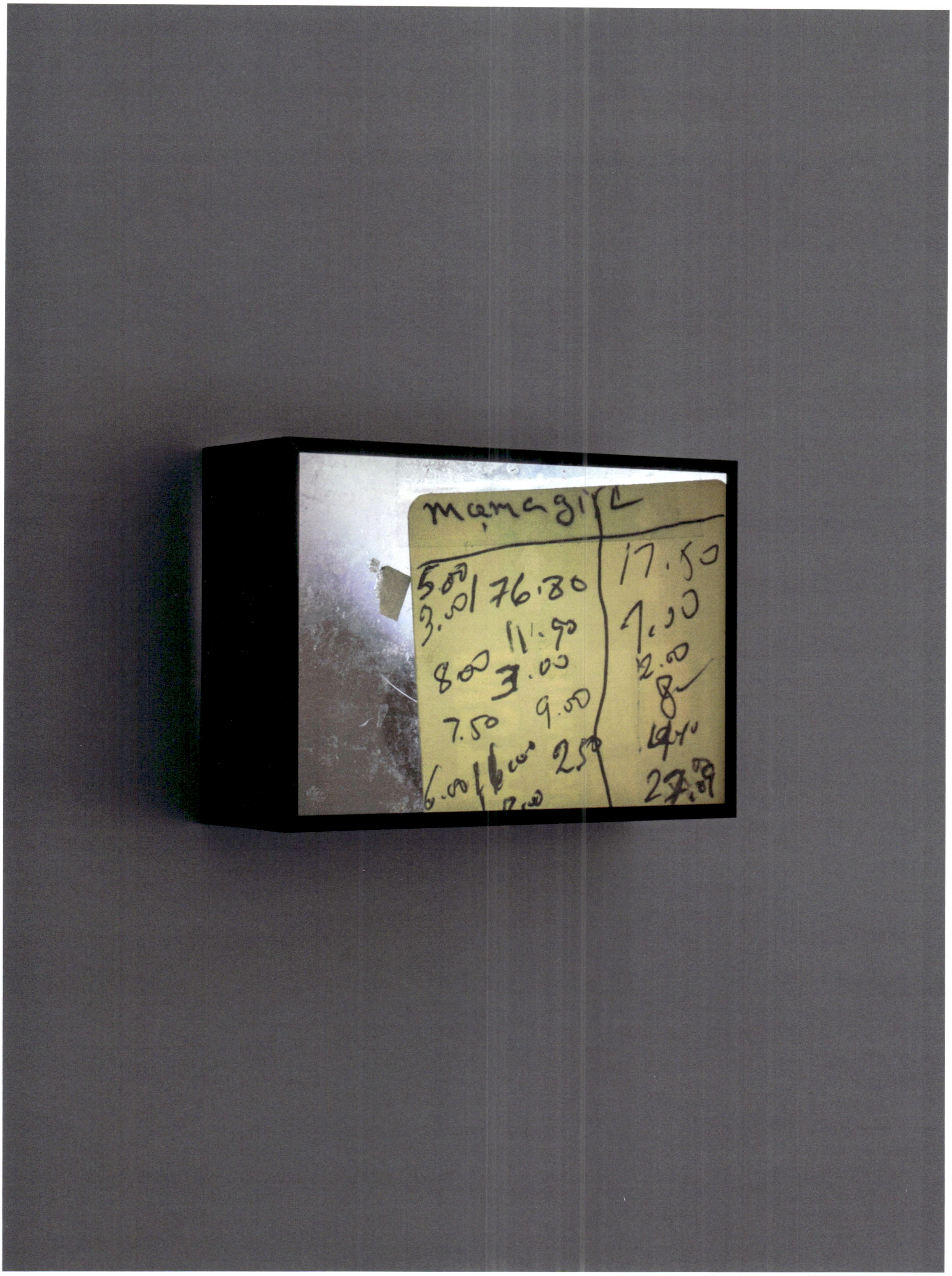

Shadi Habib Allah, *Dropping the 10th Digit*, 2018 (detail)

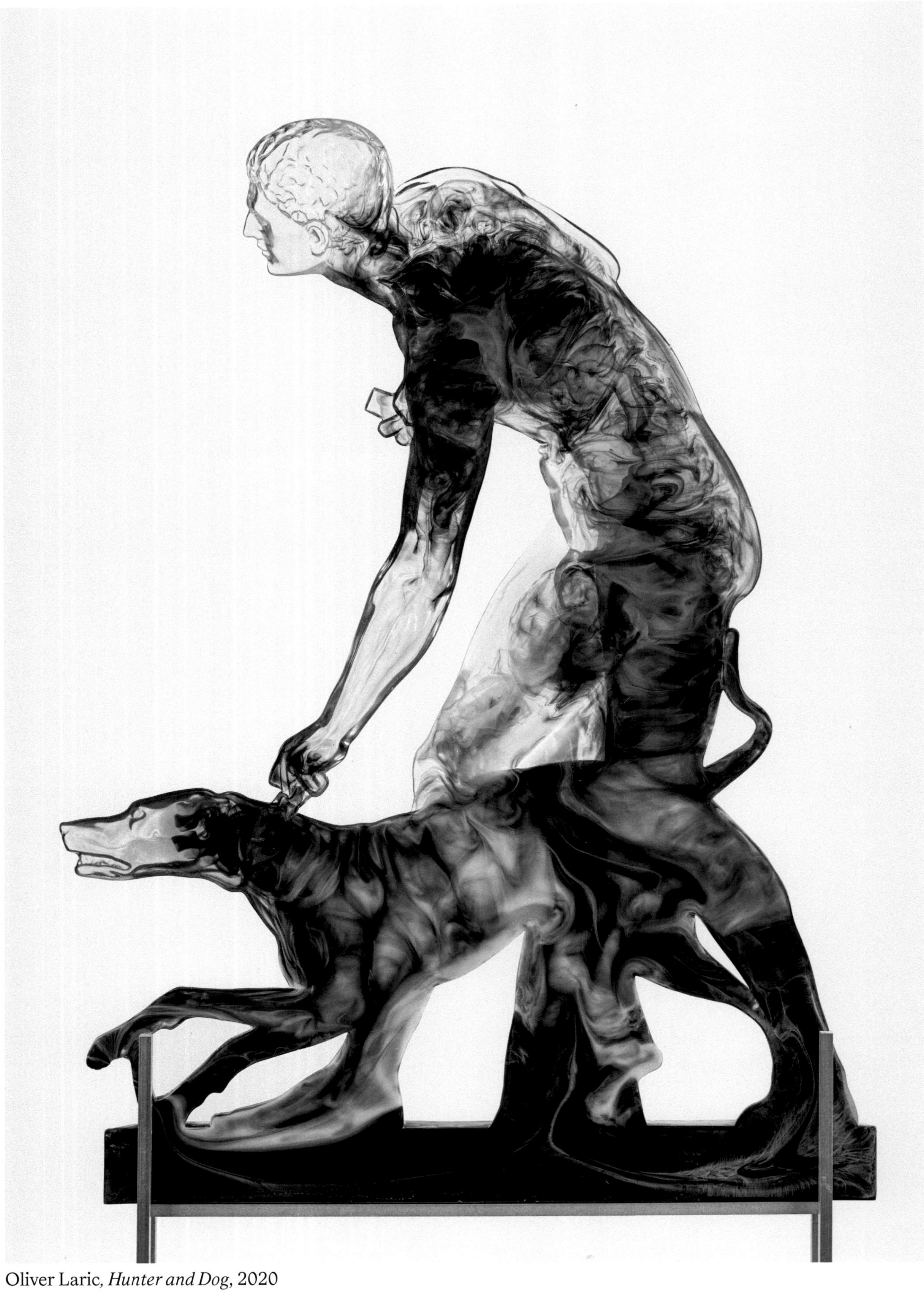

Oliver Laric, *Hunter and Dog*, 2020

Oliver Laric

Hunter and Dog (2020), *Reclining Pan* (2021), *Hermanubis* (2021) and *Ram With Human* (2021), by Oliver Laric were created from 3D scans of sculptures from different centuries. They variously depict relationships between humans and animals, or human-animal hybrids. For example, *Hermanubis* refers to a classical sculpture from c. 100 CE that combines the Greek god Hermes with the canine Egyptian deity Anubis. Similarly, *Hunter and Dog* is based upon a neoclassical sculpture by John Gibson dated c. 1847, which portrays a man holding a dog by its collar.

Rather than making faithful copies, Laric has used mostly neoclassical Greco-Roman sculptures as 'recipes or compositions for new works', which he creates using a 3D printer. By producing multiple versions of the same object, often in different sizes and colours, Laric questions notions of authorship, authenticity and originality. 'I'm not drawn to the idea of a single, precious object with

Oliver Laric a créé *Hunter and Dog* (2020), *Reclining Pan* (2021), *Hermanubis* (2021) et *Ram With Human* (2021) à partir de scans 3D de sculptures de différentes époques. Ces œuvres représentent de diverses manières les relations entre humains et animaux ou des hybrides humain-animal. Par exemple, *Hermanubis* fait référence à une sculpture antique, réalisée autour de 100 apr. J.-C. et qui combine le dieu grec Hermès avec la divinité canine égyptienne Anubis. De la même façon, *Hunter and Dog* se fonde sur une sculpture néoclassique réalisée vers 1847 par John Gibson et qui représente un homme tenant un chien par le collier.

Plutôt que de réaliser des copies fidèles, Oliver Laric a utilisé des sculptures, pour la plupart néoclassiques et gréco-romaines, comme « recettes ou compositions permettant de produire de nouvelles œuvres » qu'il réalise avec une imprimante 3D. En produisant de multiples versions du même objet, souvent dans des tailles et des

charisma…' the artist has said. 'It's not the object itself that excites me, but the idea that manifests itself in it'. While the vast majority of Laric's 3D scans were made with the consent of the museums that own them, in cases when permission was denied, the artist uses photogrammetry – a technique in which a three-dimensional model is made from hundreds of photographs – as a legal workaround.

In addition to using scans of these objects to produce his own sculptures, Laric also uploads them to the website threedscans.com, where they can be downloaded for free and used to endlessly produce new versions. By digitalising these works, Laric makes them available to an audience that far exceeds that of the museum. For instance, in 2015, Laric's model of the Gibson statue was seen by over 200 million people when it was used as part of a projected backdrop for the Italian entry to the Eurovision Song Contest. The artist has described this experience as one of the proudest moments of his career.

Oliver Laric was born in 1981 in Innsbruck, Austria. He lives and works in Berlin, Germany.

couleurs différentes, Laric interroge les notions d'auteur, d'authenticité et d'originalité. « Je ne suis pas attiré par l'idée d'objet unique, précieux et charismatique », a déclaré l'artiste. « Ce n'est pas l'objet lui-même qui me passionne, mais l'idée qui s'y manifeste. » Bien que Laric ait réalisé la majorité de ses scans en 3D avec l'accord des musées qui les possèdent, dans les cas où l'autorisation lui est refusée, il utilise la photogrammétrie – une technique consistant à produire un modèle tridimensionnel à partir de centaines de photographies – comme contournement légal.

En plus d'utiliser des scans de ces objets pour produire ses propres sculptures, Oliver Laric les publie sur le site threedscans.com, où l'on peut les télécharger gratuitement et les utiliser pour produire un nombre infini de nouvelles versions. En numérisant ces œuvres, Oliver Laric les met à la disposition d'un public qui dépasse très largement celui du musée. En 2015, par exemple, plus de deux cents millions de personnes ont pu voir son modèle de la statue de Gibson, qui fut projeté sur le fond de la scène pendant la prestation des candidats italiens au concours de l'Eurovision. Aux dires de l'artiste, cette expérience fut l'un des plus grands moments de fierté de sa carrière.

Oliver Laric est né en 1981 à Innsbruck, en Autriche. Il vit et travaille à Berlin, en Allemagne.

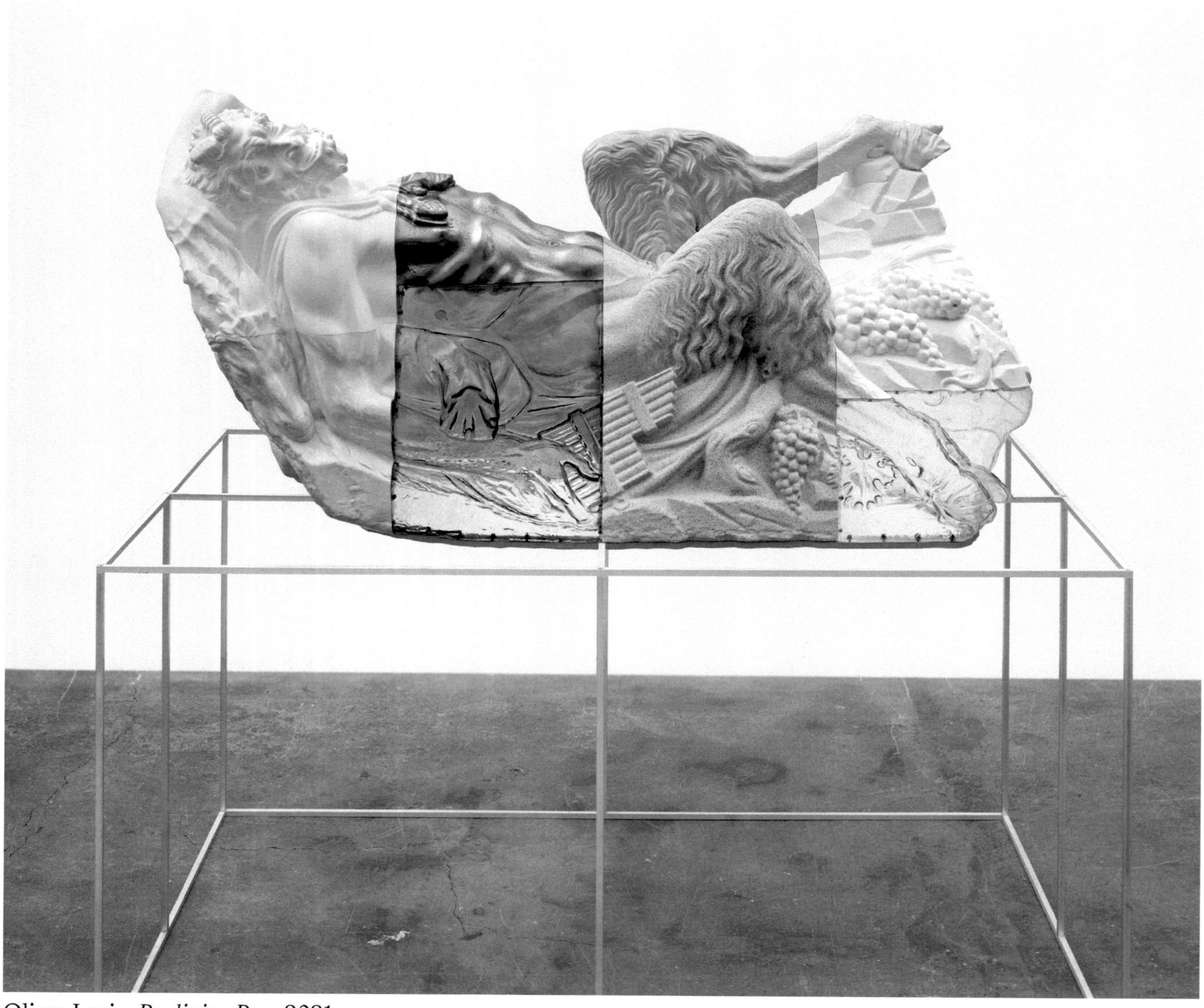

Oliver Laric, *Reclining Pan,* 2021

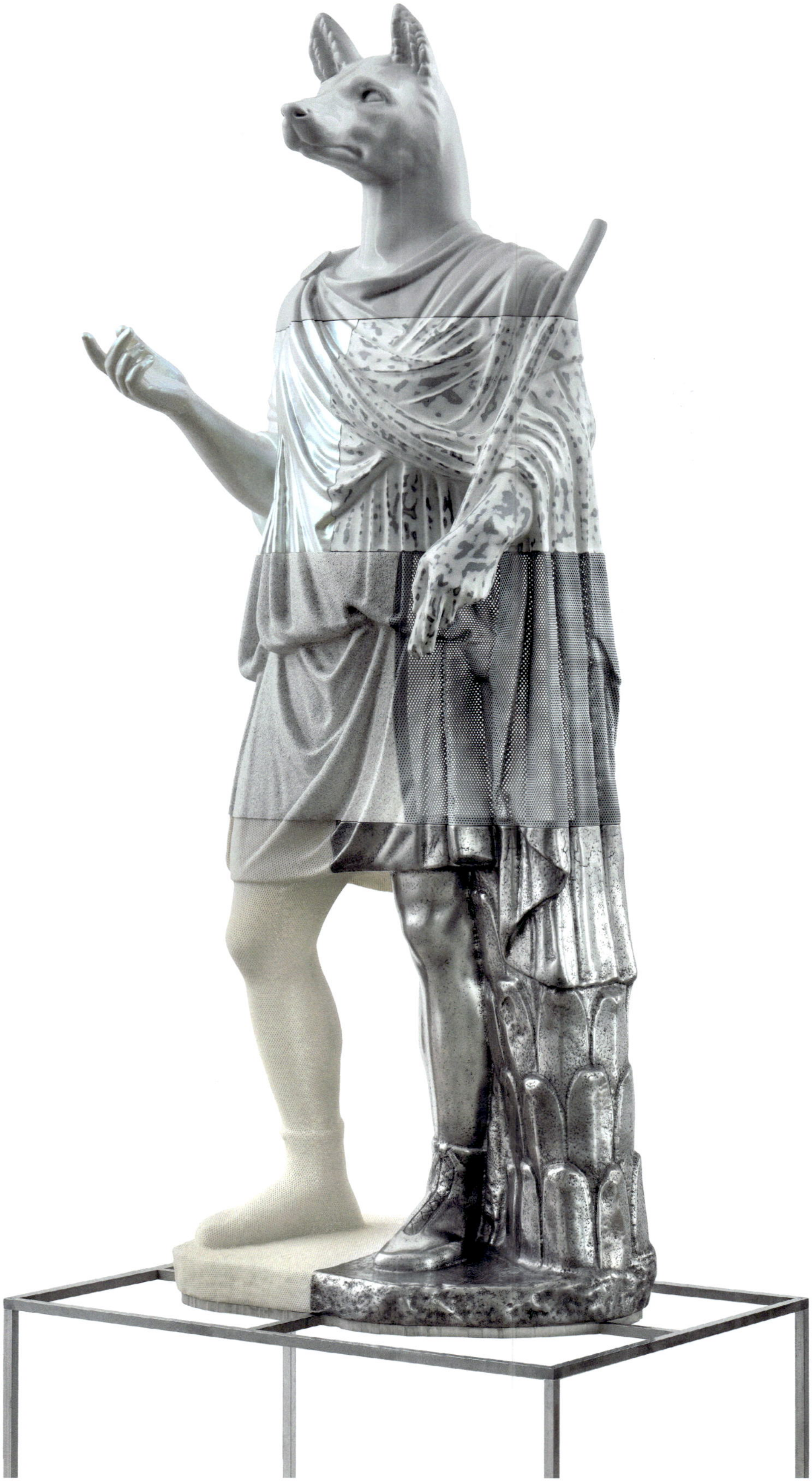

Oliver Laric, *Hermanubis*, 2021

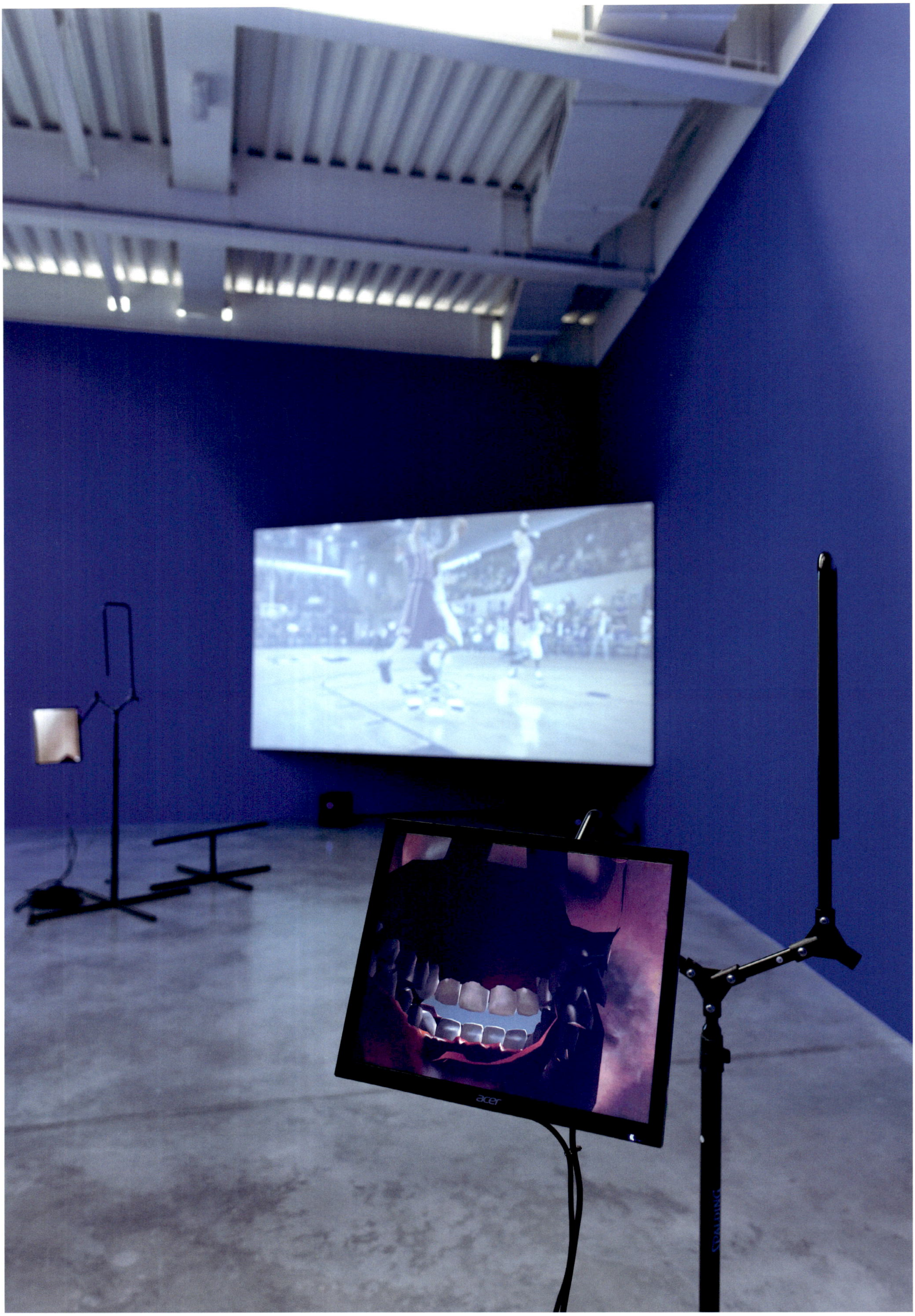

Sondra Perry, *IT'S IN THE GAME '17 or Mirror Gag for Projection and Five Universal Shot Trainers with Nasal Cavity, Pelvis, Orbit, and Axes,* 2018 (installation view)

Sondra Perry

Sondra Perry's multimedia installation, *IT'S IN THE GAME '18 or Mirror Gag for Projection and Two Universal Shot Trainers with Nasal Cavity and Pelvis* (2018), incorporates video and sculpture. The work employs the artist's signature bricolage of digital technology, cultural analysis and personal biography to examine contemporary culture with a focus on evolving technology and histories of contentious ethnographic display and racism. It features Perry's twin brother Sandy, a former college basketball player whose biometric data was sold by the National Collegiate Athletic Association to the publisher EA Sports, who used it to create a player of the same name for a popular series of video games. Excerpts from the game are collaged with footage of the siblings viewing African artefacts at The Metropolitan Museum of Art, New York and The British Museum, London. The work traces connections between the consumption and classification of

L'installation multimédia de Sondra Perry *IT'S IN THE GAME '18 or Mirror Gag for Projection and Two Universal Shot Trainers with Nasal Cavity and Pelvis* (2018) allie vidéo et sculpture. L'œuvre est caractéristique de la pratique de l'artiste, qui mêle technologie numérique, analyse culturelle et histoire personnelle afin d'examiner la culture contemporaine à travers le prisme de l'évolution technologique et de l'histoire controversée de l'exposition ethnographique et du racisme. L'œuvre traite du frère jumeau de Sondra Perry, Sandy, ancien joueur de basket à l'université dont les données biométriques ont été vendues par la National Collegiate Athletic Association à l'éditeur EA Sports, qui s'en est servi pour créer un joueur du même nom dans une série populaire de jeux vidéo. L'artiste réalise un montage à partir d'extraits de ce jeu et d'images d'elle et de son frère observant des objets d'art africains au Metropolitan Museum of Art de New York et au British

human bodies and cultures within the museum, and the objectification of Black Americans by commercial enterprises.

Personal materials, such as family photos and camera phone videos, are layered and presented over computer-generated environments and bodies that appear incomplete and unresolved. Perry points to how the monetisation of Black bodies is facilitated by the negation of individual humanity, stating: 'Abstraction isn't neutral ... And when political abstractions happen over marginalised bodies, that's a huge issue. But at the same time, there's a tremendous amount of power you can give or gain through this'.[1] Using text-to-speech, 3D scanning and design software to mimic the processes employed by the game designers, Perry enacts a 'mirror gag' (a form of physical comedy in which two actors portray one person in front of a mirror) with EA Sports' representation of her brother. Rendering physical details of her brother's body, she begins to reclaim his likeness, to a soundtrack that samples The Stylistics's 1971 R&B ballad, 'You are Everything', a song that opens with the lyric 'today I saw somebody who looked just like you'.

Perry's title for the work, itself a collage, combines these details with EA Sports' promotional slogan, 'It's in the game' and the name of the basketball equipment (Universal Shot Trainers) she has repurposed as monitor stands. These elements, which also recall easel supports, can be read as a gesture towards the history of painted portraiture. The complex arrangement of physical objects and digital images appears against walls painted with Chroma Key Blue. A shade of paint developed as an alternative to the 'green screen' background used in post-production, the blue is more effective with darker skin tones. Perry's choice of colour further highlights the inherent bias within technologies of representation.

Sondra Perry was born in 1983 in Perth Amboy, USA. She lives and works in Newark, USA.

1 Sondra Perry interview by Ella Coon, '"Abstraction Isn't Neutral": Sondra Perry on the NCAA, Subjecthood, and Her Upcoming Projects', *ARTnews*, 15 March 2016, https://www.artnews.com/art-news/artists/abstraction-isnt-neutral-sondra-perry-on-the-ncaa-subjecthood-and-her-upcoming-projects-5922 (accessed 21 May 2021).

Museum de Londres. L'œuvre établit des liens entre la consommation et la classification des corps et des cultures au sein du musée et l'objectivation des Américains noirs par les entreprises commerciales.

Elle superpose du contenu personnel, comme des photos de famille et des vidéos prises avec un smartphone, à des environnements et des corps générés par ordinateur, qui apparaissent dès lors incomplets et incertains. Sondra Perry souligne que la négation de l'humanité individuelle facilite la monétisation des corps noirs : « L'abstraction n'est pas neutre. [...] Et lorsque les abstractions politiques portent sur des corps marginalisés, cela devient un énorme problème. Mais en même temps, on peut donner ou acquérir, par là même, un pouvoir considérable[1]. » En utilisant des logiciels de synthèse vocale, de numérisation et de modélisation 3D pour imiter les processus mis en œuvre par les concepteurs de jeux, Sondra Perry déploie un « gag en miroir » (un procédé humoristique dans lequel deux acteurs jouent une seule et même personne devant un miroir) avec la représentation de son frère produite par EA Sports. En restituant les particularités du corps de celui-ci, elle se réapproprie progressivement son semblant, sur une bande-son qui sample la ballade R&B des Stylistics, « You Are Everything » (1971), qui s'ouvre sur ce vers : « *Today I saw somebody who looked just like you* » [Aujourd'hui, j'ai vu quelqu'un qui te ressemblait trait pour trait].

Le titre de l'œuvre, lui-même un collage, combine ces détails avec le slogan promotionnel d'EA Sports, « *It's in the game* » [Ça fait partie du jeu] et le nom de l'équipement de basket (Universal Shot Trainers) qu'elle réassigne en pieds d'écrans. Ceux-ci rappellent aussi des chevalets, dans un clin d'œil à l'histoire du portrait en peinture. Cet agencement complexe d'objets physiques et d'images numériques prend place devant un ensemble de murs peints en « Chroma Key Blue ». Cette teinte, développée comme alternative au « fond vert » utilisé pour faciliter les techniques de postproduction, est réputée plus appropriée aux peaux foncées. Par ce choix de couleur, Sondra Perry souligne encore davantage les biais inhérents aux technologies de représentation.

Sondra Perry est née en 1983 à Perth Amboy, aux États-Unis. Elle vit et travaille à Newark, aux États-Unis.

1 Sondra Perry, entretien avec Ella Coon, « "Abstraction Isn't Neutral": Sondra Perry on the NCAA, Subjecthood, and Her Upcoming Projects », *ARTnews*, 15 mars 2016, https://www.artnews.com/art-news/artists/abstraction-isnt-neutral-sondra-perry-on-the-ncaa-subjecthood-and-her-upcoming-projects-5922 (consulté le 21 mai 2021).

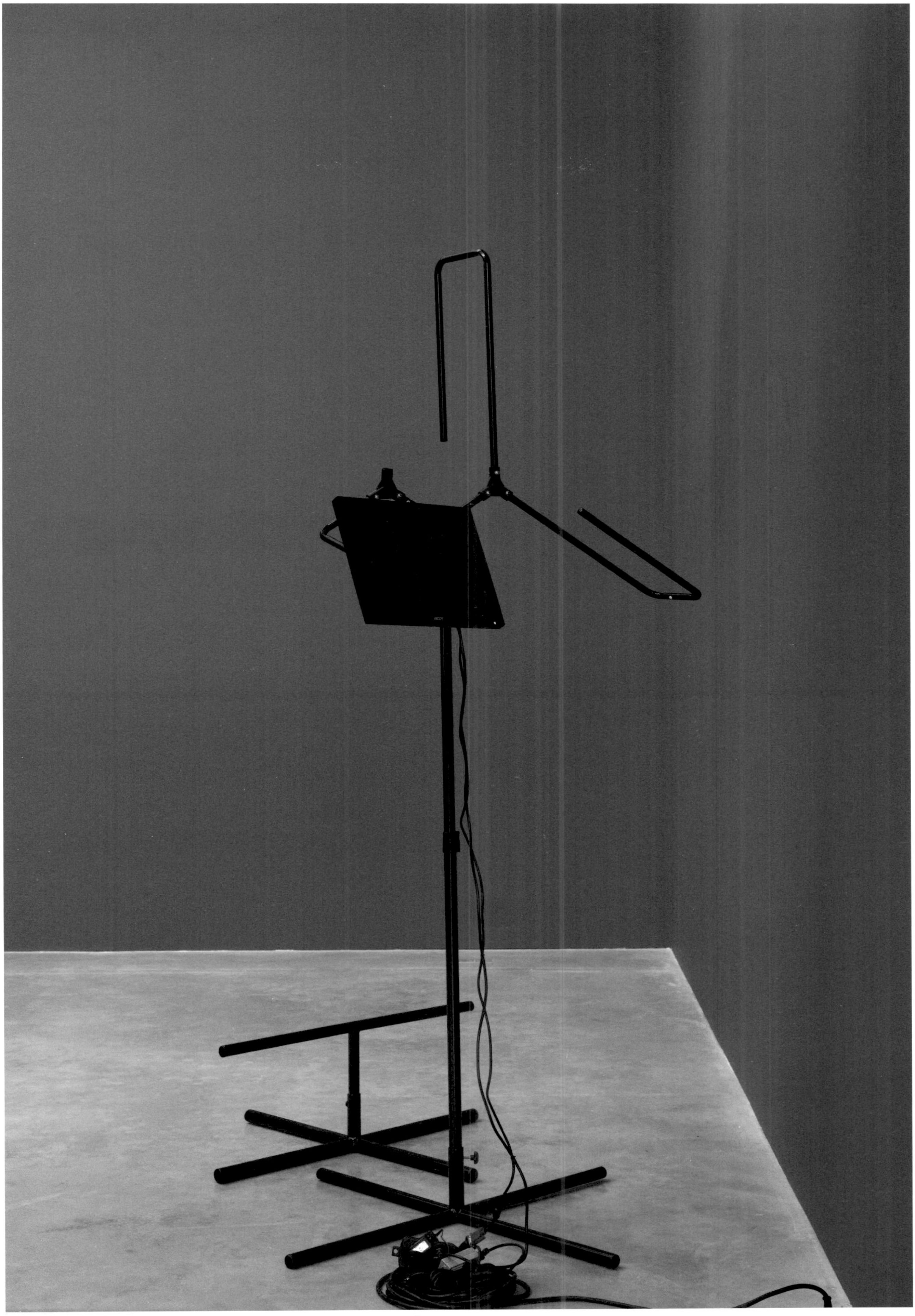

Sondra Perry, *IT'S IN THE GAME '17 or Mirror Gag for Projection and Five Universal Shot Trainers with Nasal Cavity, Pelvis, Orbit, and Axes,* 2018 (installation view)

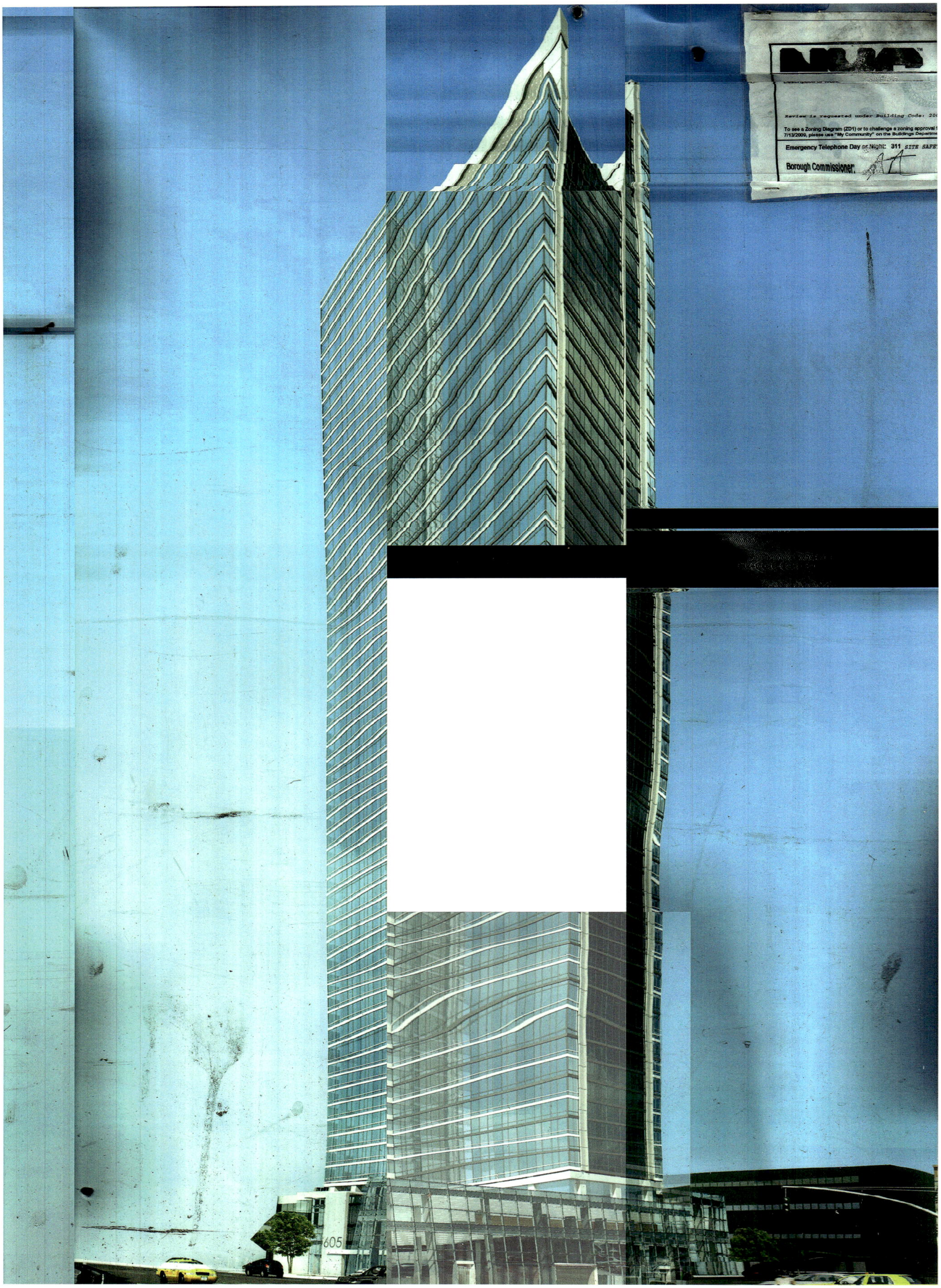

Nick Relph, *Glorifying the American Girl*, 2016

Nick Relph

Sally, So This is Marriage, The Girl from Everywhere (all 2015) and *Glorifying the American Girl* and *Annie Laurie* (both 2016) belong to an ongoing series of photographs that Nick Relph began producing in 2014. Each employs digital scans of hoardings erected around various construction sites in New York. Over the course of the last seven years Relph has made approximately 350 scans of these computer-generated architectural drawings, which are typically printed on a large scale and wrapped around sites to illustrate the designs of the buildings under construction. Captured using a portable hand-held scanner, the digital images are stitched together on a computer before being developed as Cibachrome prints. The resultant photographs offer an imperfect reproduction – registering the movement of the artist's hand and the missing fragments. They also record dirt, graffiti, fly-posts, and other ephemera adhered to the surface of the hoarding.

Sally, So This Is Marriage, The Girl from Everywhere (2015), *Glorifying the American Girl* et *Annie Laurie* (2016) font partie d'une série photographique entamée par Nick Relph en 2014. Chacune de ces œuvres repose sur des scans numériques de diverses palissades érigées autour de chantiers à New York. Au cours des sept dernières années, Relph a réalisé environ 350 scans de ces dessins d'architecte créés par ordinateur, généralement imprimés en grand format et enveloppant les sites pour donner une illustration du bâtiment en construction. Capturées grâce à un scanner portatif, ces images numériques sont assemblées par ordinateur avant d'être tirées en Cibachrome. Les photographies qui en résultent constituent une reproduction imparfaite – enregistrant le mouvement de la main et les fragments manquants, mais fixant aussi les saletés, les graffitis, les affiches et tous les éléments éphémères collés sur la surface de la palissade.

Presented out of context and without the developer's accompanying marketing texts, the incidental details of the images come into focus and the designs assume their own casual, commercial idiom. Sparsely-populated scenes show landscaped precincts and minimalist interiors; high-rise buildings are flanked with new cars and cut-and-pasted young professionals. The titles of these works are borrowed, somewhat arbitrarily, from different romantic films from the 1920s, introducing a sense of narrative and, notionally, a cast of female subjects from a bygone era of cinema.

Aspirational content and nostalgic resonances are ultimately and playfully undercut by the layers of dirt and gestural graffiti (containing the occasional topical message such as 'GEE THANKS', 'NO THANKS' or 'TRUMP 4 PREZ') overlying the designs. Relph's process of capturing the printed, computer-generated image by hand and converting digital images to analogue photography, effectively de-accelerates their content. Images that were intended to be read individually and at a glance by passers-by are reproduced to invite close reading and careful scrutiny. Collectively, the series captures the widespread gentrification of a city via generic images that illustrate capitalist desires.

Nick Relph was born in 1979 in London, UK. He lives and works in New York, USA.

Dans ces images, présentées hors contexte et sans les textes publicitaires produits par les promoteurs, ces détails secondaires se révèlent et les formes parlent sans complexe leur langue commerciale. Des scènes quasi désertes montrent des enceintes aménagées et des intérieurs minimalistes. Des gratte-ciels sont flanqués de voitures neuves et de jeunes cadres dynamiques qui semblent copiés-collés. Les titres de ces œuvres, empruntés plus ou moins arbitrairement à diverses comédies romantiques des années 1920, font émerger un récit et, potentiellement, un ensemble de sujets féminins tout droit sortis d'une période révolue de l'histoire du cinéma.

Le contenu « aspirationnel » et les références nostalgiques sont malicieusement mises à mal par les couches de saleté et les graffitis griffonnés à la va-vite (véhiculant parfois un message contextuel, comme « MERCI BIEN », « NON MERCI » ou « TRUMP PRÉSIDENT ») par-dessus les dessins. En capturant à la main l'image imprimée et produite par ordinateur et en convertissant les images numériques en photographies analogiques, Nick Relph crée de fait une décélération de leur contenu. Il reproduit des images destinées à être lues individuellement et d'un coup d'œil par des passants pour nous inviter à les examiner attentivement. Dans son ensemble, la série saisit la gentrification rampante d'une ville au travers d'images génériques illustrant les désirs capitalistes.

Nick Relph est né en 1979 à Londres, au Royaume-Uni. Il vit et travaille à New York, aux États-Unis.

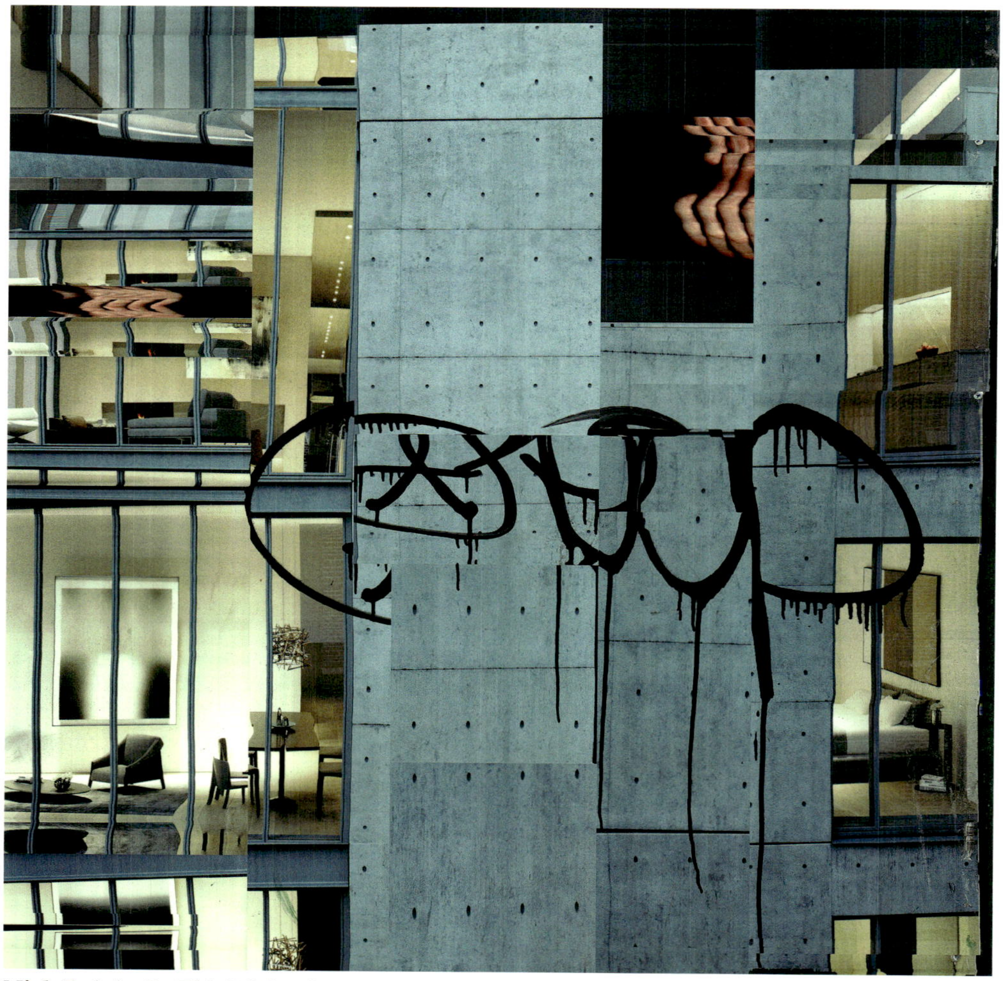

Nick Relph, *So This Is Marriage*, 2015

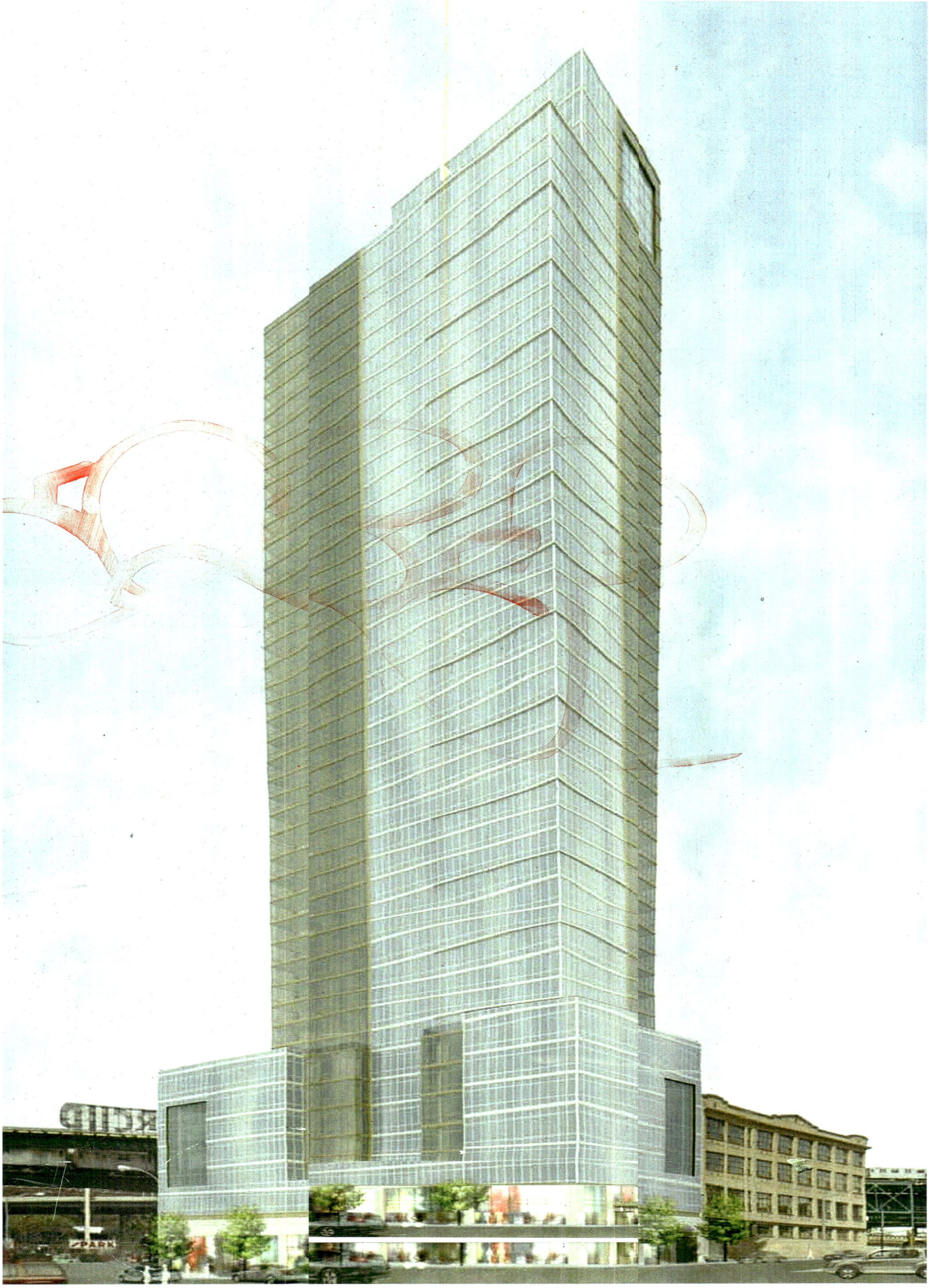

Nick Relph, *The Girl From Everywhere*, 2015

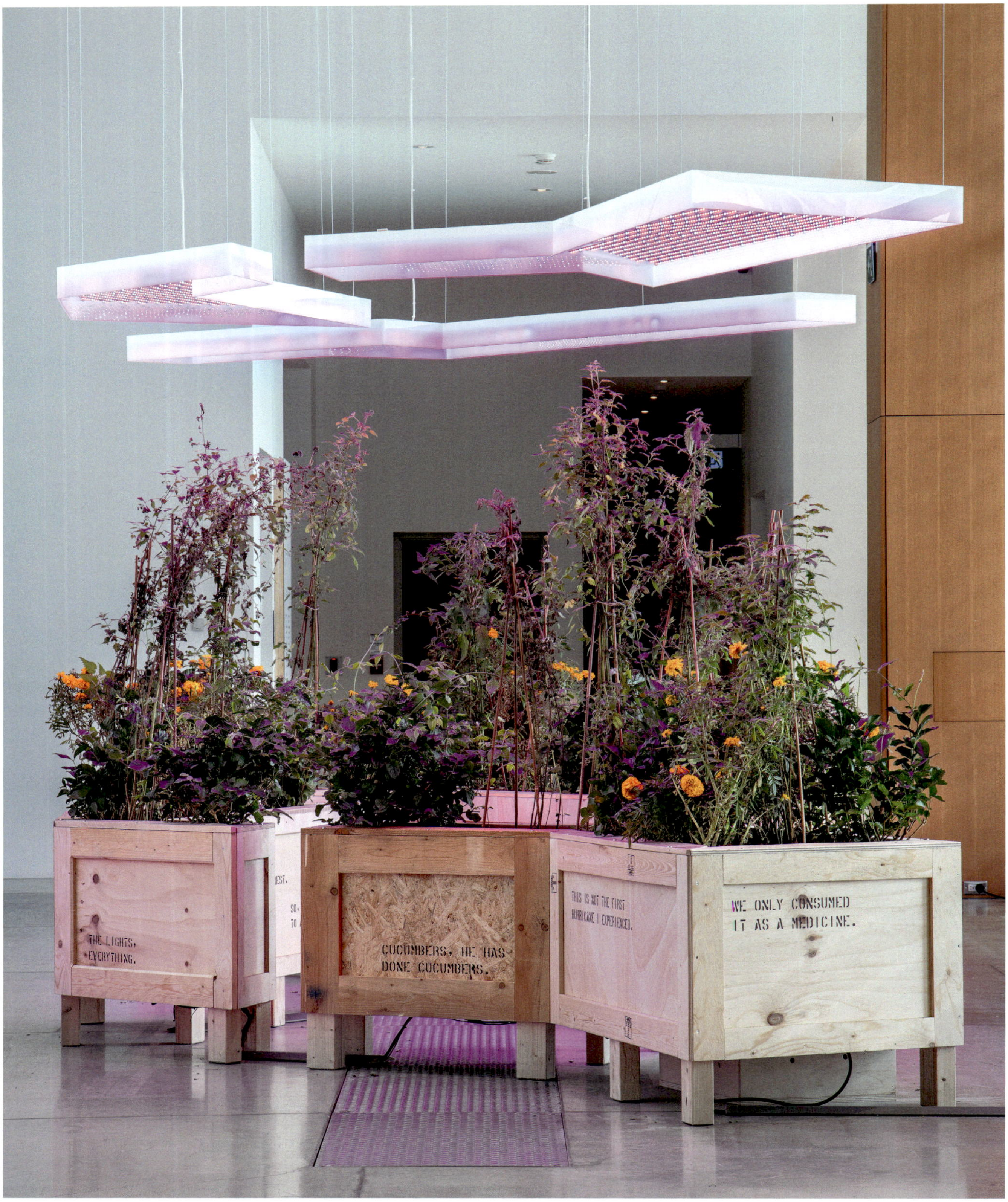

Hito Steyerl, *FreePlots*, 2019–ongoing (installation view)

Hito Steyerl

FreePlots (2019–ongoing) is an installation by Hito Steyerl, made in collaboration with Jardin communautaire Bonnevoie-Kaltreis, a Luxembourg-based community garden. It comprises a series of planters resembling shipping crates, three custom-built UV grow-lamps, compost and plants. The work was made in response to the artist's discovery that one of her artworks was stored in Geneva Freeport, a duty-free warehouse that enables clients to avoid paying taxes on luxury goods. The shape of the wooden crates refers to the architecture of this freeport, along with another in Panama. Initially financed by the (estimated) proceeds of the sale, *FreePlots* can be seen to counter capitalist frameworks by highlighting alternatives to private ownership.

This is the third incarnation of *FreePlots*, following exhibitions at the Park Avenue Armory, New York and the Art Gallery of Ontario, Toronto. In both cases, the

FreePlots (2019-en cours) est une installation réalisée par Hito Steyerl en collaboration avec le jardin communautaire de Bonnevoie-Kaltreis (Luxembourg). Il se compose d'un ensemble de bacs ressemblant à des caissons de transport, de trois lampes à UV artisanales, de compost et de plantes. L'artiste a réalisé cette installation après avoir découvert qu'une de ses œuvres était conservée dans le port franc de Genève, un entrepôt qui permet à ses clients d'éviter les taxes sur les produits de luxe. La forme des bacs fait référence à l'architecture du port franc de Genève et d'un autre situé au Panama. Financée au départ par les bénéfices (estimés) de sa vente, *FreePlots* déjoue les cadres capitalistes en mettant en lumière des modèles alternatifs à la propriété privée.

Il s'agit de la troisième incarnation de cette œuvre, qui a d'abord été exposée au Park Avenue Armory de New York et à l'Art Gallery of Ontario à Toronto. Dans les

artist worked with members of local community gardens, inviting them to choose and establish the plants. At each new presentation of the work, Steyerl also conducts interviews with members of the community, excerpts of which are stencilled on the side of the planters and relayed via a recording that forms the installation's soundtrack. 'After the first iteration I realised that it wasn't just about growing plants', the artist has said, 'it was about growing stories and communities'.[1]

For the artist, community gardens – which are often maintained by women and migrant communities – are also an important symbolic example of opposition to nationalism and xenophobia. 'We need to learn from experiences all over because we are under extreme pressure from right-wingers, especially in Germany', she has commented, 'who claim that their soil belongs to them – that they are the only ones to own the territory and to have any claims to it'.[2]

Hito Steyerl was born in 1966, in Munich, Germany. She lives and works in Berlin, Germany.

1 Hito Steyerl, 'Artist Talk: Drill', 20 June 2019, Park Avenue Armory, New York.
2 Gelek Badheytsang, 'The Story Behind Hito Steyerl's Parkdale-inspired Art Installation', *Now Toronto*, 29 October 2019.

deux cas, l'artiste a travaillé avec des membres de jardins communautaires locaux, qu'elle a invités à choisir les plantes et à les mettre en terre. À chaque nouvelle présentation de l'œuvre, Hito Steyerl effectue aussi des entretiens avec des membres du jardin communautaire : elle en reproduit des extraits au pochoir sur le côté des bacs et en diffuse les enregistrements, qui constituent la bande-son de l'installation. « Après la première version, a expliqué l'artiste, je me suis rendu compte qu'il ne s'agissait pas seulement de cultiver des plantes, mais de cultiver des histoires et des communautés[1]. »

À ses yeux, les jardins communautaires, qui sont souvent entretenus par des communautés de femmes et de migrants, sont aussi un symbole important de l'opposition au nationalisme et à la xénophobie. « Nous avons besoin d'apprendre d'expériences venues de partout, parce que, particulièrement en Allemagne, nous sommes soumis à une forte pression de la droite, qui prétend que son sol lui appartient – qu'elle est la seule à posséder le territoire et à pouvoir en revendiquer la propriété[2]. »

Hito Steyerl est née en 1966 à Munich, en Allemagne. Elle vit et travaille à Berlin, en Allemagne.

1 Hito Steyerl, « Artist Talk: Drill », Park Avenue Armory, New York, 20 juin 2019.
2 Gelek Badheytsang, « The Story Behind Hito Steyerl's Parkdale-inspired Art Installation », *Now Toronto*, 29 octobre 2019.

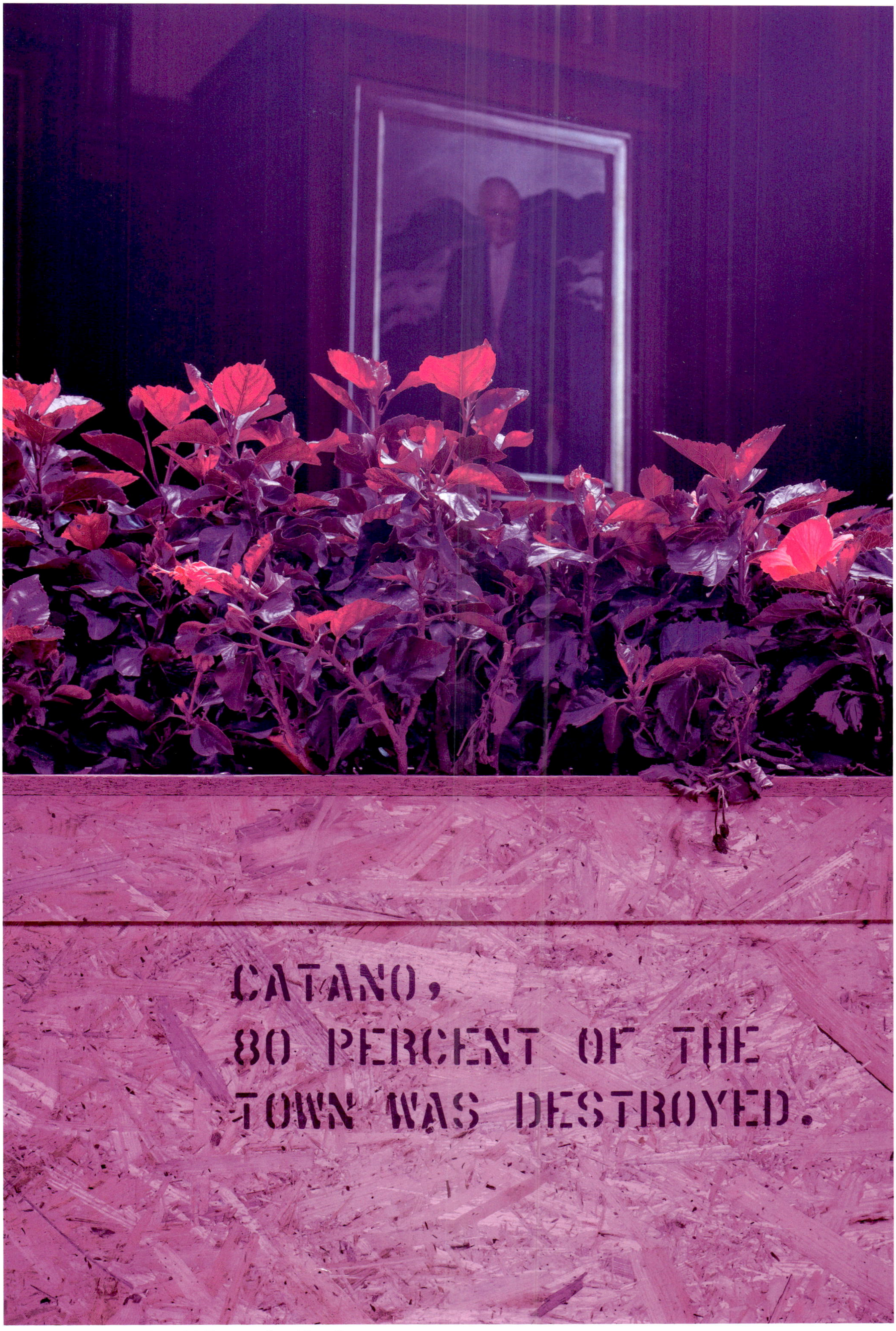

Hito Steyerl, *FreePlots*, 2019–ongoing (detail)

AUTHORS

James Bridle is a writer and artist based in London. Bridle is the author of *New Dark Age: Technology and the End of the Future* (Verso, 2018). Their writing has appeared in publications including *Wired*, *The Atlantic*, *The New Statesman*, *The Guardian* and *The Observer*.

Heike Geissler is a writer of fiction based in Leipzig. She is the author of *Seasonal Associate* (Semiotext(e), 2018) and received the Alfred Döblin Prize for her novel *Rosa* (Deutsche Verlags-Anstalt, 2001).

Richard Seymour is a writer and broadcaster based in London. He is the author of *The Twittering Machine* (Indigo Press, 2019), *Corbyn: The Strange Rebirth of Radical Politics* (Verso, 2016), and *Against Austerity: How We Can Fix the Crisis They Made* (Pluto, 2014), among other books. He has contributed to publications including *The New York Times*, the *London Review of Books*, and *The Guardian* and is an editor at *Salvage* magazine.

Hito Steyerl is an artist and writer based in Berlin. She is the author of *Duty Free Art* (Verso, 2017) and *The Wretched of the Screen* (Sternberg Press, 2012) and is a regular contributor to publications including *e-flux*. She is a Professor of New Media Art at the Berlin University of the Arts.

McKenzie Wark is a writer and academic based in New York. She is the author of *A Hacker Manifesto* (Harvard University Press, 2004), *Gamer Theory* (Harvard University Press, 2007), *Capital Is Dead: Is this Something Worse?* (Verso, 2019) and *Reverse Cowgirl* (Semiotext(e), 2020), among other books. She teaches at the New School for Social Research and Eugene Lang College in New York.

Shoshana Zuboff is the Charles Edward Wilson Professor Emerita at Harvard Business School. She is the author of *In the Age of the Smart Machine: The Future of Work and Power* (Basic Books, 1988) and *The Age of Surveillance Capitalism: The Fight for a Human Future at the New Frontier of Power* (Profile Books / PublicAffairs, 2019).

Sarah Beaumont is an Assistant Curator at Mudam Luxembourg – Musée d'Art Moderne Grand-Duc Jean.

Michelle Cotton is the Head of Department, Artistic Programmes and Content at Mudam Luxembourg – Musée d'Art Moderne Grand-Duc Jean.

Clémentine Proby is an Assistant Curator at Mudam Luxembourg – Musée d'Art Moderne Grand-Duc Jean.

Chloe Stead is a writer and editor based in Berlin. Her criticism has appeared in *art-agenda*, *Artnet*, *frieze* and *Spike Art Magazine*, amongst others.

Joel Valabrega is the Curator of Performance and Public Programme at Mudam Luxembourg – Musée d'Art Moderne Grand-Duc Jean.

Lauren Wetmore is a Curatorial Research Fellow at Mudam Luxembourg – Musée d'Art Moderne Grand-Duc Jean.

AUTEURS

James Bridle est un·e écrivain·e et artiste basé·e à Londres. James Bridle est notamment l'auteur·e de *New Dark Age: Technology and the End of the Future* (Verso, 2018). Ses écrits sont parus dans de nombreuses publications, notamment *Wired*, *The Atlantic*, le *New Statesman*, *The Guardian* et *The Observer*.

Heike Geissler est une écrivaine basée à Leipzig. Elle est notamment l'auteure de *Seasonal Associate* (Semiotext(e), 2018). Elle a reçu le prix Alfred Döblin pour son roman *Rosa* (Deutsche Verlags-Anstalt, 2001).

Richard Seymour est un écrivain et présentateur de radio basé à Londres. Il est notamment l'auteur de *The Twittering Machine* (Indigo Press, 2019), *Corbyn: The Strange Rebirth of Radical Politics* (Verso, 2016), et *Against Austerity: How We Can Fix the Crisis They Made* (Pluto, 2014). Il a contribué à des publications telles que le *New York Times*, la *London Review of Books* et *The Guardian*. Il est l'un des rédacteurs en chef du magazine *Salvage*.

Hito Steyerl est une artiste et écrivaine basée à Berlin. Elle est l'auteure de *Duty Free Art* (Verso, 2017) et de *The Wretched of the Screen* (Sternberg Press, 2012), et contribue régulièrement à des publications telles que *e-flux*. Elle est professeure en Art des nouveaux médias (New Media Art) à l'Université des arts de Berlin.

McKenzie Wark est une écrivaine et universitaire basée à New York. Elle est l'auteure de *A Hacker Manifesto* (Harvard University Press, 2004), *Gamer Theory* (Harvard University Press, 2007), *Capital Is Dead: Is this Something Worse ?* (Verso, 2019), et *Reverse Cowgirl* (Semiotext(e), 2020), entre autres. Elle enseigne à la New School de New York.

Shoshana Zuboff est professeure émérite Charles Edward Wilson à la Harvard Business School. Elle est l'auteure de *In the Age of the Smart Machine: The Future of Work and Power* (Basic Books, 1988) et *The Age of Surveillance Capitalism: The Fight for a Human Future at the New Frontier of Power* (Profile Books / PublicAffairs, 2019).

Sarah Beaumont est assistante curateur au Mudam Luxembourg – Musée d'Art Moderne Grand-Duc Jean.

Michelle Cotton est chef de département, programmation artistique et contenu au Mudam Luxembourg – Musée d'Art Moderne Grand-Duc Jean.

Clémentine Proby est assistante curateur au Mudam Luxembourg – Musée d'Art Moderne Grand-Duc Jean.

Chloe Stead est une écrivaine et rédactrice basée à Berlin. Ses écrits et critiques sont parus dans *art-agenda*, *Artnet*, *frieze*, et *Spike Art Magazine*, entre autres.

Joel Valabrega est curateur des performances et du programme public au Mudam Luxembourg – Musée d'Art Moderne Grand-Duc Jean.

Lauren Wetmore est chargée de recherches curatoriales au Mudam Luxembourg – Musée d'Art Moderne Grand-Duc Jean.

Ei Arakawa
How to DISappear in America (Duration: multiple times in total of 9 hours, & approx. 60 hours on preparation, Honorarium: 3,500 EUR, 0.72 EUR per minute)
2020
4364 LED (WS2813 100m black) on hand-dyed fabric with grommets, 1 T300-K Controller, 1 SD card (2 GB) with 1 LedEdit 2014 data (.led), 2 5V40A power supplies with 22 AWG stranded wire
80 cm diameter
Sammlung Haus N, Kiel / Athens

Ei Arakawa
YouTube Our Unemployment (Post-Capital)
2021
7384 LED (WS2813 100 / m black) including altered LED tips, on hand-dyed fabric with grommets, 1 T300-K Controller, 1 SD card (2 GB) with 1 LedEdit 2014 data (.led), 3 5V40A power supplies with 22 AWG stranded wire, 1 Tectonic TEAX25C10-8 / SP transducer, double corrugated cardboard, Lepai LP-2020TI amplifiers, MP3 player. Music: Ei Arakawa, Lyrics: Ei Arakawa and Dan Poston
107 cm diameter
Courtesy of the artist and Galerie Max Mayer

Mohamed Bourouissa
All-in
2012
Video, colour, sound
5:41 min
Courtesy of the artist and kamel mennour, Paris / London
Co-production kamel mennour / La Monnaie de Paris

Cao Fei
Asia One
2018
Video, colour, sound
63:20 min
Courtesy of the artist; Vitamin Creative Space, Guangzhou; and Sprüth Magers, Berlin / London / Los Angeles
Commissioned by the Solomon R. Guggenheim Museum, New York, for The Robert H. N. Ho Family Foundation Chinese Art Initiative

Simon Denny
Amazon worker cage patent drawing as virtual Aquatic Warbler cage (US 9,280,157 B2: "System and method for transporting personnel within an active workspace", 2016)
2020
Powder coated metal, MDF, iOS Augmented Reality interface
293 × 222 × 253 cm
Kunstsammlung Nordrhein-Westfalen, Düsseldorf
Acquired 2021

Simon Denny
Document Relief Study 1 (Amazon Worker Cage Patent)
2019
Inkjet print on archival paper, glue, custom metal wall mount
30 × 21.4 × 15 cm
Kunstsammlung Nordrhein-Westfalen, Düsseldorf
Acquired 2021

Simon Denny
Document Relief Study 2 (Amazon Worker Cage Patent)
2019
Inkjet print on archival paper, glue, custom metal wall mount
29.8 × 21.4 × 11.9 cm
Kunstsammlung Nordrhein-Westfalen, Düsseldorf
Acquired 2021

Lara Favaretto
Clandestine Talks [Thinking Head]
2017–ongoing
'Series of meetings behind closed doors, no spectators'. The audio recording of the talks can be accessed as a livestream from mudam.com and thinking-head.net. Transcriptions of the talks will be archived on the website thinking-head.net.
Courtesy of the artist and Galleria Franco Noero, Turin

GCC
CO-OP
2014
Video, colour, sound
5:41 min
Collection Mudam Luxembourg – Musée d'Art Moderne Grand-Duc Jean
Donation 2015 – Stephanie and Patrick Majerus

GCC
Royal Mirage
2014
Oil on canvas, aluminium frames, digitally printed wallpaper
Dimensions variable
Collection Mudam Luxembourg – Musée d'Art Moderne Grand-Duc Jean
Donation 2020 – Nadine Zeidler and Amadeo Kraupa-Tuskany

Guan Xiao
A Sinking Blue Field
2019
Brass, fibreglass, coloured rope, knee protectors, LED lamp
151 × 60 × 90 cm
Courtesy of the artist; Kraupa-Tuskany Zeidler, Berlin and Antenna Space, Shanghai

Guan Xiao
Chicken House
2019
Brass, fibreglass, wood, drill extension
99 × 81 × 88 cm
Collection of Sabine DuMont-Schütte, Cologne

Guan Xiao
The Daughter of Tree
2019
Brass, fibreglass, silver foil, paper, parasol, camera tripod, coloured rope
160 × 100 cm
Collection of Alexander V. Petalas, London

Shadi Habib Allah
Dropping the 10th Digit
2018
8 lightboxes, photographic print on Duratrans
34.3 × 50.8 × 12.7 cm
Courtesy of the artist and Reena Spaulings Fine Art, New York / Los Angeles

Roger Hiorns
The retrospective view of the pathway
2017–ongoing
MiG 21, dried earth, peristaltic pump, silicone tubing, suspension of liquified pizza
Dimensions variable
Courtesy of the artist; Luhring Augustine, New York; Galerie Rudolfinum, Prague

Oliver Laric
Hunter and Dog
2020
Polyurethane, pigments, steel
184 × 70 × 55 cm
Courtesy of the artist and Tanya Leighton, Berlin / Los Angeles

Oliver Laric
Reclining Pan
2021
SLS Nylon, SLA Resin, pigments, acrylic paint, aluminum
145.7 × 151.7 × 83.7 cm
Courtesy of the artist and Tanya Leighton, Berlin / Los Angeles

Oliver Laric
Hermanubis
2021
SLS Nylon, SLA Resin, pigments, acrylic paint, aluminum
155 × 40.5 × 57.5 cm
Courtesy of the artist and Tanya Leighton, Berlin / Los Angeles

Oliver Laric
Ram with Human
2021
SLS nylon, SLA resin, pigments, paint, aluminium
162 × 93 × 32 cm
Courtesy of the artist and Pedro Cera, Lisbon

Liz Magic Laser
In Real Life
2019
Five-channel video, colour, sound, UV printed fabric and polyurethane foam seating elements
Dimensions variable, 112 min
With Alabi Adebayo Akintunde (nollygfx on Upwork), Zahid Iqbal (thelancersinc on Fiverr), Cardy O'Donnell (PeoplePerHour), Nikki (PeoplePerHour), Kiki Wong (K1wngg on Fiverr), Count Marco (Fiverr and PsychicMix), Louise Papadopoullos (Mind Body Design).
Video Producer: David E. Guinan, Edited by: Laura Geisswiller, Trailer Editor / Assistant Editor: Jonathan Turton, Producer: Charlotte Horn, Written by: Liz Magic Laser, Cardy O'Donnell, Vanessa Thill, Whiteboard Animator: Alabi Adebayo Akintunde, Graphic Design: Zahid Iqbal, Voiceover Artist: Kiki Wong, Social Media Content Creator: Nikki, Researcher: Vanessa Thill, Research Assistant: Penelope Pardo, Motion Graphics: Patrick Bate, Frostmotion, Graphicsplayer, David Guinan, Yoshi Sodeoka, Jonathan Turton, 3D Animation: David Guinan, Sound Designer: Jared Arnold, Composer: Gobby, Sound Re-recording mixer: Chris Liang, Technical Advisor: Mark Murphy, Additional Music by: Chris Liang and Sonnymusic1 (on Fiverr), Additional Animations by: Yoshi Sodeoka, Additional filming by: Carl Davies, Atanas Paskalev and Maria Ruban, Special Thanks to Maneesh Sethi of Pavlok.
Courtesy of the artist; Various Small Fires, Los Angeles / Seoul; and Wilfred Lentz, Rotterdam.
Commissioned by FACT as part of *The Future World of Work*, a project commissioned by Culture Liverpool as part of the Liverpool 2018 programme. Supported by the US Embassy London. Supported using public funding by Arts Council England and Liverpool City Council.

Katja Novitskova
Pattern of Activation (jumping spider, termite cathedral mounds, growth potential)
2015
Digital print, aluminium, polyurethane, steel
240 × 450 × 300 cm
Collection of Fondazione Sandretto De Rebaudengo, Turin

Katja Novitskova
Pattern of Activation (emu)
2014
Digital print, aluminium cut-out display, polyurethane, steel
Cutout print: 241 × 143 × 35 cm, Arrow: 106 × 220 × 25 cm
Gaby and Wilhelm Schürmann Collection, Herzogenrath

Laura Owens
Untitled
2015
Oil, silkscreen inks, Flashe, acrylic and gesso on linen
274.3 × 213.4 × 3.8 cm
Collection of Alexander V. Petalas, London

Yuri Pattison
the ideal (v/0.3.2)
2015–ongoing
Video, colour, sound. Warehouse racking, monitor, media player, BITMAIN Antminer C1, PC water cooling unit, custom dam reservoir (by Mountain Storm / RW Keeton), Dadu River stones, 1⁄12 scale miniatures, BROCKHAGE® Clear Demonstration & Practice Padlock, print on static cling sticker, cables, packaging, purified water, dust.
Dimensions variable, 30:02 min
Courtesy of Klosterfelde Edition, Berlin

Sondra Perry
IT'S IN THE GAME '18 or Mirror Gag for Projection and Two Universal Shot Trainers with Nasal Cavity and Pelvis
2018
Video, colour, sound (looped), wall painted in Rosco Chroma Key blue, training hardware
Dimensions variable, 16:20 min
Collection Mudam Luxembourg – Musée d'Art Moderne Grand-Duc Jean
Donation 2019 – Allen & Overy

Josephine Pryde
Sorry Not Sorry
2016
C-print
80 × 62.5 × 3.5 cm
Courtesy of the artist and Galerie Neu, Berlin

Josephine Pryde
Einen Scheiss Muss Ich
2016
C-print
80 × 62.5 × 3.5 cm
Courtesy of the artist and Galerie Neu, Berlin

Josephine Pryde
Your Secure and Private Path
2015
C-print
80 × 62.5 × 3.5 cm
Courtesy of the artist and Galerie Neu, Berlin

Josephine Pryde
Here Do You Want To
2014
Giclée print
79 × 57.5 × 3.5 cm
Courtesy of the artist and Galerie Neu, Berlin

Josephine Pryde
Küsse sind das
2014
C-Print
79 × 57.5 × 3.5 cm
Courtesy of the artist and Galerie Neu, Berlin

Josephine Pryde
Für Mich
2014
Giclée print
79 × 57.5 × 3.5 cm
Courtesy of the artist and Galerie Neu, Berlin

Nick Relph
Sally
2015
Cibachrome mounted on aluminium
127 × 121.9 cm
Courtesy the artist; Herald St, London and Standard (Oslo)

Nick Relph
So This is Marriage
2015
Cibachrome mounted on aluminium
127 × 121.9 cm
Courtesy of the artist; Herald St, London and Standard (Oslo)

Nick Relph
The Girl From Everywhere
2015
Cibachrome mounted on aluminium
127 × 121.9 cm
Courtesy of the artist; Herald St, London and Standard (Oslo)

Nick Relph
Glorifying the American Girl
2016
C-print
127 × 101.6 cm
Courtesy of the artist and Herald St, London

Nick Relph
Annie Laurie
2016
C-print
127 × 101.6 cm
Courtesy of the artist and Herald St, London

Cameron Rowland
Handpunch
2014
Photograph
35.6 × 25.8 cm
Courtesy of Essex Street / Maxwell Graham, New York

Cameron Rowland
Handpunch
2014
Photograph
35.6 × 25.8 cm
Courtesy of Essex Street / Maxwell Graham, New York

Cameron Rowland
Handpunch
2015
Photograph
35.6 × 25.8 cm
Courtesy of Essex Street / Maxwell Graham, New York

Cameron Rowland
Handpunch
2015
Photograph
35.6 × 25.8 cm
Courtesy of Essex Street / Maxwell Graham, New York

Cameron Rowland
Handpunch
2015
Photograph
35.6 × 25.8 cm
Courtesy of Essex Street / Maxwell Graham, New York

In businesses where employees' time is one of the most valuable assets, the Handpunch time clock secures this time. Manufactured by Schlage (the American lock company) the Handpunch uses biometric readings of employees' right hands to inhibit false clock-ins and payment for false hours. Biometric recognition was developed to replace photography as a superior form of criminal indexing.

Hito Steyerl
FreePlots
2019–ongoing
3 custom-built wooden planters, 3 custom-built UV grow lamps, plant grow bags, compost, plants, sound
Dimensions variable
Courtesy of the artist; Andrew Kreps Gallery, New York and Esther Schipper, Berlin

Martine Syms
Mythiccbeing
2018
Video, colour, sound, adhesive vinyl
Courtesy of the artist and Sadie Coles HQ, London

Nora Turato
eeeexactlyyy my point.
2021
Wall painting
Courtesy of the artist; LambdaLambdaLambda, Pristina
and Galerie Gregor Staiger, Zurich

Nora Turato
Wish it were that simple
2021
Digital print on paper
Courtesy of the artist; LambdaLambdaLambda, Pristina
and Galerie Gregor Staiger, Zurich

Nora Turato
If you don't mind, it doesn't matter
2021
Digital print on paper
Courtesy of the artist; LambdaLambdaLambda, Pristina
and Galerie Gregor Staiger, Zurich

Nora Turato
Very good 08/10
2021
Digital print on paper
Courtesy of the artist; LambdaLambdaLambda, Pristina
and Galerie Gregor Staiger, Zurich

Nora Turato
pool 5
2021
Performance
Courtesy of the artist; LambdaLambdaLambda, Pristina
and Galerie Gregor Staiger, Zurich

TEXT CREDITS

pp. 37–40
Excerpt from McKenzie Wark, *Capital Is Dead: Is this Something Worse?*, London: Verso Books, 2019, pp. 41–49.
© McKenzie Wark 2019. Reproduced with permission of the Licensor through PLSclear.

pp. 46–47
Excerpts from:
Heike Geissler, *Seasonal Associate*, translated by Katy Derbyshire, Los Angeles: Semiotext(e), 2018, pp. 67–69; pp. 71–73.
© Text: Heike Geissler: *Saisonarbeit*; Spector Books, Leipzig, 2014
Original edition published in German in the *Volte* series, issue 2 edited by Jörn Dege and Mathias Zeiske with Spector Books, 2014 © Semiotext(e) 2018

pp. 81–85
Excerpts from Shoshana Zuboff, *The Age of Surveillance Capitalism: The Fight for a Human Future at the New Frontier of Power*, London: Profile Books, 2019, pp. 93–97; pp. 345–348.
© Shoshana Zuboff, 2019

pp. 86–91
Excerpts from Shoshana Zuboff, *L'âge du capitalisme de surveillance*, trad. française Bee Formentelli et Anne-Sylvie Homassel, Paris, Éditions Zulma, 2020.
© Zulma, 2020, pour la traduction française

pp. 92–94
Excerpt from Richard Seymour, *The Twittering Machine*, London: The Indigo Press, 2019, pp. 52–56.
Extracted from *The Twittering Machine* by Richard Seymour © 2019, published by The Indigo Press

pp. 129–132
Excerpt from Hito Steyerl, *Duty Free Art: Art in the Age of Planetary Civil War*, London: Verso Books, 2017, pp. 77–83.
© Hito Steyerl 2017, 2019. Reproduced with permission of the Licensor through PLSclear.

pp. 133–136
Excerpt from Hito Steyerl, *De l'art en duty free – L'art à l'époque de la guerre civile planétaire*, « Chapitre 7 – Duty Free Art », trad. française Armelle Chrétien, Dijon, Les Presses du réel, 2021.
© Armelle Chrétien © Les Presses du réel

pp. 137–140
Excerpts from James Bridle, *New Dark Age: Technology and the End of the Future*, London: Verso Books, 2018, pp. 106–109; pp. 113–116; pp. 118–119.
© James Bridle 2018, 2019. Reproduced with permission of the Licensor through PLSclear.

pp. 141–145
Excerpts from James Bridle, *Un nouvel âge de ténèbres. La technologie et la fin du futur*, trad. française Benjamin Saltel, Paris, Éditions Allia, 2022.
James Bridle, New Dark Age © Éditions Allia, Paris, 2022

IMAGE CREDITS

All works detailed in the *List of Works* unless otherwise specified.

Cover:
Josephine Pryde, *Your Secure and Private Path*, 2015
Courtesy of the artist; Galerie Neu, Berlin; Reena Spaulings Fine Art, New York and Simon Lee Gallery, London / Hong Kong

p. 15
© Liz Magic Laser 2019
Courtesy of the artist; Various Small Fires, Los Angeles / Seoul and Wilfried Lentz, Rotterdam

pp. 16, 66, 69
Courtesy of Yuri Pattison; Helga Maria Klosterfelde, Berlin and mother's tankstation Dublin | London

pp. 17, 26, 154, 157
Photo: Useful Art Services
Courtesy of Shadi Habib Allah; Reena Spaulings Fine Art, and the Renaissance Society at the University of Chicago

pp. 18, 27, 150, 153
© GCC

pp. 19, 28, 118, 120, 121
Courtesy of Josephine Pryde; Galerie Neu, Berlin; Reena Spaulings Fine Art, New York and Simon Lee Gallery, London / Hong Kong

p. 20
Courtesy of Oliver Laric

pp. 24, 98, 100–101
© Adagp Mohamed Bourouissa / Courtesy the artist and kamel mennour, Paris / London

p. 25
Courtesy of Nora Turato; LambdaLambdaLambda, Pristina and Gregor Staiger, Zurich

p. 50
Ei Arakawa, *Family Dollar (Social Capital)*, 2020
7384 LED (WS2813 100m black) including altered LED tips, on hand-dyed fabric with grommets, 1 T300-K Controller, 1 SD card (2GB) with 1 LedEdit 2014 data (.led), 4 5V40A power supplies with 22 AWG stranded wire, 1 Tectonic TEAX25C10-8 / SP transducer, double corrugated cardboard, Lepai LP-2020TI stereo amplifiers, any MP3 media player
100 cm diameter
Music: Ei Arakawa, Lyrics: Ei Arakawa and Dan Poston, Arrangement: ZALA from Mish-Mosh
Photo: Katja Illner / Courtesy of the artist and Galerie Max Mayer, Düsseldorf

pp. 52–53
Photo: Katja Illner / Courtesy of Ei Arakawa and Sammlung Haus N, Kiel / Athens

pp. 54, 56, 57
Courtesy of Cao Fei; Vitamin Creative Space, Guangzhou and Sprüth Magers, Berlin / London / Los Angeles

pp. 58, 61
Photo: Jesse Hunniford / MONA
Courtesy of Simon Denny and Stiftung Kunstsammlung Nordrhein-Westfalen, Düsseldorf

p. 62 (top)
Installation view from the exhibition *REAL WORK*, FACT, Liverpool, 12 July–06 October 2019.
Photo: Rob Battersby © Liz Magic Laser 2019

pp. 62 (bottom), 64–65
© Liz Magic Laser 2019 / Courtesy of the artist, Various Small Fires, Los Angeles / Seoul and Wilfried Lentz, Rotterdam.

p. 68
Yuri Pattison, *the ideal (v. 0.2)*, 2015
BITMAIN Antminer C1 PC water cooling unit, custom dam reservoir (by Mountain Storm / RW Keeton)
Kangding riverbed stones, 1⁄12 scale miniatures, flatpack steel racking Perspex, BROCKHAGE®, Clear Demonstration & Practice Padlock, protective film, print onstatic cling sticker black MDF, HD monitor, media player & SD card with video file, packaging
Dimensions variable, 30:02 min
Courtesy of the artist; Helga Maria Klosterfelde, Berlin and mother's tankstation Dublin | London

pp. 70, 72, 73
© Cameron Rowland / Courtesy of the artist and Maxwell Graham / Essex Street, New York

p. 74
Martine Syms, *Mythiccbeing*, 2018
Infinite loop, interactive video on LED panels (4:3); Stereo Speakers / Sub / DAC
Installation view as part of *Grand Calme*, Sadie Coles HQ, London, 6 September–20 October 2018.
Photo: Robert Glowacki © Martine Syms / Courtesy of the artist and Sadie Coles HQ, London

pp. 76, 77
© Martine Syms / Courtesy Sadie Coles HQ, London

pp. 84, 89
© Shoshana Zuboff / Courtesy of Shoshana Zuboff and Profile Books, London

pp. 102, 104
Photo: Mareike Tocha
Courtesy of Guan Xiao; Kraupa-Tuskany Zeidler, Berlin; Antenna Space, Shanghai and Bonner Kunstverein, Bonn

p. 105
Installation view from the exhibition *Guan Xiao: Products Farming*, Bonner Kunstverein, Bonn, 2 February–20 April 2019.
Photo: Mareike Tocha
Courtesy of Guan Xiao; Kraupa-Tuskany Zeidler, Berlin; Antenna Space, Shanghai and Bonner Kunstverein, Bonn

pp. 106, 108
Photo: Roger Hiorns © Adagp Paris, 2021
Courtesy of the artist; Galerie Rudolfinum, Prague and Luhring Augustine, New York

p. 109
Roger Hiorns, *The retrospective view of the pathway*, 1990–2016
Aircraft burial, Ipswich, Suffolk, UK
Photo: Roger Hiorns © Adagp Paris, 2021
Courtesy of the artist; Corvi-Mora Gallery, London; Annet Gelink Gallery, Amsterdam and Luhring Augustine, New York

p. 110
Photo: Hans-Georg Gaul
Courtesy of Katja Novitskova and Kraupa-Tuskany Zeidler, Berlin

pp. 112–113
Photo: Gunter Lepkowski
Courtesy of Katja Novitskova and Kraupa-Tuskany Zeidler, Berlin

pp. 114, 116, 117
Laura Owens, *Untitled*, 2014
Acrylic, silkscreen ink, oil, Flashe, gesso on linen
349.3 × 304.8 cm
Collection of Aïshti Foundation, Beirut
Photo: Annik Wetter © Laura Owens
Courtesy the artist; Sadie Coles HQ, London and Galerie Gisela Capitain, Cologne

p. 122
Nora Turato, *wow this huge wooden horse is great!*, Documentation of performance (film still) at Galerie Gregor Staiger, Milan, 2 September, 2020
Photo: Alessio Costantino
Courtesy of the artist and Galerie Gregor Staiger, Zurich

pp. 124–125
Courtesy of Nora Turato and Galerie Gregor Staiger, Zurich

p. 146
Lara Favaretto, *Thinking Head*, 2017–ongoing
Pure water, ultra-fine mist nozzles, fog pipes and hoses, pump stations, remote control
Installation view, 58th Venice Biennale, 11 May–24 November 2019
© Ela Bialkowska / Courtesy of the artist and Galleria Franco Noero, Turin

p. 149 (top)
Lara Favaretto, *Thinking Head*, 2017–ongoing
Location view at the Central Pavilion, Arsenale, at the 58th Venice Biennale, 11 May–24 November 2019
© Ela Bialkowska / Courtesy of the artist

p. 149 (bottom)
Undisclosed location, Luxembourg
Photo: Joel Valabrega / Courtesy of the artist

p. 152
Installation view, FIAC, Paris, 2014
© GCC / Courtesy of GCC and Kraupa-Tuskany Zeidler, Berlin

p. 158
Photo: Dirk Pauwels / Courtesy of Oliver Laric and Tanya Leighton, Berlin

pp. 160, 161
Photo: Gunter Lepkowski / Courtesy of Oliver Laric and Tanya Leighton, Berlin

pp. 162, 165
Installation view, *À Cris Ouverts,* 6th edition of Les Ateliers de Rennes – Biennale d'art Contemporain in Rennes, France, 28 September–2 December, 2018
Photo: Aurélien Mole / Courtesy of Sondra Perry and Bridget Donahue, New York

pp. 166, 168, 169
© Nick Relph / Courtesy of the artist

p. 170
Installation view, *Hito Steyerl: This is the Future*, 21 October 2019–23 February 2020, Art Gallery of Ontario
Photo: Dean Tomlinson © Art Gallery of Ontario
Courtesy of the artist; Andrew Kreps Gallery, New York and Esther Schipper, Berlin

p. 173
Installation view, *Drill*, Park Avenue Armory, New York, 20 June–21 July, 2019
Photo: James Ewing
Courtesy of Hito Steyerl; Andrew Kreps Gallery, New York and Esther Schipper, Berlin

ACKNOWLEDGEMENTS

Mudam would like to thank the artists, authors, and Antenna Space, Shanghai; Galeria Pedro Cera, Lisbon; Sadie Coles HQ, London; Sabine DuMont-Schütte, Essex Street / Maxwell Graham, New York; FRAC Lorraine 49 Nord 6 Est, Metz; Herald Street, London; kamel mennour, Paris / London; Klosterfelde Edition, Berlin; Kraupa-Tuskany Zeidler, Berlin; Andrew Kreps Gallery, New York; LambdaLambdaLambda, Pristina; Tanya Leighton, Berlin / Los Angeles; Wilfried Lentz, Rotterdam; Luhring Augustine, New York; Galerie Max Mayer, Düsseldorf; Sammlung Haus N, Kiel / Athens; Galerie Neu GmbH & Co. KG, Berlin; Galleria Franco Noero, Torino; Kunstsammlung Nordrhein-Westfalen, Düsseldorf; Alexander V. Petalas; Fondazione Sandretto Rebaudengo, Torino; Galerie Rudolfinum, Prague; Esther Schipper, Berlin; The Heins Schürmann Collection, Herzogenrath; Reena Spaulings Fine Arts, New York / Los Angeles; Standard (Oslo); Galerie Gregor Staiger, Zurich; Various Small Fires, Los Angeles / Seoul; Vitamin Creative Space, Guangzhou; and Sprüth Magers, Berlin / London / Los Angeles; who have loaned work for this exhibition.

We also thank those lenders who wish to remain anonymous.

Mudam would also like to thank the Jardin Communautaire de Bonnevoie-Kaltreis for their collaboration on the production of *FreePlots* by Hito Steyerl.

The exhibition is partly made possible thanks to the support of the Institut für Auslandsbeziehungen (IFA), the Italian Embassy in Luxembourg and its partners (as part of the Italian Contemporary Art Day), and the Mondriaan Fund.

The curators would also like to thank Julia Alfert, Sara Antman, Patrick Armstrong, Henry Babbage, Lisa Baldelli, Harriet Balfour, Thomas Ballot, Helen Barr, Ulrike Baumgart, Devrim Bayar, Sven Biscop, Samantha Bok, Vanessa Boni, Leila Bou-Nasr, Chloë Bourdon, Lorenza Brandodoro, Henriette Bretton-Meyer, Galerie Buchholz, Köln / Berlin, Michael Carter, Pedro Cera, Jan Černý, Mallory Cohen, Sadie Coles, Alice Conconi, Eli Coplan, Tommaso Corvi-Mora, Mercedes Costa, Will Davies, Inge Devogelaere, Bridget Donahue, Stéphane Duguin, Cédric Durand, Rose Eastwood, Hamida El Aroud, Ludwig Engel, FACT, Liverpool, Phillipe Fettes, Nic Flood, Peter and Erin Friedland, Susanne Gaensheimer, Pierre Ghiraldini, Martine Gillen, Fanny Gonella, Simon Gowing, Maxwell Graham, Hannes Grassegger, Friederike Gratz, Hillary Halter, Peter Hammond, Sasha Helinski, Sigrid Hermann, Helen Hester, Sophie Heyligers, Yves Hoffmann, Charlotte Horn, Roy Huschenbeth, Nicole Isaac, Marketton, Finola Jones, Sarah Khabirpour, Omar Kholeif, Frank Kintzinger, Alfons Klosterfelde, Anne König, Sylvia Kouvali, David Korecký, Amadeo Kraupa-Tuskany, Anette Kruszynski, Anaëlle Lec'hivien, Erin Leland, Rachel Lepley, Veronika Lindova, Laura Lord, Geert Lovink, Christian Lübbert, Carla Mantovani, Charlotte Masse, Max Mayer, Minnie McIntyre, Alia McKellar, Marta Mente, Markus Missien, Nathalie Moerman, Therese Möllenhoff, Mothers Tankstation, Dublin / London, Hendrike Nagel, Carla Mantovani, Kamel Mennour, John O'Doherty, Friedrich Petzel, Christina F. Olsen, Emiliano Pistacchi, Lucy Price, Anamaria Fernández Purón, Jacques Putz, Patrizia Sandretto, Rebaudengo, Elsa de Rémur, Caterina Riva, Marco Rovacchi, Tanja Rochow, Esther Schipper, Alexander Schröder, Anne Schulte, Wilhelm Schürmann, Christopher Schwartz, Poppy Sebire, Markéta Stará Condeixa, Dan Solbach, Gregor Steiger, Claes Storm, Zdenek Svobodnik, Julia Speed, Nick Srnicek, Xunzhi Sun, Sarah Johanna Theurer, Michael Thouber, Rob Tufnell, Leah Turner, Sam Tsao, Claire Valageas, Maité Vanhellemont, Adelina Vlas, Catherine Wang, Simon Wang, Heather Ward, Paul Whang, Fillipo Weck, Xiong Xu, Nicole Yip, Jackie Wang, Alan Yulun Wu, Claudine Zahlen and Nadine Zeidler for their help with the exhibition and publication.

IMPRINT

Post-Capital: A Reader is published on the occasion of the exhibition
Post-Capital. Art & the Economics of the Digital Age
02 October 2021–16 January 2022,
Mudam Luxembourg – Musée d'Art Moderne Grand-Duc Jean

17 September 2022–15 January 2023,
Kunsthal Charlottenborg, Copenhagen

Exhibition curated by Michelle Cotton, assisted by Clémentine Proby, Nelly Taravel and Joel Valabrega

Post-Capital Research Group:
Sarah Beaumont, Michelle Cotton, Caroline Hoffmann, Ioanna Madenoglu, Bob Mersch, Nelly Taravel, Joel Valabrega

Published by
Mudam Luxembourg – Musée d'Art Moderne Grand-Duc Jean, Mousse Publishing

Editor: Michelle Cotton
Graphic design: Dan Solbach, Anamaria Fernández Purón
Editorial management: Deborah Lambolez, Clarisse Fahrtmann

Texts: Sarah Beaumont (p. 63), James Bridle (pp. 137–140), Michelle Cotton (pp. 13–22, 103–104, 167–168), Heike Geissler (pp. 46–47), Clémentine Proby (pp. 59–60, 99–100), Richard Seymour (pp. 92–94), Chloe Stead (pp. 51, 55, 67, 71, 107–120, 159–160, 171–172), Hito Steyerl (pp. 129–132), Joel Valabrega (pp. 123–124, 147–148), McKenzie Wark (pp. 37–40), Lauren Wetmore (pp. 75, 151–156, 163–164), Shoshana Zuboff (pp. 81–85)

Translations: Simon M. Benedict (pp. 63, 99–100), Armelle Chrétien (pp. 133–136), Bee Formentelli and Anne-Sylvie Homassel (pp. 86–91), Boris Patrick Kremer (pp. 23–33, 41–45, 48–49, 95–97), Benjamin Saltel (pp. 141–145); Nicolas Vieillescazes (pp. 51–60, 67–75, 103–124, 147–172)

Copyediting: Camille Didelon, Hélène Remaud, Rosemary Sheridan

Mudam Luxembourg – Musée d'Art Moderne Grand-Duc Jean
3, Park Dräi Eechelen
L–1499 Luxembourg
mudam.com

MUDAM
Musée d'Art Moderne Grand-Duc Jean

Kunsthal Charlottenborg
Kongens Nytorv 1
1050 Copenhagen K
Denmark
kunsthalcharlottenborg.dk

KUNSTHAL
CHARLOTTENBORG

Distributed by
Mousse Publishing
Contrappunto s.r.l.
Corso di Porta Romana 63
20122, Milan–Italy

Available through:
Mousse Publishing, Milan
moussepublishing.com
DAP | Distributed Art Publishers, New York
artbook.com
Vice Versa Distribution, Berlin
viceversaartbooks.com
Les presses du réel, Dijon
lespressesdureel.com
Antenne Books, London
antennebooks.com

First edition: 2021

Printed in Germany by DZA Druckerei zu Altenburg GmbH

Typeface: Magister, Laurenz Brunner, Goldman Sans, Dalton Maag
Paper: Performa White, Gardamatt Art

ISBN 978-88-6749-477-4
€ 40 / $ 45

Legal deposit: October 2021

The publishers would like to thank all those who have kindly given their permission for the reproduction of material for this book. Every effort has been made to obtain permission to reproduce the images and texts in this catalogue. However, as is standard editorial policy, the publishers are at the disposal of copyright holders and undertake to correct any omissions or errors in future editions.

Mudam Luxembourg remercie l'ensemble des donateurs et des mécènes, et en particulier pour leur soutien exceptionnel

The Leir Foundation, JTI, Luxembourg High Security Hub, M. et Mme Norbert Becker-Dennewald, Allen and Overy, Banque Degroof Petercam Luxembourg, Cargolux, Œuvre Nationale de Secours Grande-Duchesse Charlotte, The Loo & Lou Foundation

et également

Arendt & Medernach, Baloise Group, Banque de Luxembourg, Capital*at*Work Foyer Group, PwC, Atoz, AXA Group, Banque Pictet & Cie (Europe), Bonn & Schmitt, Fondation Indépendance, Soludec SA, Dussmann Services Luxembourg, Fondation Sommer, Indigo Park Services SA, Les Amis des Musées d'Art et d'Histoire, American Friends of Mudam, Helmut Dorner et Galerie Nosbaum Reding.

Mudam Luxembourg est financé par le Ministère de la Culture.

MUDAM Musée d'Art Moderne Grand-Duc Jean

LE GOUVERNEMENT DU GRAND-DUCHÉ DE LUXEMBOURG
Ministère de la Culture